Studies in Emotion and Social Interaction

Paul Ekman
University of California, San Francisco

Klaus R. Scherer
Justus-Liebig-Universität Giessen

General Editors

Conversations of Friends

Studies in Emotion and Social Interaction

This series is jointly published by the Cambridge University Press and the Editions de la Maison des Sciences de l'Homme, as part of the joint publishing agreement established in 1977 between the Fondation de la Maison des Sciences de l'Homme and the Syndics of the Cambridge University Press.

Cette collection est publiée co-édition par Cambridge University Press et les Editions de la Maison des Sciences de l'Homme. Elle s'intègre dans le programme de co-édition établi en 1977 par la Fondation de la Maison des Sciences de l'Homme et les Syndics de Cambridge University Press.

Conversations of friends
Speculations on affective development

Edited by
John M. Gottman and Jeffrey G. Parker

Department of Psychology
University of Washington,
Seattle

Department of Psychology
University of Illinois,
Urbana-Champaign

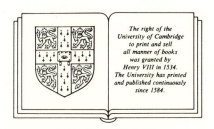

The right of the
University of Cambridge
to print and sell
all manner of books
was granted by
Henry VIII in 1534.
The University has printed
and published continuously
since 1584.

Cambridge University Press

Cambridge
London   New York   New Rochelle
Melbourne   Sydney

Editions de la Maison des Sciences de l'Homme

Paris

Published by the Press Syndicate of the University of Cambridge
The Pitt Building, Trumpington Street, Cambridge CB2 1RP
32 East 57th Street, New York, NY 10022, USA
10 Stamford Road, Oakleigh, Melbourne 3166, Australia
and
Editions de la Maison des Sciences de l'Homme
54 Boulevard Raspail, 75270 Paris, Cedex 06

First published 1986

Printed in the United States of America

Library of Congress Cataloging-in-Publication Data
Conversations of friends.
(Studies in emotion and social interaction)
Bibliography: p.
Includes index.
1. Childhood friendship. 2. Social interaction in
children. 3. Interpersonal communication in children.
4. Friendship. I. Gottman, John Mordechai. II. Parker,
Jeffrey G. III. Series.
HQ784.F7C66 1986 155.4'18 86-20778
ISBN 0 521 26321 2

British Library Cataloging-in-Publication Data applied for.

R00648 52744

Two are better than one
because they have a good reward for their labour
For if they fall, the one will lift up his fellow;
But woe to him that is alone when he falleth,
and hath not another to lift him up.
Again, if two lie together, then they have warmth;
but how can one be warm alone?

Ecclesiastes 4:9–12

To my parents, Salomon and Lina Gotthelfsman,
who all their lives filled
their home with warmth, coffee, pastry,
and the conversations of friends

John Mordechai Gottman

To Sue, who teaches me a little about
friendship every day; to my parents, Stan
and Dorothy; and to Carol Rupe, who
started my interest in studying children

Jeffrey Parker

Contents

IV EXTENSIONS

Contributors

Dorothy Ginsberg
  *Langley Porter Neuropsychiatric
  Institute
  University of California,
    San Francisco*

John M. Gottman
  *Department of Psychology
  University of Washington*

Anne Hope Heflin
  *Department of Psychology
  Duke University*

Gwendolyn Mettetal
  *Department of Communications
  Purdue University*

Jeffrey G. Parker
  *Department of Psychology
  University of Illinois*

Jennifer Parkhurst
  *Department of Psychology
  University of Illinois*

Martha Putallaz
  *Department of Psychology
  Duke University*

Preface

In 1972 I became interested in learning how children become friends. My goal was to help socially isolated children, but I was convinced that it was necessary to teach a child to make friends the way *children* naturally do, not the way I, an adult, thought they ought to. I assumed that developmental psychologists had studied the subject thoroughly and that this knowledge surely existed somewhere in the research literature. I was surprised to discover that it did not. It seemed that finding out what I needed to know would take only a few months and then I could get back to the job at hand. What began as a brief excursion has lasted 14 years.

From the outset, it was amazing how rich the conversations of children were. In some sense they seemed magical. Young children playing in their rooms at home were often engaged in high adventure, taking trips to the moon, becoming robots whose batteries needed charging, flying, building cities, taking revenge on bad things, or racing supersonic cars. They went on these adventures involved with one another's minds, with drama, with animation, and with great invention.

Often on the same audiotapes one could hear the conversations of adults in the home. These were soothing, they were calm, with a limited range of volume, pitch, energy, and dramatization. By contrast, the speech of the children was highly varied in pitch, volume, emotional tone, and drama. For example, one could hear the adults discuss their furniture while their children rushed a feverish baby to the hospital at breakneck speed and then performed the necessary surgery as doctor and nurse.

I began systematically collecting children's conversations with Jennifer Parkhurst in 1975. We were fortunate enough to stumble on a way of making audiotapes – in homes, with parents' help – that recorded very rich and natural conversations. The conversations were nothing like what

I had expected from the view prevailing in the research literature at that time. The literature characterized young children as being much more limited in social skills than what I was observing.

It has taken this long to produce only two pieces of writing on this work, an interim paper from the *Minnesota Symposium on Child Psychology* in 1980 and a monograph of the Society for Research in Child Development in 1983. Looking back, I can explain why it took so long only by saying that it is difficult to see the obvious. Once noticed, a process that children employ in their conversations is henceforth glaringly apparent. However, until it is noticed it is baffling to discover what organizes children's interaction. For example, I used to get headaches listening to tapes of children apparently jumping randomly from one topic to another. In 1982, when I designed the MACRO coding system, I suddenly noticed the process I called escalation and deescalation. From then on, these processes were immediately apparent; and the tapes no longer gave me headaches.

In 1977 I presented a paper at the Society for Research in Child Development's biennial meeting entitled "Developing May Not Always be Improving." In this paper I reported evidence that young children are superior to older children in some important social skills. Very young children use coordinated fantasy play with their friends in a way that often demonstrates an impressive ability to be with their friends undistracted, truly in the moment. They are also very careful about their management of conflict and the clarity of their communication. I was extremely impressed. It has taken me all these years to arrive at some perspective on children's strengths and weaknesses at each developmental level I have studied so far, to see what their concerns and tasks are, and to relish the beauty of each period. As we shall see, in some senses I was right in 1977. Development is not linear. It is not a steady, gradual approximation to the Mature Competent Adult. We give things up when we grow up. To be sure, we also gain, but in the process we make trade-offs. The conversations we present in this book show each age group in terms of its own world. We trace the development and reorganization of important social processes in the two major contexts studied: friendship and acquaintanceship. For me, preparing this material was an experience in learning what development is.

Now there is this book. It is an edited volume, but all the work was begun in the same laboratory, with the same goal: to observe and describe the peer social world of childhood. Thus, the book should have considerable unity.

Only recently have we begun the task of explaining. Jeffrey Parker's laboratory work with the "extraterrestrial" to explore the processes of friendship formation in young children and Martha Putallaz's examination (at Duke University) of mothers of accepted and unaccepted children represent initial attempts at explaining.

This book begins in Chapter 1 by examining the importance of friendship. In Chapter 2 our observational methods are described. Psychology is an exciting science at the moment, because we are forming our questions and our methods at the same time. Chapter 2 describes the main observational category systems we have developed and employed. One of the goals of this book is to combine qualitative and quantitative methods so that the children will somehow "emerge" from the pages. Chapter 3 is a summary of the observational work on how children become friends. It also describes the early laboratory work on children making friends with an "extraterrestrial." Chapter 4 is a description of same-sex and cross-sex friendship in young children. Chapter 5 is an extension of the research on conversations of friends through adolescence. In that chapter a theory of social and affective development is presented. This theory is a major contribution of this book. Chapter 6 is an extension of the work on conversations of friends to young adulthood, in a study of college roommates. Chapter 7 describes progammatic research on children's entry into peer groups, which is an extension of the work on conversation to larger groups. Chapter 8 is an analysis of the pragmatics of children's discourse within the acquaintanceship and friendship contexts. Chapter 9 is an initial attempt to describe the role of friends in helping people cope with stressful life events such as divorce.

This is a book about friendship and its formation. Though important for their own sake, the conversations of friends are also a special means of examining the social and emotional development of children. I would argue that friendship is one of the most important contexts for the study of social and emotional development. Our group of researchers has been very fortunate because we have been blessed with very natural data. What is emerging is an interesting theory about human development as well as some knowledge about an important area of our lives, the time we spend in the company of friends.

The research that forms the basis of this book was supported by Research Grant PHS MH 35997 from the National Institute of Mental Health. I am indebted to Paul Ekman for his suggestions on the research grant application and for the encouragement of Joel Goldstien, who was then executive secretary of the study section that reviewed the grant proposal. Paul Ekman encouraged the publication of this book by requesting that it appear in his series of books with Cambridge University Press. I am also indebted to Susan Milmoe for her continued support at Cambridge. This work would not have been possible without the release time provided by a National Institute of Mental Health Research Scientist Development Award (RSDA K200257), which I have held since 1979. None of the proper atmosphere for research would have existed without the superb intellectual climate provided by my wonderful colleagues in the Department of Psychology at the University of Illinois and by the leadership of our department head, Emanuel Donchin.

Steve Asher's continuing concern with moving away from "micro" descriptions to larger organizational constructs in childhood has had a great influence. I hope he will smile as he recognizes the influence of his important thinking on children's goals in social interaction.

Some of the best ideas in this book were inspired during poolside chats with Ross Parke. These chats were brief moments of peace, joy, laughter, and sanity, and swimming was at times what Parke calls a "symbolic gesture." I have never encountered a mind quite like Parke's. He has a special gift for ideational flight and for the construction of theory. If in analyzing the conversations presented in the following chapters I have gained a sense of what *development* is, I owe it to Ross. Thinking about development has been the exhilarating part of writing this book.

John Gottman
Urbana, Illinois

I. Purposes

1. The importance of friendship

DOROTHY GINSBERG, JOHN GOTTMAN, AND
JEFFREY PARKER

"There comes a time in every rightly constructed boy's life when he has a raging desire to go somewhere and dig for hidden treasure," wrote Mark Twain. "This desire suddenly came upon Tom Sawyer one day and he sought out Huck Finn, who was willing to dig for it with him. Next they had to decide where to dig for it. This was how their day together started."

Friends can create a world of great involvement and high adventure, and they can do it at the tender age of 3 or 4. They must coordinate their efforts with all the virtuosity of an accomplished jazz quartet, and they must manage the amount of conflict between them. These things require enormous social skill.

The world of children's friendships is always under our feet; it can be heard, if we care to listen, in most homes that have children and in the parks and schoolyards where children play. This world is commonplace, but it goes largely unnoticed by most adults.

This book offers a view of the everyday world of children's friendships, as it is revealed in the conversations of children. The goal of the book is not only to describe, but also to try to understand these important relationships among children. Because these relationships are so important to children, understanding them is also a step toward understanding social and emotional development. Among the questions that the chapters of this book address are the following. How do children make friends? What social skills are important in this process? Does this process change with development, and if so, why? How are close friendships different from the interactions of people just getting to know one another? How does the interaction of friends change developmentally? Why does it change?

The studies reported in this book are based almost entirely on observation. The use of any kind of observational research in develop-

3

mental psychology is quite rare; Patterson (1982) estimated that only about 8% of all published research in developmental psychology is observational. Instead, a common strategy is to ask children what they do. However, young children are at a great disadvantage when they are asked to describe what they do. What they actually do is far more complicated than what they can report.

In fact, adults may also have difficulty in articulating the social processes they engage in, unless these social events are highly formal and ritualized, such as a wedding. For example, Duncan (1972) and others (for summaries of the literature, see Argyle, 1969; Harper, Wiens & Matarazzo, 1978) have described the rules by which people in a conversation exchange turns at speaking. Listeners who wish to speak, for example, direct their gaze to the speaker, lean forward, use a series of vocal and nonvocal "backchannels" that communicate to the speaker that they are tracking the speech (e.g., they nod their head frequently and vocalize occasionally: "uh," "um," "uh huh," "well," "uh well," etc.). There are also social rules by which speakers hold the speaking turn and do not yield the floor (see Duncan and Fiske, 1979). Other sociologists and psychologists have described the hidden rules in greeting, riding elevators, and so on (see Argyle, Furnham, & Graham, 1981). These social rules are dances we engage in without much awareness. When we hear an account of them, we may recognize the truth of the description, but it is not intuitively clear that these are the same behaviors we would have described if we ourselves had been asked to characterize conversational turn taking. Direct observational methods are a necessity. This is not to say that children's (or adults') reflections on social events are not interesting in their own right, but the premise of our research is that it is best to begin by *watching* young children.

This book is also about development. We are interested in the organization of children's social world and how and why this organization changes with development. Our approach to these questions is very similar to the approach of ethologists. We observe children with their peers in as natural a context a possible. We organize and summarize our observations, both qualitatively and quantitatively. We try to account for variation in the intimacy of relationships and in progress toward friendship of unacquainted children. We move to the laboratory to test some of our notions in an experimental context. On the basis of all this we propose a theory of social and affective development, built from the ground up, in an empirical tradition.

Though interesting in its own right for both theoretical and applied reasons, the study of close relationships throughout development may also teach us a little about ourselves: who we are and how we got to be that way. If we can learn something from children, let us be wise enough to do so.

In this introductory chapter we argue that acquaintanceships and close friendships are important in people's lives at all ages for a variety of reasons. Furthermore, we argue that we need to know a great deal more than we do about the *specific social processes* involved in having a close friend.

1.1. The importance of friendship in childhood

Much has been written about the positive, promotive influence of general peer interaction on children's current and long-term adjustment and maturity (see Asher, 1978a; Hartup, 1979; 1983; D. W. Johnson, 1980; Piaget, 1932; Sullivan, 1953; Youniss, 1980). For example, the opportunity to interact with other children is said to be essential for full cognitive (Piaget, 1932), social-cognitive (Selman, 1980), moral (Damon, 1977; Kohlberg, 1964), and linguistic (Bates, 1975) maturity; for mastery of aggressive impulses (Hartup, 1978); and for the acquisition of appropriate sex-role behavior (Fagot, 1977; Fine, 1980). Participation in children's groups is said to afford children access to informal academic "tutors" (Allen, 1976; Cooper, Marquis, & Ayers-Lopez, 1982); to important information on topics adults are unwilling or unable to discuss, such as sexuality (Fine, 1981); and to sources of comfort during times of acute and chronic stress (Freud & Dann, 1951; Ispa, 1981).

These are claims about the importance of peers generally. Yet children are not interested in peers in general; they are interested in specific peers, namely, their friends. As Hartup (1982) notes "Children want the company of Judy or Caleb, not just any child, and they want to share concerns, interests, information, and 'secrets' with them" (p. 540).

What, then, is the importance of children's friendships specifically? What functions do children's friendships serve that are not otherwise captured by research on the functions of peer interaction generally? In this section we first consider several salient functions of friendship in childhood. We then consider the importance of friendship in childhood in another way by examining the consequences for long-term adjustment of the absence of friends in childhood.

Functions of friendship in childhood

Wright (1978, 1984; Wright & Keple, 1981) proposed a theory of adult friendship based on a conception of self that regards friendships as one important way in which individuals "live out" various self-referent motives related to concern for their own well-being and self-image. These motives include the desire to affirm one's sense of individuality, to affirm one's important attributes, to evaluate one's self positively, and to change toward positive self-growth. According to Wright, friendship involves investments of self in a relationship characterized by the partners' voluntary interdependence and personalized concern for one another. This investment, entailing expenditures of time, personal resources, and concern, yields dividends or direct rewards experienced concretely as a partner's ego support value, self-affirmation value, stimulation value, and utility value.

Weiss (1974), too, has theorized that people seek to satisfy a number of social needs in their friendships and other interpersonal relationships. According to Weiss, different interpersonal relationships (e.g., parent–child, sibling, friendship) supply different "relational provisions," such as affection, reassurance of worth, instrumental help, companionship, and intimate disclosure. Friendships, in Weiss's view, are formed primarily to meet needs for companionship and reassurance of worth.

Whatever their accuracy, formulations such as those of Wright and Weiss are important in calling attention to the functional quality of friendships at any age. As Wright (1984) notes:

> The friendship relationship is rewarding – sometimes profoundly rewarding – in a number of specifiable ways. People are often able to articulate quite clearly what they "get from" their different friends (or their different friendships) that makes each one special, and they are generally more detailed and articulate in this respect about their stronger than their weaker friendships [p. 115].

This functional quality of friendship is not lost on children: All but the very youngest of children are capable of articulating what they value in their friends and friendships, their expectations of their friends and friendships, and how friendship obligations and rewards differ from those of other relationships (e.g., Bigelow, 1977; Bigelow & LaGaipa, 1975; Furman & Bierman, 1981; Gamer, 1977; Selman, 1980; Wright & Keple, 1981; Youniss & Volpe, 1978).

We consider next six functions of friendship in childhood –

companionship, stimulation, physical support, ego support, social comparison, and intimacy/affection – drawing, where possible, on empirical research on children's friendships and their friendship expectations.

Companionship. Friendship provides children with a reliable, familiar partner and playmate, someone who is willing to spend time with them and join in collaborative activities in the spirit of Huck Finn and Tom Sawyer cited at the opening of this chapter. In fact, in very young children preferential play partnership is taken as a reliable *index* of the existence of a friendship (George & Krantz, 1981; Howes, 1981; Rotheram & Phinney, 1982; Vandell & Mueller, 1980). But differential allocation of time is not solely the province of young friendships; writing of adolescent friendships, Richey and Richey (1980) note that "the best friend is a more or less constant companion" (p. 537) and that

> friends spent a great deal of time together, most seeing each other every day outside of classes. They also used the telephone to keep in touch, more than half calling 2–3 times a week or more (10% calling more than once a day!) [p. 536]

Children are acutely aware of the companionship aspect of friendship: Virtually every study of children's friendship descriptions and expectations has found a dimension of companionship and mutual activity. It appears as early as preschool (Hayes, 1978), remains prominent at least through early adolescence in girls and middle adolescence in boys (Bigelow & LaGaipa, 1975; Douvan & Adelson, 1966; Furman & Bierman, 1981; LaGaipa, 1981; Reisman & Shorr, 1978), and is more characteristic of close than distant friendships (Hayes, Gershman, & Bolin, 1980). Furthermore, children who lack friends and the companionship they provide report loneliness (Asher, Hymel, & Renshaw, 1984; Cohn, Lohrmann, & Patterson, 1985).

Stimulation. Another function of friendship in childhood is that of providing children with interesting information, excitement, and amusement. Of course, children get information, excitement, and amusement from other, nonfriend peer relationships. But when children interact with friends, their play involves more extended, nonstereotyped fantasy play (Gottman & Parkhurst, 1980; Roopnarine & Field, 1984) and more talking, laughter, smiling, and humor (Foot, Chapman, & Smith, 1977; Newcomb, Brady, & Hartup, 1979) than it does when they interact with nonfriends.

Physical support. Wright (1978, 1984; Wright & Keple, 1981) has written of the "utility value" of adult friendships:

> Some people are valued as friends because of their willingness and ability to use their own time and resources to help the individual meet his or her needs or reach various goals [Wright, 1981, p. 561].

Like those of adults, the friendships of children involve the provision of time, resources, and assistance. In fact, Berndt (in press) has noted that the degree to which friends share and help one another is often taken as an index of how close their relationship is and how much positive influence their friendship has on their social behavior in general.

Clark (1981) has argued that physical support is exchanged in friendships in ways that are unlike resource exchange in other relationships. Clark likened children's friendship to a communal relationship, such as that which exists among kin or romantic partners. In a communal relationship members feel a special obligation to be responsive to one another's resource needs. This is in contrast to an exchange relationship, such as that between business partners, in which members are responsible for benefiting one another in direct proportion to benefits received, without any specific sense of obligation to fulfill unmet needs.

The empirical literature on children's friendships supports all of these contentions. At the same time it suggests that these formulations do not fully capture the complexity of the processes involved in physical assistance in children's friendship. When children of all ages are interviewed about their friendships, their remarks almost always contain references to friends' obligations to share and help one another (e.g., Berndt, 1981; Bigelow, 1977; Douvan & Adelson, 1966; Furman & Bierman, 1981; Hayes, 1978; LaGiapa, 1979; Sharabany, Gershoni, & Hofman, 1981).

Research on friends' actual behavior, however, suggests that sharing and helping among friends is more contextually dependent than children's verbal reports would suggest. Berndt (1981) reviewed this evidence and concluded that in situations structured so as to allow children to work toward equality of outcomes (i.e., noncompetitive situations), friends share and help each other more often than nonfriends, particularly as they get older. However, when sharing and helping are assessed in situations structured so that one child gains at the other's expense (i.e., competitive situations), friends may be *less* likely to share and help than nonfriends. Berndt speculated that this occurs because friends have a greater tendency to compare their performance with that of the other and wish to avoid appearing inferior to them.

There is also evidence that friends are particularly inclined to share when they perceive that their relationship is threatened (Staub & Nuerenberg, 1981), suggesting that physical support serves not solely as a reward of friendships, but also as a mechanism of friendship repair.

Ego support/enhancement. Another function of friendship that receives attention both in the writing of friendship theorists (e.g., Duck, 1984; Wright, 1978) and in the comments of children themselves (e.g., Bigelow, 1977; Douvan & Adelson, 1966; LaGaipa, 1979; Richey & Richey, 1980) is ego support/enhancement. This refers to the expectation that friends will be supportive and encouraging and in general will help an individual to maintain an impression of him- or herself as a competent, attractive, and worthwhile person (Wright, 1978).

When children lack friends or when they perceive their friendships as lacking ego support, children's self-esteem (Greenberg, Siegel, & Leitch, 1983), self-acceptance (Reese, 1961), and perceptions of self-competence (Harter, 1985) may suffer, and they may become depressed (Vosk, Forehand, Parker, & Rickard, 1982).

Duck (1984) noted that the ego support/enhancement function of both adults' and children's friendships may be both direct and indirect:

> . . . one reason that we appreciate friends is because of their contribution to our self-evaluation and esteem. Friends can do this both directly and indirectly: they may compliment us or tell us about other people's good opinions of us. . . . But they can also increase our self-esteem in other ways: by attending to what we do, listening to us, asking our advice and generally acting in ways that indicate the value they place on our opinions [p. 25].

Elkind (1980) offered another way in which children's friendships can provide ego support/enhancement. Elkind noted that, in early adolescence, friendship in children takes on a "strategic coloration" that belies children's conscious and unconscious efforts to build a positive self-image, in their own eyes and in the eyes of an imaginary audience:

> [A physically] attractive girl may befriend a less attractive one, in part, at least, to enhance the impression of attractiveness to the imaginary audience. But the contrast also confirms her sense of being specially, uniquely attractive. Similar motives operate for the less attractive girl, who hopes to impress the audience by the very fact of being associated with the attractive girl.

Hurlock (1973) has made a similar point with regard to adolescents' desires to be friends with popular children.

Social comparison. Another function of children's as well as adults' friendship is social comparison; in Duck's (1984) words, friendships "help us see where we stand *vis-à-vis* other people and whether we are doing OK" (p. 19). In other words, friends provide us with a standard against which to gauge our important views and attributes.

As we shall take up later in this chapter, a great deal of research has been conducted on both the objective and the perceived (by children) importance of similarity in children's friendships. At virtually all ages, friends are similar in age, sex, and race; and from about early adolescence, friends are similar in such attitudinal respects as orientation toward school and contemporary teen culture (see Berndt, 1981; Epstein, 1986).

The opportunity to compare and contrast one's views and attributes within the relatively safe interpersonal environs of friendship may be especially important for traits and views that are idiosyncratic or not otherwise common in the peer group at large. Ball (cited in Berndt, 1981) identified one pair of girls who had a common interest in horses. Three boys seemed to be friends because they were in scouts together.

Intimacy/affection. Intimacy and affection are, of course, the hallmark of friendship at any age, the facet that most clearly distinguishes close friends from distant friends, acquaintances, and activity partners (Oden, Herzberger, Mangione, & Wheeler, 1984; Serafica, 1981). Sullivan (1953) is generally credited with first calling attention to the intimate, affectionate quality of friendship in childhood. He contrasted the intimacy of child friendships with that of parent – child love:

> All of you who have children are sure that your children love you; when you say that you are expressing a pleasant illusion. If you will look closely at one of your children when he finally finds a chum – somewhere between eight-and-a-half and ten years – you will discover something very different in the relationship, namely, that your child begins to develop a real sensitivity to what matters to another person [p. 245].

According to Sullivan, the intimate, affectionate aspect of friendship largely does not appear until middle or late adolescence. At that point, it can be seen most clearly in the form of intimate self-disclosure, that is, in the tendency of friends to share personal or private thoughts and feelings with friends.

There is research to support both Sullivan's general claim of the intimate, affectionate quality of children's friendships and his specific claim that this aspect of children's friendships does not develop fully until after preadolescence. Research on children's friendship expectations, for example, has revealed that, although references to sharing intimate thoughts and feelings are apparent at all ages, such comments increase dramatically between middle childhood and adolescence (Berndt, 1981; Bigelow, 1977; Douvan & Adelson, 1966; Furman & Bierman, 1981; Riesman & Shorr, 1978; Youniss, 1980).

Observational research also shows that it is not until sometime after middle childhood that children's conversations with friends contain a notable amount of self-disclosure or intimate problem solving in relation to self-disclosure (see Chapter 5). Perhaps for this reason, children younger than about 12 years cannot report with any accuracy on the intimate, personal attributes and feelings of their best friends (Diaz & Berndt, 1981; Ladd & Emerson, 1984).

Later adjustment of children without friends

Peer groups do not afford each child an equivalent set of social experiences in terms of acceptance. That much is obvious to anyone who has ever spent more than a few minutes carefully watching children in classrooms or at recess. Instead, some children have many friends, are generally popular, and command most of the attention, affection, and loyalty of their agemates, whereas others have few, if any, friends and are rejected. Asher (1978) wrote:

> "If you hate Graham, sign here." This petition was making the rounds in one fourth grade classroom not long ago. Fortunately, the teacher intercepted the paper just before it reached Graham's desk. This time, at least, Graham was spared [p. 23].

Such differences arise quickly even in small groups of children (Dodge, 1983) and are relatively stable over time (Busk, Ford & Schulman, 1973; Coie & Dodge, 1983; Roff, Sells, & Golden, 1972; LaFreniere & Charlesworth, 1983; Bukowski & Newcomb, 1984). Most important, psychologists and educators are coming to accept that such differences may constrain children's development and eventual adaptation. This is the so-called "at-risk" view of low acceptance: that, without intervention, children who have difficulty making and keeping friends and experience little acceptance run a greater risk of developing social and personality disturbances than more socially successful agemates. This at-risk view has become particularly widespread in recent years and has led to a number of attempts to delineate the social skills that determine peer acceptance and to several interventions designed to aid friendless children (for reviews see Asher & Renshaw, 1981; Conger & Keane, 1981; Hops, 1982; Oden, 1980; Wanless & Prinz, 1982).

Yet for all the impact of this view, relatively few empirical studies bear directly on the question of peer acceptance and later adjustment (for a comprehensive and critical review see Parker & Asher, 1985). Researchers generally address the issue in one of two ways. One is to ask whether deviant (e.g., schizophrenic) adults and nondeviant adults differed as children in terms of their adjustment with peers. The second approach is to ask whether accepted and nonaccepted children differ in terms of their incidence of later behavioral abnormalities. These are known as "follow-back" and "follow-up" approaches, respectively. As we shall see, the two approaches tell us somewhat different things about the relationship between acceptance and later adjustment.

Do disturbed adults have a history of low acceptance?   The notion that disturbed adults have a history of low acceptance is very much a part of conventional wisdom regarding psychopathology and criminality. It is not uncommon, for example, to hear, as Duck (1984) claimed in a popular book on friendship, that "the most famous mass murderers of almost every country (e.g. Christie, the Black Panther, Blue Beard, the Michigan Murderer, the Boston Strangler, and others) have invariably been found to have had abnormal social experiences in childhood, or to have been left without adult help or guidance when they ran into difficulties with their peers" (p. 115).

Consistent with these impressions, interviews with psychiatric patients or relatives and friends of psychiatric patients very often suggest that a high proportion of such individuals had difficulties with peers as children. For example, Kohn and Clausen (1955) interviewed 45 adult schizophrenics and a matched group of nondisordered control subjects and found that 18% of the disordered subjects reported that they, as children, had played alone nearly all of the time, and an additional 27% reported that they had played "primarily alone, but occasionally with a crowd, close friends, or siblings." By comparison, these rates among nondisordered adults were about 2%. Similarly, Bower, Shellhammer, and Dailey (1960) interviewed the former teachers of adult male schizophrenics and found that, relative to controls, the schizophrenics were recalled as having been less well liked, having been less interested in their environment, having shown fewer leadership skills, having been less interested in the opposite sex, and having participated less frequently in athletics. When sorted case by case on the basis of background, four of the schizophrenics, but none of the controls, were best described as "pathologically shy." Authors reporting essentially similar findings include Bowman (1934); Birren (1944); Edwards and Langley (1936); Kasanin and Veo (1932); Pollack, Woerner, Goodman, and Greenberg (1965), Pollin, Stabenau, Mosher, and Tupin (1966); and Schofield and Balian (1959).

The problem with retrospective interviews, of course, is that they invite conscious or unconscious distortion by soliciting information from respondents who are often disturbed, guarded, defensive, denying, or guilt ridden (see Garmezy, 1974; Yarrow, Campbell, & Burton, 1970). Furthermore, even if such distortions can be minimized – Bower et al., for example, went to elaborate lengths to ensure that their respondents did not know the true purpose of the interview – one still has to contend with the unreliability inherent in asking someone to recall events that may have happened as much as a decade earlier.

Several authors have avoided these criticisms by turning to available child guidance clinic records to gain an understanding of the disordered individual's peer adjustment history (e.g., Frazee, 1954; Friedlander, 1945; Roff, 1963; Nameche, Waring, & Ricks, 1964; Ricks & Berry, 1970; Rolf, Knight, & Wertheim, 1976). The advantage of this approach is that the peer relations data were collected more or less systematically by teachers and social workers *while the patient was still a child*, thereby avoiding potential inaccuracies from memory limitations and selective recall. Illustrative of this approach is a series of pioneering studies by Roff published in the late 1950s and early 1960s (Roff 1957, 1960, 1961, 1963).

Roff searched military service records to locate servicemen who, in middle childhood, had been referred to either of two guidance clinics in Minnesota and who later showed problematic military adjustment. Problematic military adjustment meant either a diagnosis by military psychiatrists as neurotic (Roff, 1957, 1960) or psychotic (Roff, 1961) or a dishonorable discharge for antisocial conduct (Roff, 1963). The child clinic records of these servicemen were then compared with those of former clinic patients who had exemplary later military service records.

Specifically, a complex weighting scheme was designed to evaluate these data for evidence of peer relations difficulties. Subjects were said to have had "poor" peer relations if they showed signs of active dislike by the general peer group, inability to keep friends, and being regarded as "odd," "peculiar," or "queer" by other children.

Roff's analyses indicated a strong association between disorder and poor childhood peer relations. Specifically, about one-half of the neurotic servicemen, but only one-eighth of the nonneurotic servicemen, had shown poor peer adjustment when seen at the clinic. Similarly, about two-thirds of the psychotics, but only one-fourth of the nonpsychotics, had shown poor peer adjustment. Finally, 54% of the servicemen dismissed for antisocial conduct, but only 24% of matched controls, had shown poor peer adjustment. In short, depending on the psychiatric or behavioral disorder, disordered servicemen were anywhere from two to four times as likely as nondisordered servicemen to have had a history of poor peer relations.

Roff's findings are roughly consistent with those of other follow-back researchers working with child guidance clinic files (Frazee, 1954; Friedlander, 1945; Fleming & Ricks, 1970; Namache, Waring, & Ricks, 1964; Ricks & Berry, 1970). For example, Frazee (1954) examined the child clinic files of 23 adult schizophrenics and 23 adults with no history of psychiatric hospitalization and found that 12 (52%) of the later schizophrenics had had no friends and had been isolated from agemates in childhood, compared with only 5 (22%) of the controls. Indeed, none of the psychotics had "evidenced anything approaching normal associations with other children." Similarly, Ricks and colleagues (Fleming & Ricks, 1970; Namache et al., 1964; Ricks & Berry, 1970) examined the clinic files of schizophrenic adults and noted that, compared with controls, preschizophrenics "showed long-standing histories of difficulty in establishing or maintaining peer relationships" (Fleming & Ricks, 1970, p. 249). Adults with impulsive character disorders, like schizophrenics, had also evidenced very poor peer relations according to their clinic files. It is interesting, however, that alcoholic adults had a history of relatively good peer relations and integration into the peer group. In fact, prealcoholics appeared to have been almost excessively dependent on their peers, often at the expense of relationships with parents and siblings.

Collectively, then, follow-back studies with child clinic samples add credence to the notion that disordered individuals have a history of peer disturbance. However, though an improvement over retrospective interview studies, such studies are themselves subject to several limitations (see Garmezy, 1974; Offer & Cross, 1969; Parker & Asher, 1985; Neale & Oltmanns, 1980; Robins, 1972). Most of these center in one form or another on the question of whether the findings can be generalized to the majority of disordered adults. Most schizophrenics, for example, have no history of child clinic contact (Neale & Oltmanns, Ch. 8, 1980). Children seen at guidance clinics obviously represent a very select subset of children: a sample of children with one – or even several – adjustment difficulties severe enough to warrant their referral for evaluation or treatment (e.g., Achenbach & Edelbrock, 1981). Fortunately, there is another set of follow-back studies that have avoided some of the problems of generalization endemic to child guidance clinic studies and thereby provide the most pertinent data yet on the general issue of whether disturbed adults have histories of problematic peer acceptance. These studies use samples of school children.

Perhaps the most well known study to use an unselected school sample and compare disordered and nondisordered individuals in terms of their adjustment with peers is that conducted by Cowen and colleagues (1973) at the University of Rochester in New York. As part of a program for early detection and prevention of school maladaptation, a battery of school adjustment measures had been administered to a large cohort of third-grade children and their teachers. This included indices of poor physical health (school nurse referrals, absenteeism), intellectual capacity (IQ scores), achievement (standardized test scores, grade-point average, over- or underachievement), and socioemotional adjustment (behavioral ratings, anxiety, self-esteem). In particular, the children had been asked to select from among their classmates those children who they thought would be most appropriate for certain desirable and undesirable roles in a hypothetical class play (Bower & Lambert, 1965). Presumably, the children who received many class play nominations for undesirable roles (e.g. "a bully") would be those who were generally disliked by their classmates. The fortuitous establishment of a countywide psychiatric registry shortly thereafter made it possible to establish which of the third-grade children, 11 to 13 years later, had received public or private psychiatric care. Registry adults were matched with former classmates whose names did not later appear in the psychiatric registry, and the two groups were compared in terms of their class play nominations.

The results indicated that, compared with nonregistry adults, adults under psychiatric care had received significantly more class play nominations for undesirable roles, a greater proportion of undesirable to total role nominations, and more overall nominations (desirable and undesirable). In short, registry adults had been viewed quite negatively by their peers. Moreover, the authors were surprised to find that class play scores were the *only* childhood index to discriminate reliably between registry and nonregistry adults – proving more effective than indices of physical health, intelligence, academic achievement, and socioemotional well-being.

The findings of Cowen et al. are not the only results of this type, though they are the most dramatic and probably the most methodologically sound. Authors reporting similar results include Watt and colleagues (Lewine, Watt, Prentky, & Fryer, 1978; 1980; Watt 1972; 1978; Watt & Lubensky, 1976; Watt, Stolorow, Lubensky, & McClelland, 1970), who examined the ad-lib comments of teachers in the cumulative records of pupils who later did and did not develop schizophrenia, and reported that preschizophrenics were less socially competent, personable, extroverted, and secure than controls and more emotionally labile, disagreeable, and passive; Warnken and Siess (1965), who reported that preschizophrenics had been frequently described by teachers as shy, timid, and withdrawn and less often described as well liked; and Barthell and Holmes (1968), who noted that preschizophrenics were less likely to have participated in social extracurricular activities in their senior year.

Moreover, psychiatric patients are not the only group of later disordered individuals to show evidence of problematic peer acceptance in childhood. Conger and Miller (1966) studied the comments of teachers in the cumulative records of later juvenile delinquents and nondelinquents. They presented compelling evidence that, as early as third grade, future delinquents are distinguishable from future nondelinquents in the quality of their peer acceptance. Teachers rate future delinquents much lower than future nondelinquents in social acceptability. They are also less likely to comment spontaneously that future delinquents are well liked, accepted, friendly, and considerate of others and are more likely to comment that predelinquents do not get along well with others or are highly aggressive.

Lambert (1972) examined the fifth-grade class play scores of students who were either successful or unsuccessful academically or non-academically in their last year of high school. She reported that seniors with low (versus average or high) academic "success" (high grade-point averages and achievement test scores) or high "unsuccess"

(reports of discipline problems, remedial instruction, probationary academic standing, and/or dropping out) tended to be those children who,
in fifth grade, had received a disproportionate number of undesirable
role nominations, suggesting that they were viewed quite negatively by
peers.

Finally, several studies indicate that students who drop out of school
have a history of low acceptance. Kuhlen and Collister (1952), Ullmann
(1957), and Bowman and Matthews (1960) indicated that high school
dropouts of both sexes receive, on average, less than one-half as many
friendship choices in elementary school as later graduates. Ullmann
reported that the biserial correlation between acceptance and later
dropout status is − .39. And Amble (1967) found that almost half of all
future dropouts are described by their teachers as socially rejected or, at
best, simply tolerated by their peers.

In summary, there seems to be consistent empirical support for the
common-sense view that disturbed adults have a long-standing history
of problematic peer relations suggestive of low acceptance, although the
empirical picture is not quite as dramatic, perhaps, as the earlier quote
by Duck (1984) implies. This pattern is not limited to adults with serious
psychiatric disorders, but also may be characteristic of juvenile delinquents, dropouts, and high school students who do poorly academically
and socially. Moreover, it seems relatively unaffected by changes in
methods of collecting childhood peer data since it occurs in studies that
use retrospective interviews, studies that abstract guidance clinic
records, and studies that use school records. Childhood peer adjustment variables under some circumstances may even distinguish disordered from nondisordered adults when many other intellectual, behavioral, and demographic variables do not (Cowen et al. 1973).

Are children who are not well accepted likely to be maladjusted later? Several
authors (e.g., Garmezy, 1974; Kohlberg, LaCross, & Ricks, 1972; Parker
& Asher, 1985; Robins, 1972) have pointed out that follow-back studies
such as those described above, though useful for suggesting connec-
tions between adult symptoms and childhood behavior, cannot provide
data interpretable in terms of predictive risk, that is, that children with
a certain level or type of acceptance, when compared with others with
higher or more adaptive types of acceptance, have an increased likelihood of experiencing later maladjustment. Such probabilistic prediction
is possible only from studies that first identify samples of accepted and
nonaccepted children and then follow these children over time to

determine the proportion of children in each of these two groups that subsequently develop disorder. Kohlberg et al. (1972) illustrated this point well with data from Robins (1966). Robins collected both follow-back and follow-up data on truancy and later alcoholism. Follow-back analyses indicated that 75% of all alcoholics had once been truants, compared with only 26% of later nonalcoholics. This suggested that truancy might be a useful *predictor* of later alcoholism. However, follow-up data indicated that this was not the case; only 11% of truants became alcoholics, compared with 8% of the remaining population. Thus, although our understanding of the causes of alcoholism is aided by knowing that most alcoholics were once truants, this understanding does not generate a useful probabilistic prediction of the fate of truants, because the vast majority of truants never become alcoholic. If these percentages applied to low acceptance instead of truancy, it is easy to see that we would probably not wish to declare that poorly accepted children represent a group "at risk" for alcoholism.

For fairly obvious reasons, there are fewer follow-up than follow-back studies of acceptance and later adjustment. Follow-up studies are more expensive, are less flexible, and may require decades to complete. Moreover, in order to ensure that a sufficiently large number of individuals later develop some specific disorder, acceptance data must ideally be gathered on a large number of individuals in childhood. Nonetheless, several follow-up studies that included measures of peer acceptance have been conducted; one such study was conducted by Kupersmidt (1983) and one by Janes and colleagues (Janes & Hesselbrock, 1978; Janes, Hesselbrock, Myers, & Penniman, 1979).

Kupersmidt first obtained fifth-grade children's nominations of their best friends (positive nominations) and children they did not particularly like (negative nominations). Using a scheme proposed by Cole, Dodge, and Coppetelli (1982), she then identified two types of poorly accepted children: rejected children – children who received many negative nominations and few, if any, positive nominations; and neglected children – children who received few positive *and* few negative nominations. The former children are overtly disliked by their peers whereas the latter are simply overlooked by or isolated from their peers. For comparison purposes, Kupersmidt also identified those children who received many positive nominations and few negative nominations (popular children) and children who simply did not stand out in terms of their peer acceptance (average children). Finally, she followed all the children for six years, noting which children became truants, were retained in grade, dropped out, and/or became delinquent. Kupersmidt asked two questions: (1) To what degree does relative social acceptance predict negative adjustment, especially after important variables, such as the child's sex and prior grade-point average, are controlled for? (2) Are children with different types of low acceptance differentially at risk, and does this depend on the specific outcome (truancy, delinquency, grade retention, dropping out)?

In general, children's social preference (number of positive minus number of negative nominations) was not strongly predictive of the total number of problems (academic and delinquent) they subsequently experienced. However, rejected children experienced, on average, significantly more problems in adolescence than neglected, popular and average children. Furthermore, social preference scores did predict a small, but significant amount of the variance in the total number of subsequent academic-related adjustment problems (truancy, dropping out, school failure), and did so even after the child's sex and prior grade-point average, among other things, were statistically controlled for.

The most complete picture emerged, however, when both the type of low acceptance and the type of outcome were considered. Both rejected and neglected children were more than twice as likely as children of average acceptance, and more than three times as likely as popular children, to be truant in at least two subsequent years. Most average children and most popular children were never truant or were truant in only one subsequent year. However, rejected children (30%) were more likely than average (21%), neglected (10%), or popular (4%) children to later drop out of school. Similarly, almost half of the rejected children, but only one-quarter of the neglected, one-fifth of the average, and one-eighth of the popular children, were later retained in grade at least once, although these differences represented only a marginally significant association. Finally, perhaps because so few delinquents were detected, there was no significant association between acceptance and later delinquency. Yet it is noteworthy that rejected children were twice as likely as either average or popular children, and more than four times as likely as neglected children, to be in trouble later with the law.

Janes et al. (1979) located and interviewed 187 adult men and women who, approximately 12 years earlier, had been referred to a child guidance clinic. At the time of their clinic referral, the subjects' elementary school teachers had completed a 31-item behavioral checklist that assessed classroom academic performance and attitudes, relationships with other children, shyness and withdrawal, neurotic behaviors, and leadership. The follow-up interview covered myriad adult adjustment outcomes, ranging from educational and employment progress to contacts with police to psychiatric hospitalization. In addition, clinicians rated each subject in terms of the quality of their present social adjustment.

The results indicated that the teacher item most frequently related to negative adult adjustment was the simple notation that the child "failed to get along with other children." This item related to six separate adulthood variables. Compared with boys whose teachers did not check this item, boys whose teachers indicated that they failed to get along with other children were twice as likely to report later not finishing high school, having been fired because of something they had done, having been in trouble with the law, and/or having been arrested. They were also somewhat more likely to enter the military and/or to report that they had been hospitalized for psychiatric disorder. (Girls were not examined in this analysis.) No other teacher item, including undue aggressiveness, was associated with more than two later problematic outcomes, and shyness did not predict any problematic adult outcomes. In addition, boys and girls who failed to get along with other children, as adults had significantly lower clinician adjustment ratings than other children, even after intelligence and socioeconomic status had been statistically controlled. Janes et al. (1979) noted:

> The diversity of adulthood behaviors to which [failing to get along with peers] is related is striking and demonstrates that in this clinic population, poor peer relations serves as an ominous sign for future adjustment . . . The present results allow us to conclude that a teacher's perception that a child was not getting along well with other children could have served as a warning light for diverse adulthood problems and to conclude that the other teacher-rated behaviors do not singly forecast impending trouble [p. 468].

Of course, we must be wary of the fact that Janes et al. were working with a clinical sample and therefore that their results might not be generalizable to other children. However, Janes and Hesselbrock (1978) noted that their sample included an unusually broad spectrum of disorders – some severe, but most very mild – and suggested therefore that the generalizability might be relatively good.

Although the Kupersmidt and Janes et al. studies represent the most recent and most instructive studies in this area, at least three other studies provide follow-up data on the long-term risk of poorly accepted children. Gronlund and Holmlund (1958) examined dropout rates among elementary school children of sociometrically high and low acceptance. Consistent with the findings of Kupersmidt and Janes et al, they reported that the incidence of dropping out among poorly accepted children was several times that among highly accepted children and about twice that of children of average acceptance. Similarly, Barclay (1966) found that the incidence of dropping out among sociometrically poorly accepted boys was twice as high as base rates in the school district as a whole and nearly five times as high as that among highly accepted children specifically. Poorly accepted girls were also about twice as likely to drop out as district girls in general and about two and one-half times as likely to drop out as highly accepted girls. Finally, Roff, Sells, and Golden (1972) reported that a child's risk for later delinquency was inversely related to the extent of his or her peer acceptance as determined by positive and negative sociometric nominations from children and teacher ratings, although this relationship did not hold true in schools located in the economically deprived urban areas.

The findings described above and the earlier discussion of the functions of friendships in childhood converge on the very important conclusion that friendships play a critical role in meeting children's current and long-term psychological needs. Given this, it is not surprising that friendships also play an important role in people's mental, physical, and subjective well-being in adulthood. We turn to this issue next.

1.2. The importance of friendship in adulthood

Friendship influences on mental and physical health

Clinicians and researchers have long believed that adults have a fundamental psychological need to establish close emotional ties with others (e.g., Adler, 1927; Jourard, 1964; Sullivan, 1953). Consistent with this belief, correlational data from several research areas indicate that achievement of satisfying relationships may have important psychological and physical consequences. In this section we examine these data.

Although there are some inconsistencies in the research findings, social epidemiologists have established positive correlations between close relationships and emotional and physical well-being. For example, Berkman and Syme (1979) conducted a nine-year longitudinal study of

2,229 men and 2,496 women aged 30 to 69 in 1965, randomly sampled from Alameda County, California. The presence of four kinds of social ties (marriage, contact with friends, church membership, and formal or informal group associations) predicted the probability of a person dying in the next nine years. The trends held for both sexes across ages; however, marriage had the strongest benefits for men, whereas contacts with friends had the strongest benefits for women. Berkman and Syme constructed a social network index that tapped the number of close friends, the number of relatives their subjects felt close to, and the number of times these people were seen each month. The index was significantly related to mortality even after age, initial physical health status, socioeconomic status, health practices (smoking, alcohol consumption, obesity, physical activity), and utilization of health services were statistically controlled.

Other, perhaps less dramatic studies have provided similar results. For example, Brown, Bhrolchain, and Harris (1975) found that an intimate, confiding relationship between a woman and a male friend or spouse reduced the probability of depression after a stressful event. Similarly, Cobb (1976) reviewed evidence indicating that adequate social support can protect people in crisis from a wide variety of mental and physical health problems. These problems include complications with pregnancy, arthritis, death after an illness, depression, and suicide.

The attainment of a close relationship may serve a protective function at times of stress, and the absence of a close relationship is associated with mental and physical health problems. Miller and Ingham (1976) found that women who reported the lack of a close confidant also reported more fatigue, anxiety, depression, and irritability than women who reported having such a relationship. The absence of many casual, less intimate friends was also associated with higher symptom levels, both psychological and physical (e.g., backache, headache, dizziness). Although the results were not as clear for men, they showed the same trend. In another study, Miller (1967) analyzed the factors associated with community stay or rehospitalization of more than a thousand mental patients. He concluded that those patients who experienced close social relationships, regardless of sex or type of family, were more likely to remain in the community; isolates were more likely to be rehospitalized.

An experimental study by Arnetz, Theorell, Levi, Kallner, and Enroth (1983) randomly assigned elderly people living in a senior citizens' apartment building to an experimental, social activation group or to a control group. Social activity increased threefold in the experimental group. People in the control group *decreased in height* more than people in the experimental group. These changes were linked to changes in hormonal functioning in the experimental group. Plasma levels of testosterone, dehydroepiandrosterone, and estradiol increased significantly in the experimental group compared with the control group over a six-month period.

Finally, close relationships have also been associated with positive psychological states. Wilson (1967), in a review of correlates of avowed happiness, concluded that the most impressive finding was the relationship between happiness and successful involvement with people. Several aspects of social relationships seemed to be important, including being satisfied with one's friends and making friends easily. There is some evidence that close friendships are more important to a person's general sense of well-being than are relationships with acquaintances. Brenton (1974) noted that the Midtown Manhattan study of 1954 involving 1,660 men, women, and children supported the association between friendship and mental health: A very high risk of *poor* mental health was associated with the absence of close friends. The number of neighbors with whom the interviewees were friendly and the number of organizations to which they belonged were only moderately associated with sound mental functioning. Friendships played a much more important role.

Friendship and loneliness

From what we know, loneliness is an extremely widespread complaint of modern humankind. Weiss (e.g., 1982) distinguished between loneliness related to a need for close relationship and loneliness related to a need for community. Existential loneliness can also be distinguished. All forms of loneliness are important to understand, but loneliness caused by the lack of a close relationship is probably the most common (see Peplau and Perlman, 1982).

Rubenstein and Shaver (1982) placed a questionnaire in six American newspapers asking readers, among other things, how loneliness feels. They reported the results from a subset of 3,500 respondents ranging in age from 18 to 87 years. As the authors acknowledged, their findings were subject to the biases of the people who chose to fill out the questionnaires. The most common feelings of individuals who labeled themselves "lonely" were sadness, depression, boredom, self-pity, and longing to be with one special person. A factor analysis of all responses yielded four factors called Desperation, Impatient Boredom, Depression, and Self-deprecation. Rubenstein and Shaver speculated that Depression and Self-deprecation might best be conceptualized as reactions to loneliness. They suggested that prolonged loneliness or repeated rejection may lead to self-blame and finally depression. Because of their correlational nature, however, their data do not support conclusions about cause-and-effect relationships.

In another study, Paloutzian and Ellison (1979) examined the questionnaire responses of more than 400 people to items about emotional and physical feelings associated with loneliness. This sample, like the previous sample, was not randomly selected from the general population. Feelings that were significantly correlated with loneliness were helplessness, depression, rejection, being misunderstood, being unwanted, emptiness, worthlessness, frustration, isolation, and being unloved. There was also a significant negative correlation between self-esteem and emotional and physical feelings experienced during loneliness. Significant, but low correlations were found between loneliness and feelings of chest tightness and fatigue, but not for other physical complaints. Thus, these studies provide evidence that loneliness is associated with negative cognitive, emotional, and physical states.

When people feel lonely, the actions they take to deal with their loneliness appear to determine whether the loneliness will persist. By examining the effectiveness of strategies used to cope with loneliness, we can obtain a better understanding of the factors that alleviate feelings of rejection, alienation, and depression. It makes sense to assume that increased contact with others will reduce feelings of loneliness. Whether loneliness is actually dealt with in this way and whether it is an effective coping strategy has only recently been the focus of scientific investigation (see Chapter 9). At least two studies have addressed the way individuals cope with loneliness.

In the Rubenstein and Shaver study mentioned earlier, readers were asked which of 24 activities they were likely to perform when they felt lonely. The most common were reading, listening to music, and calling a friend. When all reactions to loneliness were factor-analyzed, the largest proportion of the common variance was a factor called Sad Passivity (crying, sleeping, sitting and thinking, doing nothing, overeating, taking tranquilizers, watching television, drinking, or smoking marijuana). This was found to be characteristic of those who reported severe loneliness. Rubinstein and Shaver described this as "a state of lethargic self-pity which may well contribute to a vicious cycle of low self-esteem and social isolation." It was also found to be highly correlated with both Depression and Self-deprecation.

The other three factors representing "solutions" to loneliness were found to characterize people who labeled themselves "infrequently lonely." These factors were Active Solitude (studying or working, writing, listening to music, exercising, walking, working on a hobby, going to a movie, reading, playing music), Spending Money (spending money, going shopping), and Social Contact (calling a friend, visiting someone). Rubenstein and Shaver (1979) suggested that these reactions were more constructive and positive solutions to feelings of loneliness, stating that

> active solitude . . . portrays a creative and rewarding use of time spent alone; it is an alternative to loneliness. The profligates, who react by Spending Money, compensate themselves for negative feelings – or at least attempt to distract themselves. . . . Social Contact . . . deals with the problem of loneliness head-on, by "calling a friend," or "visiting someone." For people who use this strategy loneliness is likely to be a transient state [p. 19].

This study has implications for the function of friendship. Social contact, among other things, may dispel loneliness and circumvent negative self-attributions that lead to hopelessness and depression. The failure to find constructive alternatives to loneliness may result in the set of behaviors called Sad Passivity.

A study by Paloutzian and Ellison (1979) examined 23 activities people reported engaging in when lonely and the perceived effectiveness of these behaviors in coping with loneliness. The greatest percentage of people were moderately to highly likely when lonely to remain alone to think, listen to music, talk to a close friend, read, spend time with close friends, or eat. Attempts to cope with loneliness by being alone to think were the most frequent, and establishing social contact was the next most frequent. The greatest percentage of people felt that making contact with close friends was the most effective way to cope. Thus, this study demonstrates that people who are less lonely than others report dealing with loneliness by getting together with others.

How loneliness is related to the characteristics of a person's social network is unclear. Studies that have examined the relationship between loneliness and self-reports of social contact or activities have resulted in mixed findings. For example, in daily recordings of social interaction, Jones (1981) found that loneliness was not related to the total number of interactions, average length of interactions, or perceived intimacy level of interactions. In contrast, McCormack and Kahn (1980) found that lonely subjects reported spending significantly less time with intimate others. No differences were found in satisfaction with the contact. Cutrona and Peplau (1979) found that dissatisfaction with one's friendships, dating partners, or family were better predictors of loneliness than self-reports of dating frequency, number of close friends, or frequency of contact with family.

Given such contradictory findings, it would be important to examine not only the amount of interaction but the content of the interaction. It is likely that having a mutually satisfying relationship is more important than the number of friends one has. The interpersonal behaviors and social processes that lead to judgments about relationship satisfaction should be observed. It is necessary to investigate systematically how qualitative aspects of a person's social relationships are influenced by loneliness.

Very few studies involving direct assessment of the social behavior of lonely individuals have been reported. One study conducted by Hockenbury, Jones, Kranau, and Hobbs (1978) measured behavioral differences associated with loneliness more directly than other studies. They found that in videotaped interactions of opposite-sex stranger dyads, lonely people differed from people who were not lonely in several ways. Lonely people made fewer statements focusing on the partner, asked fewer questions, changed the topic of discussion more frequently, and responded more slowly to the previous statement of their partners. Thus, the interpersonal behavior of lonely subjects with opposite-sex strangers was more self-focused and less responsive than that of other subjects. (For a similar pattern in children unaccepted by their peers, see Chapter 7.) Jones (1981) proposed that such behavior may have an inhibitory effect on friendship formation. It could be that, by focusing attention inward, lonely subjects fail to notice various cues of friendship or affection from other people. Also, lonely subjects may provide less attention and responsiveness to others than other subjects which might make them seem less attractive as potential friends. This study, linking loneliness to actual behavior during interpersonal interactions, represents a promising direction for future research.

In summary, the findings of this and the preceding section are intriguing and suggest that friendship at all ages may be important for our emotional and physical well-being. North Americans armed with this knowledge about health and friendships might be a very interesting group to observe. The vast amount of energy, time, and resources we spend planning our diets, taking vitamins, jogging, and exercising shows how interested we are in our health and longevity. What would happen if we invested the same energy, time, and resources in our close personal relationships?

However, most of these studies leave us with very little descriptive information about the kind or quality of support that is protective. Even if satisfying, close relationships are necessary for healthy functioning, the processes by which they operate are not understood. What are the important characteristics of friendship? What are the ingredients of friendship that affect the health of an individual? At present, these questions remain unanswered. Indeed, one goal of this book is to begin this task of description. But though we lack firm answers to the question of how friendships affect adjustment, we do not lack hypotheses. In the next two sections we examine two such hypotheses: that friendship provides social support during stress and that friendship is the basis for confidant relationships.

1.3. Friendship and social support

Social support and stressful life events

There is a great deal of research linking stressful life events to the occurrence of both physical and mental illness (Dohrenwend & Dohrenwend, 1974; Holmes & Masuda, 1974; Jacobs, Prusoff & Paykel, 1974; Kellam, 1974; Nuckolls, Casel & Kaplan, 1972; Rabkin & Struening, 1976). Although many observers have noted this relationship, there is considerable dissatisfaction with the evidence. There are numerous methodological and conceptual problems that require resolution in future research to establish more definitively the relationship between stress and illness (for a review see Dean & Lin, 1977). Nonetheless, the hypothesis is alive and well and the target of considerable research.

One recent popular hypothesis to account for the variability in the stressfulness of specific life events posits social support as a stress-mediating or buffering system. This hypothesis is that people who can count on the support of close friends or relatives in the face of adversity are less likely to experience negative physical and emotional consequences than people who cannot.

One of the most frequently cited studies on the stress-moderating role of social support was conducted by Nuckolls, Cassel, and Kaplan (1972). They attempted to examine the degree to which "psychosocial assets" are protective against complications during pregnancy in the face of other life changes. Psychosocial assets were measured by a self-report inventory of the subject's feelings about herself, her life in general, and her relationships with her husband, her extended family, and her friends. The subjects were 170 military wives who gave birth in a military hospital. Measures of psychosocial assets and life changes were obtained retrospectively before pregnancy and then at two different times during pregnancy. It was found that, taken alone, neither life changes nor psychosocial factors were significantly related to complications. When psychosocial assets and life changes were considered together, however, a significant relationship was found. If the life change score was high both before and during pregnancy, women with more pychosocial assets had fewer complications than women with fewer assets. In the absence of many life changes, there was no significant relationship between psychosocial assets and complications. This study supports the hypothesis that social support moderates the impact of stressful life events rather than having a direct influence on health.

A retrospective study by Myers et al. (1975) also revealed that social factors moderate the relationship between life events and psychiatric symptoms. They interviewed 720 adults twice over a two-year period about their degree of social integration, life crises that occurred during the previous year, and physical and mental health. Individuals who reported few psychiatric symptoms but many stressful events were more socially integrated than individuals who reported many symptoms but few stressful events.

Although these studies tend to support the notion that social support is an intervening variable, there are conflicting findings. For example, Andrews, Tennant, Hewson, and Valliant (1978) found that neither coping style nor any of their measures of social support had any mediating effect on the relationship between life event stress and psychological impairment. They found that good coping ability and support had independent effects on psychological well-being.

There are many methodological problems with this research, including a tendency to rely on retrospective accounts as well as self-report data. Nonetheless, these early findings are encouraging. At the same time, it is probably the case that the relationship between social support and mental health is reasonably complex. Pearlin and Schooler (1978) suggested that effective copers may be those who have the capacity to gather support from others but that the effectiveness of any particular coping strategy depends on the kind of situation one is dealing with. For example, if one has little control over a particular situation, such as being fired from a job, it makes sense to use a coping strategy that will minimize the importance of such a situation or alleviate the stress. Job problems and marital problems, however, may lend themselves to very different solutions. One cannot as easily demean the importance of a spouse as one can devalue a particular job or an unattainable life style. Thus, the nature of the problem must be taken into consideration in determining the most effective coping strategy.

However, we do not yet know which situations lend themselves to the utilization of social resources. In some cases social support seems to be helpful, and in others relying on one's personal resources appears to be adequate. In coping with loneliness, for example, individuals who reported engaging in individual activities (e.g., reading, listening to music, shopping) felt less lonely than individuals who did not. This was also true of individuals who dealt with their loneliness by getting together with friends (Rubenstein & Shaver, 1982). In this case, both individual action and reliance on others seemed effective. In another study (Paloutzian & Ellison, 1979), although subjects preferred an individual coping strategy to deal with loneliness, they reported that getting together with friends was more effective. The effectiveness of drawing on social resources undoubtedly is influenced by the quality of one's relationships with others. The amount of trust, warmth, and commitment between two people, as well as the ability to communicate distress or the need for help, are likely to be important variables in the ability to gather support.

Another factor that may influence the effectiveness of drawing on social resources at times of stress is the expertise provided by the social network. Here both educational level and practical experience with a particular situation may make a difference. Those who have undergone a similar experience may be more aware of potential problems and alternatives for coping than those who have not. The educated may have professional competence with which to advise or render service to the person in distress that the less educated cannot provide. Also, access to monetary resources allows a person to hire those with legal, psychological, and medical expertise, which can do much to reduce the impact of a crisis. Indirect evidence for this is provided by the inverse relationship between social class and psychiatric status. More specifically, members of the lowest social class are more likely than members of higher classes to be diagnosed with more severe psychiatric categories of psychopathology (Dohrenwend & Dohrenwend, 1969; Dohrenwend, 1974; Levy, 1974). Myers, Lindenthal, and Pepper (1975) have suggested that individuals of higher socioeconomic status are more likely to have friends with money and education and can avail themselves of these resources in a crisis. Often, being classified as severely disturbed is the only way that lower-income people can receive free or low-cost psychiatric services.

One final study is of importance. Tolsdorf (1976) compared the social networks of 10 male hospitalized psychiatric patients (all first-admission schizophrenics) with 10 male medical inpatients matched on demographic variables. The social networks of the schizophrenics were kin-dominated, with kin frequently reported as hostile. The medical patients reported giving and receiving an equal amount of support, whereas the schizophrenics received more than they gave. Schizophrenics considered it inadvisable and potentially dangerous to draw on their networks in times of stress. There is evidence that this perception is veridical. Familial criticism, called "expressed emotion," predicts relapse of schizophrenic patients (see Doane et al. 1981; Milkowity et al. 1983, 1984; Vaughn & Leff, 1976). Hirsch (1981) has noted that previous family research suggests that families of schizophrenics discourage the development of nonfamily friendships and that this fact may be related to the excessive dependence of schizophrenics on their families and their lack of social skills.

Unfortunately, most of the research on coping has given greater emphasis to inner psychological resources than to social resources or to specific methods for coping. This leaves us with little scientific information about how social support helps an individual cope with stress. Most studies that focus on support as an intervening variable between stressful life events and psychopathology obtain only global measures of social support such as having or not having a confidant (Brown, Bhrolchain, & Harris, 1975).

The loss of social support

A growing body of research has focused on the deleterious effects of the loss of support through death, separation, or any change in the environment that disrupts existing social relationships. The loss of important social relationships can precipitate intense and complex emotional reactions. In his clinical observations of the recently separated, Weiss (1975) noted emotional reactions that he referred to as "separation distress." This is marked by a focusing of attention on the lost person and a great deal of discomfort because of the person's inaccessibility. The individual feels apprehensive, anxious, or, at times, euphoric. According to Weiss, an increased sense of vulnerability is experienced, even though in reality individuals may be just as capable of coping with threat as they were when their spouse was present. He also noted that separation frequently involves loss of self-confidence, increased feelings of worthlessness, and rejection.

Hetherington, Cox, and Cox (1977) found that divorced parents felt more anxious, depressed, angry, rejected, and incompetent than married couples. Ilgenfritz (1961) reported on a group educational program for 12 single mothers and identified the major problems that were discussed. These were fear of being alone, concern with the loss of self-esteem as a woman, hostility toward men, practical problems of living, specific concerns regarding child rearing, and interest in the development of self-help strategies. Loss of support through marital disruption has also been found to have negative consequences for the children of the disrupted family (see Hetherington, 1972; Hetherington et al., 1977; Kelly & Wallerstein, 1975, 1976; McDermott, 1968, 1970; Pemberton & Benader, 1973; Wallerstein & Kelly, 1974, 1975).

Blau (1961) has shown that marital disruption may be stressful not only because of loss of support from the spouse but because it may decrease other important social contacts. A change in marital status that puts one in a different social position than one's peers reduces the opportunity to maintain old friendship ties. According to Blau, the change signifies a shift in interests, experience, and interpersonal resources that differentiates the individual from peers. This diminishes the commonality that served as a basis for friendship. Thus, the overall number of friendship ties for such a person may be depressed.

Although people may react to the news that an individual's marriage has ended with warmth and compassion, this is not always the case. In fact, some have observed that people reject and avoid lonely others. There may be a social stigma attached to being divorced or lonely. Weiss (1973) wrote that "our image of the lonely often casts them as justifiably rejected" (p. 12). Gordon (1976) noted that even being single may be regarded negatively: "to admit to being single would be to admit to having committed a cardinal sin in our culture – that of being unable to attract or hold a mate" (p. 217). The extent to which negative stereotypes actually influence responses to the divorced or separated is unknown. Although no empirical evidence exists, the extent to which negative reactions prevail may contribute to feelings of rejection.

What psychological mechanisms account for the link between the loss of support and psychopathology? Brown, Harris, and Copeland (1977) address the role of loss in the etiology of depression. They emphasize that the loss of a close friend or relative often means the loss of someone who valued and appreciated the bereaved person. Being deprived of an important source of value may result in a loss of self-esteem. This kind of speculation, however, does not allow one to make predictions about the aspects of relationships that make one feel valued and appreciated (e.g., being needed, sharing activities). Brown et al. also assert that a person deprived of important sources of value can develop a profound sense of hopelessness, which is a central feature of depression. Whether this occurs, according to Brown et al., depends on one's ongoing self-esteem, the perceived ability to control one's world and thus change things for the better, and one's confidence that, in the end, alternative sources of value will become available. According to this viewpoint, the perception of control and ability to reestablish adequate social support influences the etiology of depression.

There are, of course, individual differences in the degree of stress experiences at the loss of a loved one. If, as Kaplan et al. (1977) suggested, loss of support results in needs being unmet, one would expect to find fewer psychological problems in individuals who develop and obtain support in alternative relationships. Thibaut and Kelley's (1959) concept of comparison level of alternatives may be relevant here. Individuals who perceive alternative relationships with high reward potential may be less affected by loss. Mueller (1980) made a similar point:

> The availability of alternative support relationships within the network when one is cut-off from usual support sources seems critical. Individuals who lack such alternatives would appear to be especially vulnerable to loss events or exits from the social field. In short, the degree to which network disruption can be absorbed without psychological damage to the focal individual may be dependent, in large part, on the availability of adequate substitutes for the disrupted or lost relationship(s) [p. 157].

There is empirical evidence for this notion. If the notion is connected with the greater dependence of men on the spouse as a confidant, it could account for the well-known sex difference in the impact of bereavement on the mortality of the survivor; the impact is generally greater for men than for women (for a review see Van Dyke & Kaufman, 1983).

Lowenthal and Haven (1968) showed that an individual who has been widowed within seven years and who has a confidant has an even higher morale than a person who remains married but lacks a confidant: "In fact, given a confidant, widowhood within such a comparatively long period makes a rather undramatic impact on morale. Among those having confidants, only 10% more of the widowed than of the married are depressed, but nearly three-quarters of the widowed who have no confidant are depressed, compared with only about one-half of the married who have no confidant" (p. 27).

White and Asher (1976) interviewed 30 divorced men 6 to 12 months after they were divorced concerning their marital disturbances and postseparation adjustment. In general, the men who made the most successful adjustment to the divorce were those who had *not* been as dependent on their wives, but had established a social life that was somewhat independent of the marriage. Maddison and Walker (1967) found that the perceived supportiveness of the social environment by widows at three months after the spouse's death was associated with the widows' health status at one year. Those who perceived more support had fewer health problems at one year.

The findings of these studies converge on a number of important problems faced by persons who have lost a loved one, particularly a spouse. This would include a generally weakened social support system, economic and child-care problems, psychological reactions to the loss (e.g., depression, loss of self-esteem, anger), and the need for resocialization into the community as a single person.

1.4. The importance of having and being a confidant

Among adults, confidant relationships appear to provide a sense of psychological intimacy that may not be found in other relationships. Crawford (1977) interviewed 306 middle-aged married couples about their closest friends. The two definitions of intimate friendship given most frequently were "A friend is someone I can talk to and trust" and "A friend is someone I can call on for help." Phillips and Metzger (1976) found that the largest proportion of their respondents defined friendship in terms of being able to discuss personal matters. Similarly, a survey of *Psychology Today* readers (Parlee, 1979) indicated that the qualities of friends most valued were loyalty, warmth, and the ability to keep confidences. Although random samples were not used in some of these studies, it would appear that one of the functions of a friend in adulthood is to play the role of a confidant.

An important issue in the literature on social support and mental health is whether the diffuse support of many casual friends and acquaintances helps, or whether only a close relationship with a trusted confidant is helpful. Some researchers have investigated the different consequences of these two types of social support by making a distinction between emotional and social isolation (e.g., Fischer & Phillips, 1979; Weiss, 1973). Emotional isolation refers to the absence of a confidant, whereas social isolation refers to the absence of less intimate friends and acquaintances.

A few studies have addressed the issue of whether there are different psychological consequences of emotional and social isolation. These studies have resulted in mixed findings. In some studies only close relationships were judged to be important for emotional well-being (e.g., Brown, Bhrolchain, & Harris, 1975; Lowenthall & Haven, 1968). In other studies both close and casual relationships seemed to make a difference (e.g., Henderson, Byrne, Duncan-Jones, Adcock, Scott, & Steele, 1978; Miller & Ingham, 1976), and in one study the number of casual friends a person had was more strongly related to feeling pleased or happy than was having or not having a confidant.

Unfortunately, most of these studies suffer from the same methodological problems as those of the social network correlates of mental health. In particular, this research is characterized by the exclusive use of self-report measures of questionable reliability and validity to operationalize both social relationships and mental health.

It is also likely that the importance of various types of relationships varies as a function of the age, sex-role identification, marital status, and socioeconomic status of the individuals involved. For example, it may be more important in young adulthood than it is in middle age to have many friends, because this is a way to establish a sense of personal competence (Campbell, Converse, & Rodgers, 1976) and because younger adults are "between families" (Shulman, 1975).

Also in need of further study are the conditions under which having a confidant influences mental health. For example, in the Brown et al. (1978) study the confidant relationship was of primary importance only when women were under stress. It is possible, then, that the influence of a confidant on mental health is limited to moderating the impact of life event stress rather than having an impact on mental health independent of the presence of stressful events. As another example, we know that married men tend to have much smaller social networks than their wives, and if they are happily married their wives are their primary confidants. This is not true of their wives, for whom friends and kin are primary sources of confidant relationships (Komarovsky, 1962; see also Komarovsky, 1976, on college men's confidant relationships, and Berkman and Syme, 1979, on married men and women).

The measures used to assess social support and mental health contribute to the ambiguity of the findings. There is a need for more detailed questioning, monitoring, and observation of the confidant relationship than these studies have undertaken. Even if the discussion of personal matters is a general criterion of an intimate relationship, this leaves a great deal unknown. What kind of information is disclosed, at what level of intimacy, and how does this come about? Also, what is the response to the disclosure? Is it problem solving, nurturance, empathy, reciprocal disclosure, or engagement in various activities together? Dyadic social processes have not been examined.

Furthermore, a self-report assessment of a relationship may simply be a measure of relationship satisfaction rather than a specific description of relationship characteristics. This is not an unlikely possibility, given the results of the past 45 years of research on marriage using primarily questionnaires and interviews. In the area of marriage it has been empirically discovered (see Burgess, Locke, and Thomes, 1971) that almost any questionnaire about the marriage correlates extremely highly (high .80s) with measures of marital satisfaction. This is so because of common method variance, a critical problem. Unhappy couples endorse almost any item that describes something that could be wrong with their marriage, and happy couples tend to endorse almost any positive item. Thus, almost all questionnaires on marriage tap this same fundamental dimension of marital satisfaction (for a brief review see Burgess, Locke, and Thomes, 1971). Burgess suggested in the 1950s that sociologists of marriage were all measuring the same dimension because their measures correlated so highly, despite the fact that each of the measures were called something other than marital satisfaction. Even today Burgess's point is often ignored. Every few years a new self-report measure of the quality of the marital relationship emerges in the literature (e.g., focusing on some theoretical construct such as equity); in subsequent years the new measure is invariably shown to correlate with old measures of marital satisfaction in the .80s. This methodological shortcoming is one strong reason for employing multiple methods of measurement in the study of relationships, and the chances are that this also holds for the study of the confidant relationship.

Another problem is that the measures used to assess psychological well-being vary greatly from one study to another. For example, in a study by Fischer and Phillips (1979) a measure of positive affect was used, and in the Miller and Ingham (1976) study indices of negative affect and physical illness were used. This makes it difficult to compare findings across studies. Furthermore, none of these studies was able to account for the direction of effect in the social support/mental health equation.

Identity of the confidants

Several investigators have specifically studied the identity of the confidant. According to Bloom, Asher, and White (1978), marital status is one of the most consistent social correlates of mental health. Perhaps the role of the spouse as confidant is an important contributing factor. A study by Roy (1978) compared, among other things, the confiding nature of the marital relationship of 84 depressed women and 84 women in a matched control group. On the basis of the results, Roy concluded that the lack of a confiding marital relationship was one factor associated with depression in working-class women. Fischer and Phillips (1979) also examined the identity of the confidant. They found that spouses were "very disproportionately" named as confidants, *especially by men with regard to disclosure of personal worries.* Men were more likely either not to have a confidant or to have only one (their spouse) than were women, who tended to have confidants in addition to their husbands outside the home. Similarly, Booth and Hess (1974) found that, among married people, a larger proportion of all friendships reported by women were characterized by confiding behavior. Lowenthal and Haven (1968) also found that the characteristics of a person having a confidant and the identity of the confidant were related to the person's sex and marital status. They found that women were more likely than men to have an intimate confidant. The married were most likely to have a confidant, single persons were least likely, and the widowed fell in between. Husbands were the least frequently mentioned by women, whereas wives were the most frequently mentioned by men. As we noted previously, this is a reasonably consistent finding in the literature.

Even though women were likely to have confidants other than their husbands, being married seemed to decrease the amount of confiding that both men and women did to individuals other than their spouse (Fischer & Phillips, 1979). Fischer and Phillips wrote:

> For both genders, being married meant a greater chance of no extra-household confidants. These results suggest that in acting as confidants, spouses often substitute for more than one other person. This is especially so for males, where the spouse often substitutes for no confidant at all [p. 13].

Thus, marital status seems to influence the choice of individual in whom one confides. As we noted earlier, there appear to be distinct sex differences in husbands' and wives' social networks with respect to confidants.

In any discussion of confidants, the issue of sex differences in self-disclosure inevitably arises. In our view the literature on sex differences in self-disclosure within the context of close relationships is in need of serious reappraisal. In her 1976 book *Dilemmas of Masculinity*, Komarovsky stated on the basis of her 1962 study of 58 blue-collar couples that the blue-collar male is generally not emotionally expressive, is not self-disclosing, and does not view his wife as someone with whom he can talk things out. However, she did not analyze her data statistically, and her conclusion is unwarranted. We analyzed her tables 10a and 10b (p. 362) and found a strong statistical relationship between marital satisfaction and self-disclosure for both men [$X^2(1) = 14.09$] and women [$X^2(1) = 16.25$]. These results show that, in her sample, blue-collar husbands *do* self-disclose when they are happily married. Further analysis revealed that in *happy marriages* there are no statistically significant differences between husbands and wives in the amount of self-disclosure.

Komarovsky's data reveal that husbands and wives differ in the area in which they show emotional reserve. Women tend to hold back information and disclosure in the most personal areas (worries about health, dissatisfaction with self, hurts, dreams and aspirations for themselves and their families, transgressions, and reminiscences), whereas men tend to hold back only in concerns about their jobs. Women self-disclose in these areas to close female friends and female kin, whereas men primarily do not disclose except to their wives. Thus, on the basis of this reanalysis of Komarovsky's data and our discussion so far, it appears that men have a smaller and more intense social network than women, which may explain, in part, why they are more vulnerable than women to bereavement when they lose a spouse (see Van Dyke, 1983).

In distressed marriages, however, the evidence is that men withdraw whereas women do not. Findings on marital grievances from the earliest studies (Terman, et al., 1938) reveal sex differences. Men complain that their wives are too conflict engaging, whereas women complain of their husbands' withdrawal.

J. Gottman and R. Levenson (unpublished data) proposed that, in distressed marriages, men withdraw from high levels of negative affect because their autonomic nervous system differs from that of women. Men are more labile physiologically in response to stress, have higher autonomic base rates, and recover more slowly than women. Autonomic arousal may be more punishing for men than for women, and they may therefore try to manage the level of negative affect so that conflict does not escalate. This hypothesis would account for such results as men being described as "rational" and women as "emotional" and for the observed sex differences in marital interaction (e.g., see Raush et al., 1974).

Other evidence on sex differences in expressiveness should be reexamined as well. For example Shennum and Bugental (1982) noted that, although women smile more than men, they often mask a negative affect with a smile, whereas men prefer to inhibit any facial expression as an emotional control strategy. In a paper entitled "Perfidious Feminine Faces," Bugental, Love, and Gianetto (1971) reported that children trust their fathers' smiles more than their mothers' as indicating positive affect because mothers often also smile when they are angry or upset. Hence, obtained sex differences in expressiveness (e.g., see the review by Hall, 1979) must be closely reexamined. Despite this need for reexamination, the view lives on that men's relationships and emotional lives are impoverished compared with women's.

The definitive work on these questions has yet to be done, and, indeed, even ground-breaking descriptive research is often lacking. Many differences may be a function of how questions are asked or how interviews are conducted. For example, although it is well accepted that depression is more common among women than men, there is now evidence that, if one asks about the *recent* past, the responses of men and women do not differ (Angst & Dobler-Mikola, in press). Similarly, Averill (1983) reported no sex differences in the expression of anger when he employed a daily diary procedure. Men and women express anger about as often and primarily in the same contexts (close relationships) and for the same reasons.

Even the context in which data are collected may be critical in determining the kind of sex differences one observes. For example, specifically in relation to friendship, Brenton (1974) wrote:

When I interviewed working-class men in formal settings the image they usually presented was conventionally masculine – strong, tough, self-contained, little emotion showing through. When I interviewed similar men in more relaxed settings – for instance, having drinks with them at veterans' posts – many became freer about revealing their feelings, and certainly much less unemotional. "I love this guy, I really do!" exuberantly cried a telephone company lineman at a V. F. W. post near Boston after he had introduced me to a buddy for the third time. . . . these men were affectionate with their friends too – showing them off to me with evident pride; kidding, clowning, bear-hugging them, being physical with them in the kind of way men are when they want to be demonstrative with each other but also reassure the world about their masculinity [p. 43].

However, Brenton found that white-collar executives and businessmen (in either formal or informal interviews) are guarded about their feelings, either when sober or after having had a few drinks. "They conformed to the image of the close-mouth executive," he wrote (p. 43).

An interesting issue raised by these studies is whether other network relationships can provide an adequate *substitute* for a strong supportive relationship with the spouse. That is, can close ties with other network members compensate for the lack of a confiding relationship with the spouse?

Bott (1957, 1971) examined how the marriage itself is related to people's involvement with other members of their social network. She hypothesized that "the degree of segregation in the role-relationship of husband and wife varies directly with the connectedness of the family's social network" (Bott, 1971, p. 21). In other words, the more clearly defined and separated are the roles of husband and wife, the more likely is each spouse to have his or her own separate network to confide in. Segregated roles are characterized by a clear division between the tasks of husband and wife. The wife is usually responsible for household tasks, and husband and wife tend to have separate interests and activities. Their roles tend to be complementary and independent. Joint roles, on the other hand, are characterized by a sharing of tasks and interests between husband and wife. Bott (1971) found that in segregated role relationships husband and wife usually had separate circles of same-sex friends. Their separate social networks tended to be closely knit, with kin playing an important part. Bott suggested that, with separate and closely knit networks, each spouse derived more emotional support from external relationships and as a result less was needed or demanded from one's spouse.

However, when spouses had joint roles, a different pattern was found. In these cases, husbands and wives tended to have friends in common (e.g., other couples) rather than separate same-sex friends. Bott found that these couples usually had more loosely knit social networks, with kin playing a less important part. Marriages in which roles were shared and in which networks were loosely knit were more likely to be mobile both socially and geographically. Bott suggested that, in these marriages, husband and wife must rely more on each other for emotional support and satisfaction than couples with separate closely knit networks.

This study suggests that the lack of a confiding relationship with the spouse may be more problematic in marriages characterized by joint roles and loosely knit networks. In these cases strong emotional support may be less available from network members. In segregated role relationships with separate closely knit networks, the lack of a confiding relationship with the spouse may be less problematic. Adequate substitutes may be available in the social network. However, if something cuts off one's contact with friends or kin, such as a move, physical disability, or the loss of a job, this could place new demands on the segregated marital relationship.

Although these studies suggest the importance of having a relationship in which personal matters can be discussed and in which emotional intimacy is expressed, practically nothing is known of the process whereby intimacy develops. In later chapters of this book we shall show that studies on self-disclosure suffer from serious methodological problems due to the lack of validity of self-report measures of self-disclosure.

1.5. What do we know about friendship?

Friendship appears to be a distinct form of human relationship. Its existence transcends legal sanctions, social institutions, and family ties. Brain (1977) wrote that "no culture fails to emphasize the essential loyalty and love between friends." He reported that many cultures such as that of the Bangwa value friendship far above kinship. Not only is friendship a highly valued relationship but, according to Brain, it is nearly a universal characteristic of human society. There has been increasing interest in the topic of friendship among behavioral scientists in recent years. Sociologists are studying the nature and sociometric patterns of naturally occurring friendships among children (Corsaro, 1978; Hallinan, 1978). Developmental psychologists (Asher et al., 1977) and special educators (Strain, Cooke, & Appolloni, 1976) are beginning to focus on peer relations as an important factor in a child's social development. Social psychologists are publishing an increasing number of articles and books about the growth and decline of close relationships (Altman & Taylor, 1973; Levinger & Raush, 1977; Rubin, 1973).

Despite the increasing interest in friendship, there has been very little descriptive research on its natural formation and maintenance in ongoing relationships. Little is known about what friends talk about or do together, or what the function of various kinds of activities may be, or how mutually satisfying relationships are maintained or fail to be maintained, and so on. There is, therefore, a need for basic descriptive research in this area.

Most work has been conducted in the laboratory (see Byrne, 1971). Levinger and Snoek (1972) noted that most of these laboratory studies deal with attraction based on first impressions between strangers rather than with factors that promote and maintain attraction in long-term relationships. Thus, there is a large body of research associated with the earliest stage of the acquaintance process and little that focuses on well-established relationships. This dearth of knowledge about the processes of friendship and acquaintanceship has resulted in a very small data base for generating hypotheses and constructing theories about the nature of friendship in adults.

Theoretical models of relationship development

Theoretical models of the development of relationships have dealt primarily with courtship and marriage (Lewis, 1972; Murstein, 1970; Ryder, Kafke, & Olson, 1971; Stambul & Kelley, 1978). More recently, however, models have been developed that have a greater degree of generality and attempt to account for the formation and maintenance of all interpersonal relationships (Altman & Taylor, 1973; Huesmann & Levinger, 1976; Leik & Leik, 1976; Levinger & Huesmann, 1974; Levinger & Snoek, 1972; Scanzoni, 1978). These models are based on the social exchange theories of Homans (1961) and Thibaut and Kelley (1959). They focus on reward – cost factors, proposing that individuals will positively evaluate a relationship and will be more likely to continue moving through the stages of acquaintance if they perceive the relationship to be more rewarding than costly. Two of these models, incremental exchange theory proposed by Levinger and Snoek (1972) and social penetration theory proposed by Altman and Taylor (1973), will be considered next.

Incremental exchange theory. Levinger and Snoek (1972) view dyadic relationships as varying in degrees of "relatedness." The dimension of relatedness is characterized by three levels ranging from awareness of each other without contact to superficial interaction to a deeper relationship characterized by interdependence and emotional investment. The notion of interdependency pertains to the ability of individuals involved in a relationship to determine the outcomes (i.e., rewards and punishments) for the other directly.

According to Levinger and Snoek (1972) a relationship begins when one person becomes aware of another. If two people enter into "surface contact," they can each sample the actual outcomes of the joint interaction. If this outcome compares favorably with the outcomes the individual expects in general, as well as with those available in other relationships, Levinger and Snoek predict that the relationship will continue. At this second level of relationship, Levinger and Snoek describe communication as containing no self-disclosure and almost never concerning personal matters outside of stereotyped role requirements. If the relationship continues to be favorably evaluated, it moves into a level of mutuality characterized by "unique interpersonal depth." At this level, there is self-disclosure containing personal feelings, shared knowledge, and open evaluation of how the individuals feel about the relationship. Within this third level of relationship, there exists a range of mutuality with greater degrees of intimacy, characterized by increasing degrees of reciprocal self-disclosure. The intimacy of items for potential disclosure are conceptualized by Levinger and Snoek as a continuum ranging from easily disclosed and publicly accessible information to emotionally laden and privately held information about the self.

Social penetration theory. Altman and Taylor's social penetration theory postulates that interpersonal relationships follow a developmental course similar to that proposed by incremental exchange theory. They suggest that interpersonal interaction changes over time in terms of breadth (i.e., the amount of interaction per unit of time) and depth (i.e., the intimacy of an interaction). This results in a relationship progressing from "highly superficial" to "highly intimate." Once again, exchange theory is central. The balance of rewards and costs in a relationship determines whether the dyad will move toward a greater or lesser degree of involvement. If the rewards outweigh the costs, the relationship will progress; if this balance becomes negative, "depenetration" will occur. The empirical evidence for these theories will now be considered.

Evaluation of the empirical evidence. Although few studies have systematically investigated the developmental nature of a relationship, there is an extensive literature in social psychology on interpersonal attraction (for reviews see Berscheid & Walster, 1969; Byrne, 1969; Lott & Lott, 1965; Secord & Backman, 1964). Interpersonal attraction is relevant to the present discussion because it can be seen as a measure of relationship development. Most of the studies, however, do not consider whether this attraction actually leads to affiliative behavior or the maintenance of a relationship.

Many of the empirical findings on attraction support the principles of reinforcement theory and suggest that individuals evaluate one another in terms of the perceived reward potential. Factors that lead to attraction include similarity of personality (Cattell & Nesselroade, 1967; Izard, 1960), similarity of social background (Festinger, 1950; Goodnow & Taguiri, 1952), similarity of attitudes (Brewer & Brewer, 1968; Byrne & Clore, 1966; Veitch & Griffitt, 1973), physical attractiveness (Byrne, Ervin, & Lamberth, 1970; Dion, Bersheid, & Walster, 1972) and cooperativeness (Deutch, 1960; Solomon, 1960). Physical proximity and frequency of contact increase the likelihood that individuals will notice these and other characteristics of others that make them attractive (Byrne & Buehler, 1955; Festinger, Schachter, & Black, 1950). Little research, however, has focused on which factors are rewarding at various stages of relationship development. Different factors may lead to initial attraction and maintenance of a relationship at later stages of acquaintance (Murstein, 1976; Lewis, 1972).

Even if studies of interpersonal attraction have added to our knowledge of how people become initially attracted to each other in order to form a relationship, we know little about friendship itself. Two shortcomings in the literature are the failure to examine social processes in established, rather than superficial, relationships and the paucity of research that employs measures of interaction processes as opposed to self-report measures.

Although a few studies have investigated attraction in ongoing relationships, they have been limited to the attitudinal rather than behavioral components of attraction. Longitudinal studies have investigated the connection between attraction and similarity, complementarity in needs, and personality "fit" in friends (Newcomb, 1961) and dating couples (Kerckhoff & Davis, 1962; Levinger, Senn & Jorgensen, 1970). Most of these studies have used self-report measures of attraction and variables that affect it rather than behavioral indices of attraction. Little is known about the connection between attraction and interaction processes in ongoing relationships. Understanding how relationships develop might best be advanced by approaches that relate attraction or other indices of relationship development to actual interaction sequences.

Content-laden theorizing. According to both incremental exchange theory and social penetration theory, the development of a relationship includes reciprocal behaviors that can be analyzed in terms of reward–cost factors. Each model proposes a theory that is essentially content free. That is to say, each model remains relatively unconcerned about specifying the nature of the interaction at each stage. It is as if these models viewed specifying the *type* of exchange as relatively trivial compared with specifying the reward–cost matrix of the exchange for each participant. Various types of interaction may include problem solving, praise, advice, self-disclosure, or derogatory comments. Perhaps these theorists view the type of interaction as idiosyncratic and not lawfully or theoretically central to the acquaintanceship process. This may, in fact, be a reasonable assumption. It is, however, an assumption that warrants further investigation. The precise nature of salient social processes must be described accurately *before* theory characterizing relationship formation and maintenance can be constructed. This critique is not meant to invalidate the use of behavior exchange theory, but rather to amplify and elaborate it. The critique is the basis for our interest in observational methods.

Similarity

It has been observed that, in North American culture, nonkin friends tend to be of the same age, sex, and race (Nahemow & Lawton 1975; Weiss & Lowenthal, 1975). There are exceptions to this, of course, but the idea of similarity as a necessary component of friendship has been the focus of a great deal of investigation.

Results of studies about similarity are mixed, with some data showing an association (Duck, 1973a; McCarthy, Duck, 1976) between similarity and attraction and others failing to reveal one (Curry & Kenny, 1974; Levinger, 1972; Duck, 1976). The important question here is not whether similarity leads to attraction, but rather what kinds of similarity are important, how important they are, and for whom (Huston & Levinger, 1978). As we shall see in this book, the establishment of similarity serves different functions and goals at different points in social development. Studies attempting to determine the role of similarity in the formation of friendship have failed to clarify these issues.

Similarity to another person in background attitudes, and other characteristics gives promise of that person's future liking toward us. Information about another's similarity to us is frequently interpreted to mean that the other is likely to be benevolent (Johnson & Johnson, 1972; Sole, Marton, & Hornstein, 1975), to be compatible (Sussman & Davis, 1975), or to have greater ability to provide rewards than someone who is dissimilar to us (Brickman, Meyer, & Fredd, 1975). These studies suggest that similar individuals may have more favorable expectations about the outcome of future interaction and therefore are more likely to interact. Thibaut and Kelley (1959) have argued convincingly that the degree to which social interaction is rewarding is in large part a function of the degree to which norms and values are shared by the participants.

In sum, there is indirect evidence that similarity may be an important aspect of friendship. The kind of similarity, its purposes, the conditions and stage of relationship in which it is important are unclear. Furthermore, the reasons for the importance of similarity and its influence on interaction must be empirically established. It seems likely, however, that similarity along dimensions that are important to an individual makes interaction more rewarding and self-validating.

Descriptions of friendship

Although little is known about the behavioral processes of friendship, some studies have obtained self-reports of what friendship is like. Several illustrations of this approach are considered here.

Reisman and Shorr (1978) interviewed 330 male and female subjects ranging in age from 7 to 65. They attempted to determine, among other things, what people expected from their friends. They found that younger respondents mentioned pleasure more often than older respondents ("A friend is nice to play with") and that this expectancy declined significantly with age. Older respondents were significantly more likely than younger respondents to mention utility ("Someone to talk to," "A help when you need help"). Thus, friendship expectations appear to change from providing pleasure and entertainment to being useful. This suggests that the functions of friendship may vary over the life span.

Weiss and Lowenthal (1975) also found certain similarities in written descriptions of friends of various ages ranging from high school students to older people facing retirement. Most of the 1,700 descriptions had to do with the nature of relationships. A content analysis of the descriptions based on preestablished categories revealed a cluster of items related to "doing things together." Friends were described as people with whom one has shared interests, experiences, and activities and with whom one feels comfortable talking. Friends were also seen as supportive, dependable, understanding, and accepting.

Bigelow (1977) asked children ranging in age from 6 to 14 years to write an essay about what they expected from their best friends in contrast to acquaintances. A question should be raised about studies requiring young children to *write* descriptions of friendship. It is possible that such a task is too demanding and that the results do not accurately reflect the nature of friendship at that age. In fact, considerable age-related differences in expectancies were found. There were, however, responses that did not change with age. Expectations that best friends would provide ego reinforcement and reciprocity of liking accounted for most of the consistency. This was also true in another study conducted by Bigelow and LaGaipa (1975). On the basis of these findings Bigelow asserted that the more cognitive aspects of friendship may change over time, but the affective value of friendship may remain basically unchanged. Similarly, Duck (1973) argued that the basic function of friendship at all ages is psychological or ego support.

In short, although there are certainly differences in the functions of friendship at various ages, there also appear to be substantial consistencies. Aspects of friendship that appear to be present at all ages include similarity, emotional supportiveness, shared activities, confiding, and reciprocal liking, trust, and acceptance.

The research discussed above grouped all friends into a single category. Some studies have made distinctions between types of friends along various qualitative dimensions. Murstein and Spitz (1973) asked female college students to rate friends of four different types: their best friend, their most admired friend, their most useful friend, and their most enjoyable friend. An 80-item bipolar checklist contained items judged to represent pleasure, utility, and virtue. Best friends were described mainly by traits of virtue, and most useful friends by traits of utility. Most admired friends also were described by traits of utility.

LaGaipa (1977) examined dimensions of friendship at four levels of involvement: social acquaintance, good friend, close friend, and best friend. A greater ease of self-disclosure was reported for best friends. What distinguished close from good friends was that close friends could be counted on to be helpful and supportive. Thus, the greater the involvement in the relationship, the more likely was the friendship to be perceived as providing supportive functions.

Accounts of developmental trends in friendship expectations are informative, but they tell us very little about how such expectations are realized in actual interaction. To rely on common sense in this regard can be misleading. For example, knowing that support is a common feature of both children's and adults' friendships could lead one to the mistaken conclusion that openly expressing one's understanding of the other's feelings or actions is desirable in a friendship. This is not necessarily the case. One of the few studies that has examined actual content of interaction provides some clues. Reisman and Yamokoski (1974) compared the communications of friends with those of therapist and client. In the context of discussing a personal problem, they found that friends rarely expressed direct empathy. Instead, they typically responded with either interrogative statements, expository statements, suggestions, or self-disclosures. Moreover, when subjects were asked how they liked their friends to respond to them during the discussion of a personal problem they indicated that the communication they most favored was expository. That is, subjects wanted their friends to offer an *analysis* or *explanation* of the problem, behavior, or possible course of action. They tended not to want their friends to be empathetic. It would have been difficult to predict this result.

1.6. Summary

In this chapter we have outlined evidence that friendship, the ability to make friends, and the ability to be generally well accepted by one's peers are important in several dimensions of life. We reviewed evidence that friendship is important in childhood because it fulfills needs for companionship, stimulation, physical support, ego support/enhancement, social comparison, and intimacy/affection, as well as evidence that children who have difficulty making and keeping friends are at relative risk for adjustment difficulties in later life. We also reviewed evidence suggesting the importance of friendship in adulthood for physical and psychological health. We reviewed evidence that loneliness is another dimension of living that can, to some degree, be ameliorated by close relationships with friends. Finally, we reviewed evidence that throughout our lives we will probably be better off if we can gather social support, have and be a confidant, and can replace the loss of social support, particularly through major life transitions.

We have also tried in this chapter to make a case for our approach to research. There is a need for careful observation and description, for research that is developmental, and for content laden theory construction.

II. Methods

2. The observation of social process

JOHN GOTTMAN

The greatest challenge in observational research is the discovery of a method for recording something difficult to define – namely, natural behavior. This requires a great deal of pilot investigation, which must be done anew for observations in different settings or with children of different ages. In the laboratory or playroom, for example, it is very difficult to capture the same high level of fantasy play, self-disclosure, and gossip that preschool children engage in at home. Video cameras disrupt fantasy play and gossip and so does the presence of the mother (see Chapter 4). Even a visible microphone can be a problem.

It is easy to tell when interaction is natural. There are few references during the interaction to the research, the recording equipment, or the artificiality of the situation (a code we call "reactive"). Also, there is a relaxation, spontaneity, and richness that is simply missing if people feel constrained.

It is much more difficult to design a coding system that categorizes unconstrained interaction, but it is well worth doing because it takes essentially as much time to code stilted behavior as it does to code unstilted behavior.

This chapter is a journal of our attempts to describe key social processes during the conversations of children and young adults with their friends and acquaintances. Although the focus of this chapter is on our coding systems and the methodological issues that guided their development, our hope is that interested readers will also learn how children talk to one another. How do they get one another's attention? What is a tag question or a summons–answer sequence? How do children manage a given level of conflict? How do 5-year-olds disclose their fears and worries?

This chapter describes two coding systems we have developed and their variations. The first, now called the MICRO system, took approximately five years to develop and was first published in a descriptive study of acquaintanceship in preschool and early childhood (Gottman & Parkhurst, 1980). Modifications of MICRO were introduced even before its publication, however, as it became apparent that the system had limitations. In particular, the MICRO system did not take into account the problems sociolinguists were confronting about indirect directives. As a result, a variety of categories considered in the MICRO system to be expression of feelings were actually indirect directives. For example, "I need to cut this" can be an indirect way of making a demand that saves face if it is ignored, compared with the direct form: "Please pass the scissors." After modifying the MICRO system, we recoded all our original tapes. This process took an additional two years and resulted in the comparisons of directive usage between friends and strangers and hosts and guests presented in Chapter 8.

The MICRO system was modified again for a study of college roommates (see Chapter 6); among other things, detail was added to the gossip and self-disclosure categories. This revision took us approximately five years but made a considerable difference in accounting for variation in closeness between roommates.

The second coding system, the MACRO system, was developed in the course of a study on how children become friends (Gottman, 1983). This system employed a larger interactional unit than the MICRO system did. The MACRO system *coded* for specific interaction sequences of interest, and it used more global categories. It was initially designed for peer interaction between children aged 3 to 9 years (all dyadic sex compositions: male/male, male/female, and female/female) but was subsequently expanded to code the interaction of children from 3 to 17 years of age (see Chapter 5).

The results of these efforts were three separate coding manuals (available on request). This chapter summarizes each of these coding systems and presents reliability data appropriate for the stringent task of sequential analysis of the data. First, however, it is useful to describe briefly the methods of sequential analysis we employ.

2.1. Sequential analysis

Many options exist for the sequential analysis of observational data (J. Gottman and A. Roy, in preparation). Most observational data are presented as rates or relative frequencies of specific code categories, and any sense of temporal pattern is lost. However, it is precisely in the study of temporal pattern that we can discover the social rules implicit in interaction. Sequential analysis can add precision to hypotheses about social interaction.

The relatively recent interest in the observational study of interacting systems, such as the parent–infant system, has led to the development of new techniques for sequential analysis (Bakeman, 1978; Gottman and Bakeman, 1979; Gottman and Notarius, 1978; Sackett, 1977; Allison and Liker, 1982). Much of this work has its roots in ethological approaches, which employ the mathematics of information theory to define a communicative sequence.

A communicative sequence occurs when the behavior of one organism reduces uncertainty in the behavior of another organism. Gottman and Parkhurst (1980) present the following illustration:

> Consider the social behavior of an organism for which we have no prior knowledge of which behaviors have communicative significance. For example, suppose we were studying spider crabs. We would notice that these crabs do not move very often; in fact, the unconditional base rate of crab B moving is about .03. To understand the communicative significance of a single chilepid raise of crab A, we may look at the conditional probability of crab B moving on those occasions following crab A's single chilepid raise. We find it is .03. The single chilepid raise of crab A has resulted in no reduction of uncertainty in crab B's behavior. But when we look at the forward chilepid extension of crab A, we find that the conditional probability of crab B's movement is .65. The forward chilepid extension has definite communicative value [p. 200].

The conditional probability of an event A, given a prior event B, is written $p(A/B)$. We shall use this notation throughout this book.

Thus, *the detection of sequences involves the comparison of conditional and unconditional probabilities.* In this chapter the z-score statistic initially proposed by Sackett (1977) and later modified first by Gottman (1980) and then independently by Allison and Liker (1982) is used to compare conditional with unconditional probabilities. The latter statistics are not radically different. The Sackett statistic is more conservative than the Allison and Liker (AL) statistic. Neither is actually normal, except asymptotically, that is, for a relatively large number of observations. In the research presented in this book, we used the z-score as a statistic in an analysis of variance or regression, rather than referring it to a standard normal table (see also Margolin and Wampold, 1983; Wampold and Margolin, 1983).

Event sequential data – data in which no code can follow itself (Bakeman, 1978) – were almost always used in the present research. This eliminated the need to be concerned with lag 1 autocontingency in the data in computing the z-score index of cross-contingency. However, there are times when this collapsing is misleading, for example, if we are interested in durations. Hence, if we want to see if children in middle childhood gossip more than young children, event sequential data will tell us only whether the two groups differ in the number of separate episodes of gossip, not whether the length of episodes is different for the two groups.

2.2. Reliability for sequential analysis

For a general introduction to the assessment of reliability for observational data, see Bakeman and Gottman (1986). Two statistics are recommended: Cronbach's alpha from an appropriate generalizability study (see Cronbach, Glaser, Nanda, & Rajaratnam, 1972) and Cohen's kappa. Cronbach's alpha assesses the amount of variance due to a relevant facet of the experimental design (e.g., subjects) compared with an irrelevant facet. Cohen's kappa controls for interobserver agreement by chance alone. When important codes are infrequent, we cannot reliably compute Cronbach's alpha; instead, we must collapse data across subjects and can meaningfully compute kappa only. A generalizability study addressing issues raised by Cronbach et al. (1972) was conducted on the MICRO and MACRO systems. Reliability involves the claim that most of the variance in the occurrences of a particular code is accounted for by subject variance and not coder variance or Coder × Subject interaction (see Wiggins, 1973, ch. 7).* This approach to reliability assessment was first applied to observational data by Jones, Reid, and Patterson (1975). They calculated total frequencies of a particular code for observer and independent reliability checker over codes. However, their analysis was appropriate only if the data were not analyzed sequentially, because high reliability could be obtained in the analysis if both coders observed a similar number of a particular code, regardless of where in a transcript these occurrences were observed. Observers might thus not agree at all on specific utterances, and this analysis would still yield a high coefficient of generalizability.

A more stringent procedure for sequential analysis is to tie agreement

---

* $\alpha = \dfrac{(MS_s - MS_e)}{(MS_s + MS_e)}$ (Wiggins, 1973), where the subscripts s and e denote standard and error, respectively.

Table 2.1. *Computing generalizability coefficients*

	Observer 1		
Observer 2	A	B	C
A	5	0	1
B	1	12	1
C	2	3	40

Note: The first step for each transcript is the confusion matrix, here for transcript 1 (see Table 2.2).

Table 2.2. *Sample data for computing generalizability coefficient for code A*

Transcript no.	Diagonal	Diagonal plus off-diagonal
1	5	6
2	•	•
3	•	•
•	•	•
•	•	•
N	•	•

Note: See Table 2.1.

to specific utterances. A matrix of agreements and disagreements can be tallied for the two coders by proceeding through the transcript unit by unit. Suppose that there are three codes, A, B, and C, and the matrix for a particular transcript is as displayed in Table 2.1. Diagonal entries represent agreement on particular utterances. For Code A, we can calculate two numbers: the total number of diagonal entries (five in this case) and the total number of diagonal plus off-diagonal entries. These two numbers form the entries in the repeated-measures design illustrated in Table 2.2. Perfect agreement is tied to specific units of transcript. In the perfect-agreement case, the variance is accounted for entirely by variance across subjects, as in the Jones et al. (1975) analysis, but agreement is localized at particular utterances. There are two relevant generalizability claims: (1) High reliabilities are obtained for each coding category, and (2) codes discriminate across subjects (or dyads) and not across irrelevant facets such as observers, time of the coding within the study, or location of the reliability segment within the transcript. Detail on computations can be found in Bakeman and Gottman (1986).

As previously mentioned, in many cases it is not meaningful to compute Cronbach's alpha – for example, if there are not enough instances in the reliability sample of specific codes to rely on the frequencies for these codes on a tape-by-tape basis. This is the case for many codes in the MACRO coding system, because this system employs a larger interaction unit and there are thus fewer codes in each tape. In this event, Cohen's kappa provides an estimate of interobserver agreement that controls for chance levels of agreement. Cohen's kappa is computed from the confusion matrix, as described in Bakeman and Gottman (1986). Cohen's kappa still ties agreement to specific time points, so that it is appropriate for sequential analysis.

2.3. A MICRO to MACRO understanding of social processes

A coding system is useful only to the extent that it provides a window to social processes of interest. We began designing coding systems at a microanalytic level, as reflected by the MICRO coding system and its decendants. As we got to know our data and how our codes were used by observers, and as we conducted sequential analyses of our MICRO data, we began to use specific codes and specific sequences of codes to index *social processes* we were interested in. Our interest had been at this process level of analysis to begin with, but the MICRO system provided the precision necessary to arrive at this level. As testimony to the usefulness of this approach, we found (Gottman, 1983) that with a few MICRO codes and code sequences it was possible to account for 80 to 90% of the variance in predicting whether two unacquainted children between 3 and 9 years of age would "hit it off" and progress toward friendship.

With knowledge of the variables that indexed important social processes, it was then possible to design the MACRO system, which coded for social processes more directly. As will be seen, the MACRO system was very different from the MICRO. First, it *coded* for sequences of social acts. Second, the dyad – not the individual child – was the unit of study. Third, a larger interaction unit was employed. Fourth, new categories were devised, categories that became apparent only through this empirical building process. Finally, MACRO was much faster than MICRO.

In continuing the building process, we sought to understand how the social processes were organized with respect to one another. The first level of organization was temporal, that is, the sequencing of social processes within the same interaction session. The results of this analysis are presented in detail in Gottman (1983) and briefly in Chapter 3. The second level of organization was developmental, as will be summarized later in this chapter (see Section 2.11) and in considerable detail in Chapter 5.

Thus, we see a kind of overall progression in this observational research, designed so that at the final, most global and theoretical level our discussions will still be grounded in precision.

2.4. The MICRO coding system

The MICRO coding system uses 42 content codes and 6 double codes to derive 20 mutually exclusive and exhaustive summary codes. These summary codes, in turn, can be used to index 6 conversational social processes: communication clarity and connectedness, information exchange, establishing common ground, the resolution of conflict, positive reciprocity, and self-disclosure. They also can be used to index the extent to which two previously unacquainted children hit it off and progress toward friendship. A detailed presentation of the MICRO system is presented in Gottman (1983) and is also available in manual form (Gottman, Parkhurst, & Bajjalieh, 1983). The following discussion outlines the coding unit and coding procedure and summarizes the code categories and their reliabilities as calculated in two studies of Gottman (1983). Next the derivation of the summary codes is presented. Then the use of the MICRO summary codes to index the six social processes and hitting it off is discussed. Finally, the results of a methodological study are presented. The purpose of that study was to examine the impact of using audiotapes rather than videotapes to code with the MICRO system.

The coding unit

The MICRO system uses a unit called the thought unit, which is one expressed idea or fragment. A wide variety of units have been used in previous research on conversation. The three most common units are the utterance, which is any speech separated by pauses; the phrase, which is separated by punctuation; and the sentence. Each unit has shortcomings. People do not always express ideas without pausing, as in "I'm going to make mine [*pause*] green." It does not seem sensible to make this two units. Moreover, people do not always complete their sentences, as in the following examples: "Something's broken. Right here!" "My daddy for!" "Going underwater!" "Under there!" "Going bells!" (ringing bells). The sentence unit is clearly not manageable; in conversation, verbs are often discarded, fragments are repeated, ideas intrude parenthetically during speech, and speech disturbances (Mahl, 1956) are common.

The thought unit derives from research on the conversation of married couples (Gottman 1979). This unit can be one utterance or several, and it can be either a phrase or a sentence. Reducing the coding to event sequential data is a data-reduction technique; for example, a series of utterances that give instructions could be considered one code even though they are interrupted by pauses (e.g., "First you put this on this [pause] then you snap this on [pause] when you're finished . . . "), or two utterances that give reassurance could be considered one sympathy code (e.g., "Don't cry [pause] your daddy'll be back soon"). The thought unit can be somewhat more global than the utterance; for example, a thought unit can be referred to the code that involves assigning roles to both children or sharing, whereas if the utterances were coded separately they might be coded as two commands. However, the thought unit has its own limitations. For example, it loses information about time; it assumes that conversation is segmented by meaningful speech units. Clearly the choice of a unit is an important issue, and it is not independent of the design of the coding system.

The coding procedure

Coders use both audio- and videotape and the accompanying verbatim transcripts. A randomly selected section of several pages from each double-spaced typewritten transcript (about 7 minutes) of each tape is independently coded. Generalizability indices do not vary greatly when 4 or 2 pages are used, except for infrequent codes. For very infrequent codes, data must be combined across subjects and Cohen's kappa computed. Every tape is checked in this fashion. In a long study in which two years are required to code the tapes this procedure yields reliability increment and not decay (Reid, 1972) over time (see Gottman, 1979).

Code categories and Cronbach alphas

Six double codes can co-occur to some extent with one another and with 42 content codes (to be discussed later). The double codes are the following:

1. *Fantasy,* coded whenever a child spoke in role within the framework of a fantasy. For example, "Help, help, they're tying me up!" (alpha = .998, .999 for Studies 1 and 2 of Gottman, 1983, respectively).
2. *Question,* coded whenever a statement was made to sound like a question. For example, "Is that mine?" (alpha = .959, .993).
3. *Joke,* coded whenever an utterance was accompanied by laughter, giggling, chuckling, or silliness. Examples include formally told jokes, bathroom humor, and puns (alpha = .933, .976).
4. *Squabble,* coded for angry, annoyed, disgusted, aggressive statements or other squabbling, which included insults, yelling, whining, sarcasm, verbal or physical aggression, threats, retaliation, or tattling (alpha = .777, .856).
5. *Gossip,* coded as statements about other people, regardless of the content or evaluative nature of the comment. For example, "Her mother and father sleep naked" (alpha = .917, .977).
6. *Positive,* coded for statements said with warm, approving, admiring, affectionate, loving, or enthusiastic tone of voice (alpha = .651, .747).

Not all double-code combinations are logically possible. Fantasy and gossip cannot logically co-occur, nor can squabbles and positive.

There are 42 content codes; these codes are mutually exclusive, but they can co-occur with any number of double codes. Table 2.3 lists these codes as they are grouped in the manual, with an example of each code and the reliabilities obtained in Studies 1 and 2 of Gottman (1983). Table 2.3 shows that nearly all of the codes were highly reliable. Low reliabilities were obtained only when codes occurred infrequently in the random reliability sample. This is not a problem with the coding system, but with the hazards of the reliability checking procedure; when the codes were more frequent, reliabilities were high.

Summary codes

To study friendship formation in young children (Gottman, 1983), the 42 content codes and 6 double codes of the MICRO system were aggregated to form 20 mutually exclusive and exhaustive summary codes for coding conversational processes. This not only served as a data-reduction device, but corrected to some extent the problem of low reliability among infrequent codes. This aggregation scheme was derived on both logical and empirical grounds and is shown in Table 2.4. This table shows, for example, that the four demands for the pair (hafta wanna, let's, let's in question form, and roles for both) are combined into a category called *we demands*. All four of these codes extend inclusion to the other child in an attempt to initiate a joint activity; they are thus functionally similar. Likewise, positive, an infrequent double code, is absorbed by the *agreement code*.

The validity of these aggregating decisions is presented in detail in

Table 2.3. *Content codes*

Code	Example	Cronbach α Study 1	Study 2
Demands for the other child			
1. Command (COM)	"Gimme that."	.983	.944
2. Polite requests (PRE)	"That one, please."	1.000	1.000
3. Polite request in question form (QPRE)	"Would you gimme that?"	.983	.935
4. Suggestion (SUG)	"You could make that black."	.994	.949
5. Suggestion in question form (QSUG)	"Why don't you make that black?"	1.000	.965
6. Asking permission (QASK)	"Can I play with that now?"	1.000	.942
7. Demands in the form of an information statement (IND)	"I think my crayons are next to you."	.663	.862
8. Demands in the form of a question for information (QIND)	"Have you got any sixes?"	.000	.921
9. Wanna (WA)	"I wanna play house."	.961	.924
10. Question wanna (QWA)	"Do you wanna play house?"	.970	.819
11. Requirements for the other child (REQ)	"You should stay in the lines."	.906	.862
12. Asks help (AH)	"Would you tie this for me?"	1.000	1.000
We demands (demands for the pair)			
13. Hafta wanna (HWA)	"We have to take a nap."	1.000	.933
14. Let's (LTS)	"Let's play house."	.997	.978
15. Let's in question form (QLTS)	"How about drawing now?"	.872	.944
16. Roles to both (ROL)	"You be the cop and I'll be the robber."	.900	.791
You and me			
17. We both (WE)	"We're both four."	.884	.871
18. Me too (TOO)	"So am I."	.992	.950
19. We against others (WEG)	"We hate Jason."	.697	.975
20. Joining in (JOI)	A: Brm brrm. B: Brrm brmm.	.943	.991
Self-focus statements			
21. Me (ME)	"I finished it so fast."	.970	.969
22. Attention getters (ATT)	"You know what?"	.971	.974
Emotive statements			
23. Feelings of the speaker (FE)	"I'm mad at Sally."	.951	.916
24. Questions about the other child's feelings (QFE)	"Are you tired?"	.990	.963
25. Feeling inferred (FI)	"That must have hurt."	.929	.981
26. Sympathy and comfort (SY)	"Don't worry."	.486	.000
27. Offers (OF)	"I made this for you."	.703	.107

Table 2.3. *(Cont.)*

Code	Example	Cronbach α Study 1	Cronbach α Study 2
28. Agreement and acknowledgment (AG)	"Right."	.991	.976
29. Question for agreement (tag question) (QAG)	"Right?"	.999	.982
30. Disagreement (DG)	"It is not."	.985	.991
31. Disagreement with rationale (DG/CM)	"No, cause I'm using it."	.958	.950
32. Clarified agreement (AG/CM)	"Yeah, or a dog maybe."	.952	.940
Social rules			
33. Rule (RU)	"You have to take turns."	.864	.863
Information exchange and message clarification			
34. Information (IN)	"White and red makes pink."	.955	.952
35. Question for information (QIN)	"What does this one do?"	.930	.981
36. Information about the other child (YOU)	"You have big trucks."	.899	.895
37. Questions for information about the other child (QYOU)	"Do you read a lot?"	1.000	.990
38. Narration of other child's actions (INX)	"You're painting it blue."	.415	.715
39. Request for clarified message (QCM)	"Which one?"	.879	.847
40. Clarified message[a] (CM)	"The gray one with red on it."	.949	.922
41. Nonclarified message (NCM)	"*That* one."	.949	.934
42. Request for repetition (QRE)	"What?"	.980	.977
Transcript markers			
43. Inaudible (IA)	—	.991	1.000
44. Speaking to others (OTH)	"Mommy, where's my coat?"	.998	.996
45. Dummy code (segment break)[b] (DU)	—	1.000	1.000
46. Fragment (FR)	"It, uh . . ."	.986	.836

[a] Message clarification is also used after a disagreement code if a child gives a reason for the disagreement.
[b] Dummy codes index breaks in the action, such as when the children left the room and then returned. The dummy code was used to avoid joining codes from the end of one segment to the beginning of the next in the sequential analyses.
Source: Gottman (1983).

Gottman (1983). Parkhurst, approaching the issue from the perspective of the pragmatics of communication (Chapter 8), presents other evidence of the validity of aggregating the demand types specifically. Table 2.4 also shows that *all* 20 summary codes have high reliabilities, as calculated from Studies 1 and 2 of Gottman (1983).

2.5. Social processes of the MICRO system

As noted earlier, the MICRO coding system was derived as a precise means of indexing (1) whether two unacquainted children hit it off and (2) six conversational processes of interest in understanding how children make friends. It is important at this juncture to clarify the notion of *index* variables. As pointed out elsewhere (Gottman, 1983), a particular code or code sequence that is selected to index a complex social process need not "equal" that process, but merely index it in the sense that, *if that process occurs more or less often, the index variable should correspondingly increase or decrease in the data.* A particular sequence may thus represent an entire cluster of variables indexing a type of social event. Thus, the variables selected need *not* be taken as operational definitions of the social processes, but as indices of these processes. However, the flexibility to choose variables that index but do not define a particular process brings with it a responsibility to provide some validation, either internal or external, of the proposed index variables. For evidence of the validity of each of the index variables to be described next, the reader is referred to Gottman (1983).

The selection of social processes for study was, of course, informed by the literatures on acquaintanceship and friendship, and in the discussions that follow reference is made to these literatures as appropriate. But the selection was also determined empirically. This is because one is forced to select a set of social processes that provide an adequate summary description of how children actually talk. Suppose, for example, that a researcher decided to focus only on reciprocal self-disclosure in naturally occurring conversations. Trying to write a script of a conversation that contained *only* reciprocal self-disclosure would be absurd. It might sound like the following:

A: I was once in a mental hospital.
B: My mother is having an affair with the mailman.
A: Last summer I had an abortion.
B: My house was destroyed by a tornado.
A: I detest college.

It is difficult to write a reasonable script of purely reciprocal self-disclosure because so many other things are involved in a natural

Table 2.4. *MICRO summary codes for friendship formation studies.*

Lumped summary code	Subcodes
1. Weak demands (WEA) 1 = .969 2 = .816	Polite request Polite request in question form Suggestion in question form Asking for permission Demands in form of information statement Demands in form of a question for information Question wanna
2. Strong demands (STR) 1 = .977 2 = .959	Command Suggestion Wanna Requirements for the other child Asks help Offers
3. We demands (WEDE) 1 = .996 2. = .971	Let's Let's in question form Hafta wanna Roles to both
4. You and me (YM) 1 = .939 2 = .991	We both Me too We against others Joining in
5. Attention (ATT)	Attention
6. Me (ME)	Me
7. Feeling (FE)	Feeling
8. Question about feeling (QFE)	Question about feeling
9. Disagreement (DG)	Disagreement
10. Agreement (AG) 1 = .990 2 = .976	Agreement Sympathy Positive double code, co-occurring with any content code
11. Question for agreement (QAG)	Question for agreement
12. Clarifies message (CM) 1 = .945 2 = .930	Clarifies message Rule
13. Nonclarified message (NCM)	Nonclarified message
14. Information (IN) 1 = .956 2 = .950	Information Feelings inferred Information about the other child Narration of other child's actions

Table 2.4. *(Cont.)*

Lumped summary code	Subcodes

15. Questions (Q)
  1 = .935
  2 = .970
	Question for information
	Question for repetition
	Question for clarification

16. Gossip (G)	Gossip, with any content code
17. Fantasy (F)	Fantasy, with any content code
18. Jokes (J)	Jokes, with any content code
19. Squabbles (S)	Squabbles, with any content code

20. Blub (BL)
  1 = .995
  2 = .983
	Inaudible
	Speaking to others
	Dummy code
	Fragment

Note: Double-code co-occurrence rules: Fantasy and gossip cannot co-occur logically (code as gossip). Both take precedence over jokes. Jokes take precedence over squabbles and positive, which cannot co-occur. Positive and squabbles take precedence over questions.
Source: Gottman (1983).

conversation of this sort, including social comparison, humor, empathy, support, disagreement, exploring feelings, and so on. In short, the transcripts of children's conversations themselves influence the set of social processes one must include for study.

Furthermore, the set of process variables one decides to study also depends to a great extent on the literature one is addressing. For example, sociolinguists are often interested in how context affects language use. It makes a great deal of difference if one is primarily a linguist studying social interaction as a context for understanding how language is used in discourse or primarily a developmental social psychologist who uses language to understand relationships. For example, Dore, Gearhart, and Newman (1978), in their analysis of nursery school conversation, have a category called "evaluations," which are personal judgments or attitudes (e.g., "That's good"). Thus, they lump agreement and disagreement into one summary code. No *social* psychologist since Bales (1950) would combine these two codes because one would then lose a great deal of the power of being able to describe the affective climate of the interaction. In contrast, consider the following examples of the tag question, which is a question that asks for some form of agreement: (1) "He's coming home, right?" and (2) "He's coming home, isn't he?" The first statement represents a lower level of *linguistic* competence because it employs a universal tag instead of a specific transformation of the stem "He's going home." This distinction on a dimension of linguistic competence would be of less interest to the social psychologist, who would see in both forms a request for agreement.

Indexing hitting it off

If one wishes to understand friendship formation, it is not adequate to describe what unacquainted children do when they are together, because there is a great deal of variability in how unacquainted children get along. Instead, it is necessary to construct a criterion variable that indexes how well two children have hit it off. On the basis of a literature review, Gottman (1983) evaluated 10 MICRO variables as potential criterion variables of hitting it off. Four of these proved to be valid indices: the proportion of agreement (AG; see Table 2.3), the proportion of disagreement (DG), the agreement-to-disagreement ratio (AG/DG), and the difference between the proportions of agreement and disagreement (AG − DG). Validity in each case was established by requiring the variable to (1) distinguish children playing with their best friends from children playing with strangers and (2) predict an independent maternal assessment of each child's progress toward friendship with a stranger.

These findings are consistent with those obtained in other areas. For example, Markman (1977, 1981) found evidence for the predictive validity of indices of positive interaction in the conversations of couples planning to marry to predict relationship satisfaction in a five-year longitudinal study. There is also a great deal of evidence that the interactions of nondistressed families and married couples are more positive than the interactions of their distressed counterparts (see Gottman, 1979). Furthermore, this is true regardless of the source of the distress (Birchler, Weiss and Vincent, 1975; Cheek, 1964; Lennard and Bernstein, 1969; Mishler and Waxler, 1968). Similarly, Riskin and Faunce (1972), in a review paper, concluded that agreement-to-disagreement ratios provide excellent discrimination across studies between distressed and nondistressed families and between pathological and normal families, despite disparate definitions of these terms across studies.

Similarly, Putallaz and Gottman (1981) reviewed research evidence that preschool and kindergarten children low in peer sociometric status are less positive to their acquainted peers than those high in sociometric status. This was also true for school age children both in situations of dyadic play and in attempts at entry into a dyadic peer group. Putallaz and Gottman (1981) found this result specifically for agreement, disagreement, and agreement-to-disagreement ratios. In a subsequent study, Putallaz (1981) employed the entry procedure with unacquainted children. Child actors were employed as confederates who systematically varied their behavior. The subjects were children who were studied during the summer before their entry into school. Sociometric data were obtained four months later, once the subjects had entered school and had been in class for several months. Putallaz found that the proportion of disagreement correlated highly and negatively with the sociometric rating measure. The proportion of agreement minus the proportion of disagreement, which is similar to an agreement-to-disagreement ratio, also correlated highly with the sociometric rating measure.

Social process index variables

The social processes of the MICRO system are neither exotic nor novel; each has been discussed to some degree in the literature. However, much of the theoretical writing about these processes has either obscured or oversimplified them, and many have not systematically been made operational in the context of naturalistic social interaction. Thus, there was often no precedent for selecting observational measures for these social processes. In the discussion that follows, each social process and the specific MICRO variables that index it are presented against a backdrop of literature from which the process was derived.

Communication connectedness and clarity. Perhaps the most basic dimension of social competence is the connectedness of the interaction. Piaget (1930) characterized the conversation of preschool children as collective monologue. This characterization has effectively been challenged in a series of naturalistic studies (e.g., Garvey and Hogan, 1973; Mueller, 1972). Garvey and Hogan used acquainted preschool dyads, whereas Mueller used unacquainted preschool children. The connectedness of the interaction can be related to the degree of acquaintanceship. Research on toddler interaction reviewed by Vandell and Mueller (1980) suggests that, as toddlers become friends, their interaction becomes more connected.

Closely related to connectedness is the clarity of children's communication. The clarity of communication in social interaction has been considered important in many fields – for example, in a comprehensive review by Jacob (1975) on family interaction. Research on referential communication in children has focused on a speaker's ability to specify to a listener what he is referring to. However, research on referential communication among children has largely abandoned naturalistic observation in favor of experimental tasks that make it possible to program a speaker's intent and to assess the listener's reception of the message. The decision may have been made at great cost, because it is not at all clear to what extent performance on these laboratory tasks can be generalized to social interaction (see Asher, 1979). In peer interaction, it is valuable to study communication clarity in situ.

A solution to the problem of the difficulty of using observational methods is to study *specific* sequences in which a speaker's intent is known. Such a state of affairs exists when a listener is observed making a request for clarification from a speaker. Garvey (1977) brought these speech events to our attention in her suggestion that the "contingent query" is a basic "modular component of discourse" (p. 64). She was not interested in the same issue, but in the use of the contingent query in the regulation of speech. However, an alternative to using laboratory tasks to assess the extent to which children communicate clearly and how this varies with age and other contextual variables is to perform sequential analyses of children's response to requests for clarification from their peers.

Thus, to index connectedness and communication clarity, the MICRO system uses sequences that represent a request for clarification of a message ("Which truck do you want?") followed by an appropriate clarification of the message ("The dumpster") (notation:Q → CM). The argument is that we know that children communicate clearly to the extent that we detect predictable sequences between a request for clarification by one child and an appropriate clarification by the other child – for example, A: "Hand me the truck"; B: "Which truck?" A: "The red one." The last two utterances represent a sequence of a question for clarification of a message followed by a clarification of the message.

Information exchange. Garvey and Hogan (1973) discussed Schegloff's (1968) summons–answer routine as a characteristic method used by preschool children for exchanging information. This pattern is a sequence found in conversational openings. It is of the following form. (1) Speaker A summons Speaker B (e.g., "Hey, you know what?"); (2) Speaker B answers (e.g., "No, what?"); (3) Speaker A responds (e.g., "Sometime you can come to my house"). Garvey and Hogan found 23 examples of this routine, but the examples were complex and displayed considerable variety, including jokes ("Hey, you know what?" "What?" "You're a nut") and the "rhetorical gambit." There are so many variations of the summons–answer sequence in the data – for example, (1) A: "Hey, you know what? You're coloring that green"; (2) A: "Hey!" B: "This crayon's the one you want, right?" A: "Right"– that it makes sense to *index* its occurrence with the relative frequencies of the attention-getting and information codes, ATT and IN, respectively.

Children's success in asking questions for information and eliciting relevant information can be indexed by the z-score that relates questioning and information exchange. This z-score is $z(Q \rightarrow IN)$ for one child's question for information followed by relevant information given by the other. Note that this sequence provides greater precision than variables that collapse over time, such as the proportion of one child's questions.

Establishing common ground. There are two ways that children establish common ground: They find something they can do together, and they explore their similarities and differences.

An index variable that is counterindicative of establishing common-ground activities is the proportion of me statements (the ME code), which represent the narration of one's own activity. Compliance to we demands (WE), indexed by the z-score $z(WE \rightarrow AG)$, in which AG is agreement, is indicative of establishing common-ground activities.

The role of similarities and differences between people in interpersonal attraction has been studied extensively, though not by naturalistic observation of interaction in relationships as they form. Hinde's (1979) review of this literature concluded that similarity is attractive, that people who are initially more similar to one another than are others are more likely to progress toward a relationship, and that people who are in a satisfying relationship become more similar over time, whereas people in an unsatisfying relationship become less similar over time. There is also some evidence that people find differences between them attractive, if they are assured of being liked (Walster & Walster, 1963). Subjects in the Walster and Walster (1963) study who were assured of being liked said that they would prefer to interact with people who were dissimilar rather than similar to themselves. Thus, exploring both similarities and differences may be critical social processes in building common ground.

These social events can be indexed using the MICRO system as follows. One index of building similarity is agreement to tag questions. The tag question is a question for an agreement. For example, "My dolly's going to sleep, right?" The ending "right?" is a tag question. This tag question/agreement sequence is represented by the z-score z(QAG → AG), one child's question for agreement followed by agreement by the other. A second index of building similarity is direct agreement with the partner's direct expression of feelings (the FE code). This is indexed by the z-score z(FE → AG), one child's agreement with the other child's feelings. The exploration of differences is indexed by disagreement with the partner's feelings, that is, with z(FE → DG). Note that the exploration of differences is also *positively* correlated with hitting it off.

Resolution of conflict. Three sets of variables are of interest. First, Gottman and Parkhurst (1980) and later Gottman (1983) reported that giving a reason for disagreeing is related to the deescalation of squabbling over time. Hence, this simple tactic appears to be an effective conflict resolution strategy. These sequences are represented by the z-score z(DG → CM), a child giving a rationale for disagreeing following his or her own disagreement.

A second conflict resolution strategy stems from Brown and Levinson's (1978) theoretical work on politeness and face saving. It involves using polite demand forms to soften one's requests and increase the likelihood of compliance. This is indexed by z(WEA → AG), one child's compliance to weak demands by the other. This index is consistently negatively related to squabbles (the S code) and the escalation to squabbles (DG → S sequences; see Gottman, 1983).

Finally, the MICRO system indexes conflict resolution by noting its failure through the presence of disagreement chains. An example of a disagreement chain is the following excerpt from a conversation of two young girls:

H: This is stretchy.
G: No, it's not.
H: Uh huh.
G: Yes.
H: Uh uh.
G: It's dirty.
H: Uh uh.
G: Uh huh.
H: Uh uh.
G: Uh huh.
H: Uh uh.
G: Uh huh.
H: Uh uh. It's not dirty.

This disagreement chain continues for some time and reappears in various forms throughout the conversation. It is assessed by z(DG → DG), one child's disagreement followed by the other child's disagreement. For long reciprocal disagreement chains two scores will be nearly equal; asymmetry is also possible. Disagreement chains are highly correlated with conflict resolution failure, as evidenced by the escalation of disagreement to squabbles (see Gottman, 1983).

Positive reciprocity. A variety of operational definitions of positive reciprocity have emerged in the literature on social interaction, and it has become clear that it is not an easy construct to define. A review of all these definitions would require a separate chapter (for reviews specific to acquaintanceship, see Altman and Taylor, 1973, and Foot, Chapman and Smith, 1980). However, a few comments and distinctions are in order.

A common logical error in the assessment of temporal reciprocity is assessing reciprocity as a correlation across subjects of rates or frequencies of a behavior between people in a dyad. For a review of studies that have employed this assessment procedure see Gottman (1979). This correlation merely means that people within a dyad are displaying similar rates or relative proportions of a behavior; they could be doing so entirely independently of one another in a temporal sense. The notion of temporal reciprocity *requires* the assessment of temporal contingency. Here reciprocity is defined as temporal reciprocity. This is a contingency-based definition, which means that, for example, if one child jokes, this will increase the probability (beyond base rate) that the other child will now joke.

In the theoretical literature on positive reciprocity it has often been assumed that well-functioning relationships are characterized by positive reciprocity. But reciprocity of positive interaction does not necessarily characterize well-functioning close relationships. Murstein et al. (1977) found that adherence to a quid pro quo belief about relationships (i.e., that relationships function by positive reciprocity) was positively correlated with relationship satisfaction among roommates but negatively correlated with relationship satisfaction among married couples. Despite the fact that Murstein et al.'s study was neither about acquaintanceship, nor based on observational data, it does suggest that positive reciprocity may not always be characteristic of well-functioning close relationships. The hypothesis may be supported even in acquaintanceship if people think that there is an opportunity to form a close relationship. An experimental study by Clark and Mills (1979) supports the contention that, if unacquainted people desire a close relationship, positive temporal reciprocity reduces interpersonal attraction.

The case can be made stronger by considering the more specific notion of positive temporal reciprocity, which may be productive in the early stages of relationship formation but counterproductive later. This can be understood in the following way. Temporal reciprocity means that the interaction system is tightly linked in immediately mirroring one positive behavior with another of the same sort. Temporal linkage means constraint in information-theory terms; this means that less information is conveyed by a message, because more redundancy exists by virtue of temporal structure. Gottman (1979) reported evidence that dissatisfied married couples could be distinguished from satisfied married couples by more negative affect *and* more positive affect reciprocity. These findings are consistent with others in the family interaction literature (e.g., Haley, 1964) that show that distressed families are more tightly and rigidly linked than nondistressed families.

In general, however, little is known about the functions of temporal reciprocity in relationship development. Our work with young children getting acquainted indicates that indices of positive reciprocity become less important over time in accounting for progress toward friendship (Gottman, 1983). In fact, they are the only indices to show such a temporal decline. It may be that, on first acquaintance, positive temporal reciprocity communicates that the other person is responsive to his or her partner or that a reciprocal attention structure exists (see Chance & Larsen, 1976). As relationships develop, however, temporal reciprocity may no longer serve this function.

The MICRO system indexes positive reciprocity by the z-scores representing sequences in which a particular code by one child is followed by the same code by the other child; for example, $z(F \rightarrow F)$ represents fantasy reciprocity, and $z(J \rightarrow J)$ represents joking reciprocity.

Self-disclosure. Self-disclosure has rarely been investigated in the context of relationship formation by means of observational methods, especially with children. Studies with adults have tended to use self-report measures; the most widely used measure is Jourard's self-disclosure questionnaire (the JSDQ; see Jourard and Lasakow, 1955). A full discussion of this approach to self-disclosure is deferred to Section 2.7 on extensions of the MICRO system.

The MICRO coding system indexes self-disclosure by coding the direct exploration of feelings, using the following sequence: questions about feelings by one child followed by the expression of feelings by the partner, $z(QFE \rightarrow FE)$. It should be noted that this sequence only *indexes* the complex process of self-disclosure; it does not equal this complex process. As discussed earlier, many social events naturally co-occur with the expression and exploration of feelings.

2.6. Audiotape versus videotape MICRO coding

A study was conducted to assess what might be different about coding with audiotapes or videotapes. The question can be answered only with respect to a particular coding system. Videotapes are not always better than audiotapes. For example, information about appearance (attractiveness, weight, etc.) may bias observers, so that they are less observant of those aspects of the interaction considered salient by the coding system.

In this study 10 pairs of female best friends, aged 4 to 6, were videotaped in the laboratory in a free-play session. The laboratory room was designed to be similar to a home setting. It was carpeted, and had drapes and low-level incandescent lighting. Cameras were concealed behind bookcases, although the children were aware of being video-taped and their consent had been obtained.

The videotapes were coded independently by two groups of coders. One group used both audio and video information, whereas the video screen was blocked for the other group of coders. One child was arbitrarily designated the host, the other as the guest. Both groups of coders had a verbatim transcript.

Table 2.5 presents the results of the MICRO coding for both the nonsequential and sequential variables employed in this book. Of 50 repeated-measures analyses of variance, only one was significant at a .05 alpha level, for the variable of gossip reciprocated by the host. This *pattern* was more likely (i.e., higher z-scores) for the coders who had full audio and video information. In general, both unconditional probabilities and z-scores were comparable for these tapes across both conditions. If anything, there was an overall tendency (not significant) for audio-based coding to underestimate the strength of sequential connection, compared with video-based coding. For the most part, for the variables used in this book from the MICRO coding system, audiotapes provided information quite parallel to that provided by videotapes.

2.7. Extension of the MICRO system: conversations of college students

Ginsberg (see Chapter 6) extended the original MICRO system to account for variation in the closeness of college roommates. One of the

Table 2.5. *Comparison of audio- and videotape coding with MICRO*

	Mean		
Variable	Audio	Video	F Ratio[a]
Host agreement	.05	.05	.13
Host disagreement	.04	.04	1.95
Host fantasy	.03	.03	.76
Host jokes (humor)	.04	.04	.46
Host squabbles	.01	.01	.08
Host information	.05	.05	.18
Host me	.06	.06	1.62
Host attention	.03	.03	.07
Host gossip	.01	.01	.13
Guest agreement	.05	.05	.01
Guest disagreement	.03	.03	.05
Guest fantasy	.02	.03	2.57
Guest jokes	.05	.05	.93
Guest squabbles	.003	.003	.52
Guest information	.05	.05	.41
Guest me	.06	.06	.19
Guest attention	.03	.04	.56
Guest gossip	.015	.014	.14
Host disagreement → host squabbles	−.12	−.35	1.10
Host gives reason after disagreement	5.97	6.60	.43
Host disagreement → guest disagreement	2.71	1.84	3.01
Host disagrees → guest squabbles	.49	−.22	2.34
Host fantasy → guest fantasy	6.71	7.65	.33
Host humor → guest humor	6.53	7.59	1.15
Host squabble → guest squabble	.51	1.23	1.82
Host clarification request → guest clarifies	1.68	1.07	.84
Host question info → guest info	3.17	4.03	1.34
Host tag question → guest agreement	4.60	5.31	.74
Host question about feelings → guest feeling	.74	1.39	1.28
Host feeling → guest agreement	.63	1.07	.40
Host feeling → guest disagreement	.40	.18	.15
Host weak demand → guest agreement	1.73	2.28	.66
Host we demand → guest agreement	1.52	1.28	.21
Host gossip → guest gossip	1.52	4.98	9.59*
Guest disagreement → host disagreement	1.92	1.54	.42
Guest disagreement → host squabbles	.44	.91	.31

Table 2.5. *(Cont.)*

	Mean		
Variable	Audio	Video	F Ratio[a]
Guest disagreement → guest squabbles	−.14	−.09	.42
Guest gives reason after disagreeing	7.87	7.71	.02
Guest fantasy → host fantasy	6.89	8.12	.45
Guest humor → host humor	6.02	5.55	.14
Guest squabble → host squabble	1.24	.69	1.90
Guest clarification request → host clarifies	2.71	2.07	.72
Guest question for info → host info	5.25	5.47	.06
Guest tag question → host agreement	2.41	3.32	.68
Guest question about feelings → host feelings	2.78	4.99	2.98
Guest feeling → host agreement	1.01	.92	.03
Guest feeling → host disagreement	−.29	.29	2.36
Guest weak demand → host agreement	1.24	2.37	3.09
Guest we demand → host agreement	1.29	1.56	.32
Guest gossip → host gossip	4.73	5.24	.07

[a]Degrees of freedom, (1, 9).
*$p. < 05$.

most interesting aspects of the conversations of late adolescents and young adults is their preoccupation with understanding themselves (called "self-exploration" by Gottman, 1983). In extending the MICRO coding system to this age group, several changes had to be made to better reflect the group's seeming preoccupation with self-exploration: Some original MICRO codes were modified, others were dropped, and four new codes were added. Also, examples relevant to young adult conversation were used. In this section, we first present the extended MICRO and its relation to the original MICRO system. Then we consider how the extended MICRO codes were aggregated into a smaller number of more reliable summary codes in Ginsberg's college roommate study. In the next section, we consider how this extended MICRO system can be used to index eight social processes related to friendship among college roommates.

MICRO extension coding system

The extended MICRO codes are listed in Table 2.6, along with their definitions and examples of each. There are 5 double codes (fantasy, question, joke, squabble, gossip) and 33 content codes – 29 original codes and 4 new codes. The new codes are mindreading, opinion, repetition, and reactive. Cohen's kappa was computed for the content codes and double codes separately. A statistic was computed across all codes, summed across all transcripts. For the content codes, Cohen's kappa was .890. For the double codes, Cohen's kappa was .882. Except for these code changes, the procedures for coding with the extended MICRO system are essentially identical to those of the original system.

Summary codes for roommate study

As in the original acquaintanceship study, the codes of the extended MICRO system were aggregated into a smaller number of summary codes to increase reliability and simplify data analyses. This was done on logical grounds and involved lumping some codes and splitting others (for a more detailed discussion of the considerations that guided this process, see Chapter 6). For example, because one of the goals of this research was to examine self-disclosure as a function of the intimacy of the information exchanged, the feeling code (FE) was divided to distinguish superficial feelings (FE1) from intimate feelings (FE2). The ME code was divided into exclamations (ME1), simple self-statements (ME2), and personality-revealing self-statements (ME3). Then two summary codes were created: high-intimacy self-disclosure (HSD), composed of the FE2 and ME3 subcodes, and low-intimacy self-disclosure (LSD), composed of FE1, ME2, and the opinion subcodes. In all, 19 mutually exclusive and exhaustive summary codes were created. These codes are shown in Table 2.7; their alpha coefficients of generalizability as calculated in the college roommate study are shown in Table 6.4a.

2.8. Social processes of the MICRO extension

In all, eight social processes related to self-exploration were explored among college students. The first two were self-disclosure and gossip. The literature on gossip and that on self-disclosure have not been integrated, nor have their relative roles been investigated. For this reason these two processes are discussed in some detail below. The

Table 2.6. *Extended MICRO coding system (college roommate study)*

Code	Meaning	Definition	Examples
		Double codes	
F/	Fantasy	Pretending to be someone else or speaking within a framework of a fantasy	"You don't grasp these concepts" (speaker imitating his or her instructor). "I'm flying."
Q/	Question	A statement made to sound like a question	"May I have this?"
J/	Joke	Any utterance accompanied by laughter, silliness, or joking; includes bathroom humor, good-natured teasing, giggling, exuberance	"Oh, poop!" (said mischievously). "Whee! Whee! Whee!"
S/	Squabble	Angry, annoyed, disgusted, or aggressive behavior; includes insults, yelling, whining, sarcasm, verbal or physical aggression, threats, retaliation, tattling	"Cut it out." "Fight, fight, fight, that's all you two ever do."
G/	Gossip	References to a third person or persons the speaker is personally familiar with	"Mary's in my class." "I think he's nice."
		Content Codes	
COM	Command	Direct imperatives	"Give me that." "Water the plants."
ATT	Attention getters	An utterance used to get the other's attention; includes greetings and salutations	"You know what?" "See."
Q/PRE	Polite requests	Polite requests for a response of something from the other	"Would you gimme that?"
SUG	Suggestions	Advice or a suggestion to do something	"You could put it under the bed." "Invite him to the hospital."

Table 2.6. *(Cont.)*

Code	Meaning	Definition	Example
FE	Feeling	Statements about the speaker's feelings, wants, likes, dislikes, opinions, and needs; includes feelings and opinions about other people	"I like peanut butter." "I'm tired."
MR	Mindreading	The attribution of feeling, motive, personality trait, experience, behavior, or opinion to the other person	"You don't like Ray." "You can't take a compliment."
ROL	Roles to both	Statements that unite the speaker with the other person to work for a common goal by assigning roles or tasks to each of them	"You make the hotdogs and I'll toast the buns."
WE	We both	"We" statements that show solidarity by describing both persons with a common label	"We're friends." "We're so classy."
TOO	Me too	Statements that directly express similarity with some aspect of the other person	"Same here." "I have one like that, too."
WEG	We against others	"We" statements that show solidarity by aligning with the other against a common enemy.	"We're much better than she is." "We hate Jason."
REP	Repetition	Statements or portions of statements repeated by the other	"I'm going to get up," and the other person says,"I'm going to get up."
JOI	Joining in	Usually occurs in song singing when one starts singing and the other joins in; also joining in, in wit.	"Oh, my heart," and the other joins in with "Oh, my heart, my hero!"

Table 2.6. *(Cont.)*

Code	Meaning	Definition	Example
IN	Information	Factual information that is asked for or given	"There's a whole box left." "Is the mail here yet?"
CM	Clarifies message	Clarification that is asked for or given in order to avoid or eliminate confusion; includes giving instructions clearly	"What do you mean?" "The one up *there*. *The one with red on it*." (The italicized portion clarifies "there")
AG	Agreement	Agreement, approval, or a positive attitude with regard to the other; includes acknowledging a statement of the other, praise, compliments, and politeness	"You're the smartest person in the class." "Thank you."
OP	Opinion	Opinions or generalizations about the state of the world; note that this is a less personal opinion than those included in the feeling category	"It's still a man's world." "You can't overstudy in college."
DG	Disagreement	Negativity, noncompliance, or disapproval toward the other; includes disagreements, criticism, insults, sarcastic teasing, and refusal to share	"Don't get so upset!" "Your room is a mess!"
SY	Sympathy and comfort	Attempts to console, protect, defend, or ease the distress of someone who is unhappy	"Don't worry, he'll probably call again." "It's OK, it'll work out."
OF	Offers	Helpfulness, thoughtfulness, or generosity	"I'll clean it for you." "You can use mine if you want to."
AH	Asks help	Request for help or assistance	"Can you show me what to do?"

Table 2.6. *(Cont.)*

Code	Meaning	Definition	Example
RU	Rule	Rules or principles for behaving or proceeding that are implied, invoked, or created	"We're not supposed to play the stereo after midnight."
NCM	Failure to clarify message	Inadequate or illogical responses to a question or the failure to clarify a message in response to the other's confusion	"Which one?" *"You know."* (the italicized sentence would be coded NCM)
REAC	Reactive	Reference to the tape recorder, experimenter, or experimental procedure	"Is the tape recorder on?" "I wonder if we should be talking about this now."
DG/CM	Disagreement with clarification	Disagreement in which an explanation is implied	"Let's use this." *"I'm using it."* (The second sentence would be coded DG/CM because it shows noncompliance with a reason implied)

other social processes investigated were mindreading (comments about the other person, such as psychological interpretations or trait attributions), the amount of affect in the interaction, extended conflict, extended humor, the exploration of similarities, and the exploration of differences.

Self-disclosure

Mutual self-disclosure has been suggested to be the process by which people gradually develop psychological closeness. Jourard (1971b) noted that "the amount of personal information that one person is willing to disclose to another appears to be an index of the closeness of the relationship, and the affection, love, or trust that prevails between the two people" (p. 13). The relationship between self-disclosure and interpersonal attraction has frequently been investigated in the context

Table 2.7. *Summary codes of extended MICRO (college roommate study)*

Summary code	Subcodes
Fantasy (FANT)	Fantasy (F/) double code in combination with any content code, including content codes in which F/ co-occurs with the double codes joke (J), question (Q/), squabble (S/), and gossip (G/)
Joke (JOKE)	Joke (J/) double code in combination with any content code, including content codes in which J/ co-occurs with the double code Q/
Questions (QUES)	Question (Q/) double code in combination with any content code, including content codes in which Q/ co-occurs with the double code G/
Gossip (GOS)	Gossip (G/) double code in combination with any content code
Negativity (NEG)	Squabble (S/) double code in combination with any content code; content codes without double codes: disagreement (DG), disagreement with clarification (DG/CM)
Controlling statements (CONT)	Command (COM), attention getters (ATT), polite requests (Q/PRE), suggestions (SUG), question suggestions (Q/SUG), asking permission (Q/ASK), demands as questions for information (Q/IND), wanna (WA), question wanna (Q/WA), we'll have to (HWA), let's (LTS), rule (RU), asks help (AH), question let's (Q/LTS), roles to both (ROL)
You and me (YM)	We're both (WE), me too (TOO), we against others (WEG)
Acknowledgment (ACK)	Acknowledgment (AGI), repetition (REP), joining in (JOI)
Information (IN)	Information (IN), clarifies message (CM)
Support (SUP)	Sympathy (SY), Offers (OF)
Exclamations (EXCL)	Exclamations (MEI)
Praise (PRA)	Praise (AG2)
Other-directed statements (YOU)	Mindreading(MR)

Table 2.7. *(Cont.)*

Summary code	Subcodes
Low self-disclosure (LSD)	Simple self-statements (ME2), superficial feelings (FEI), opinions (OP)
High self-disclosure (HSD)	Personality-revealing self-statements (ME3), intimate feelings (FE2)
Failure to clarify message (NCM)	Failure to clarify message (NCM)
Reactive (REAC)	Reactive (REAC)
Tape off (OFF)	Tape off (OFF)
Inaudible (INAU)	Inaudible (INAU)

of theories of social penetration and social exchange (e.g., Daher and Banikiotes, 1976; Derlega, Wilson & Chaikin, 1976; Morton, 1978).

According to social penetration theory, individuals tend to disclose more information as a relationship develops. This means that they share information about a greater number of topics, that within each topic a greater amount of information is disclosed, and that disclosure becomes increasingly intimate. Furthermore, at each stage of the relationship, there is hypothesized to be more disclosure of superficial information than intimate information. Two examples of longitudinal studies that provide evidence for this pattern of self-disclosure include a study by Taylor (1968) of dormitory roommates and a study by Altman and Haythorn (1965) of groups of naval recruits socially isolated for 10 days. Both these studies used self-disclosure questionnaires to assess the number of items revealed to others (breadth) and the intimacy of items revealed (depth).

Although by this view self-disclosure would appear to be an important factor in moving a relationship toward greater intimacy, it has rarely been investigated in the context of close relationships. Most self-disclosure research is conducted in laboratory settings with strangers who will never see each other again. There is evidence that two strangers meeting in this kind of setting will reciprocate disclosure no matter how intimate the topic. Cozby (1972) and Savicki (1972) found, contrary to expectations, that even exceptionally high intimacy of disclosure from a confederate resulted in an increase in disclosure by the subject. This reciprocity of self-disclosure independent of the intimacy of the topic does not appear to characterize the beginning stages of conversation in relationships that will have a history. Murdoch, Chenoweth, and Rissman (1969) found that subjects who anticipated seeing each other again disclosed significantly less information than subjects who expected the experiment to be over at the end of the session. Thus, laboratory-based conceptions of self-disclosure may not be readily generalized to naturally occurring relationships.

Studies that do examine self-disclosure in well-established relationships have tended to use questionnaires or self-reports of the content disclosed to other persons rather than behavioral indices of self-disclosure (Jourard, 1971a; Taylor & Haythorn, 1965). As previously noted, the most widely used instrument for assessing individual difference is the JSDQ, described in Jourard and Lasakow (1958). In a review article, Cozby (1973) noted that the JSDQ does not accurately predict actual self-disclosure. In fact, in his review, *he was unable to find a relationship between the JSDQ and actual disclosure in a situation or ratings of actual disclosure made by peers.* In addition to lacking predictive validity, questionnaire research cannot provide direct information about the day-to-day or minute-to-minute dynamics of the social exchange process. Unless self-disclosure is observed as it occurs in everyday relationships, theoretical frameworks cannot adequately explain how or why it stops once it is started. For this reason, research on the function of self-disclosure in interpersonal relationships must have an observational methodology. We can see this most clearly in a discussion of the reciprocity of self-disclosure.

Disclosure reciprocity. One of the most consistent findings in the self-disclosure literature is the importance of the reciprocity of self-disclosure. A number of studies provide evidence that intimate disclosure by one person leads to intimate disclosure by the other person when the initiator is the experimenter, a confederate, another subject, or an imaginary subject (see Chaikin & Derlega, 1976). Closer examination of the methods used to measure the reciprocity of self-disclosure, however, indicates that the definitions of reciprocity in the various studies are not equivalent. In the literature on self-disclosure there are at least two approaches to the study of reciprocity: (1) experimental manipulations of self-disclosure and (2) nonexperimental self-report studies of self-disclosure. These approaches represent two different concepts: contingency-based and noncontingency-based reciprocity (see Gottman, 1979).

Contingency-based reciprocity is established when the behavior of one person changes the probability of subsequent behavior by the other. Evidence for contingency-based reciprocity is provided by studies that examine the effects of experimentally manipulating the intimacy level or the number of statements produced by a confederate or a subject on the self-disclosure of another subject (e.g., Derlega, Wilson, & Chaikin, 1974).

Non-contingency-based reciprocity, or rate matching, means that two members of a dyad displayed similar rates of particular behaviors, whether or not the behavior of one changed the probability of subsequent behavior by the other. Noncontingency-based reciprocity is frequently studied in long-term relationships by means of self-report measures (e.g., Jourard & Landeman, 1960; Jourard & Richman, 1963). In these studies correlations are obtained between what subjects said they revealed to various significant others and what they indicated the other disclosed in return. The term "reciprocity" ought not to be used. Two individuals may disclose equally large amounts of intimate information. The individuals in the dyad have matched rates of self-disclosure, but this does not necessarily mean that there is any contingency between their behaviors. They may, for example, have similar personality characteristics that predispose them to interact at high levels of intimacy. The disclosure of one individual and the disclosure of the other would be considered contingently reciprocal only if they were connected in the probability change sense. Although this point on contingency in most concepts of reciprocity is straightforward, it has not been well understood by some social scientists. One common critique of this argument is that a moment-to-moment definition of reciprocity overlooks the possibility of delayed reciprocity. This critique fails to understand that, if an experimenter uses the term "reciprocity" in a delayed sense, contingency must *still be demonstrated* by sequential analysis; the length of time is immaterial to the conceptual argument.

In addition to the previously mentioned problems concerning the validity of self-report data, a shortcoming of these studies is that the process by which information is disclosed and the way in which the level of intimacy was arrived at cannot be established. Nonetheless, high correlations between the level of intimacy reported by a subject and the reported intimacy of input from another have been interpreted as evidence of mutual reciprocity.

Moreover, one of the few studies to examine actual interaction processes did not provide evidence for mutual reciprocity. Davis (1976) found that, even though partners increased intimacy at the same rate as well as disclosed equally intimate information, matching was not achieved as a result of mutual reciprocity. He found that *reciprocity was asymmetric*. That is, the more disclosing partner behaved independently in selecting the intimacy levels of his or her disclosures while the other partner assumed the reciprocating role. This contradictory evidence suggests that understanding the effect of self-disclosure on the disclosure of another person may be better advanced by examining actual interaction processes. In Chapter 5 we shall see an interesting example of reciprocal self-disclosure among two adolescents. However, it is clear from the content of the interaction that the reciprocation is in the service of explaining a line of questioning that only one friend is conducting in solving the other person's problem. In other words, what is apparently symmetric reciprocity may not be symmetric after all.

A significant contribution of the Ginsberg extension of the MICRO system is that it enables one to study contingency-based self-disclosure reciprocity in the context of actual interaction, through the use of sequential analytic techniques.

Disclosure, topic intimacy, and friendship. In a theoretical paper on disclosure reciprocity, Altman (1972) suggested that rules governing reciprocity may differ depending on the stage of the relationship and the intimacy of the topic. Altman speculated that, in general, reciprocity plays a greater role in the early stages of a relationship than in the later stages. Direct support for this hypothesis was reported by Gottman (1983). Some support for this position was also provided by Derlega, Wilson, and Chaikin (1976), who examined contingency-based reciprocity of self-disclosure in dyads composed of strangers and friends. They found that, although low intimacy was reciprocated in a laboratory encounter by both groups, high intimacy was reciprocated by strangers only. They suggested that the obligation to reciprocate may be more important with casual acquaintances to prove one's trustworthiness than between close friends. Close friends presumably have relationships based on trust and spontaneity that do not require constant monitoring to assess what is obligatory. Friends may respond in a less stereotyped fashion according to their mutual needs without concern that the other will be offended by their failure to reciprocate. It may also be that positive reciprocity is important in intimate relationships after high levels of negative affect. For example, if after a conflict one partner did something positive, a lack of reciprocation by the friend would be a strongly negative act. It would seem important to investigate reciprocity as a function of the topic of disclosure and the closeness of a relationship.

Although some work has been done on the reciprocity of self-disclosure and on the depth of self-disclosure, little has been done on the content of information disclosed (see Cozby, 1973). For example, gossip is assumed to be an intermediate step between the exchange of factual information and self-disclosure (Levinger and Snoek, 1972). However, gossip has rarely been investigated by social psychologists.

Gossip

Although psychologists seem to have disregarded the phenomenon of gossip, sociologists and anthropologists have shown a great deal of interest in it (see Hannerz, 1967; Rosnow & Fine, 1976). Ideas about the functions of gossip are numerous and varied. A rich, nonquantitative, descriptive literature suggests hypotheses about how gossip is used in individual impression management, how it exerts control over the behavior of others, and how it functions in a community. Some of the proposed functions of gossip investigated include social comparison (Suls, 1977); the preservation of group unity (Rysman, 1977); competition (Haviland, 1977); support of occupational ideology (Rysman, 1976); socialization, evaluation, impression management, and skill development in children (Fine, 1977); and information exchange and social control (Szwed, 1966).

Whatever its function, a certain amount of familiarity or trust between two people has been proposed as a prerequisite of gossip (Abrahams, 1970; Gluckman, 1963; Hannerz, 1967; Yerkowich, 1977). This suggestion has a certain amount of common sense. Gossipers must recognize the same names, and arriving at this recognition is part of the process of becoming familiar with someone (see Yerkowich, 1977). Despite the appeal of this viewpoint, there is evidence that unacquainted girls from 11 to 17 years of age use gossip as a way of becoming acquainted. They create a common stereotype of someone they both know and both disapprove of (e.g., a gym teacher). We can see that theories about gossip may be wrong even when conclusions seem obvious and intuitively appealing. Nonetheless, gossip may have specific functions in relationships between familiar peers.

Although sociologists and anthropologists have done much preliminary hypothesis-generating research, gossip has not been investigated systematically in the context of everyday conversation. Also, the failure of these investigators to use quantitative methods weakens one's confidence in their findings. Without an empirical analysis, we have little information about when or how gossip is initiated, what its social consequences are, or how it is related to other important social processes such as self-disclosure. We have little information about the kinds of relationships or the stage of acquaintance in which gossiping is likely to occur.

Gossip reciprocity and gossip as a forecast. A consistent theme of social penetration theory and incremental exchange theory is that relationships progress from superficial to intimate levels of exchange and from established areas of interaction to new ones. Before people disclose intimate information, they are likely to explore their partner's views and reactions to decide whether to progress to more intimate interaction. Ginsberg (Chapter 6) hypothesized that one way to anticipate someone's reactions and their values well enough to decide whether to disclose intimate information is to gossip about other people. Thus, gossip can be a lead indicator of self-disclosure. For example, a woman may not be likely to reveal the fact that she had an abortion to an individual who reacted with disapproval to news of another woman's abortion.

It is generally believed that, as a relationship develops, more intimate information is disclosed (see Cozby, 1973). Not as well known are the antecedents to intimate disclosure and the nature of interactions on which forecast assessments are based.

Mindreading

Mindreading refers to attributions that people make to their partners' action, motives, or personality (e.g., "You don't care about this game") (Gottman, 1979). Mindreading can be functional or dysfunctional, depending on the affect with which it is delivered. In research on marital interaction, Gottman (1979) found that, if it is delivered with neutral or positive affect, it is responded to as if it were a sensitive probe about the partner's feelings; it is agreed to and elaborated (e.g., A: "You always get tense at my mother's"; B: "Yeah, I do. I wish she wouldn't be so critical of the way I discipline Jason"). If it is delivered with negative affect, it is responded to as if it were a criticism; it is disagreed with and a self-defensive elaboration follows (e.g., A: "You always get tense at my mother's"; B: "I don't *always* get tense. I think it's mostly her fault for criticizing me. And what do you do? You defend her!"). Mindreading was an integral part of self-exploration in the college roommates' conversations.

Amount of affect

The interactions of young women with their close friends has been described as more emotional than the interactions of young men with their close friends (e.g., see Kon, 1981). The interactions of men with their friends has been described as more matter-of-fact and informational than emotional (e.g., see Brenton, 1974). In the study with college roommates these variables were assessed by the probabilities of negative affect, humor, and information.

Extended conflict

Hinde (1979) wrote about the potential functions of conflict in relationships; he suggested that it could have beneficial or harmful effects. Kaplan, Burch, and Bloom (1964) found negative affect and physiological coupling (i.e., correlation in skin conductance) only among pairs of people who mutually disliked one another; this suggests the dysfunctional nature of extended chains of negative affect. Levenson and Gottman (1983) found that negative affect mediated physiological coupling among married couples and, furthermore, their measure of physiological coupling was able to account for more than 60% of the variance in marital satisfaction. Gottman (1979) found that negative-affect reciprocity characterized the interaction of unhappily married couples. Among friends the question has been empirically investigated by Parkhurst and Gottman (1980) and Gottman (1983). In the college roommate study extended conflict was assessed by "negative-affect" chains and extended humor by "joking" chains.

Extended humor

McGhee (1979) proposed that extended laughter, humor, "hilarity," or "glee" characterizes the interactions of people who like one another. The "amity" concept and our findings about its role in successful acquaintanceship (Gottman, 1983) support this proposal.

Similarities, differences, and intimacy

As in the conversations of young children, college roommates explore their similarities and differences. However, the *function* of this process is very different in young adulthood, highlighting a major theme of this book: The same codable interaction segment may have a very different function at different points in development and may have to be considered as comprising different social processes. We elaborate this theme in Chapter 5.

One possible function of friendship is that it provides an opportunity for social comparison. Social comparison theory (Festinger, 1954) states that, when nonsocial means are not available, people employ comparison with others.

Evidence indicates that, all other things being equal, people are attracted to those who agree with them and tend to reject those who disagree with them (Byrne, 1971), though there is some evidence that people prefer differences if they are assured of being liked (Walster & Walster, 1963). The sequences used to operationalize these processes in the college roommate study were the same as those used with young children, namely, the expression of feelings by one person followed either by agreement or acknowledgment or by disagreement or negativity. In the college roommate study a distinction was made between high- and low-intimacy expressions of feelings.

2.9. The MACRO system

As we have noted, the social processes selected from MICRO as candidates to account for variance in whether two unacquainted children hit it off were by no means exotic processes. All of them have been extensively discussed either in the literature on social development or in the literature on relationship formation. But these literatures did not suggest *specific* observational measures for assessing these processes in naturalistic conversation. The MICRO system gave us a means of specifying these processes. Furthermore, the extent to which children were able to exchange information, establish a common-ground activity, explore their similarities and differences, resolve conflict, reciprocate joking, gossip, and fantasy, and engage in self-disclosure was related to the extent to which the children progressed toward friendship. Thus, the importance of the MICRO variables that index these processes, and hence the importance of the processes themselves, has been demonstrated (for a review see Chapter 3).

However, many important questions could not be answered by MICRO. First, although the variables selected to measure each social process were sensible, they did not *define* processes they measured; instead, they *indexed* these processes. What, precisely, are the content and structure of information exchange or establishing a common-ground activity? What events *define* rather than index these processes?

A second limitation of MICRO is that the model relating the six social processes to the progress of unacquainted young children toward friend-ship (see Gottman, 1983) was not a dynamic model. Although we discovered that some processes became more important over sessions (e.g., self-disclosure) and some became less important (e.g., reciprocity), we had no idea of the temporal relationships *between* the processes within the session. Do children begin an interaction with information exchange? What happens when they fail to establish a common-ground activity? Do they return to information exchange, which suggests that this is an easier exchange to maintain? These and other questions remained unanswered. Answering them required a different level of analysis.

The MACRO system led to a dynamic model because, instead of being used to index social processes, it created a set of mutually exclusive and exhaustive codes. Transition diagrams between codes then could be employed to create a dynamic model (see Gottman, 1983).

The coding system described in Tables 2.3 and 2.4 employed the thought unit as the smallest code unit, with the proviso that the data were transformed to event sequential data for analysis. However, because sequence analysis was employed, the variables that indexed the social processes often involved larger units, such as sequences within one child (e.g., disagreement followed by a reason for disagreeing) and sequences between children (e.g., gossip reciprocity). When the variables were relative frequencies of codes (e.g., information), they alluded to a family of sequences too varied to specify except in general morphology.

In part what was required in modifying MICRO was a reorganization of the data using a larger unit of analysis. To build a temporal model relating the six social processes, the appropriate minimal unit would be the two-turn unit, that is, all of one child's talk before the floor is yielded and then all of the next child's talk before the floor is yielded. The units of coding would then be (1) Turn 1 (Child 1)/Turn 1 (Child 2); (2) Turn

1 (Child 2)/Turn 2 (Child 1); (3) Turn 2 (Child 1)/Turn 2 (Child 2), and so on, in this interlaced fashion.

A larger coding unit introduces problems, however, if a coding system is to remain reasonably detailed. One problem is that the data may become so sparse that it is not possible to analyze them parametrically with the dyad as the unit of analysis. In such cases, it is necessary to collapse data across subjects and to employ nonparametric statistics. This introduces additional problems. Collapsing data across subjects makes the assumption of homogeneity of sequential structure across subjects; nonparametric statistics also tend to be less powerful than parametric statistics. Fortunately, it is possible to test the assumption of homogeneity of sequential structure (see Gottman, 1983).

It would seem reasonable that the MICRO data might be reorganized into higher-level sequences by constructing some logical definitions and extensions of each social process. It would also seem possible to construct a hierarchical decision rule in the event that two or more processes occurred within the two-turn unit. However, this requires human judgment rather than a computer program that automatically reorganizes coded data. This is true because once one specifies the objective of building a temporal model relating the six social processes, new social events become apparent that (1) further define each process and (2) play the role of interstitial processes.

For all these reasons a MACRO coding system was devised and used to study friendship formation in young children (Gottman, 1983). Table 2.8 summarizes this coding system and describes its relationship to the original MICRO coding system. A training manual is available. The categories of the MACRO system are dyadic states; they characterize the dyad in a two-turn unit, not each individual. Note that the MACRO system codes assess social processes directly rather than using sequences of codes to index processes as the MICRO and extended MICRO systems do. The MACRO system is considerably more efficient than MICRO. Instead of 30 hours to code 1 hour of tape, MACRO required only 2 hours; 1 hour was required to watch the tape in real time without coding and 1 hour was necessary for coding.

MACRO codes

In the process of creating MACRO, we devised eight codes: (1) escalation and deescalation, (2) common-ground activity, (3) amity, (4) self-disclosure, (5) gossip, (6) mindreading, (7) message clarification, and

Table 2.8. *The MACRO coding system and its relationship to the MICRO system*

Category	Definition and relationship to other coding system	Example
Information exchange		
Success	1. HQIN → GIN 2. GQIN → HIN 3. HATT 4. GATT 5. HIN 6. GIN 7. HATT → HIN or GAG 8. GATT → GIN or HAG	A: What's this? B: This is my room right here. This is my farm here. Look how very, very large.
Failure	1. HQIN → GNCM 2. GQIN → HNCM 3. HATT → GNCM 4. GATT → HNCM	A: How come we can't get this off? B: You know, I'm gonna get the rolling pin so we can roll this.
Common-ground activity		
Success	There is a hierarchy of successful conversation in common-ground activities, organized in terms of the responsiveness demand.	
	1. Parallel play, collective monologue; unconnected ME codes.	A: I'm making this blue. B: Staying in the lines, there, there.
	2. Parallel play, connected dialogue: ME → ME chains of connected statements.	A: I'm making mine blue. B: I'm making mine brown.
	3. Narration of the other child's play: INX statements.	A: You're using blue to color that.
	4. Asymmetrical exchange, in which at least one child affects the other's activity, with demands, compliance, and noncompliance.	A: I'm putting pink in the blue. B: Pass the blue. A: I think I'll pass the blue.
	5. Symmetric exchange in which the children affect each other.	A: And you make those for after we get in together, OK? B: 'Kay.

Table 2.8. *(Cont.)*

Category	Definition and relationship to other coding system	Example
		A: Have to make those.
		B: Pretend like those little roll cookies too, OK? Flat cookies, I mean.
		A: And make, um, make a, um, pancake too.
		B: Oh, rats, this is a little pancake.
	6. Successful initiation of a joint activity (HWE → GAG, GWE → HAG).	A: Yeah, let's play house. B: Okay, play house.
Failure	Initiation is ignored or disagreed with; activity does not develop for even one two-turn unit.	A: Let's play house. B: Nope, nope, nope, nope, nope. A: Because you're coloring that brick wall? B: Yep.
Escalation		
Success	An attempt is made to escalate the responsiveness demand of the common-ground activity and it results in a new play.	A: Guess what color I'm going to put between those. B: What? A: You have to guess. B: Brown.
Failure	The attempt to escalate is ignored or rejected. Rejection also occurs if the previous activity continues unchanged.	A: I'm the mommy. B: Who am I? A: Um, the baby. B: Daddy. A: Sister. B: I want to be the daddy. A: You're the sister. B: Daddy! A: You're the big sister. B: Don't play house. I don't want to play house.
Deescalation	Is similar to escalation except that the attempt is to reduce the amount of responsiveness required. This code also has two states, success and failure, depending on the response.	A: You can play your own game and I can play mine. OK?

Table 2.8. (Cont.)

Category	Definition and relationship to other coding system	Example
Conflict	Squabbles codes, or disagreement chains.	A: This is stretchy. B: No it isn't. A: Uh huh. B: Uh uh.
Conflict resolution	HDG → HCM; GDG → GCM; HWEA; GWEA; reciprocated joking in the service of conflict reduction.	A: Is it OK if I unbutton her?
Message clarification		
Success	HQCM → GCM; GQCM → HCM (includes request for repetition followed by repetition)	A: Which one? B: The blue one.
Failure	HQCM → GNCM; HQCM → GNCM	A: What's a dumb straw? B: Your dumb straw.
Gossip reciprocity		
Success	HG → GG or GG → HG	A: Why does he come here all the time? B: Because he does, because my mommy asks him.
Failure	Unreciprocated gossip	A: Well, my dad gave those to me. B: Well, what are these?
Similarity	WE, WEG, TOO, JOI	A: Mine's almost finished. B: Mine's too.
Contrast	Children note that they are not the same.	A: I'm gonna be five at, in my birthday. B: Well, I'm five now.
Self-disclosure	1. HQFE → GFE 2. GQFE → HFE 3. HFE → GFE 5. Any personal statement about one's feelings that is intimate. This excludes low-intimacy statements (e.g., ''I love chocolate''), even if they are strongly stated.	A: She didn't say anything about the dress. She said leave me alone. B: Why'd she say that? A: She doesn't love me.

Table 2.8. *(Cont.)*

Category	Definition and relationship to other coding system	Example
Amity	1. Validation or approval of the other person 2. Affirmation of the relationship 3. Sympathy (SY) 4. Offers (OF) 5. Affection 6. Wit (J) 7. Hilarity (HJ → GJ; GJ → HJ) 8. Shared deviance	A: [kisses B] B: Oh gosh. A: What? B: You just kissed me on the cheek. Thank you. A: I'll kiss you on the forehead. B: I'll kiss you.

Note: H, host; G, guest; QIN, question for information; IN, information; ATT, attention; AG, agreement; NCM, failure to clarify message; DG, disagreement; CM, message clarification or reason for disagreeing; WEA, weaker form of demand; G, gossip; QFE, question about feelings; FE, feelings; WEG, we against others; JOL, joining in; and J, joking.
Source: Gottman (1983).

(8) information exchange. Also, a distinction was made between whether these processes were successes or failures. Details of these codes can be found in Gottman (1983). In this section we describe briefly common-ground escalation and deescalation, amity, and self-disclosure.

Common-ground escalation and deescalation

Children often initially established a relatively simple common-ground activity (such as coloring side by side) that made low demands on each child for social responsiveness. For example, in coloring side by side each child narrated his or her own activity (e.g., "I'm coloring mine green"). This involved extensive use of the ME codes. However, in the Gottman (1983) studies the common-ground activity was usually escalated after a while. For example, both children might begin narrating their *own* activities; then one child would narrate the other child's activity (e.g., "You're coloring in the lines"); next, a child would begin giving suggestions or other commands to the other child (e.g., "Use blue. That'd be nice"). The activity would escalate in each case in terms of the responsiveness demand it placed on the children. A joint activity might

Table 2.9. *Cronbach alphas for the codes of the*
extended MACRO system

Code category	Alpha
Conflict	.999
Amity success	.924
Amity failure	.000
Gossip codes	
Negative-evaluation success	.925
Positive-evaluation success	.910
Neutral-evaluation success	.886
Negative-evaluation failure	1.000
Neutral-evaluation failure	.928
Negative-evaluation success	
about a stereotype	1.000
Escalation success	.692
Mindreading	1.000
Common-ground success	.990
Message clarification success	.826
Message clarification failure	1.000
Similarity	.923
Difference	1.000
High-intimacy self-disclosure	.776
Low-intimacy self-disclosure	.794
Information success	.974
Information failure	.640

Note: The following were not computable: conflict
resolution, common-ground failure, relationship talk,
escalation failure, deescalation success and failure, and
other forms of stereotyped gossip (failure and
success).

then be suggested and the complexity of this activity would be escalated
from time to time.

Sometimes this escalation process was smooth, but sometimes it
introduced conflict. When it did, the children often deescalated the
activity, either returning to a previous activity they had been able to
maintain or moving to information exchange. An example will illustrate
this point. D, the host, is 4:0 and J, the guest, is 4:2. They began playing
in parallel:

18. J: I got a fruit cutter plate.
19. D: Mine's white.
20. J: You got white playdough and this color and that color.
21. D: Every color. That's the colors we got.

They continued playing, escalating the responsiveness demand by using strong forms of demand:

29. D: I'm putting pink in the blue.
30. J: Mix pink.
31. D: Pass the blue.
32. J: I think I'll pass the blue.

They next moved toward doing the same thing together (common-ground activity):

35. D: And you make those for after we get it together, OK?
36. J: 'Kay.
37. D: Have to make these.
38. J: Pretend like those little roll cookies, too, OK?
39. D: And make, um, make a, um, pancake too.
40. J: Oh, rats. This is a little pancake.
41. D: OK. Make, make me, um, make two flat cookies. 'Cause I'm, I'm cutting any, I'm cutting this. My snake.

The next escalation included offers:

54. J: You want all my blue?
55. D: Yes. To make cookies. Just to make cookies, but we can't mess the cookies all up.
56. J: Nope.

They then introduced a joint activity and began using "we" terms in describing what the activity was:

57. D: Put this the right way, OK? *We're* making supper, huh?
58. J: *We're* making supper. Maybe *we* could use, if you get white, *we* could use that too, maybe.
59. D: I don't have any white. Yes, *we*, yes, I do.
60. J: If you got some white, *we* could have some y'know.

As they continued the play, they employed occasional contextual reminders that this was a joint activity:

72. D: Oh, we've got to have our dinner. Trying to make some.

D then tried to escalate the play by introducing some fantasy. This escalation was not successful. J was first allocated a low-status role (baby), then a higher-status role (sister), then a higher-status (but still not an equal-status) role (big sister).

76. D: I'm the mommy.
77. J: Who am I?
78. D: Um, the baby.
79. J: Daddy.
80. D: Sister.
81. J: I wanna be the daddy.
82. D: You're the sister.
83. J: Daddy.
84. D: You're the *big* sister!
85. J: Don't play house. I don't want to play house.

The escalation failure led to a deescalation.

87. J: Just play eat-eat. We can play eat-eat. We have to play that way.

However, in this case, the successful deescalation was not accomplished without some conflict:

89. J: Look hungry!
90. D: Huh?
91. J: I said look hungry!
92. D: Look hungry? This is dumb.
93. J: Look hungry!
94. D: No!

The children then successfully returned to the previous level of common-ground activity, preparing a meal together. Common-ground activity is thus viewed in this coding system as a hierarchy in terms of the responsiveness it demands of each child and in terms of the fun it promises.

Amity

The amity code was designed to describe the following types of events of strong positive affect: (1) strong validation and approval exchanges (e.g., A: "How do you like this?" B: "That's pretty"); (2) the expression of sympathy ("Don't worry about that; it'll come off. It was on before and it came off before. Just don't worry about it, 'cause I'm not worried") and support (e.g., the "we against others" code in Table 2.3); (3) affection (e.g., A kisses B. B: "Oh, gosh." A: "What?" B: "You just kissed me on the cheek. Thank you." A: "I'll kiss you on the forehead." B: "I'll kiss you"); (4) wit enjoyed by both (A: "How do you do this stupid thing?" B: "You do it in a stupid way"); and hilarity (also called "glee" by McGhee, 1979) in which both children are convulsed by their own wit.

Self-disclosure

Self-disclosure was directly examined in MACRO; instead of indexing the process with a question about feelings followed by an expression of feelings, we extended the definition to include any high-intimacy self-disclosure. All examples given in Table 2.8 come from transcripts. Furthermore, these self-disclosures did not come just from older children. For an example see Chapter 4.

MACRO reliability

Because the MACRO system employs a larger unit of interaction, fewer instances of each code within the sample of transcript are used for reliability checking. As previously mentioned, this could require combining data across subjects, a methodological implication of which is the change in the reliability statistic. For sequential analysis, agreement still must be tied to the unit of analysis, not summed over time. However, Cohen's kappa rather than Cronbach's alpha is clearly the statistic of choice because data are combined across tapes. A reliability checker coded 100 turns of each tape for the children's friendship formation study (Gottman, 1983). An overall kappa of .870 was computed for all codes.

2.10. Expansion of MACRO

It was necessary to extend MACRO once we began coding the conversations of children in middle childhood and adolescence (see Chapter 5). The expansion included the following. (1) Common ground was made a double code because it often co-occurred with other kinds of conversation among older children; this happened only when the common ground was successful. (2) Mindreading and relationship talk were added. (3) High- and low-intimacy self-disclosure were added. (4) We decided to note whether the gossip involved a real person or a stereotype, and whether it was positive, negative, or neutral; as previously mentioned, unacquainted older children often invented a stereotype or caricature of a person (e.g., macho gym coach) about whom they gossiped; we also decided to note whether the gossip involved was positive or negative ("put-downs," for example). All these changes were made because new codes became prominent for a specific age group. The codes of the expanded MACRO are presented in Table 2.9.

Reliability

On the basis of the data from our study of middle childhood and adolescence (see Chapter 5), we coded a reliability sample of 10 tapes using the expanded version of MACRO. There were 1,011 jointly coded events (about 100 per tape). The Cohen's kappa for the reliability study was .729, with a standard deviation of 0.014, which gives a highly significant $z = 52.07$. This implies that interobserver agreement was far beyond chance levels. The Cronbach alpha for each code in the expanded version of MACRO are given in Table 2.9 for those codes for which alpha was computable. (It was not computable if it never occurred in the reliability samples, which was the case for infrequent codes.) Except for amity failure, which was quite rare in these age groups, the alphas were high.

2.11 Beyond MACRO

These coding systems, MICRO and MACRO and their variations, were our tools for quantitative discovery, along with our sequential analyses. They were not our only tools, however, and indeed our goal in this book is to present an integration of quantitative and qualitative data sources. What has emerged from the effort is a new theory of social and affective development, which is presented fully in Chapters 4 and 5. The remainder of this chapter offers an explanation of the organization of our research methods with respect to this new theory.

The MACRO coding system divides social events during these conversations into *affects* (e.g., amity, conflict) and *social processes* (e.g., gossip, success). These are not mutually exclusive categories, of course. For example, one can gossip with various affects. Imagine a wagon wheel, with a hub and spokes that radiate to the perimeter. At the hub is a set of salient social processes. These processes are those that are most central at a particular period in development. They represent the things children at a particular age spend the most time on and have the most affect about. They are related to the concerns of children at that age and to their social and emotional goals. In early childhood these processes at the hub involve the coordination of play. One of the major goals of this book is to explain why the coordination of play is so salient for the young child. In middle childhood, acceptance and avoiding rejection by same-sex peers is at the hub, and with this goes the social processes of negative-evaluation gossip and support by the best friend. In adolescence, self-understanding is at the hub and the salient processes are gossip (both positive and negative), self-disclosure, and problem solving. This wheel model will be elaborated later. The objective here is to convey a sense of the differing goals, concerns, and social processes that are central at different developmental points.

At the rim, at the end of each spoke, are other social processes. Their metaphorical position implies that they are *in the service of those at the center*. For example, information exchange in middle childhood is often in the service of avoiding embarrassment, finding out what is weird, and differentiating oneself from these actions so that acceptance will be ensured. Information exchange in adolescence, in contrast, is often in the service of self-exploration.

The theory presented in this book is that *the social processes in MACRO are organized differently as a function of social and affective development*. This concept will become clear as we present these conversations.

From the standpoint of observational methods, this chapter has progressed from microanalysis to macroanalysis and, finally, beyond description toward an understanding of how these social processes are organized and may change with development or with the sex composition of a dyad and how these processes are organized both among friends and among strangers becoming acquainted (successfully or unsuccessfully). We shall see that in the understanding of this organization and reorganization we have a view of what development is. It involves what has been called second-order change, which is a change in the organization of processes with respect to one another, as well as first-order change, in which we see decrements or increments in the salience of particular processes.

III. Results and theory

3. Becoming friends: conversational skills for friendship formation in young children*

JEFFREY PARKER

The study of children's friendships has received increasing empirical emphasis in recent years (see Asher & Gottman, 1981; Hartup, 1983; Lewis & Rosenblum, 1975; Z. Rubin, 1980; K. H. Rubin & H. S. Ross, 1982). Researchers interested in the growth of social-cognitive skills, for example, have begun to chart the development of children's understanding of friendship and their friendship expectations (Berndt, 1984; Bigelow & LaGaipa, 1975; Damon, 1977; Furman & Bierman, 1981; Gamer, 1977; Reisman & Shorr, 1978; Selman, 1981; Youniss, 1980). Other researchers have described some of the ways that social interaction differs across friend and nonfriend relationships (see Berndt, 1986; Foot, Chapman, & Smith, 1980; Hartup, 1983; Serafica, 1982) and have examined how school, home, and community variables mediate friendship selection and friendship influence (Epstein & Karweit, 1983; Hallinan & Tuma, 1978; Schofield, 1982; see also Chapter 7).

Collectively, this research represents a promising advance toward understanding the nature of young children's friendships and the contextual constraints that operate within and upon them. However, it tells us very little about the natural history of such relationships. Friendship among children, in one author's words,

> is not so much a stable entity as a goal which is pursued. Children have to work to get a friendship started. Once it is established,

* I would like to thank Kathy Cain and Jackie Gilbert for splendid performances as Panduit. I would also like to thank my two excellent "naive" coders, Ellen Friman and Naomi Collins; and Kathy Scherer, Suzanne Lee, and Stephanie Lyons for their help in data collection. I am indebted to John Gottman for his helpful comments on this chapter and for his continued research inspiration and guidance. Finally, I would like to thank the dozens of children who, with their parents, made the Panduit study a reality. This manuscript was written while the author was supported by a NICHHD Traineeship (HD07205) and by a University Fellowship from the University of Illinois, Champaign–Urbana.

they have to work to keep it going. Effort is needed if only because circumstances of events and other peers continually intrude on and tend to change the relation. To move on to best or close friendship, the friends have to attend to one another and keep in mind the direction in which they want to go. And despite these efforts, we know that in most instances a friendship will not last. Eventually the friends will move apart and their relation will change so that they become less attentive to one another and hardly have contact [Youniss, 1980, p. 189].

Any complete characterization of childhood friendship must also include a description of the ways in which friendships form, are maintained, change over time, and end. To date, much less empirical effort has been devoted to describing the temporal aspects of children's friendships.

The focus of this chapter is the process of friendship formation in young children. As we shall see, how children become friends is a remarkably complex process that is still only partially understood. Yet it is important that this process be described, not only for its own intrinsic value, but for the sake of efforts to aid children who have difficulty making friends. As pointed out earlier in this volume (Chapter 1) and elsewhere (Parker & Asher, 1985), there is reason to be concerned about the psychological fate of children who have difficulty with their peers, particularly children who repeatedly meet overt rejection in their efforts to make friends.

A number of researchers have begun to design interventions on behalf of friendless, socially isolated, or rejected children (see Hops, 1982; Putallaz & Gottman, 1984; Wanless & Prinz, 1982). As Gottman (1983) notes, in many cases these interventions focus on improving the quality of the child's *dyadic* peer interactions, and in some cases they directly attempt to teach a child how to make a friend (e.g., Oden & Asher, 1977; Stocking, Arrezzo, and Leavitt, 1980). However, there is currently very little descriptive knowledge of the social skills essential for making a friend. Without such a data base, those wishing to teach children how to make friends have either (1) relied on armchair speculation, anecdotal observation, or current clinical wisdom or (2) extrapolated from the literature on the antecedents of sociometric acceptance in order to decide which social skills to include and exclude from intervention efforts.

The literature on social skills and sociometric acceptance is relatively well developed, but there is a critical distinction between acceptance and friendship (Asher & Renshaw, 1981; Duck, Miell, & Gaebler, 1980; Hartup, 1975, 1978; Mannarino, 1980; Masters & Furman, 1981; Miller & Gentry, 1980). Sociometric acceptance is a group metric; it reflects an individual's relative status in a group of children in terms of unilateral liking and attraction. Friendship is a dyadic relationship based on mutual affection. It is possible to have no friends and be well accepted by the peer group generally and, conversely, to maintain specific friendships despite generally low peer group regard (Asher & Renshaw, 1981). The social skills required to achieve adequate group acceptance may in many ways be distinct from those required to form friendships. Thus, there is a need to explicate the social skills involved in friendship formation per se.

3.1. Studying friendship formation: some research considerations

The suggestion that very little is known about the process of friendship formation among children may be somewhat surprising to researchers familiar with the literature on children's peer relations. In part, this is because, as just noted, the literature on sociometric acceptance is sometimes thought to bear on this issue and may lead to the mistaken impression that the topic has been extensively researched. However, there are several additional literatures that focus more specifically on friendship and seem on the surface to provide descriptive data relevant to friendship formation. Let us consider what these literatures can and cannot tell us.

Research on interpersonal attraction

Several decades of social psychological research with both adults and children have identified the correlates of interpersonal attraction. One basic finding, now quite replicable, is that children are attracted to other children who are similar in age, sex, and race; to children who share their own preferences for leisure activities; and to children with similar attitudes toward academic matters and deviant behaviors such as smoking (see Asher, Oden, & Gottman, 1977; Berndt, 1982; Duck, Miell, & Gaebler, 1980; Furman, 1982; Hartup, 1983; Kandel, 1978). Implicit personality traits such as intelligence seem to carry less weight.

Research on similarity and attraction is important, but it is of limited value for constructing a model of friendship formation. To begin with, such studies are rarely observationally based and therefore ordinarily reveal very little about the specific behavioral mechanisms by which similarities in specific characteristics promote friendship formation. More important, they do not address the fundamental question of why some pairs of children become friends whereas others do not. Although it is clear that children are attracted to other children who are similar to them in essential respects, it is also clear that children are attracted to many children with whom they never develop friendships. Initial interpersonal attraction is a necessary, but hardly sufficient condition for friendship formation. What is needed is a behaviorally based account of why some children go beyond initial attraction and develop a friendship whereas others do not.

Research on acquainted and unacquainted children

There is a small, but growing literature on the process of acquaintance among children. One kind of study compares strangers with children who know each other. Comparisons between acquainted and unacquainted children suggest that acquainted children are more talkative, more socially responsive, and better able to initiate and sustain complex forms of play than strangers (Doyle, Connolly, & Rivest, 1980; Jormakka, 1976; Matthew, 1978; McCormack, 1982; K. Rubin, Fein, & Vandenberg, 1983; Vandell & Mueller, 1980). In addition, a few researchers have studied the acquaintance process more dynamically by mapping how strangers interact over time (Furman & Childs, 1981; Furman, 1982; Oden, Herzberger, Mangione, & Wheeler, 1984). Furman and Childs (1981), for example, observed the process of acquaintanceship in 40 dyads of third graders during a single laboratory play session. Their preliminary analyses indicated that the first time two unacquainted children meet they usually begin by asking one another questions in order to discover their common attitudes and orientations. This process of disclosure and discovery of "co-orientation" soon leads to the establishment of mutually rewarding activities. These activities serve as the content, or substance, of the emerging relationship and, by the end of the session, can come to "individuate" this relationship from the participants' other relationships. This progression from disclosure to mutual activities to individuation of the relationship is thought to be essential to the development of an affectionate bond.

Work on the effects of familiarity on the process of acquaintanceship cannot be applied directly to an understanding of how children become friends, because children do not become friends with every child with whom they become acquainted, no matter how much repeated contact the two may have. As Gottman (1983) pointed out:

> Investigations designed to describe how children become friends must also account for natural variation in the *success* of children's attempts at making friends. Not all attempts are successful, particularly for young children (see Gottman & Parkhurst, 1980). Thus *there is a need to index the quality of the acquaintanceship and then to account for variation in this index by reference to appropriate social process variables* [p. 4; emphasis added].

As with interpersonal attraction, understanding how children become acquainted is necessary, but not sufficient for understanding friendship formation.

Research on friends and nonfriends

Interest in friendship has led a number of authors to compare the behavior of friends with that of strangers or acquaintances (e.g., Berndt, 1981; Foot, Chapman, & Smith, 1977; George & Krantz, 1981; Gottman & Parkhurst, 1980; Labinger & Holmberg, 1983; Oden, et al., 1984; Rotherham & Phinney, 1982; Sharabany & Hertz-Lazarowitz, 1981; Staub & Noerenberg, 1981). Such comparisons invariably yield differences in both the style and content of verbal and nonverbal interaction. For example, friends smile, talk, and laugh more often; communicate more successfully; are more agreeable and more disagreeable; have more extended fantasy play; and are more prosocial, but also more competitive, than nonfriends.

Comparisons between friends and acquaintances or strangers provide data on how interaction differs at differing points in friendship formation. However, Furman (1984) points out that, although such comparisons can indicate differences in phases of friendship formation, "they do not reveal what *effect* a variable has on the development of a relationship" (p. 30); that is, they do not inform us as to the dynamics of friendship formation. This is because such comparisons confound social processes that produce friendships with those that are the product of friendship. Furman noted:

> Often the differences observed in cross-sectional comparisons can be secondary in importance – in fact, they can even present a misleading picture of the processes involved. For example, acquainted children are more critical of each other than unacquainted children (Furman & Willems, 1982). It seems unlikely, however,

that criticism promotes the development of friendly relationships. Instead, the difference may reflect an increase in the acceptability of expressing feelings in the relationship. . . . The dynamic processes involved in relationship development can be delineated only by manipulating a variable experimentally or examining the pattern of relationships over time [p. 31].

Furman's last point warrants elaboration: To understand the processes involved in friendship formation it is necessary (1) to follow previously unacquainted children over time to determine which ones become friends and the social processes that might have foretold such an outcome or (2) to find a meaningful way to vary aspects of initial interaction systematically and determine the impact of these changes on the likelihood of subsequent friendship formation.

The remainder of this chapter is devoted to two recent inquiries – one longitudinal and one experimental – into the process of friendship formation in young children. These studies are part of a programmatic series of studies of this topic begun in 1975 by Gottman and Parkhurst (1980) and continued by Gottman (1983) and Parker (1984). The goal of this research has been to explicate the conversational skills that determine why some pairs of previously unacquainted children become friends whereas others do not.

3.2. The Gottman studies of friendship ontogeny

Gottman (1983) presented what appears to be the first published description of the process of friendship formation in children. In his monograph, *How Children Become Friends*, he describes the results of two studies designed to assess the role of a small set of conversational processes in accounting for variations in the success with which pairs of unacquainted children "hit it off" and progressed toward friendship.

Gottman's basic data consisted of the audiotaped play conversations of 18 dyads of unacquainted children, aged 3 to 9 years, during three consecutive play sessions in one child's home. Audiotaped play conversations were also gathered from a second sample of 13 children, aged 3 to 6 years, playing at home on different days with their best friend and with a stranger. These additional cross-sectional data were used to validate several measures used in the longitudinal analysis. In addition, the tapes of children playing with a stranger provided an opportunity to replicate any findings that might emerge from the initial session in the longitudinal sample. All tapes in both samples were transcribed verbatim, coded using the MICRO coding system described in Chapter 2, and then analyzed both sequentially and nonsequentially.

Two months after the sessions, mothers in the longitudinal sample filled out a 21-item questionnaire designed to assess the extent to which the children had progressed toward friendships. They were asked, for example, whether the two children spoke positively about one another, asked to see one another again, telephoned, visited, and so on.

Gottman's first objective was to derive, from the interaction itself, an index of the extent to which the two children had hit it off and progressed toward friendship. The most reliable and valid index proved to be the proportion of agreement expressed by the guest child (GAG; see Chapter 2). GAG correlated highly with mother questionnaire scores across sessions and distinguished friends from strangers in the cross-sectional sample.

The second task was to select, operationalize, and validate a limited number of salient conversational processes for evaluation as potential predictors of friendship formation. This process was guided both by previous research and inductively by the conversations themselves and is described in detail in Chapter 2. It is sufficient to note here that, including both the host and the guest roles, 32 such indices were derived, representing seven salient social processes: (1) communication clarity and connectedness, (2) information exchange, (3) exploration of similarities and differences, (4) establishment of common-ground play activities, (5) resolution of conflict, (6) positive reciprocity, and (7) self-disclosure. Most of these indices of conversational processes were sequentially based; for example, one index of communication clarity and connectedness was essentially the conditional probability of a question for clarification by one child being followed by an appropriate clarification by the other child. A few were nonsequentially based; for example, one index of information exchange was the relative frequency of information statements expressed by the host child.

Findings

Predicting progress toward friendship. The essential question was whether the seven social processes could account for differences among dyads in their progress toward friendship. The answer, in a word, was yes. In fact, regression analyses indicated that these variables could account for more than 80% of the variance in dyads' progress toward friendship, regardless of whether progress was indexed by guest agreement (GAG) or mothers' questionnaire scores.

Several conversational processes were related in clear ways to friendship formation. Communication clarity and connectedness was significantly related to progress toward friendship (i.e., GAG) in the first session of the longitudinal sample and marginally related in the stranger data of the cross-sectional sample. Information exchange variables and variables indexing conflict resolution correlated significantly with friendship progress in both samples, as did indices of common-ground play activities.

Somewhat more equivocal findings were found with regard to the remaining three conversational processes. The establishment of similarity and exploration of differences in the first meeting was not consistently related to progress toward friendship in either sample; in fact, there was some suggestion that this process was *negatively* related to progress in the stranger data of the cross-sectional sample. Positive-reciprocity variables were related to progress, but not in a consistent manner, in both samples. In the first session of the longitudinal sample, reciprocity of fantasy was related positively to progress, whereas reciprocity of joking was related to progress in the stranger data of the cross-sectional sample. Self-disclosure was not essentially related to hitting it off in either sample. Thus, as Gottman summarized, "The tasks of the first meeting appear to be to interact with one another in a low conflict and connected fashion in order to exchange information and establish common-ground activity" (p. 38).

The data from the second and third sessions of the longitudinal study provided an opportunity to examine the relationship between communication process variables and friendship development over repeated interaction opportunities. Communication clarity and connectedness became even more important as acquaintanceship proceeded in accounting for the extent to which two children eventually hit it off and progressed toward friendship (i.e., GAG); so did information exchange, the resolution of conflict, and the establishment of common-ground activities. Moreover, self-disclosure and the exploration of similarities and differences – two processes of limited predictive utility in initial encounters – did predict progress toward friendship in the second and third sessions. Reciprocity was the only variable to decrease in predictive significance and become unimportant over repeated interaction opportunities. Regression analyses of the second- and third-session data indicated once again that communication process variables could account for more than 90% of the variance in acquaintanceship success.

Additional analyses indicated that the relationships between process variables and acquaintanceship success did not have to be qualified very much by reference to either the ages of the children or the sex composition of the dyad (i.e., same-sex males, same-sex females, or cross-sex).

The dynamics of friendship formation. The findings above demonstrate the effect of specific conversational processes such as information exchange on the likelihood of friendship formation. They also show how these processes increase or decrease in importance over repeated interaction episodes. They do not, however, tell us how acquaintanceship is patterned *within* a session. For example, do children begin an interaction with information exchange? What happens when common-ground activities deteriorate? In other words, they do not tell us the dynamics of acquaintanceship. More to the point, they do not tell us how the dynamics of acquaintanceship differs between pairs of children who do and do not eventually become friends.

Gottman recoded all the transcripts of the stranger dyads in the cross-sectional sample using a global MACRO coding system (see Chapter 2). Briefly, there were 19 MACRO codes related to *information exchange* (success and failure), common-ground play and its successful and unsuccessful *escalation* and *deescalation, conflict* and *conflict resolution, similarities, differences, gossip* (success and failure), *self-disclosure, amity* (success and failure), and *communication clarification* (success and failure). The categories of the MACRO coding system were dyadic states; they characterized the dyad in a two-turn unit, not each individual. On the basis of proportions of guest agreement, Gottman divided the stranger tapes into dyads that hit it off (above the mean, $n = 7$) and dyads that did not hit it off (below the mean, $n = 6$).

The first thing that became apparent was that dyads that hit it off interacted for more turns than those that did not. But there were qualitative differences as well. Children who did not hit it off were more likely to experience unsuccessful amity (i.e., unreciprocated affection or humor) and were more likely to be unsuccessful when exchanging information than children who hit it off. They were also less likely than children who hit it off to reciprocate gossip, to self-disclose, and to exchange information successfully. They were *more* likely than children who hit it off to be successful in escalating play to a higher level of interpersonal responsiveness; yet their common-ground activities were no more likely to stay successful than those of children who hit it off, and their interaction was characterized by greater conflict and squabbling. Rapidly escalating play intensity without the supportive scaffolding of successful information exchange, gossip, and self-disclosure would seem counterproductive to friendship formation. This is consistent with Gottman and Parkhurst's (1980) anecdotal observation that some children take a "high-risk" approach to making friends that is sometimes highly successful but often ends in fury and adult intervention.

To examine the patterning of conversational processes within sessions, the lag 1 transition frequencies of the codes were examined for both children who hit it off and those who did not, that is, the probability of similarity, for example, being followed by common-ground success, self-disclosure, amity, escalation success, and so on, in the two groups. The two groups were similar in a few respects, but different in many – too many to present fully here. Nonetheless, some of the most interesting similarities and differences warrant brief presentation.

To begin with, nearly all children began the session with information exchange (90%), although children who did not hit it off were less successful in such attempts than children who did. When information exchange was successful, children who hit it off were likely to move to common-ground activity talk or amity. Children who did not hit it off were not. Instead, they were likely to conflict or to explore similarities and differences. In fact, it appeared that these children were almost preoccupied with the goal of establishing an early "me too" climate of agreement.

Another important way the two groups differed was in their sequences following successful common-ground activity talk. Children who hit it off were much more likely to progress to successful amity after engaging in common-ground activity talk than children who did not hit it off. Consistent with the high-risk strategy noted above, children who did not hit it off were more likely to attempt to escalate the level of play; however, when this was successful, their activity play was subsequently more likely to fail. In fact, these and other analyses indicated that the play of children who did not hit it off had a "staccato rhythm" – that is, brief periods of common-ground activity interrupted by frequent escalation attempts. When common-ground activity talk failed, a likely consequence for both groups was conflict and a return to information exchange, particularly among children who did not hit it off.

Following conflict, children who hit it off tended to move to successful information exchange and common-ground activity talk, whereas children who did not tended to move to conflict resolution exchanges. Although at a glance this might appear to indicate greater competence on the part of children who did not hit it off, other findings indicated that the interaction of children who did not hit it off was characterized by more conflict, and more extended conflict, than the interaction of children who did. Thus, there was probably a greater need for conflict resolution strategies in these dyads.

Two other differences in temporal patterns deserve mention here. First, although events following successful gossip did not differ between children who hit it off and those who did not, there was nonetheless some suggestion that gossip among the latter dyads tended to end abruptly, that is, to be unreciprocated. Among children who hit it off, on the other hand, gossip tended to be reciprocated and to lead to successful amity. Second, there was at least a suggestion in the data that self-disclosure among children who hit it off was more likely to lead to successful amity than among children who did not. The latter group may be more likely to establish similarity. Gottman noted that a simple "me too" response following self-disclosure may not be as effective in the acquaintanceship process as supportive, affectionate, and humorous comments.

The comparisons discussed above indicate clearly that there are many differences in the temporal patterning of conversations of children who do and do not hit it off, but they still do not provide much indication of the organization of the salient conversational processes during ongoing interaction. A feel for the organization of the conversational processes can be gained by examining the "state transition diagram" shown in Figure 3.1 (Gottman, 1983). It presents the sequential relationships between the conversational processes for children who hit it off with strangers in the cross-sectional sample. Its lines represent, in terms of conditional probabilities, the transitions from antecedent to consequent codes. Thus, it provides a schematic representation of a successful approach to friendship formation. The conversational processes are grouped into three categories: (1) processes that involve play – information exchange, establishing common-ground activities, and escalation; (2) processes that involve self-exploration – gossip, self-disclosure, and the exploration of similarities and differences; and (3) processes that involve the repair and maintenance of interaction – conflict resolution, deescalation, and message clarification. In addition there are two affective states: amity and conflict. Using Figure 3.1 it is possible, albeit tedious, to trace in detail the scenarios that can result from different combinations of successful and unsuccessful play, exploration, repair, amity, and conflict. Short of that, it is sufficient to note first that, in dyads that hit it off, self-exploration, play, and amity are a tightly connected cluster in a temporal sense; children move in and out of discussions of play materials to self-disclose, explore feelings, offer confirmation and support, gossip, laugh, and joke. Perhaps this is partly why rapidly and repeatedly escalating the responsiveness level of play constitutes a high-risk friendship strategy that is often unsuccessful: It may come at the expense of other important processes and is therefore too much, too soon.

In addition, amity and conflict operate as interstitial processes, providing links within and among the other three categories (play, self-exploration, repair). For example, amity provides links between play and self-exploration as noted earlier, but it also provides links within self-exploration. In other words, discussions involving gossip, self-disclosure, similarities, and differences are characterized by a great deal

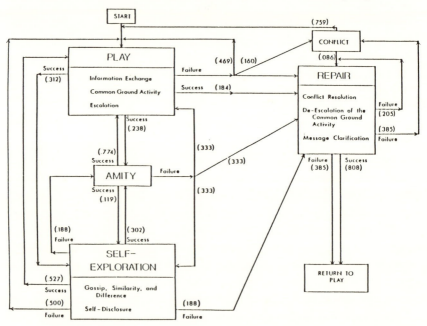

Figure 3.1. Partial state transition diagram of a temporal flow model of friendship formation processes among children who "hit it off." From Gottman (1983).

of humor and supportiveness in dyads that eventually hit it off. Conflict can provide links between play and repair, although repair can (and often does) occur in the context of play without the need for overt conflict.

Gottman suggests that a successful friendship formation strategy begins with successful information exchange. Information exchange requires that children communicate clearly and connectedly and indicates responsiveness and interest on the part of both parties. Progressing farther, however, requires that children move to common-ground activities and talk about play and play materials. If this move is unsuccessful, the dyad must return temporarily to information exchange to avoid conflict. Once common-ground activities are established, however, there is a complex "mini–max" problem to be solved: A balance must be struck between the level of responsiveness demanded by the common-ground activity and the potential for conflict. Nondemanding levels of play, such as the parallel play Parten (1932) describes, yield little conflict but offer little in terms of amity as well. Highly demanding levels of play, such as adventure fantasy play, offer much in terms of amity but run a higher risk of creating conflict. There is thus a hierarchy of play activities (in terms of the responsiveness they demand) that must be ascended by artful escalation when opportunities present themselves and deescalation when conflicts arise. Throughout, children must explore similarities and differences, reciprocate gossip, and self-disclose; they must also work continually to clarify messages and avoid and resolve conflict.

Individual differences. The analyses outlined above were deliberately carried out at the dyadic level. They describe what happens between two children when they do or do not progress toward friendship. They do not address the question of whether these social events are a function of the social skill levels of the individual children. However, using the data from the cross-sectional sample, Gottman was able to address some aspects of this issue. Specifically, he reasoned that a social skills deficit would be indicated if, while playing with their best friends, children who did not hit it off with strangers seemed more problematic in terms of the conversational processes than children who hit it off. And, in fact, this appeared to be the case. Children who hit it off with strangers were more likely than children who did not to clarify their messages with best friends, more likely to establish similarities with best friends, somewhat more likely to employ some forms of conflict resolution, and more likely to reciprocate humor with their best friends.

The findings from Gottman's ontogeny studies have been presented in detail because they represent a significant advance in our understanding of friendship formation in young children. They indicate that the emergence of friendship at this age can be accurately predicted through a detailed examination of children's conversations upon first meeting. In particular, six specific conversational processes seem to hold considerable predictive power in this regard: the extent to which two children communicate clearly and connectedly, exchange information successfully, explore similarities and differences, successfully establish common-ground activities, resolve conflicts amicably when they arise, and to a lesser extent disclose private thoughts and information. There is also evidence that children who are successful at making friends use common-ground activity talk as a springboard to self-exploration and amity, use information exchange as a "home base" when conversation goes awry, and artfully escalate and deescalate levels of play as the situation demands. Finally, there is some evidence that individual children differ in their adeptness at carrying out many of these conversational processes. Taken together, the findings suggest that these social processes, or some subset of these processes, play a role in determining whether two children will progress toward friendship. They may, in effect, represent friendship formation "skills." If true, this has important implications for researchers interested in helping children who have difficulty making friends. Because Gottman's data are correlational they cannot be used to address this possibility directly, however. What is required is an assessment of the effect of an independent manipulation of these conversational processes on subsequent friendship formation – in other words, an experimental study. The remainder of this chapter is devoted to the discussion of such a study.

3.3. Making friends with an "extraterrestrial": the Panduit experimental study

A study was designed to determine whether a gross manipulation of the six important conversational processes Gottman identified would systematically alter the subsequent likelihood of the development of a friendship between a child and a stranger (Parker, 1984). To do this, two problems had to be overcome: (1) An experimental procedure had to be designed in such a way that it preserved as much as possible the spontaneity and richness of children's conversation but allowed tight experimental control over specific verbal processes, and (2) the dyadic conversational processes Gottman identified as critical to predicting progress toward friendship had to be operationalized into a set of specific individual behaviors.

The Panduit paradigm

The first task was that of gaining experimental control over children's conversation while preserving much of its spontaneity and richness. With older children, a same-age child can be solicited and trained to act as the experimenter's confederate (e.g., Putallaz, 1983). With preschool-aged children, however, the confederate approach, as such, seemed counterindicated for fairly obvious reasons related to the cognitive complexity of the task. Nonetheless, it seemed possible to create, in effect, a "surrogate" child that might act as an experimental confederate. This was accomplished by constructing a 2-foot-tall cloth talking doll, dubbed Panduit, that resembled a small green child in silver clothing (Figure 3.2). Although the doll did not move, it stood upright, was portable, and contained a hidden wireless electronic receiver/speaker

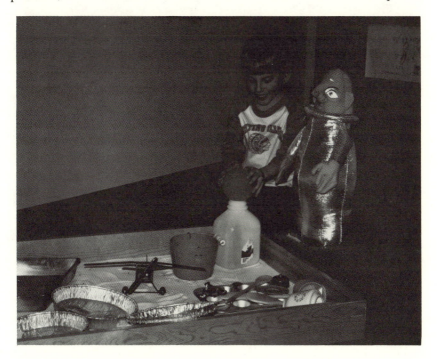

Figure 3.2. Panduit and child during play session.

that allowed an assistant behind a hidden two-way mirror to act as its voice and converse interactively with the children in an age-appropriate manner. Extensive pilot work indicated that almost all children enjoyed meeting the doll, spoke to it unguardedly when adults were absent, and viewed it as unusual but very much alive. A few children considered it a robot, computer, or outer-space boy or girl.

Operationalization of the process variables

The most difficult task involved operationalizing at the level of discrete behaviors the dyadic conversational sequences Gottman identified using the MICRO coding system. To appreciate this difficulty, it is necessary to realize that Gottman (1983) did not claim to have *described* the social processes he studied – only to have *indexed* them in the sense that

> if that process occurs more or less often, the variable should correspondingly increase or decrease in the data. A particular sequence may thus represent an entire cluster of variables indexing a type of social event, without necessarily being an operational definition of the social event [p. 19].

What follows is an overview of the operationalization of the six conversational processes manipulated in the Panduit experimental study, with emphasis on the specific behaviors used to represent skilled and unskilled behavior in these respects. The examples given are taken from the audiotapes used in Gottman's cross-sectional study (A and B examples) or from pilot work with the Panduit paradigm (P and C examples). A manual that specifies the operationalization of these conversational processes in detail is available.

In some cases operationalization could, in part, follow directly from Gottman's index variable. For example, Gottman considered the sequence "host request for clarification followed appropriate clarification" (HQ → GCM) to index communication clarity. Therefore, skilled behavior with regard to communication clarity could include the prescription to follow all requests for clarification by the child with an appropriate clarification. Unskilled behavior, on the other hand, could include following a request for clarification with inappropriate repetition, as this example from pilot work illustrates:

Panduit: Take me over there, please [*Does not specify where.*]
Child: Over where? [*Requests clarification.*]
P: Please. [*Fails to clarify following request.*]
C: Over where? [*Repeats request.*]
P: Over there. [*Repeats without any added clarification.*]

Every attempt was made to include in operational definitions the specific index sequences Gottman identified, but this was not always possible or sufficient. In such cases, operationalization was aided by reference to appropriate literature on children's discourse processes, as noted.

Communication clarity and connectedness. Connectedness simply refers to linking one's own comments to the prior comments of the other person; that is, person A speaks; person B responds; person A responds; and so on. To be considered dialogue, even the most inconsequential verbal exchanges require communication connectedness. Unconnected speech refers to talk in which children are talking about different things and during which statements neither are responses to previous statements nor are responded to. In considering communication connectedness, operationalization was aided by reference to Piaget's (1932) work on collective monologue in children and Planalp and Tracey's (1980) work on appropriate and inappropriate topic changes in adults.

Communication clarity is concerned with the ambiguity of an utterance during conversation, that is, whether it is said in such a way as to be likely to be understood by the other person. Failing to communicate clearly, then, refers to omitting prepositions or details that would provide the listener with sufficient information to allow him or her to place a statement in context or to distinguish a particular object from several possible alternatives. It can also involve using idiosyncratic words or phrases, as in "You take the Kudapah" when "Kudapah" is a nickname the other child is not familiar with. Operationalization of communication clarity was aided by research on referential communication (see Asher 1978; Asher & Wigfield, 1981), by Garvey's (1977) work on "contingent queries," and by Shuy and Griffen's (1981) sociolinguistic account of requests for clarification.

Skilled behavior means that care is taken to speak contingently, to supply adequate referential information, and to clarify ambiguous statements when asked to do so. For example:

P: Can we make up a story about that rabbit on the wall?
C: Which rabbit?
P: That rabbit, over there, on the wall. There's a rabbit on the wall.

and

P: No. But they're almost at the side of the road.
C: Toad?
P: Road.

Unskilled behavior means that important referential information is occasionally omitted and the resulting ambiguity not clarified, as in the "Over there" example earlier. In addition, words with idiosyncratic meanings are introduced without any effort to clarify or contextualize them. For example:

P: My, my suit's made of formaline. Are your clothes made of formaline?
C: What is formaline?
P: My suit's made out of it . . .
C: No, what *is* formaline?
P: My suit's made outta formaline, and, and it won't tear. It won't even rip. It's really strong, kinda.
C: Mine is too, see, watch even if I rip it, it won't rip.

and

P: . . . is that our G-force?
C: What?
P: Is that a G-force over there?
C: This?
P: No.
C: What?
P: That's a G-force, isn't it?
C: What's a G-force?
P: It's over there by the sandbox.
C: What *is* it?
P: By the sandbox.
C: What is one?
P: Oh, nevermind.

Finally, disconnected discourse is created by occasionally responding to questions with topic changes. For example, Panduit is playing make-a-cake in the sandbox:

P: . . . there's gonna be some candy in it. Candy cake. Candy cake, and I'm gonna put it in the oven.
C: What?
P: My knees are strong.
C: Oh. Your knees are strong.

Information exchange. According to Gottman, information exchange is the process by which children discuss themselves, the other, their own or other's possessions or actions, the surroundings, and things outside the present context. It does not include intimate topics, which are included under self-disclosure. Recall that Gottman found that information exchange often served as a "home base" in the conversations of children who hit it off.

Gottman identified the summons – answer routine as central to information exchange. He also noted the importance of asking questions.

Operationalization was further aided by the work of Wilkinson, Clevenger, and Dollaghan (1981) on older children's strategies for requesting information in small instructional groups, particularly their observations on the "Wh-question" (e.g., "How did you do that?") and the "yes–no" question (e.g., "Did you put out fours?").

Skilled behavior means that information exchange is enhanced by initiating summons–answer routines; asking questions regarding objects, people, possessions, and attitudes; and using attention phrases such as "Hey, you know what!" Also, the child's questions are almost always answered fully. The following are examples of skilled information exchange in context:

C: I hate gray hair, on noses.
P: Well, my mom has some, on her head.
C: I know, my grandmother has gray hair on her head too.
P: But not very much.
C: My grandmother has a lot.
P: My mom is thirty-six.
C: I think my grandmother is older than that.
P: That's pretty old.
C: She's older than your mom.

    *   *   *   *   *

P: Hey, hey, do you know, do you know Ghostbusters?
C: Um hum.
P: I know Ghost; did you see the movie?
C: Um hum.
P: You did? I didn't get to see, but my, my dad told me about it. And, and do you know "Ain't 'fraid of no ghost" [*sung*]?
C: I, I and I know the saying "Ghostbusters!"
P: Yeah, "Who you gonna call" [*sung*]?
C: "Ghostbusters" [*sung*]!
P: "Who you gonna call?"
C: "Ghostbusters!"
P: "Ghostbusters!" I know that.

    *   *   *   *   *

P: I have three sisters, but they're all bigger than me.
C: Why are they?
P: 'Cause, 'cause, I don't know. I think they were born early.
C: Yeah, they were. 'Cause I was born before my brother so I got to be four before he got to be four. I'm gonna be five in February twenty-fourth. That's close to Christmas, after Christmas though.

    *   *   *   *   *

C: Are you a boy or a girl?
P: I'm a girl.
C: I'd rather be a boy, but I'm a girl too.
P: But I could be a gas station lady.
C: I can, I can either, I can still be and I can still be a fireman.
P: Yeah, 'cause girls can do what boys can do.

C: Yeah, I know. I have, I had a library book and it was about uh girls can be anything.
P: I bet that's a good book.
C: Yeah, it was.
P: 'Cause, 'cause girls can be policeman too.
C: Yeah, girls can be anything they want to be. Just like boys.

*   *   *   *   *

P: Hey! I didn't eat dinner yet.
C: I, I did.
P: I didn't. And I'm, I'm, I'm gonna eat after this. I can't wait. I'm gonna go to Pizza Hut and have a pizza.
C: I went to the pharmacy, and Kentucky Fried Chicken.
P: I like pizza, I'm gonna eat pizza.
C: I like pizza too, but I had Kentucky Fried Chicken.

Unskilled information exchange involves responding to many of the child's questions vaguely (e.g., "I don't know") or inappropriately or keeping answers brief.

Establishing common-ground activities. Common-ground activities, according to Gottman, are any activities in which children jointly participate, including games, fantasy, and coloring. Conversation during common-ground activities centers around (1) talk regarding the objects of play:

A: It's supposed to be a jumper and it goes like this.
B: A jumper?
A: You're supposed to get this over her head.
B: How do, you said over her head or over her arms?
A: Like so, and then you try to get it to, like so.
B: Uh, I can't do it. Looks like it – now I got all mixed up [*laughs*].

(2) roles for each other:

A: Do you want to play house? Do ya?
B: Yes. I'm looking at my book. You can be the big person. You can be seven and I can be five.
A: No, I want to be your mommy.
B: OK.

(3) agendas for play:

P: Let's, let's fill it all to the top and we could pretend we were collecting strawberries. And, and these are strawberries, OK?

or (4) simply narration of activities:

P: You're poking holes in that.
C: I was.
P: Can you make a pig?
C: What?
P: Can you make a pig?
C: No, I don't want to.

It also includes verbal word play, guessing games, rhymes, songs, and jingles.

Moreover, there is a hierarchy of play, organized in terms of demandingness for social responsiveness. At the lowest levels are parallel and simple narration, as in the "pig" example above. At the highest level are cooperative and fantasy play:

C: [*drawing pictures of trees*]: And then there's soil.
P: Soil?
C: Mine has lots of apples on it.
P: Mmmm.
C: They're going all the whole round the tree.
P: Oh, that sounds so nice.
C: I bet you'll like to pick one.
P: Do you want to pretend we're going to pick apples?
C: OK.

Operationalization of this process was aided by Gottman's (1983; Gottman & Parkhurst, 1980) discussions of the hierarchy of play and by his explication of play escalation and deescalation in the MACRO coding system. It was also aided by the work of Griffin (1985) and others (Forbes, Katz, & Paul, 1982; Garvey & Berndt, 1975; Goncu & Kessel, 1983; Seidman, 1983; Tinson, Goncu, & Kessel, 1982) on metacommunication during fantasy play.

Because Panduit cannot move, there are constraints on its play activities. For example, Panduit is not able to color. However, Panduit can narrate play, add sound effects to play activities, and pretend to do some activity. Skilled behavior in this regard means using directives (e.g., "Let's . . . ," "Do this," "Come here," "Take my . . . "), offers (e.g., "Do you want . . . ," "Can we . . . ?"); requests for involvement (e.g., "Would you . . . ?" "Will you . . . ?"), and fantasy "transformations" (utterances that declare the nonliterality of an object). It also means that care is taken to avoid, through judicious use of escalation and deescalation, the staccato rhythm Gottman described.

Unskilled behavior with regard to common-ground activity means rarely initiating or escalating joint-action proposals, deescalating some joint activities, and escalating still others too soon or too rapidly, reminiscent of the high-risk strategy Gottman described.

Similarities and differences. In the course of information exchange children regularly uncover similarities and differences in their personal attributes, attitudes, and possessions. Gottman indexed similarity with "tag questions" (questions for agreement usually ending in "right?"), and direct agreement with expressed feelings. He noted that similarity has a solidarity function. He indexed differences as direct disagreements with feeling statements. These indices proved to be useful in operationalization here.

Skilled behavior involves initiating similarities by fabricating parallels during information exchange and by frequent use of tag questions. For example:

P: . . . How old are you?
C: Four.
P: You're four?
C: Um hum.
P: Hey, you know what?
C: What?
P: I'm four too.
C: Ohhh.
P: Did you have a birthday?
C: Um hum.
P: Yeah, I
C: I gonna have a birthday and I'm gonna be five.
P: Yeah, I'm gonna have a birthday and I'm gonna be five.

and

C: Are you for real?
P: Yeah. Are you for real?
C: Yeah, I'm a real grown-up.
P: You're not a grown-up.
C: Yeah, I'm a kid.
P: Yeah, so am I. I'm five.
C: I'm five too!

Differences are also fabricated occasionally, especially after lengthy similarity exchanges. For example, one girl, after learning that she and Panduit liked many of the same vegetables, asked:

C: You like string beans?
P: Yeah.
C: Uh, so do I.
P: I like, I like peas.
C: What?
P: I like peas 'cause they're little and you could roll 'em around and go like marbles.
C: I hate 'em.
P: Oh, I love 'em.

In unskilled behavior, the goal is not to acknowledge much similarity and instead to create a preponderance of differences.

Conflict resolution. Conflict resolution skills are skills for avoiding conflict or deescalating conflict once it arises. Operationalization was aided by Gottman's focus on offering rules and using weak demand forms. Other authors who have discussed children's discourse in conflict situations include Genishi and Di Paolo (1983), Forbes and Lubin (1983), and Brenneis and Liens (1977).

Skilled behavior means that when disagreements arise care is taken to state a reason, to cite a rule if appropriate, to make an appeasement offer, to change to a more polite demand form, and/or to explore feelings.

Unskilled behavior does not mean escalating conflict or initiating squabbles. It means placing more of the burden of resolving disagreements on the other by avoiding many of the specific skills described above. For example:

P: I'm so strong, I'm so strong, it's like a F-ray shield!
C: You think so! I bet ya I'm stronger than you.
P: I'm so strong as, I got the strongest, I'm very strong. I'm strong as my sister and she's really strong.
C: I'm, I'm as strong as my dad.
P: I could lift my sister up.
C: I could lift you up.
P: If I could move my arms, I could lift you up too.
C: I don't think you could.
P: 'Cause, 'cause, 'cause I'm gonna be so strong.
C: I don't think you, if she, if she eats everything your mom tells you to, you will be, maybe you'll be even stronger than me.

Self-disclosure. This refers to personal revelations about feelings, thoughts, opinions, and past behaviors. It also includes telling secrets. The level of intimacy of self-disclosure statements varies. The following is an example of children's self-disclosure:

P: [*playing in the sand*]: I'm gonna put some alligators in the moat.
C: That's pretty scary.
P: And, oh, here's a flag. I'm gonna stick a flag on top.
C: No. I'm scared of alligators.
P: Alligators are nice, 'cause they're green.
C: And you're green also.

Skilled behavior in this regard means that attention is paid to prompting the other for self-disclosures by the use of direct questioning (e.g., "Do you like . . . ?") or, conversely, offering personal information where appropriate, and especially when asked. Also, care is taken to "match" the level of intimacy of the other's self-disclosures, and a few secrets are told. The following is an example of skilled self-disclosure:

C: Are you scared swimming, taking swimming lessons?
P: Yeah, I'm scared of the water. Are you scared?

C: Not anymore.
P: Did you learn?
C: Yeah! All you gotta do is the – don't you like going under water?
P: No, all the water goes up my nose and then I cough and and I choke and it's awful.
C: Yeah. You know what? I don't like going under water. When I took swimming lessons I had to take . . .
P: And then did you go under water?
C: Yeah, one, two, three [*makes sputtering, splashing sound*] – just like that!
P: And the water, did the water go up your nose?
C: Yeah, I've learned something now, and if you fall in the water, hold your nose, and close your eyes, and just hold your breath!
    [*The two then have a "contest" to see how long they can hold their breath.*]

Note that in this example self-disclosure is integrated into a larger context of information exchange (swimming lessons) and common ground (holding-one's-breath contest). This is also an aspect of skilled self-disclosure.

Unskilled behavior in this regard involves simply not volunteering intimate facts and secrets, even if asked (i.e., "I don't know"). It is not possible, of course, to stop children from self-disclosing if they choose to.

Skilled and unskilled speech

The lengthy process of recasting each of Gottman's six conversational processes into specific behavioral polarities was necessary in order to construct two types of speech related to friendship formation: *skilled* and *unskilled*. Skilled speech, as one might expect, refers to discourse that is age-appropriately competent in all six conversational aspects. Unskilled speech, in contrast, refers to discourse that is relatively incompetent in all six aspects. Using the detailed training manual, numerous audiotapes of preschool children's actual conversations, and role playing, a female assistant was trained to speak in a childlike manner while systematically varying the age-appropriate skillfulness of her speech, thereby creating two experimental conditions: skilled-Panduit and unskilled-Panduit.

Two aspects of skilled and unskilled speech should be noted. First, the six social processes can be heuristically thought of as forming a hierarchy, each somewhat dependent on the others following it: (1) self-disclosure, (2) conflict resolution, (3) similarities/differences, (4) common-ground activities, (5) information exchange, and (6) communication clarity and connectedness. For example, Gottman's work showed that self-disclosure was often embedded in common-ground activity talk, and everything depends to some extent on communication clarity and connectedness. The higher in the hierarchy, the more latitude there is for unskillfulness. Thus, in the unskilled-Panduit condition the relative number of instances of any given type of unskilled behavior varies somewhat depending on the level of that behavior: Although it is possible to never self-disclose during a conversation, it is pointless to never communicate clearly or connectedly. For this reason there was always at least some skilled behavior, particularly information exchange and communication clarity and connectedness, in the unskilled-Panduit condition. What varied was the relative balance of skilled and unskilled behavior across the conversation as a whole.

The second point is that it was not our goal in the unskilled-Panduit condition to be aversive or obnoxious, nor simply to avoid speaking or to speak with flattened affect. The assistant was instructed to think of Panduit in this condition as "well intentioned and sociable" but unskilled and to avoid undue frustration or antagonism.

Subjects and procedure

Subjects were recruited through past newspaper birth announcements. More than 100 couples who had given birth from four to six years earlier in local hospitals and who still resided in the immediate area were first sent a letter inviting them and their child to participate in a study of how children get acquainted and were then telephoned. The first 22 boys and 22 girls whose parents consented to their participation became the subjects. Three subjects – one boy, two girls – were dropped from the study and later replaced when they became upset just before or upon meeting Panduit. The parents indicated that their child was not used to meeting strangers and was characteristically very timid and shy. All children, including these three, were paid five dollars for participating. Children ranged in age from 4 years and 3 months to 5 years and 9 months with an average age of 5 years and 1 month. There were no sex, condition, or sex-by-condition age differences. All children were white.

The study took place in a playroom in a university setting. The playroom contained toys, books, puzzles, a sandbox, a coloring/ Playdough table, and a chalkboard. There was a separate waiting area for parents. Each child was brought individually to the playroom and given a short opportunity to become acclimated to the surroundings before being told that he or she would soon meet "another boy (girl) your age" who was "special and from a place far away" and interested in meeting the child and playing in the room. The experimenter then left the room and a short time later returned with Panduit, who had ostensibly been waiting down the hall. The two were then left alone for 30 minutes to talk and play together while the parent (usually the mother) waited in the waiting room. The interaction was videotaped by the experimenter from an adjoining room. With half of the children of each sex (e.g., 11 boys and 11 girls, chosen randomly) Panduit behaved skillfully; with the remaining children, Panduit behaved unskillfully.

After this play session, the child was reunited with the parent in the waiting room for 5 minutes of unstructured conversation. The parent was asked simply to spend a few minutes learning about the child's impressions of Panduit and the play experience in any way that was natural and comfortable. The parent was told to imagine him- or herself in a similar real-life situation – for example, upon picking up the child after the child's first day at preschool. In an effort to minimize socially desirable responses, the parent was cautioned that because "Panduit does different things with different children," there was considerable individual variation in children's responses to Panduit – some children liked Panduit, and others did not. These conversations were audiotaped. At the end of this 5-minute period, a second experimenter, naive to the child's condition (skilled- or unskilled-Panduit), returned and told the child that the play session had ended a few minutes early and that the child had a choice of (1) leaving at that time, (2) playing for 5 more minutes, but with Panduit absent; or (3) playing for 5 more minutes with Panduit present. Order of presentation was counterbalanced within cells (sex by condition). The session ended either at this point or after 5 minutes of further play with or without Panduit, depending on the child's preference.

Two to four days after the play session and parent conversation, each child's parent completed a 20-item rating scale designed to assess his or her impressions of the degree to which the child and Panduit had progressed toward friendship. Included in this scale were many items similar to those Gottman included in his mother questionnaire. Information was gathered, for example, on how often the child had spoken positively of Panduit since the session, whether the child had discussed the experience with siblings and friends, whether the child had asked to return, and whether the child spoke of Panduit as a friend. In addition, the parent was asked to rate how close the child felt toward Panduit relative to other friends and how reluctant the child had been to leave that day. This scale yielded a single cumulative rating of progress toward friendship. Subsequent analyses indicated that the scale had adequate internal reliability (coefficient alpha = .84).

The "hitting it off" designation. The specific hypothesis of this study was that children who interacted with the skilled Panduit would be significantly more likely to progress toward friendship than children who interacted with the unskilled Panduit. This obviously required an appropriate dependent measure of the extent to which the child hit it off with Panduit. Olson (1977) articulated the multiple perspectives that can exist on relationships and relationship development, distinguishing those of insiders and outsiders, as well as subjective data and objective data. It seemed important to consider, as much as possible, both insider and outsider reports and subjective and objective data in designating which children did and which children did not hit it off with Panduit.

Toward this end, a convergent criterion of hitting it off was developed that incorporated (1) the child's choice to return or not return for further play with Panduit (insider–objective data), (2) the parent rating scale scores (outsider–subjective), and (3) coders' ratings of the audiotapes of the postsession conversations with a parent (also outsider–subjective). The third measure was obtained in the following manner. First, two coders naive to the child's condition listened to tapes of all the children's conversations with their parent while reading along in the transcript. The purpose was to provide a baseline from which to make comparisons among tapes. They then listened to each tape a second time and completed a 20-item rating scale that yielded a global progress toward friendship rating. The specific items tapped such things as how often the child spoke of Panduit and how much he or she remembered about the session, as well as such impressionistic judgments as how similar the child felt to Panduit, how reluctant the child was to have the session end, and how much fun the child had had. In addition, the two coders were told that after the 5-minute conversation each child had been given the three choices listed above. The coders were asked to predict each child's choice. Both coders rated all tapes independently, and the average of the two coders' scores was taken as the child's score. Intercoder reliability was high ($r = .83$, $p < .001$). Conversation ratings correlated moderately, but significantly with parental rating scale scores ($r = .43$, $p < .01$), confirming expectations that the two measures would provide only partially overlapping perspectives on progress toward friendship.

Therefore, children were designated as having hit it off if they met three criteria: (1) They chose to return and play with Panduit; (2) they were above the overall mean of the parent rating scale scores;[1] *and* (3) they were above the mean for their sex in coders' ratings of their postsession conversation with their parent.[2]

All other children were considered not to have hit it off.

Results

A check was made to determine whether the skilled-/unskilled- Panduit manipulation was clear and meaningful. It was. Two naive assistants were able to distinguish skilled from unskilled sessions with perfect accuracy in randomly paired comparisons.

To repeat, the main hypothesis of this study was that children who interacted with the skilled Panduit would be significantly more likely to hit it off than children who interacted with the unskilled Panduit. Although on the basis of Gottman's study it was expected that this hypothesis would be equally valid for both sexes, it seemed prudent to examine sex differences owing to the novelty of the study.

Table 3.1 shows the number of children who hit it off in each condition. Table 3.2 shows this same breakdown for each sex separately. To determine whether hitting it off depended on Panduit's skill and whether this pattern depended on the sex of the child, the data were subjected to a log-linear likelihood ratio chi-square analysis (Bishop, Fienberg, & Holland, 1975; Upton, 1978). This analysis took into account the three-way nature of the study's design (Panduit's Skill × Hit It Off × Sex; see Upton, 1978, for a discussion of the necessity of such an approach). There were two factors (Sex, Panduit's Skill) and one response variable (hitting it off). Following Upton (1978), the data were first fit with the saturated model, which was then used to screen for a more parsimonious model in a step-down fashion, with the constraint that any final model must include both factors and the two-way factor interaction (Sex × Panduit's Skill).

The log-linear analysis revealed two primary determinants of a child's likelihood of hitting it off. First, there was the predicted Hitting It Off × Panduit's Skill interaction [LR χ^2 (1) = 9.25, $p < .01$]: Children who interacted with the skilled Panduit were significantly more likely to hit it off than children who interacted with the unskilled Panduit. Because the criterion for hitting it off was so stringent, this is seen primarily as a decided tendency for few children to hit it off in the unskilled-Panduit condition; 12, or slightly more than half (55%), of the 22 children who met the skilled Panduit hit it off. By comparison, hitting it off in the

Table 3.1. *Number of children hitting or not hitting it off in the skilled- and unskilled-Panduit conditions*

Panduit's skill	Hit it off		Total
	Yes	No	
Skilled	12 (55)	10 (46)	22
Unskilled	3 (14)	19 (86)	22
Total	15 (34)	29 (66)	44

Note: Numbers in parentheses are percentages.

Table 3.2. *Number of children hitting or not hitting it off in the skilled- and unskilled-Panduit conditions by sex*

Sex	Panduit's skill	Hit it off		Total
		Yes	No	
Female	Skilled	8 (73)	3 (27)	11
	Unskilled	2 (18)	9 (82)	11
Male	Skilled	4 (36)	7 (64)	11
	Unskilled	1 (9)	10 (91)	11
Total		15 (34)	29 (66)	44

Note: Numbers in parentheses are percentages.

unskilled condition was rare: only 3 of 22 children (14%), or roughly one-fourth the number who hit it off in the skilled condition.

The second primary influence on the observed distribution of hitting it off and not hitting it off was a marked discrepancy in the overall probability of hitting it off [LR χ^2 (1) = 4.53, $p < .05$)]; only about half as many children hit it off ($n = 15$) as did not hit it off ($n = 29$). Such a discrepancy is not surprising given the stringent threefold criterion used to define hitting it off.

A hierarchical model defined by the hitting it off effect and the Hitting It Off × Panduit's Skill interaction[3] was fit to the observed frequencies in Tables 3.1 and 3.2. This simpler model fit the observed data well [LR χ^2 (2) = 3.40, $p < .18$], suggesting that it provided a sufficient explanation of the observed distribution of hitting it off and not hitting it off in the table. Hence, this model supports a strong effect for Panduit's communicative competence.

Although this model fit the observed data reasonably well without reference to the sex of the child, inspection of the expected and observed frequencies under this model indicated a tendency to underestimate both the number of skilled girls who hit it off and the number of skilled boys who did not. Furthermore, there was a marginally significant Hitting It Off × Sex of Child interaction [LR χ^2 (1) = 3.19, $p < .08$]; twice as many girls ($n = 10$) hit it off as boys ($n = 5$), regardless of condition. Apparently, Panduit was a somewhat more attractive partner for girls than boys. In fact, when this sex difference is taken into account, it explains nearly all of the remaining systematicity in the observed distribution of hitting it off and not hitting it off [LR χ^2 (1) = .21, $p < .65$].[4]

In sum, the results of the log-linear likelihood ratio chi-square analysis confirmed the study's hypothesis. There were three major influences on a child's likelihood of hitting it off. The largest, as predicted, was the child's condition: Children in the skilled condition were many times more likely to hit it off than children in the unskilled condition. The second largest influence was the general tendency for hitting it off to be a relatively rare event; about half as many children hit it off as did not hit it off. This reflects to a large degree the stringent threefold criterion for hitting it off. Finally, to a lesser extent the child's sex had some influence: Girls tended to be more likely to hit it off than boys. This heightened to some extent the disparity between conditions for hitting it off.

Two additional findings are of note. Thirty of the 44 children (68.2%) chose to return to play with Panduit, 9 children (20.5%) elected to leave without further play, and 5 children (11.4%) decided to play alone. This pattern was largely independent of sex and condition. This tends to support pilot impressions that children, even those in the unskilled condition, found the situation novel, interesting, and nonthreatening. Panduit was an attractive playmate under any circumstances. Four of the 5 children who elected to play by themselves – a clear rejection of Panduit – were children in the unskilled condition. Furthermore, naive coders were moderately accurate in predicting each child's choice after hearing only the conversation with the parent: Coder 1 correctly anticipated the choices of 29 of the 44 (66%) children, including all hit it off children; Coder 2 correctly anticipated the choices of 30 of the 44 children (68%), including 14 of the 15 hit it off children. Most of the inaccuracies tended to be the result of confusion between children who left and children who played alone. Apparently, when listening to the child–parent conversations, coders were indeed cognizant of the presence or absence of cues indicating progress toward friendship. Thus, we may have greater confidence in their ratings of these tapes.

3.4. The Panduit replication study

The effect of sex in the first study is interesting: Apparently girls found the situation more conducive to hitting it off than boys. A fairly obvious explanation stemmed from the fact that a female assistant had acted as Panduit's voice for both boys and girls. This was done partly to increase standardization across the sexes and partly because pilot work indicated that the higher pitch of a woman's voice relative to a man's was less threatening and more childlike. Perhaps the feminine voice was distracting to the boys. After all, all children were told that Panduit was of the same sex as they were. Some evidence of this was found in the tapes of the child–parent conversations. Many boys seemed confused about Panduit's sex. Some, for example, told their parents that Panduit was a boy but repeatedly referred to Panduit by the pronoun "she." In light of this, the decision was made to replicate the study using a male assistant to act as Panduit with the boys.

The procedure of the replication study was identical to that of the initial study, except that (1) a different female assistant acted as Panduit for the girls, and a male assistant acted as Panduit for the boys; and (2) the girls, but not the boys, returned for three play sessions with Panduit over a two-week period. Analysis of the second- and third-session data for the girls is currently under way and not considered here. Forty children (20 boys) participated in the replication study. Two children, both girls, were dropped and replaced – one because she became upset before meeting Panduit, the other because efforts to obtain parent questionnaire data proved futile. Children ranged in age from 4 years and 7 months to 5 years and 5 months, with an average age of 5 years and 0.33 month. Two children were black; the remaining children were white. Boys were paid five dollars for their single-session participation; girls were paid fifteen dollars for their participation in three sessions. Half of the boys and half of the girls were again randomly assigned to meet the skilled Panduit. The remaining children met the unskilled Panduit.

Results

Once again, a post hoc check on the skilled/unskilled manipulation indicated that naive assistants could distinguish skilled from unskilled

Table 3.3. *Number of children hitting or not hitting it off in the skilled- and unskilled-Panduit conditions: replication study*

Panduit's skill	Hit it off		Total
	Yes	No	
Skilled	11 (55)	9 (45)	20
Unskilled	4 (20)	16 (80)	20
Total	15 (37.5)	25 (62.5)	40

Note: Numbers in parentheses are percentages.

Table 3.4. *Number of children hitting or not hitting it off in the skilled- and unskilled-Panduit conditions by sex: replication study*

Sex	Panduit's skill	Hit it off		Total
		Yes	No	
Female	Skilled	8 (80)	2 (20)	10
	Unskilled	2 (20)	8 (80)	10
Male	Skilled	3 (30)	7 (70)	10
	Unskilled	2 (20)	8 (80)	10
Total		15 (37.5)	25 (62.5)	40

Note: Numbers in parentheses are percentages.

videotapes with perfect accuracy in randomly paired comparisons. Interrater agreement for the child–parent conversation ratings was again quite high ($r = .91, p < .01$).

Fifteen (37.5%) of the 40 children, 10 girls and 5 boys, hit it off in the second study. Table 3.3 shows the number of children who hit it off in each condition. Table 3.4 shows the same breakdown for each sex separately. Log-linear analysis revealed that the data were best fit [LR χ^2 (1) = 2.16, $p < .14$] by a hierarchial model based on two interaction terms.[5] The primary interaction term was the predicted Hitting It Off × Panduit's Skill dependence [LR χ^2 (1) = 5.82, $p < .05$]. Analysis of the marginal table of frequencies for this term indicated that 11 of 20 (55%) children in the skilled-Panduit condition hit it off, compared with only 4 (20%) of the children in the unskilled-Panduit condition. Thus, children in the skilled condition were almost three times more likely to hit it off than children in the unskilled condition. In addition, there was once again a marginally significant Hitting It Off × Sex of Child dependency [LR χ^2 (1) = 3.14, $p < .08$]: Regardless of condition, twice as many girls ($n = 10$) hit it off as boys ($n = 5$). The strong hitting it off/not hitting it off asymmetry found in the first study did not reemerge.

Thus, the findings of the first study were replicated almost exactly, including the tendency for girls to hit it off. This finding is further evidence that the six conversational processes Gottman identified play a causal role in friendship formation. It also rules out the possibility that boys responded less favorably in the skilled condition and more unfavorably in the unskilled condition because they found the female-voiced Panduit confusing. Perhaps an alternative explanation for the latter finding is that the general situation was more representative of girls' than boys' acquaintanceship contexts. Care had been taken to provide an equal number of masculine and feminine sex-typed toys in the room. However, in retrospect it was apparent that, aside from the sandbox play, most activities (e.g., coloring, working with Playdough, fantasy play, playing with puzzles) were relatively sedentary and deliberately designed to maximize conversation. There were almost no opportunities for gross motor play (e.g., chasing, swinging, climbing, throwing), and this fact was exacerbated by the fact that Panduit could neither walk nor move its hands (although children frequently moved its arms for it). Other researchers have shown that preschool boys prefer gross motor and rough-and-tumble play to more sedentary and structured activities, whereas girls tend to prefer the opposite (e.g., Carpenter, 1981; DiPietro, 1981).

3.5. Toward a model of friendship formation skills

Since the early 1980s several reviews have appeared on the topic of interventions on behalf of children who have difficulty making friends (e.g., Conger & Keane, 1981; Oden, 1980; Wanless & Prinz, 1982). A common conclusion of these and other authors (e.g., Asher, Renshaw, Geraci, & Dor, 1979; Putallaz & Gottman, 1984) is that much more effort has been devoted to determining *how* to change children's behavior than to *which* behaviors to change. As Gottman (1983) noted: "As much attention needs to be devoted to building the content of the intervention as to its mode of delivery. We must be precise in discovering what social processes are natural for children. Otherwise we may continue to design interventions that are not informed by the real social world in which our children must live" (p. 76).

The empirical work presented in this chapter marks a significant step toward remediating this imbalance. Gottman's longitudinal descriptive study indicates that the extent to which two children communicate clearly and connectedly, exchange information successfully, establish common-ground play, explore similarities and differences, resolve conflicts amicably, and self-disclose predicts whether they will become friends. Indeed, the conversational processes account for almost all of the variance in acquaintanceship success. The Panduit studies take the analysis a step farther by demonstrating that these conversational processes play a determining – not just a predictive – role in young children's friendship formation. Coupled with Gottman's finding that children show individual differences in their adeptness at these processes, this demonstration elevates the processes to the status of friendship formation skills.

The two studies together also make a more general point about the study of friendship formation skills. Gottman's work illustrates the fruitfulness of an inductive data-driven approach to studying social process. His work is in child psychology's long tradition of careful observation and description of children's behavior in context. The Panduit studies indicate that descriptive and experimental approaches need not be antithetical. They show that through careful operationalization and creative methodologies descriptive findings can be put to more stringent causal tests in meaningful ways. However, at the same time the Panduit studies imply that we still need further descriptive work – more grist for the experimental mill, so to speak. Only through an iterative process of description and experimentation can we arrive at a comprehensive account of friendship formation.

This chapter has begun to describe the process of friendship formation and the conversational skills that drive it. But this work is far from complete. Future work on young children's friendship formation skills with the Panduit paradigm might proceed in two opposite directions. First, it should be recognized that the skilled/unskilled manipulation in these studies was a gross manipulation of all six processes simultaneously. It was clear in operationalizing the six processes, however, that the individual processes formed a more or less linear hierarchy of importance – each process was partially dependent on the success of the processes below it. In the future, a reductionistic perspective should be taken to determine the specific contributions of each process to the overall success of the manipulation. This could be done by varying one or few of the processes at a time and determining their effectiveness.

Conversely, additional conversational processes must be studied. Gottman was, in part, led to consider these specific variables by their ubiquity in several literatures. Although they seem to be quite adequate, both predictively and experimentally, there are other potentially useful processes to consider, including several Gottman himself identified, such as gossip and amity.

This leads to another consideration. In the future greater care should be taken to examine the impact of the *patterning* of the social processes, both across multiple sessions and within a session. Gottman's work suggests that processes wax and wane in importance over sessions. His work also indicates that skills for integrating processes into ongoing interaction, such as the ability to solve the complex mini–max problem of play escalation and deescalation, can be just as important as the presence or absence of a behavior. It would be interesting to see whether differences in patterning alone can influence the likelihood of friendship formation. If so, social skills interventions must be concerned not only with building a particular skill into a child's behavioral repertoire, but also with teaching the child to use the skill appropriately at appropriate times.

In closing, I shall comment briefly on the Panduit methodology as a paradigm for studying children's conversation and communicative competence. Almost 90 children, representing more than 130 sessions, have interacted with Panduit to date. After a few moments most of these children have opened up and talked to Panduit in an unguarded manner. Many have confided intimate feelings or secrets, and in a few tapes long bouts of high-adventure fantasy play have occurred. Other children have nurtured, reassured, instructed, kidded, and even kissed Panduit. Some children have later written Panduit letters, and several anecdotal reports have indicated that children vividly remember the experience for as long as a year. In other words, nearly all children have found the context meaningful and have considered Panduit to be real and alive in some sense. This suggests that the Panduit methodology may have broader applicability to other research issues that require controlling young children's speech while preserving discourse spontaneity. At the same time, one limitation of the Panduit paradigm must be acknowledged. Our pilot work suggests that the Panduit procedure has a limited effective age range. Children younger than about 4½ years seem to find the talking doll so attractive that naturalistic discourse is disrupted. Moreover, these young children, unlike children in the 4- to 6-year-old range, seem preoccupied with the question of whether

Panduit is real and alive. One 3-year-old boy, for example, repeatedly hit Panduit with a wooden spoon while closely observing its reaction, as if to determine whether Panduit was capable of feeling pain. Conversely, children older than about 6 years approach Panduit skeptically, with discourse that is polite, but distant. It seems clear that another experimental methodology is necessary for the study of friendship formation in slightly younger and slightly older children.

4. The world of coordinated play: same- and cross-sex friendship in young children

JOHN M. GOTTMAN

In this chapter we explore friendship between young children, paying particular attention to differences in same- and cross-sex relationships. We do this from two vantage points. We begin from a distal perspective, characteristic of the peer interaction literature until recently. A study of children's peer interaction in classrooms is described as a vehicle for reconsidering same- versus cross-sex relationships in young childhood. We then take a proximal look at same- and cross-sex peer relationships in young children, within the context of the conversations of friends. The central focus of peer interaction in young childhood (approximately ages 3 to 7 years) is *coordinated play*. Describing this focus is the goal of this chapter.

4.1. Children's same- and cross-sex peer relationships

The nature of children's same- and cross-sex friendships at different ages is largely uncharted territory; this has been known for a long time in developmental psychology (see Hartup, 1983). Part of the reason that so little is known about the developmental course of these relationships is that, from a very early age, cross-sex friendships are very rare. This fact, noted anecdotally more than 75 years ago (e.g., Hall, 1904), is one of the most consistently documented sex differences in the social development literature today (for reviews see Eder & Hallinan, 1978; Foot, Chapman, & Smith, 1980; Hartup, 1983; Kandell, 1978; Karweit & Hansell, 1983; Maccoby & Jacklin, 1974). A door-to-door survey of parents done by my laboratory (Rickelman, 1981), for example, revealed that only about 36% of all best friendships are cross-sex among 3- to 4-year-olds. This rate drops to 23% for 5- to 6-year-olds and is nonexistent among 7- to 8-year-olds. Rickelman's data are consistent with the findings of other studies done in neighborhoods (e.g., Medrich, Roizen,

Rubin, & Buckley, 1982) and in schools (e.g., Eder & Hellinan, 1978; Schofield, 1981; Omark, Omark, & Edelman, 1973; Rotheram & Phinney, 1982; Roopnarine & Field, 1984). They are also consistent with reports from other cultures (Cohen, D'Heurle, & Widmark-Peterson, 1980). In fact, gender is the most potent psychological determinant of friendship choice in middle childhood, outweighing both age and race (Kendell, 1978; Rubenstein & Rubin, 1984; Schofield, 1982).

What is the basis for the marked tendency of children, especially elementary school children, to form friendships primarily with like-sex children? Serbin, Tonick, and Sternglanz (1977) note that a pattern of same-sex affiliation is found so consistently in all cultures that this tendency may be a universal characteristic of human social behavior. Others (e.g., Rubin, 1980) draw on work with nonhuman primates (Rosenblum, Coe, & Bromley, 1975) and young children (Jacklin & Maccoby, 1978; DiPietro, 1981) to argue that children prefer same-sex friends in part because like-sex children are more compatible behaviorally, especially with regard to rough-and-tumble play. Rubenstein and Rubin (1984) list three additional common explanations for the fact that children soon come to form same-sex friendships: (1) A child may prefer same-sex friendships because perceived similarity to self enhances interpersonal attraction; (2) there may be adult reinforcement of this preference; and (3) there may be sex-role stereotypes within the peer group that foster, maintain, and strengthen sex-linked preferences.

Whatever the origins, it is clear that as a result of the tendency for children to select same-sex friends boys and girls operate in very different primary reference groups throughout middle childhood. As Thorne (1982) wrote, "The gender divide is so extensive in elementary school life that it is meaningful to speak of separate girls' and boys' worlds" (p. 1). It is additionally clear that these two worlds are very different in both size and character. At least in elementary school, boys' friendship groups are larger, more age heterogeneous, and more accepting of newcomers than girls' friendship groups (Douvan & Adelson, 1966; Eder & Hallinan, 1978; Feshbeck & Sones, 1971; Lever, 1976; Omark, Omark, & Edelman, 1975; Schofield, 1982; Thorne, 1982; Tuma & Hallinan, 1979). In addition, boys' groups play more outdoor and team sports, play farther from adult supervision, and play over a greater geographical expanse than girls' groups (Burchard, 1979; Lever, 1976; Medrich, et al., 1982; Schofield, 1982; Thorne, 1982).

Waldrop and Halverson (1975) describe the relationships of boys as "extensive" and those of girls as "intensive." These terms refer to the types of games the sexes prefer, the inclusiveness of boys' large groups, and the exclusiveness of girls' smaller groups. Unfortunately, the term "extensive" has come to be used as evidence for the superficiality of boys' friendships compared with girls'. We simply do not know if this is true, but I suggest in this chapter that it is not. Because of its importance in creating an impression of boy and girl friendships, the Waldrop and Halverson study will be discussed in some detail.

The Waldrop and Halverson study

The Waldrop and Halverson (1975) study is often misunderstood and interpreted to suggest that the friendships of boys and girls of elementary school age are different. This was *not* a conclusion of this study.

There were 35 boys and 27 girls in the study. Data were obtained when the children were 2½ years old during their attendance at a five-week nursery school. When they were 7½ years old, additional data were collected.

When the children were 2½ years old, ratings were made on three (what later turned out to be highly correlated) dimensions: (1) the child's *involvement with peers* (i.e., low levels of solitary play, awareness of other children, and frequent play with other children); (2) *friendliness*, which involved positive affect toward peers, helping and responding positively to other children; and (3) *active coping*, which was defined as immediate verbal or physical attack when the child was blocked by a peer; the concept included the rapid resolution of conflict.

At age 7½ years a new set of five ratings, on an 11-point scale, was devised by the researchers; the ratings were based on several sources of information: (1) observation of the child in *solitary* play for 20 minutes, (2) an interview with the mother about a detailed diary she had been asked to keep about her child's peer activities in the neighborhood for one week (this diary included time spent with one peer or a group and initiations of activity with peers), and (3) observation of unspecified, informal interaction during refreshments. It is unclear from the procedures section of the paper whether information obtained during other testing of the child or during other interviews with the mother was also used to make the ratings. The ratings were made on several dimensions: (1) *intensiveness*, which included such items as the child frequently mentioning a best friend, the mother speaking of this friend, and almost daily contact with the best friend reflected in the diary; (2) *extensiveness*, which involved the child and mother mentioning play with a group of peers; (3) the *importance of peers,* which was based on spontaneous comments by the child or mother that other children were important to the child; (4) *social ease,* which was judged by the child's behavior with the adult examiners or the mother's comments; and (5) *dominance,* which referred to bossiness. The diary data were used to calculate hours spent with peers, hours with one peer, hours with a group of peers, and initiations of peer contact.

The *only* statistically significant sex differences reported were these: (1) Girls saw more peers than boys did, (2) girls initiated peer activity more frequently than boys, and (3) girls were rated higher than boys on the "importance of peers" dimension. There is no evidence for the oft-cited contention that boys have extensive friendships whereas girls have intensive friendships. This is especially true when "intensive" is interpreted as intimate.

Waldrop and Halverson's conclusions about sex differences in intensiveness and extensiveness are based on two principal-components analyses, one for boys and one for girls. As we shall see, the conclusions that can be drawn from these analyses are actually complex and somewhat limited. Weights of the first principal component showed that intensiveness ratings loaded on the first component for girls, whereas extensiveness loaded on the first component for boys. No statistical tests of these differential weightings were performed, and correlation coefficients of extensiveness and intensiveness with other ratings (such as social ease) were not statistically compared.

Even if these differences were found, it must be noted that these were correlations among ratings made from the diaries, interviews, and other unspecified sources of data. Because of this, the meaning of intercorrelations and the relative weights for boys and girls may have more to do with the judges' beliefs than with the children's friendships.

The results with respect to intensiveness and extensiveness were actually somewhat complex. When all the children above average in intensiveness were compared with those below average, there were no significant differences in any variable. Thus, it is not completely clear what the intensiveness dimension is related to. Although not significant statistically, boys rated above average on intensiveness had fewer friends than boys below. However, girls rated above average on intensiveness were rated higher on social ease and importance of peers and had spent more time with just one peer than those below average. Thus, we must conclude that the construct of intensiveness was used somewhat differently by the raters for boys than for girls.

A similar problem exists in the way the raters used the construct of extensiveness. Girls rated above average on extensiveness had more friends and saw more peers than girls rated below average. Boys rated above average on extensiveness were judged more socially mature, to have more friends, and to be more assertive, friendly, and peer-oriented than boys below average.

What can be concluded from this study? An examination of the correlations led Waldrop and Halverson to suggest that positive qualities are associated with ratings of extensiveness for boys and with ratings of intensiveness for girls. In their discussion of the results, Waldrop and Halverson cited a study by Sutton-Smith, Rosenberg, and Morgan (1963), who found that elementary school boys chose play activities involving unrestrained movement or pretend assault (cops and robbers, soldiers, throwing snowballs) more often than girls. Girls chose activities that involved restrained movement (dolls, dressing up, house, school, hopscotch, jumprope, or jacks) more often than boys. This discussion is consistent with Thorne's (1985) observations that boys prefer run-and-chase activities and organized games that require larger spaces and more children.

One finding of Waldrop and Halverson that ought to be cited more often concerns the results on longitudinal consistency of peer behavior, as rated by two separate sets of judges, made five years apart. In general, children who were rated sociable at 2½ years were rated more socially at ease at 7½ years. Most of the longitudinal correlations were significant. The authors wrote that "a peer-oriented child at 2½ was likely to be vigorous and not fearful both at age 2½ and at age 7½" (p. 23). This speaks well of the importance of peer interaction in children's lives.

It should be clear from this discussion that there is still much to be learned about the nature of peer interaction among young children, particularly with respect to sex differences.

The nature of cross-sex interaction in early childhood

The strong same-sex bias found in sociometric test results does not imply that there are no cross-sex friendship choices on sociometric measures, nor that cross-sex interaction does not occur. When children do interact, what is the nature of same- and cross-sex interaction? Jacklin and Maccoby (1978) found higher rates of social actions of all kinds for same-sex than for mixed-sex dyads; the effect was greater for girls than for boys. The children were unacquainted 33-month-olds who dressed so as to minimize sex differences. Jacklin and Maccoby's interaction situation was the following. A toy was presented for 4 minutes, removed, and replaced by another toy; this was repeated six times; both mothers were present. No rationale was given for this procedure, and it is unclear whether the results would generalize to other social settings. An interesting result of this study was that girls were inhibited with boys but not with other girls, whereas boys were never inhibited.

There is no study comparable to the Jacklin and Maccoby study with unacquainted children that employed situations more typical of free play. There is some research with acquainted children. However, with acquainted children the results are not clear. Garvey and Ben Debba (1974) reported no effects of the sex composition of the dyad on children's speech (the children were 43 to 67 months of age); they measured the average number of words per utterance and the number of utterances. These measures resemble Jacklin and Maccoby's rate of interaction variable. On the other hand, Langlois, Gottfried, and Seay (1973) studied acquainted 3- to 5-year-olds and reported that 5-year-olds showed more aggression, smiling, talking, body contact, and nonword vocalizations in same-sex than in opposite-sex pairs. Three-year-old boys, however, were more sociable with girls than with boys. Moely, Skarin, and Weil (1979) observed preschool boys and girls playing a game under instructions that stressed either group or individual performance. Children of both sexes who played the game with opposite-sex partners were more competitive and obtained fewer rewards than those who interacted with same-sex partners. At somewhat older ages (7 to 8 years), the tendency to vary behavior in response to sex of partner was true only of girls; boys showed a tendency to compete regardless of the sex of the partner. Savin-Williams (1981), too, has reported that preadolescent cross-sex interaction is more agonistic than same-sex interaction. Specifically, he found that ridicule and physical assertiveness are more prevalent in cross-sex than same-sex pairs of 9- to 10-year-old children.

In general, it must be concluded that results on the differences between same- and cross-sex interaction are neither clear nor consistent. The current interaction data are certainly inadequate to explain the robust sex-segregation effect in the sociometric test literature. The study of Gottman and Benson (1975), described in Section 4.2., was designed, in part, to chart the developmental course of cross-sex friendship using sociometric data and to supplement this with observational data on the frequency and quality of same-sex and cross-sex peer interaction. A second purpose of this study was to examine the interaction of sex and children's sociometric status. The questions here were whether children interact with same-sex and cross-sex peers differently as a function of their own and the other child's acceptance by peers as assessed by sociometric measures and, if so, how this interaction changes with age.

4.2. The Gottman and Benson study

Subjects

The children in four classrooms in a working-class school served as subjects in this study. Kindergarten, first-, third-, and fourth-grade classes were included. A total of 114 subjects, 59 girls and 55 boys, participated.

Procedure

Sociometric measure. Black-and-white pictures were taken of every child in each classroom and were temporarily attached to a large poster board by means of album corners. Each child was shown the pictures of his or her classmates by an adult, who gave the following instructions. "Show me the pictures of your very best friends in the class. Remember, your *very best* friends." The pictures on the board were randomly rearranged after each child's selection. The wording of the sociometric question and the allowance of unlimited friendship choices were based on a pilot study cited in Gottman et al. (1975).

A child's peer acceptance was defined in terms of the number of sociometric choices received. Children receiving more than the classroom's median number of friendship choices were defined as accepted; those receiving fewer than the classroom's median number of friendship choices were defined as unaccepted. On the average, on this sociometric measure an accepted child received 12.79 friendship choices and an unaccepted child received 6.77 choices.[1]

Classroom observations. Using the Gottman et al. (1975) variation on the interaction coding system developed by Hartup, Glazer, and Charlesworth (1967) and a clipboard with a 6-second light-emitting diode and earphone click, six undergraduate observers were trained. Training continued until the interobserver agreement was 90%. One observer was then assigned to each of the four classrooms. The observers spent the first two weeks getting to know the children's names and becoming familiar with classroom procedures.

Once parental permission slips had been returned, the pictures were taken and the sociometric measure administered by two members of the research team who had not been assigned as observers. Observations started at the beginning of the third week and continued for four weeks. The observer watched one child for 10 consecutive 6-second intervals, coding the child's behavior during each interval on a standard form, and then moved on to the next child on the list. To reduce their obtrusiveness, the observers were careful not to observe the children in the same sequence each time. Observations were sampled from the following situations: (1) lecture, storytelling, or demonstration; (2) seat work; (3) free play or unstructured activity within the classroom; (4) free play or unstructured activity outside the classroom. We decided to sample from all these observation situations, but we did not have a large enough sample of behavior within each type of situation to analyze the situations separately. Hence, data for each child were combined across situations. Each child was observed for 240 observational periods of 6 seconds each, for a total of 24 minutes of observation per child. Observations were sampled approximately equally across all four situations, except in the kindergarten, in which there was a preponderance of situations 3 and 4 and a dearth of situations 1 and 2. Although 24 minutes of observation is not much for each child, it is a respectable amount, and it is my experience that it constitutes a sufficiently large sample to give stable data for each child, provided that the child's behavior is sampled across a range of situations and that the coding system is reasonably simple.

The following very simple observational category system was employed. There were two categories of alone: (1) *alone positive*, which meant that the child was not interacting with other children but was engaged in a task and attending (e.g., doing seat work) or paying attention during a lecture or story; and (2) *alone negative*, which meant that the child was not interacting with other children and was daydreaming, "tuned out," or not paying attention to a lecture or story. There were three categories of peer interactions: (1) *positive interaction*, which included giving or receiving attention and approval, offering praise, smiling and laughing, giving help, engaging in generally positive conversation, giving or receiving affection and personal acceptance, submitting to commands or requests that were not aggressive, giving tangible objects (toys, food, notes, etc.); (2) *negative interaction*, which included aggression or negative affect (e.g., frowns, cries, whines, yells, teases, complaints, blames); and (3) *maintenance interaction*, which included behavior that was definitely interactive but was not positive or negative (e.g., whispering, attending, passing notes). Maintenance interaction appears to be affectively neutral, but the interactants are definitely engaged. Coders also noted which child initiated an act and the identities of all children involved. To create an exhaustive coding scheme, there were three categories of interactions involving children with the teacher: (1) *teacher positive*, which involved praise, encouragement, support, or other positive affects (e.g., smiles, pats, comforts, reassurance); (2) *teacher negative*, which involved commands delivered with negative affect (e.g., "Stop it" or "No" said with anger, irritation, scorn, contempt, or disgust); and (3) *teacher neutral*, which included all other teacher behaviors that were not clearly negative or positive.

From this mutually exclusive category system the frequency of the following six categories were computed: (1) initiating positive contact with a peer, (2) receiving positive contact with a peer, (3) initiating negative contact with a peer, (4) receiving negative contact with a peer, (5) initiating maintenance contact with a peer, and (6) receiving maintenance contact with a peer. The members of the research team randomly checked one another's observations at least once per week for a minimum of 10 minutes to keep interobserver reliability high. Minimum agreement of 84% was maintained throughout the study. In addition to the reliability checks in the classroom, a weekly team meeting was held during which problems in coding behaviors were discussed and resolved. During the four weeks of observation, interobserver agreement averaged 85.9%. There was no reliability decay or drift during this time.

Results and discussion

Sociometric data from the four classrooms showed the widespread preference for same-sex peers. These results were quite strong. In kindergarten 67% of the choices were same-sex [χ^2 (1) = 34.89, $p < .001$]; in first grade 68% of the choices were same-sex [χ^2 (1) = 40.78, $p < .001$]; in third grade 76% of the choices were same-sex [χ^2 (1) = 73.09, $p < .001$]; and in fourth grade 84% of the choices were same-sex [χ^2 (1) = 89.30, $p < .001$]. The increase in these percentages with grade level was marginally significant [χ^2 (3) = 7.17, $p < .10$]. The observed scores were conservatively adjusted for decreasing differences in total peer nominations with increasing grade level (see Bishop, Fienberg, & Holland, 1975).

For comparison with Rickelman's (1981) data, the interesting sociometric variable in terms of cross-sex friendship is the frequency of *mutual* cross-sex choices. The number of mutual cross-sex friendships dropped dramatically with increasing grade level: There were 12 in kindergarten, 20 in first grade, 3 in third grade, and 2 in fourth grade. This sharp drop was significant [χ^2 (3) = 23.88, $p < .001$]. Therefore, the sociometric results are parallel to Rickelman's results, they suggest that there is indeed a *dramatic decline in cross-sex friendship with increasing age* (in the age range studied).

The interactional data paint a similar picture. At each grade level there was a clear interactional preference for same-sex interaction. The chi squares for the 2 × 2 contingency tables (Boy/girl × Boy/girl) were all highly significant: 161.44, 90.96, 111.95, and 303.21 for kindergarten, first, third, and fourth grades, respectively. However, the picture that boys and girls constitute two separate social groups that do not interact has been overdrawn. The proportions of all peer interaction that was cross-sex were substantial: .30, .35, .34, and .27 for kindergarten, first, third, and fourth grades, respectively. This is consistent with Thorne's (1984) qualitative observations. The decrease in cross-sex interaction in fourth grade was significant[2] [χ^2 (3) = 12.03, $p < 0.05$]. Thus, Rickelman's survey data are supported both by classroom observations and by sociometric data.

The nature of same- and cross-sex interaction was studied as a function of the children's acceptance by their peers. Children were divided at the median in each class (as previously described), and interactions were tallied within each class as a function of the children's sex and level of acceptance by peers. Table 4.1 shows that, even in kindergarten, girls interacted with other girls as a function of their acceptance by peers. Sixty-five percent of accepted girls' interaction with girls was with other accepted girls; 61% of unaccepted girls' interaction with girls was with other unaccepted girls. This pattern of results held for all grade levels. A comparison of the accepted/accepted cell across grade levels shows that this cell increased significantly from kindergarten to first grade but did not change significantly thereafter [overall χ^2 (3) = 27.36, $p < .001$]. Freeman–Tukey (FT) deviates showed that for kindergarten girls this cell was significantly below expected value (FT = -4.28, $p < .001$), whereas for first grade, FT was 2.30 ($p < .05$), for third grade, FT was 2.30 ($p < .05$), and for fourth grade FT was .79 (n.s.).

Table 4.1. *Girl–girl total interaction as a function of sociometric measures of peer acceptance*

	Grade level			
Cell	K	1	3	4
Accepted/accepted	95	154	324	243
Accepted/unaccepted	52	36	73	93
Unaccepted/accepted	72	38	94	113
Unaccepted/unaccepted	111	60	114	147
Chi square	20.84***	52.00***	84.77***	51.49***

***$p < .001$.

Furthermore, this pattern was evident even in the *initiation* of interaction. In kindergarten, the pattern of results held only for the initiation of positive interaction toward girls [χ^2 (1) = 18.70, $p < .001$]; the chi squares were not significant for the initiation of maintenance or for the initiation of negative interaction toward girls. Sixty-six percent of all the positive interaction that accepted kindergarten girls initiated toward girls was with other accepted kindergarten girls; 72% of all the positive interaction unaccepted girls initiated toward girls was with other unaccepted girls. This is strong evidence of an early same-sex social structure among girls.

In first grade, these results on initiation held for both positive interaction toward girls [χ^2 (1) = 10.45, $p < .01$] and negative interaction toward girls [χ^2 (1) = 10.00, $p < .01$]. Seventy-six percent of all the positive interactions accepted first-grade girls initiated toward girls was toward other accepted girls; the comparable figure for unaccepted girls was 56%. For negative interaction both percentages were 100%, respectively.

In third grade, the pattern held for the initiation of both positive [χ^2 (1) = 9.50, $p < .01$] and maintenance interaction toward girls [χ^2 (1) = 49.42, $p < .001$]; for positive interaction, the respective proportions were 83 and 75%, respectively, for accepted and unaccepted girls. For maintenance, the proportions were 86 and 53%, respectively, for accepted and unaccepted girls. In fourth grade, the pattern held only for the initiation of positive interaction toward girls [χ^2 (1) = 28.43, $p < .001$], with percentages of 70 and 63% for accepted and unaccepted girls, respectively.

Table 4.2 presents analogous data for boy–boy interaction. There was no evidence of a sociometrically based social structure in the interaction

Table 4.2. *Boy–boy total interaction as a function of sociometric measures of peer acceptance*

Cell	Grade level			
	K	1	3	4
Accepted/accepted	131	234	57	172
Accepted/unaccepted	92	262	42	71
Unaccepted/accepted	82	197	119	93
Unaccepted/unaccepted	55	177	79	131
Chi square	0.60	2.58	0.17	40.67***

***$p < .001$.

Table 4.3. *Cross-sex total interaction as a function of sociometric measures of peer acceptance*

Cell	Grade level			
	K	1	3	4
Accepted/accepted	80	181	182	179
Accepted/unaccepted	113	103	53	23
Unaccepted/accepted	47	153	105	168
Unaccepted/unaccepted	55	173	122	24
Chi square	0.58	17.29***	47.47***	0.12

***$p < .001$.

of boys with other boys until fourth grade. These results are consistent with Waldrop and Halverson's suggestion that the social network of boys with other boys is more extensive than that of girls with other girls. By the fourth grade, however, 71% of the interaction of accepted boys with boys was with other accepted boys, and 58% of the behavior of unaccepted boys with boys was with other unaccepted boys. Examining initiation of interaction, these results held for the initiation of positive interaction [χ^2 (1) = 17.32, $p < .001$]. Seventy-three percent of the positive interaction initiated by accepted boys toward boys was toward other accepted boys; the comparable percentage for unaccepted boys was 56%.

Table 4.3 presents comparable data for cross-sex interaction. The major finding is that, except for kindergarten and fourth grade, there was evidence of the same pattern of interaction defined by peer acceptance. In kindergarten there was no evidence of patterning.

However, in fourth grade the pattern of cross-sex interaction was quite complex. Accepted boys were more likely to interact with accepted girls than with nonaccepted girls; 89% of the cross-sex interaction of accepted boys was with accepted girls [χ^2 (1) = 120.48; $p < .001$]. However, unaccepted fourth-grade boys also interacted primarily with *accepted* rather than unaccepted girls [79% of the time; χ^2 (1) = 108.00, $p < .001$]. An examination of initiation shows that 100% of unaccepted boys' cross-sex maintenance interaction was with accepted girls [χ^2 (1) = 6.00, $p < .05$]. Also, 79% of accepted girls' initiation of maintenance was with *unaccepted* boys. No other significant differences were obtained for initiations in fourth grade.

This pattern of initiation is reminiscent of that of some low-ranking male nonhuman primates who affiliate with high-ranking females. They provide child care in exchange for protection (G. Stephenson, personal communication). Thorne (1982) also noted a similar phenomenon in the interaction of boys and girls in elementary schools.

A study of cross-sex *initiations* is particularly important in understanding cross-sex interaction. If there is evidence of a social system organized by sociometric measures of peer acceptance, as there is in the first and third grades, is the interaction more likely to be initiated by one sex than another?

In first grade, significant chi squares were obtained for initiating maintenance (χ^2 = 6.70, $p < .05$) and negative interaction (χ^2 (1) = 19.73, $p < .001$]. Specific examination of the interactions separately by whether boys or girls initiated revealed that only boys initiated maintenance with girls as a function of peer acceptance [boys initiating, χ^2 (1) = 6.82, $p < .05$; girls initiating, χ^2 (1) = 1.40, n.s.]. For initiating negative interactions, both boys and girls initiated as a function of peer acceptance [boys initiating, χ^2 (1) = 9.07, $p < .01$; girls initiating, χ^2 (1) = 5.10, $p < .05$]. In third grade, the initiation of all three categories of peer interactions showed the same pattern of cross-sex preference for peers similar in acceptance [for positive interaction, χ^2 (1) = 3.96, $p < .05$; for maintenance, χ^2 (1) = 33.06, $p < .001$; for negative interaction, χ^2 (1) = 10.22, $p < .01$]. A breakdown of these interactions on the basis of whether they were initiated by boys or by girls yielded nonsignificant effects for positive interaction [boys initiating, χ^2 (1) = 2.12, n.s.; girls initiating, χ^2 (1) = 3.40, n.s.], significant effects for maintenance [boys initiating, χ^2 (1) = 17.46, $p < .001$; girls initiating, χ^2 (1) = 12.71, $p < .001$], and significant effects for negative interaction [boys, χ^2 (1) = 10.58, $p < .01$; girls, χ^2 (1) = .51, n.s.].

Taken together, these results suggest that, when a cross-sex interactional social structure exists as a function of peer acceptance, boys have a greater role in initiating this interactional structure than girls. *Boys are thus not extensive in their interaction with girls; rather, girls are extensive in their interaction with boys,* particularly when one considers the accepted fourth-grade girls' interaction with unaccepted boys. This conclusion is different from that of Waldrop and Halverson.

To summarize, evidence was obtained for a same-sex preference in all grades, on both sociometric and observational measures. There was also evidence that cross-sex mutual friendship dropped off sharply after first grade. However, cross-sex *interaction* did not decrease until fourth grade. There was evidence that same-sex interaction among girls was patterned as a function of peer acceptance; as early as kindergarten, girls interacted primarily with girls similar in acceptance. On the other hand, this effect did not occur among boys until fourth grade. However, cross-sex interactions were essentially patterned by peer acceptance after kindergarten. An examination of the initiation of this pattern of cross-sex interaction shows that boys are more responsible for the pattern than girls.

These results suggest that classrooms become rapidly organized into at least four social membership groups (accepted boys, accepted girls, unaccepted boys, unaccepted girls) as children become older. In kindergarten, girls were extremely aware of their social status and limited their same-sex interaction to girls of similar status. In contrast, the same-sex interaction of young boys was more permeable. These results are consistent with those of Pitcher and Schultz (1983), who noted that "our data revealed a year's lag in the development of same-sex positive relations among the preschool boys, compared to the girls" (p. 20). In our study this difference was not due to the fact that young boys are unaware of their peers' social status, since they are extremely aware of the social status of girls.

The results also showed that the interaction of girls with boys was more permeable than that of boys with girls. This is consistent with a report by LaFreniere, Strayer, and Gauthier (1984). They examined 15 peer groups across three years. The children ranged in age from 1 to 6 years. The authors documented age changes in same-sex peer preference. At the youngest age (about 17 months) the percentage of affiliation to same-sex peers was not different for boys and girls and very close to 50%. At 27 months, boys and girls were strikingly different from one another and different from chance. Girls' means were about 67% and boys' were about

53% (still significantly greater than chance). In the oldest group (66 months) the pattern was reversed. Although both boys and girls still preferred same-sex peers, now boys exceeded girls in this preference (boys about 76%, girls about 65%). LaFreniere et al. (1984) wrote,

. . . girls began to prefer same-sex peers earlier than boys, who subsequently surpassed girls in sexual discrimination [p. 1958].

There is only a limited amount we can learn about children's relationships from the kind of observations made in the Gottman–Benson study in classrooms. Knowledge of the quality of children's close relationships is better obtained from the detailed study of children's interactions. The remainder of this chapter discusses research I have conducted on children's conversations with friends, based on recordings made at home.

4.3. The conversation of young friends

In this section we continue the discussion of two themes: (1) same- and cross-sex peer interaction and (2) development. However, we move from the broad, distal arena of the organizational structure of classrooms to the rich, detailed arena of children's friendships as reflected in dyadic play at home.

There is essentially no descriptive knowledge of the conversations of friends. Because of this, we focus in this section on the conversations of young friends using *qualitative* data to describe the children's interaction and to generate hypotheses. The data base for this qualitative study came, in part, from Study 1 of Gottman (1983); there were 16 dyads of best friends. Data also came from two 1-year longitudinal studies of two pairs of 4- to 5-year-old cross-sex best friends (22 repeated tapings). This year-long study was repeated with another pair of 4- to 5-year-old cross-sex best friends in another city.

Children in these studies were aware of the tape recorder. One pair of 5-year-olds even discussed what they thought might become of the data. One girl, M (age 5:9), said she thought the purpose of the study was to help parents understand 5-year-olds:

M: You know where this [tape] probably will be taken? To some kind of work like where they try to send it to everybody who's gonna have a five-year-old sometime, to everybody who has babies.

Her friend, A (age 5:6), agreed about the importance of the data:

A: Everybody who has babies will want it.

M then said that perhaps the purpose of the tape was to learn how children "know how to act":

M: Well, they'll know how you know how to act, you know. I'm not *sure* of
that, but I think that's what might happen.

As we shall see, although the presence of the tape recorder had an
effect on the children, the effect of the mother's presence, even when
she was instructed not to interact with the children, was dramatic and
powerful.

Coordinated play

This chapter is titled "The world of coordinated play" because play is at
the center of young children's interaction with their friends. It is what
friends do most often, and the level of play coordination also determines
whether two unacquainted strangers will "hit it off" and progress
toward friendship. Among friends, the possibilities for varying the
constituents of coordinated play are enormous.

Coordinated play can offer extreme adventure and excitement and
high levels of fun and joy. The well-known robbers' cave adventure in
Mark Twain's *Tom Sawyer* is but one kind of adventure typical of the
everyday interactions that two young friends can generate in their
rooms. Coordinated play can also offer a variety of play options far less
involving than this high level of adventure. For example, the gentle,
peaceful companionship children experience coloring side by side as
well as the more demanding activities children do together (common-
ground activities) are also part of coordinated play. Repetition of play
themes and working out personal issues through fantasy play are
among the options offered by coordinated play. Intricately interlaced
with this play is conversation itself, which with young children often
involves personal self-exploration.

The ability to *coordinate* play with a friend requires skill in maintaining
clear communication, managing the level of conflict, agreeing far more
than disagreeing, and shifting continually from one's own perspective
to that of one's friend. Without this coordination of points of view and
feelings, the kind of marvelous adventures that children invent during
play would not be possible (see also Forbes, Katz, & Paul, 1982; Garvey
& Berndt, 1975; Griffin, 1985). Two egocentric children cannot possibly
coordinate play at levels that require continual renegotiation and playing out the story line in action.

Coordinated play is an extremely important context for learning how
to manage one's emotions. If play is coordinated, it is simply not always
possible to get one's own way. Children must learn to inhibit action, to
delay getting what they want in the service of the overall adventure, to

give and to receive influence, to deal with negative affect such as anger, and to manage positive affect such as joy and excitement in the context of interaction.

Maccoby (1980) suggested that the period of young childhood involves the development of emotional control. She noted that the *inhibition of action* is the basis of the organization of behavior. Children learn to delay actions until the consequences are more appropriate. If goal-directed activity is blocked, they learn to find a way around the barrier instead of persevering with the goal activity, they learn to avoid the disorganization of a tantrum, and they learn to concentrate, blocking out irrelevant stimuli. Learning emotional control is one basis for the ability to organize behavior and thinking. Maccoby connected the development of emotional control during the years of early childhood to the development of reflective thinking, to the ability to delay gratification, and to the control of excitement. If one thinks of the requirements of coordinated play with friends, it is obvious that emotional control is learned in the context of friendship as well as in the family.

In some ways the peer context is unique. Vandell and Mueller (1978) pointed out that social development can be accelerated by peers for several reasons. First, peers are unlikely to be willing or able to do a great deal of the message clarification work that parents do when their children are not clear. Second, since peers are at a similar developmental level, it may be much easier for them to learn from and imitate one another.

We shall examine one aspect of emotional development that is a major theme of coordinated play among young friends: *working on fear*. We shall discuss children's fears, the apparent attraction of children to being afraid, and the way children get over these fears. Same- and cross-sex friends seem to do this in different ways.

Coordinated play among young friends also involves children's exploration of self. Self-exploration is not only the province of adolescents, although certain patterns do not emerge until adolescence (see Chapter 5). A major theme of young friends' play involves exploring both constancy and transformation of their personalities. This is connected with a central dialectic of young childhood – wanting to grow up and wanting to stay little.

The power of shared fantasy. There is a special character to fantasy play among young children. To explore this character we can begin by asking, For a young child what secret is inherent in pretending to play mechanical crane? The answer is that one must *become* the crane. Consider the following example:

Eric: That would be fun. Ya! Pretend I'm the winding thing and all kinds of
        parts. All the parts. OK.
Naomi: I would like to share this with you.
E: How about you will pretend that this thing . . .
N: No, this is the same thing . . .
E: OK, you can pretend that that's the same thing. OK, down, down, down.
        That's good. Now, down, now put the rope into the plumer drummer.
N: The block.
E: Block, block, down, down, now, down, that's good. Now open up the
        mouth. OK, up, up, up, up, OK, up, up.

Another example is the following. Naomi and Eric are sitting in their
room pretending to drive their sick baby to the hospital. Naomi pleads
with Eric not to drive so fast. She is (I think) actually frightened. She is
on the way to the hospital, and it is a life-and-death situation for their
baby. If she were not really frightened, this would hardly be an
adventure.

The special character to young children's fantasy play is *involvement*.
The secret of playing with a crane is to become the crane, and the reward
for high involvement is, in fact, the intense relationship children have
with one another at this moment. This is not to suggest that young
children are so involved that they cannot tell fantasy from reality. We
know from the work of Garvey (1974), Griffin (1985), and Schwartzman
(1978) on pretend play that this is certainly not the case. Nonetheless,
there is still a high level of involvement, reminiscent of many ritualized
trance states.

Fantasy requires a high ratio of agreement to disagreement (AG/DG).
Most interaction between friends that is reasonably positive has AG/DG
ratios slightly larger than 1.0. Strings in which friends are squabbling
have AG/DG equal to .11; strings that involve laughter or joking have
AG/DG equal to 1.08; fantasy strings have AG/DG equal to 2.24
(Gottman, 1983). Thus, fantasy play requires a high level of involvement, but not self-involvement. The involvement is the willingness to
go on an adventure with someone else, to influence and to accept
influence. *Fantasy play is the highest level of coordinated play.* Its demands
are as great as the rewards it offers to young children.

Eric and Naomi and others

It is my impression that, up to about age 7, cross-sex best friendships are
very intense emotional relationships, not unlike some marriages. One of
the first dyads I began studying in 1974 was a pair of children, Eric and

Naomi. They lived across the street from each other and had been best friends for several years. They considered themselves engaged to be married. Apparently Eric had discussed the wedding plans with his mother, who expressed her eagerness for him to be on his own, in the classic way mothers do, by telling him that she would be happy to dance at his wedding. He took her literally and told Naomi:

E: Hey, do you know . . . You see where my, where my, when me . . . and when you and me are married . . . um my mother is going to dance in the wedding.
N: Yeah.

Their affection for one another was common in their play, and it was often directly expressed:

E: Do you know, I love you and I'm going to marry you, Naomi.
N: I love you too and I'm going to marry you [*voice breaking with emotion*]. I hope you'll give me a ring.
E: Oh, yah, well, but I have to get some dollars, a million dollars. A lot of dollars.
N: But we'll have a little bit of dollars. Here's your balloon.

Their plans to be together were elaborate and certainly involved living together and sleeping in the same bed. For example:

E: Hey, can I have this tugboat too? You want this tugboat?
N: Yeah.
E: Here's the tugboat. Naomi, I wish this tugboat was mine.
N: You can keep it if you want to.
E: For ever and ever?
N: If you like, I will lend you . . .
E: Yes, and I'll, I'll live with you.

Getting married became a common theme of their play. They sometimes called it "the marry game":

E: Hey, Naomi, I know what we can play today.
N: What?
E: How about, um, the marry game. You like that.
N: Marry?
E: How about baker or something? How about this. Marry you? OK, Naomi, you want to pretend that?
N: Yes.
E: OK, Naomi, do you want to marry me?
N: Yeah.
E: Good, just a minute, Naomi, we don't have any marry place.
N: We could pretend this is the marry place.
E: Oh, well, pretend this, ah, there'll have to be a cake.
N: The wedding is here first.
E: OK, but listen to this, we have to have a baby, oh, and a pet.
N: This is our baby.
E: And here's our pet, a bunny. Watch how much he can hop.
N: [*Laughs, shrieks.*] He did it again!

Another time they said they would marry each other when they grew up:

E: And I could be this is the little boy and he has money and this is the money box and they came to buy something.
N: Yes, and I come here. And when we grow up we'll . . .
E: Marry each other.
N: Yeah.

Working out fears. Eric and Naomi used this affection and attachment for one another in powerful ways. Although young children do self-disclose and discuss their concerns with one another directly, they do so rarely. I believe the reason for this is that essential problem-solving abilities are not apparent in friends' conversations until adolescence. However, fantasy provides a safe mechanism for expressing fears, since these fears belong to pretend characters. Fantasy also provides a mechanism for resolving these fears. The mechanism is simple: (1) Make the story have a happy ending and (2) keep rehearsing variations of the story. Repetition is critical. I suggest that dramatic play may be a vehicle among young children for solving problems because these children lack the ability to fully represent social concerns symbolically; that is, they may be unable to list the alternative courses of action in a problem situation, evaluate them against some criterion, and then choose a best alternative. Instead, they play through the situation many times, until they discover a best course of action empirically.

Returning to the theme of the exploration of fear, young children seem to enjoy pretend play in which they *select* something to be afraid of, rehearse the fear (in a milder form, in which they have more control), and then master the fear, often by pretending to be or to conquer the feared object. For example, a 4-year-old recently told me about a trip he took to the zoo:

Nate: I went to the zoo today and saw the sea lions and they were real scary. They went underwater real fast.
Gottman: That's great. Sounds like you had fun.
Nate: Maybe sometime you can go to the zoo and get scared by the sea lions too. Know what else?
Gottman: No, what else?
Nate: I swam underwater today.
Gottman: Just like a sea lion!
Nate: Yeah.

The fearful object has a great deal of attraction.

Friends often invent pretense themes that center on power and powerlessness. They use fantasy to explore their fears and worries, much as a play therapist would. Some of Eric's repeated concerns were people making fun of him, people calling him a "dumb dumb," issues of his power and powerlessness, and his fear of being abandoned by his parents. The following is an example of his fear of being called dumb and Naomi's support of him:

E: Hold on there everyone. I am the skeleton, I'm the skeleton. Ohh, hee. Hugh, ha, ha. You're hiding.
N: Hey, in the top drawer, there's the . . .
E: I am the skeleton. Whoa.
N: There's the feet [*clattering*].
E: [*Screams.*] A skeleton, everyone, a skeleton!
N: I'm your friend. The dinosaur.
E: Oh, hi, dinosaur. You know, no one likes me.
N: But I like you. I'm your friend.
E: But none of my other friends like me. They don't like my new suit. They don't like my skeleton suit. It's really just me. They think I'm a dumb dumb.
N: I know what. He's a good skeleton.
E [*yelling*]: I am not a dumb dumb.
N: I'm not calling you a dumb dumb. I'm calling you a friendly skeleton.

These themes kept recurring, and Eric and Naomi's friendship served as a way to cope with the fears. For example, the following excerpt shows that this play theme was one that Eric and Naomi kept repeating. Notice their *continual reference to remembering* the cues for this theme. Repetition is an obvious part of the behavior of young children. The comfort and familiarity it provides presumably give children a sense of organization, order, and mastery:

N: Huh, this is nice. Wow, where are you going? We're going back to our house.
E: This is my house, *remember?*
N: Where are your parents, *remember?*
E: My parents? I don't have any parents. My mommy and daddy went; they didn't like me anymore.
N: So they went someplace else?

Not only is the statement of the catastrophic fear well rehearsed; so is the solution, which is the solution described so dramatically by Freud and Dann's (1951) case history of children who survived the holocaust of World War II by the strength of their friendships:

E: I live here all alone. Hey, you can live with me.
N: Yes, and keep you company. I'll cook the food.
E: OK, that's a great idea. You can make my bells. My ding-a-ling bells.
N: And we all can go to bed too.
E: Yeah, I'm going to bed. It's past my bedtime right now. My nap.
N: You'd better get in.

Naomi keeps reassuring Eric in these excerpts that she thinks he (or the skeleton) is not alone and not a dumb dumb.

During the period of time that Eric and Naomi's conversations were recorded, Naomi was afraid of the dark and slept with a night light. The theme of their pretense play often involved dolls being afraid of the dark. They would turn the lights off and Naomi, pretending to be the doll, would scream and then, as the mommy, comfort the doll. Eric would also comfort the doll. After a few months, Naomi announced to her parents that she no longer needed the night light. Also, the theme of being afraid of the dark disappeared from their fantasy play. Both Naomi and the doll were cured.

Boys' friendships. I have noticed a same-sex versus cross-sex difference among boys in the use of fantasy play for dealing with fear. It appears that, if there is a girl in the dyad and fear is expressed (either in conversation or in fantasy), then emotional support and love are used to comfort, soothe, and ease the fear. This is a relationship-oriented way of coping with expressed fear. In contrast, pairs of young boys use a mastery approach rather than social support to deal with fear. They do this in two ways: with fantasy or with humor.

The difference can be dramatic. Let me illustrate it. Billy and Jonathan (4 and 3 years old, respectively) start out playing with water. In the midst of this play, they discuss what they used to believe about soap:

B: We'll go wash our hands, OK? Let's pretend we go wash our hands, Jonathan.
J: OK.
B: Let's go get some soap.
J: Why do you want that water all soapy?
B: 'Cause I like it that way.
J: Why do you?
B: I just, well, because, I thought of soapy when I was a baby; then I started to like it.
J: You know what I thought when I was a baby?
B: What?
J: I thought it was poison.
B: Yes, and it was.

This is a mixed theme of fear and assertion that babies are afraid but that one is not afraid when one grows up. The theme leads Billy and Jonathan to discuss dangerous things:

J: I didn't want to have any [soap] when I was a baby.
B: Yeah, like kryptonite hurts Superman? And that's poison.
J: Yeah.

This leads to a discussion of things that can kill:

B: And rattlesnakes are poison.
J: Ark!
B: Yes, they are.
J: No, they rattle their tail before they bite people.
B: Yeah, that makes them sick.
J: Or a person shot the snake. The snake would be hurt.
B: Yeah, 'cause I hate snakes.
J: Yech!

During this conversation the children work up to a high level of excitement, and it leads them to their ultimate fearful object: the shark. They employ a strategy characteristic of the fantasy of boys of mastery and involvement, namely, pretending to *be* the thing or pretending to devour it, kill it, or conquer it:

B: And I hate sharks. But I love to eat sardines.
J: I love to eat shark.
B: Yeah, but they're so big!
J: But we can cut their tail.

They continue exploring the power of the shark, realizing that they are up against no easy enemy:

B: Yeah, what happens if we cut them to two?
J: It would bite us, it would swim, and we would have to run. Run very fast, run to our homes.
B: Yeah, but ummm . . .
J: By the trees. Mr. Shark bited the door down and we would have to run way in the forest.
B: Yeah, but . . . but if he bited all the trees down . . .
J: And then we would have to shoot him. Yeah, and the shark is poison.
B: But pink is. Red is, yellow is.
B: Yeah, but people are too. What happened if the shark ate us?
J: We would have to bite him in, on his tongue.
B: Yeah, what happened if we bite him so far that we made his tongue metal?
J: Yeah.
B: Then he couldn't have breaked out of metal.
J: He can eat metal open. Sharks are so strong they can even bite metal.
B: Yes.
J: How about concrete? Concrete could make it.

Here we have the ultimate means of resolving the fear. The creature is capable of almost infinite metamorphoses – capable of moving from sea to land, capable of biting down all the trees in the forest so that one cannot hide, capable of turning into metal. The creature is finally contained by the correct metaphor – concrete. This solution is somehow both magical and logical. It makes sense at some cognitive level, but certainly not entirely at the problem-solving level. That does not seem to matter.

Boys' second strategy for dealing with fear involves humor. In the following example two boys go on a fantasy adventure in which they will have to deal with ghosts and monsters. Bob is fixing their getaway car with a device called a "trouble shooter." Joe is the lookout:

B: Yeah. Let's get back to work. I'll work on the trouble shooter.
J: And I'll watch out for monsters.
B: Yes. And in case I see a ghost, I'll use my specter detecter.

After a few sentences they elaborate these roles:

J: I'm the one that watches out for, for monsters.
B: And I'm the one who watches out for ghosts.
J: I'm a soldier.

They now defuse the fear inherent in this adventure by turning into photograhers from *"Ghost Chasers' Magazine."*

B: Yes, and my name is Ted. I'm from *Ghost Chasers' Magazine.*
B: . . . Uh oh, I see a ghost. A ghost don't even need a vest, a suit.
J: Well, I saw a monster.
B: Uh oh, there's a coat, a ghost.
J: And you can't shoot him. 'Cause I'm from *Ghost Chasers' Magazine.*
B: I can just put some stuff in a magazine, ghost. Hey, I got a picture if this come right out. A picture of a ghost's hand. The hand, it's a ghost. We'll put that in our magazine.

Girls' friendships. My impression is that in girls' conversations, including those during fantasy play, fear is not dealt with to the extent that it is in conversations between a boy and a girl. This is true, in part, because *boys seem to be the ones who introduce danger and risky, frightening adventure themes into play.* Girls devote their play almost entirely to domestic fantasies (see Gottman & Parkhurst, 1980, for a system for classifying fantasies). I have noticed that, in cross-sex friends' play, boys are as likely as girls to introduce babies into domestic fantasies. However, what *they* want to do with a baby is quite different from what girls want to do. Girls tend to want to love, dress, and care for the baby and to take the baby around to visit pretend friends. Boys want to do things like rush a dead baby to the hospital in a fast vehicle and operate on it, eventually saving its life. After the operation, boys are often willing to visit friends with "Mom" and the baby.

When two girls do explore their fears, they use reassurance to comfort. For example:

C: OK, turn the car on.
M: No! No! No! No! No!

C: Rrrum!
M: No! No! Nooo! [*Screams.*] You can't go on fast, you stop . . .
C: I stopped the car but I'm not going.
M: Oh, yeah, you're not going. Oh, oh, oh, my baby! Where is he? Where is he? Help! My bunny, where's my bunny? Need my bunny [*whining*].
C: I don't know. Here, bunny, bunny.
M: Mommy, where's my bunny?
C: Here? . . .
M: I can't find it anywhere. [*Starts to cry.*] Bunny! He's lost! I can't find him. I'm looking, I can't find it . . .
C: Yes, you can.
M: OK, I'll take my blanket.
C: OK. Now turn the car on.
M: Yeah.

These differences are pervasive. Even the exceptions are interesting because they underscore these sex differences. Only one pair of girls in our studies played an adventure fantasy that involved danger. Even this fantasy was a variation of a domestic fantasy in which one girl was the powerful, protective mommy and the other the baby. They were going to the baby store near the zoo.

A: Oh, you know what?
B: What?
A: This is a baby store, and this will shoot somebody down. And then when, when somebody comes, the naughty customer, this will work because this is a bangta knife of yours. I want the knife now. Bang, bang, bang, bang! Uh oh, he's dead, that boogy monster, that's bad.
B: Oh, good Mommy. Are we at the zoo yet?

Among girls, danger does not necessarily take the form of adventure, but can involve talking about things that are frightening. For example, two children were discussing babies when one girl said she knew a baby boy who did not grow. The notion of the boy who does not grow (reminiscent of Gunther Grass's *The Tin Drum*) is frightening for young children. Here, the children deal with this fear by building solidarity on the basis of their similarities and affirming the superiority of girls over boys.

D: Well, my sister's, um, I have a friend, Sharon. He's two, but he doesn't grow.
J: Yes, he does.
D: Uh uh. He's just two all the time.
J: Why doesn't he grow/
D: Because.
J [*pausing*] We grow, don't we?
D: Huh?
J: We grow.
D: Yep.
J: Why doesn't he grow?

D: 'Cause Sharon's a boy.
J: What?
D: 'Cause Sharon's a boy.

Constancy and transformation of self. Perhaps in connection with the subject of fear, the play themes of many children are concerned with growing up and becoming powerful. This is clearly illustrated by an excerpt in which Eric has wet his pants:

E: I wet my pants. It's kinda warm, but it'll dry out. Don't tell your mother, OK? Tell your mother when I'm gone, OK? Both of us will keep it a secret right now. I don't want her to see me when I'm here. Look it my muscles, how big they are now. They're so big that . . .
N: I'm . . .
E: Naomi, just a minute!
N: Don't do that. It hurts my hands.
E: Well, Naomi, see I'm so strong at the butterscotch chair back home that I can lift one side of it.
N: And I can lift one side of my bed.
E: Watch *me* lift it!
N: Watch me lift *this!*
E: Watch me – Naomi. Let go of that!
N: I can lift it.
E: Well, that's light.
N: Well, I can even carry heavy things like this.
E: Oh, Naomi, no don't lift it.

Eric and Naomi are very concerned with their change and development, and the theme of metamorphosis itself is very powerful in their play. In the following excerpt we see a philosophical profundity remarkable for 4-year-olds. In this example, Eric wonders what happened to the personality of Flip, the caterpillar, when it changed into a butterfly. He also remembers that he did not want Flip to change but that Flip changed nonetheless.

E: I'm gonna make something. Let's see if you can guess what it is.
N: What, I betcha it's a worm.
E: A worm?
N: A pet worm.
E: Do you remember Flip, my pet worm, I mean my pet caterpillar? I didn't want him to change into a butterfly. But he did. I still don't know which is Flip. Do you?
N[*pausing*]:   No.

Eric and Naomi ponder the question of the continuity of identity in the face of transformation and growth. What happened to Flip the caterpillar when he became a butterfly? Was his personality lost? Did it change? Which one was Flip? They realize that these are difficult questions.

The theme of growing up is important in these conversations, and children express great ambivalence about the process. They want to grow up, but they also do not want to. Growing up involves facing unknown fears, including the terror of no longer being taken care of by one's parents. However, children also discuss the benefits of growing up, one of which, they believe, is never having to be afraid. This is reflected in their conversation, especially in their fantasy play. The following example illustrates this theme:

E: . . . when I was a little smaller, about this small, I was up high and I was so scared but now I'm so big that I'm not scared anymore.
N: I'm not scared either.
E: No, I'm going on top. I got climbing shoes. When I was littler I couldn't use these shoes. But now I can use them. Isn't that great, Naomi?
N: We're not going to be scared anymore.

There are also the great unknowns about growing up, as illustrated by the following excerpt from the conversations of a 4-year-old (Matt) and a 5-year-old (Jessica). This excerpt also illustrates the fact that young children do not always use the context of fantasy play to discuss a fear. Matt and Jessica openly discuss menstruation, a fear of Jessica's about growing up. Matt has heard about this mysterious bleeding but does not know much about it. Thorne (1984) suggested that children's fear of menstruation is the basis of many "pollution" run-and-chase games in which the touch of a girl has the primary power to pollute. Note in this excerpt how supportive the children are of one another:

J: Mary Ellis knows how to play it.
M: What? What is it that person that you know?
J: Um, Susie, Susie probably knows how. She's wild.
M: Yeah! She's a lot older.
J: Oh, that old. She has to put these things over your vagina. You have to and it's terrible and you always have to change it every few minutes.
M: [*Laughs.*]
J: Her mommie didn't. She got to do that, didn't she? But she didn't know about that. It would never happen to you. But once you get over that happens your whole life. And the, and then when you get older you quit it, right?
M: No!
J: Quit it for, let's see, and then you go back to it. And then when you're grown up you finally have it until you die.
M: Uum, um, but that won't happen to me, because I'll quit, with my . . .

Matt is quite upset, but Jessica calms him down by telling him that it does not happen to boys. However, Jessica envies boys:

J: No! Boys don't have it.
M: Yeah, I'm glad, gosh, so it could only happen to girls.
J: I wish I had a penis so I could pee standing up.
M: And she wouldn't have to stoop down. So she could go pssh, pssh, and that would be from here. This is true, Jessica, a penis from here to here.
J: It's long. Take it out. Now go on and pee, . . . and pee, and pee.

Next Matt tries to reassure Jessica that it may not be so bad:

M: You know what? *I've* had a lots more of bleeding stuff than that.
J: I know, once, once I've had blood run down my leg, that much . . .
M: You know, once I had, once I had this much blood run down my leg, all around my leg, I had a big chunk of it, all round up to my knee.

As I noted, growing up and metamorphosis are common themes in the conversations and fantasy play of young friends. It is important to note that these themes can be accompanied by joy, not just fear. Jonathan and Genevive, both 4 years old, discuss growing up:

G: Do you like dinosaurs?
J: Yeah.
G: I don't. Hey, could you like to train a dinosaur?
J: Would you?
G: That way I . . . I am, know how many things I am?
J: How many?
G: A studier, and a ordinary dancer, and a Indian, and a dinosaur trainer. How do you think that is?
J: Ah, when, when I grow up I'm going to be all the things. I'm going to be a fireman, a policeman, and a rocketship man, and dinosaur person. Did you know nobody can really fly?

The theme of transformation reappears in the same play session between Jonathan and Genevive, when Jonathan suggests that they enact a birth fantasy. Note the reference to staying a baby and the enactment of the conflict about growing up and staying little:

J: Pretend I was inside your stomach.
G: You got out of my stomach and you popped out. You were just a little baby. Pop!
J: Pop!
G: And you went "Waa . . . waa . . . waa."
J: And you did "Moo-ma, moo-ma."
G: Oh, stay that way little baby, you'd better.
J: Naa, naa, naa. Let me out of your stomach.
G: And you can't get on the stomach. You're pulling, you're pulling my stomach apart, little bubba, bubba.
J: Bubba, bubba, bubba ba, ba, bubba, ba, ba.
G: [*Laughs and giggles.*] Wait! Stop! You're wiggling around [*Laughing*]!

Gossip, self-disclosure, and problem solving. Among young children, gossip usually occurs (1) primarily in dyads that contain a girl and (2) in the context of building solidarity using a summary description that I call "we against others." Gossip usually consists of brief comments made in the context of play. For example, consider the following conversation of two young cross-sex friends:

B: Danny and Jeff did that. They did. They're dumb, aren't they?
S: Yeah.
B: Aren't they?
S: Yeah.

Gossip usually includes direct references to we-ness. For example:

S: Go! We want her to go away [*hammering*].
B: We don't want Allison here to bother us again.
S: We're very mad at her.
B: We are very mad.

Sometimes this anger at another child can be very extended. It then tends to include a special kind of fantasy, namely, imagining revenge. For example, Matt and Jessica are about to take a nap.

M: I think it's time . . .
J: To lay down and take a very little nap . . .
M: We really won't be asleep, we'll just be taking a little [*inaudible*]. Isn't my cozy blanket . . . I wish I had my cozy blanket here, don't you?
J: Uh huh. It's made out of cotton. You know that day that Jeffrey made a hole? He got in trouble?
M: Hole – he unzipped it. But not all the way, just a little bit. He made . . . 'cause he made a very big hole on his [*inaudible*].
J: Yeah, and . . . someday he'll really be in trouble because you tell him and he bust one of my pigeons and after he did though really kill him, I will. You know what I'll do, I'll bring my hand and punch him. Uh huh.
M: He'll say, "Ooh boy, I'm leaving," right?
J: Right.
M: Everytime he tries to do that I'll bust him back. One day he'll be in very big trouble, right?
J: And then he'll go to the hospital [*inaudible*].
M: I don't think . . .
J: And he'll come over, and . . . ahhh . . .
M: And he'll be in real big trouble, won't he?
J: Uh huh.
M: One day I'm really gonna do that and someday you'll want to do like him too, right?
J: Right.
M: [*Inaudible.*] One day when Ray comes to my house and you'll have to do that, say "sunshine," and he'll do it.
J: Ha ha, you are in trouble, buster.

They let each other know that they are good, not like Jeffrey:

M: You know what? He really is a fat mouth. He, he, he for no reason he just does something bad, right?
J: Uh huh.
M: That's why he does it, right?
J: Uh huh.

Among preschool children, gossip can be a temporal precursor of self-disclosure. This is the same organization of gossip and self-disclosure that exists among adolescents, for whom self-disclosure occurs frequently (see Chapter 5). The following conversation is not between friends, but between two 4-year-old girls who are just becoming acquainted, Angie and Kimberly. Angie is concerned about Jimmy, a man her mother is dating. She cannot understand why Jimmy and her mom take so many naps. Angie and Kimberly are coloring.

A: Like, if Jimmy, he's a little boy and playing with us, he would take that brown if he need it, right?
K: Huh?
A: He would take that brown, wouldn't he?
K: Jimmy who?
A: That big man downstairs.
K: Your brother?
A: He's not my brother. He's a friend of ours.
K: Why does he come over all the time?
A: Because he does. Because my mommy asks him.
K: All the time?
A: She even goes out; he even goes places without *me*.
K: Where do you stay?
A: Home.
K: Why? You're afraid?
A: No. Why?
K: I'm afraid, 'less I stayed with you.
A: Are you afraid to stay with me?
K: Un un. I said I was afraid of my mommy, if she leaves me.

Gossiping about Mom and Jimmy leads naturally to self-disclosure. Later in Angie and Kimberly's interaction, they try to figure out why Mom and Jimmy are always taking naps.

A: She said, "Never come in here with me and Jimmy."
K: That's what she said?
A: Her and Jimmy are sleeping.
K: Huh?
A: You aren't, are you?
A: We're not asleep.
K: But he is.
A: My mom is not asleep.

They are convinced of their superiority in requiring less sleep than this adult who always visits Angie's mother. The whole business of the naps is very confusing and upsetting to Angie, who feels excluded. Later she and Kimberly are playing dress-up with Angie's mother's clothes. They are not sure that this is all right:

A: This one is too . . . this one. I don't know what she says. I don't know what she says. She doesn't say. Oh, I guess I'll put it on.
K: Did she not say, did she not say, did she not say?
A: She didn't say anything about the dress. She said, "Leave me and Jimmy alone."
K: Why'd she say that?
A: She doesn't love me.
K: Why?
A: 'Cause I get near you . . . my mom and Jimmy. Look how long these things are?
K: Oh, gosh.

Angie apparently feels rejected by her mother and threatened by Jimmy's presence. Notice, however, that these young children do not know quite what to do once they have disclosed their feelings. As we shall see in Chapter 5, it is not until adolescence that children know what to do with a self-disclosure, that is, how to deal with the negative feelings that arise when they try to solve a problem.

Young children rely instead on fantasy play to act out a story that begins with a self-disclosure. Fantasy gives negative feelings a kind of closure. The following examples illustrate this. Christina's anger at her mother (though later *disclosed* to a friend) is worked through with a stranger:

J: Let's ask her if we can use her set.
C: I don't know if she will. I'll ask her [*exits*]. Maybe she will . . . Um, no, when she doesn't want me to have something she said, she does, she lost it . . .

Christina knows that her mother says she lost something only to keep Christina from having it. She talks about this later:

C: When she said, when she doesn't want you to have something, have her hair curlers back, then she says she doesn't, then she says she doesn't have it, or she says it's lost . . . But she's stupid, 'cause one day I saw that she had a haircut. And guess what? I'll tell you why. She says she doesn't have any.
J: How many?
C: She says she lost it, 'cause I took it away and hid it. Want me to get it?
J: Yeah. Oh, is it down here?
C: I didn't hide it there. Upstairs is the best place to hide it.

So when Christina's mother says that she has lost something, Christina makes sure that this becomes prophecy by hiding it so it *will* never be found. The next time Mom wants her curlers they will be difficult to find.

Christina's anger toward her mother was expressed in conversation during activity play with a stranger. When she plays with her best friend, she can finally deal with anger in nonstereotyped fantasy, a common form that I call "shared deviance," because in this fantasy Christina is planning a "crime," the murder of her mother, with her best friend. Christina is pretending to make a special poisonous brew that she will add to her mother's cooking:

C: I'm gonna mix this up. Quick. Guess what I'm going to do? I'm not gonna eat, but I'm gonna say, "Mom, here! You can cook all this." And she'll cook it without knowing there's poison in the seeds. OK? Yeah.
P: Oh, she'll see then, I know.
C: No, but she'll cook beans. She'll, she'll put them on the stove and they'll cook and she won't know where the black seeds are in there, but in the apples, OK?
P: OK.

Fantasy play seems to provide a mechanism by which young children deal with the feelings they self-disclose. They can *pretend* to carry out the actions the feelings suggest, and this seems to provide satisfying closure.

4.4. Observational study

The preceding qualitative discussion will, I hope, convince the reader that the conversations of friends are a rich source of data. This section discusses the results of an observational study that will seem somewhat pale in the context of the qualitative discussion that preceded it. However, this quantitative study had a limited set of goals and was designed primarily to extend to friendship the work on acquaintance-ship (see Chapter 3). Hence, the same social processes were studied.

The study was designed to assess the extent to which variation in a dyad's social skill was related to the dyad's closeness, as assessed by questionnaires completed by the mothers of the children. Six social processes were studied by employing dyad-by-dyad sequential analysis of the observational data: (1) connectedness and communication clarity, (2) information exchange, (3) establishing common ground, (4) the resolution of conflict, (5) positive reciprocity, and (6) self-disclosure.

Detailed discussions of each of these social skills, their measurement and validation were presented in Gottman (1983). Specific interaction code categories and sequences assessed each of these processes. For example, communication clarity was assessed by the message clarification sequence Q → CM: a request for clarification of a message (Q) by one child followed by an appropriate clarification of the message (CM) by the other child. Table 4.4 summarizes these codes and code sequences with examples.

This study also assessed whether, across this age range of 3 to 9 years, within the context of children's conversations with friends, there was evidence of change in the social processes of fantasy, self-disclosure, and gossip. Gottman (1983) found little evidence of change. He hypothesized that these processes may change very slowly.

In addition, this study was designed to assess variation in the social processes as a function of age and the sex composition of the dyad. Gottman and Parkhurst (1980) observed that preschool cross-sex friends in their small sample showed the most extended nonstereotyped fantasy play of all dyads; this play involved self-disclosure and exploration of personal problems (e.g., fear of the dark, fear of being mocked, fear of

Table 4.4. *Codes and code sequences used to measure the six social processes studied*

Process	Variables [notation]	Example
Communication clarity	Request for clarification of a message (Q) followed by appropriate clarification (CM) [Q → CM]	A: Gimme the truck. B: Which truck? A: The dumpster.
Information exchange	1. Attention-getting message [ATT]	1. Hey, you know what?
	2. Information [IN]	2. I climb up there to go to sleep.
	3. Request for information (Q) followed by appropriate information (IN) [Q → IN]	3. A: Did you get this for Christmas? B: Yeah.
Common-ground activity	1. We demand (WE) followed by agreement (AG) [WE → AG]	1. A: Let's play house. B: OK.
	2. Me statements (ME) (negatively correlated with common-ground activity)	2. I'm making mine green.
Common ground: similarities/differences	1. Tag question (QAG) followed by agreement (AG) [QAG → AG]	1. A: My dolly's going to sleep, right? B: Right.
	2. Feeling (FE) followed by agreement (AG) [FE → DG]	2. A: I love chocolate. B: Yeah.
Conflict and conflict resolution	1. Desagreeing (DG) with a rationale (CM) for the disagreement [DG → CM]	1. No, cause we only have blue crayons.
	2. Disagreement chains [DG → DG]	2. A: This is stretchy. B: Is not. A: Uh huh. B: Uh uh.
	3. Weak demand (WEA)	3. A: Please pass the scissors. B: Here.
	4. Squabbling (any negative paralinguistic cues: anger, irritation, whining, sadness, crying, etc.) [S]	
Reciprocity	1. Joking reciprocity [J → J]	1. Both children laughing

Table 4.4. *(Cont.)*

Process	Variables [notation]	Example
	2. Gossip reciprocity [G → G]	2. A: We're getting a new baby sitter. B: What happened to the old one?
	3. Fantasy reciprocity [F → F]	3. A: Help! Help! Superman. B: Up, up, and away!
Self-disclosure	1. Question about feelings (QFE) followed by an expression of feelings (FE) [QFE → FE]	1. A: Are you mad? B: Yeah. You know that wasn't very nice to take that away from me.

being abandoned by parents). However, among older children, girls have anecdotally been described as having more intense friendships, with more self-disclosure, than boys (e.g., see Rubin, 1980, chapter 7). There is a need for systematic *quantitative* research on this question.

The final purpose of the study was primarily methodological. Pilot research suggested that the presence of an adult had a strong effect on children's conversation. Previous research on children's speech had ignored this factor (e.g., Schachter et al., 1974). The present investigation systematically varied the presence or absence of the mother in a repeated-measures design.

This manipulation may also have a theoretical meaning. It is interesting to determine which social processes for which types of dyads are more fragile (i.e., disrupted by external events) than others. I propose that the most fragile processes are those that are most salient and emotionally central to the dyad. Robust processes are probably well established and not emotionally central. For example, in pilot research I have found that fantasy play among preschool children is fragile (i.e., easily disrupted), whereas activity-based play (e.g., narrating one's own play – "I'm coloring mine green") is not fragile. In the home, fantasy play is common among preschool friends, whereas in the unfamiliar laboratory playroom it is rare; activity-based talk (e.g., "I'm almost finished coloring this") is robust; that is, it is present in both environments. Fantasy play is a process of central concern to preschoolers; it has the potential for great fun and adventure and for resolving issues of personal concern, as I have noted. This argument is consistent with Corsaro's (1981) suggestion that preschool children playing in dyads reject an entering child to protect "interactive space." His idea is that young children are less capable of maintaining the complex interactive structures of fantasy play in triads than in dyads. Children reject an entering child because they are protecting fragile social processes, ones that are particularly salient. The generalization is that those processes that are more easily disrupted are more salient to the dyad than more robust processes. Testing the validity of this theoretical speculation was another motivation for the experimental portion of the present investigation.

Method

Subjects. Thirty host children and their best friends were recruited (through advertisements) to fill the cells of a 2 × 3 design, with two levels of age (younger/older) and three levels of sex composition of the dyad (0 boys, 1 boy, 2 boys). There were five dyads in each cell of the design. Younger girls ranged in age from 5:2 to 5:8, with a mean age of 5:3 and a standard deviation of 2.5 months; older girls ranged in age from 5:11 to 8:3, with a mean age of 7:3 and a standard deviation of 11 months. Younger boys ranged in age from 3:9 to 5:5 with a mean age of 5:3 and a standard deviation of 9 months; older boys ranged in age from 6:11 to 8:5, with a mean age of 7:7 and standard deviation of 8 months. Younger cross-sex friends ranged in age from 3:00 to 4:9, with a mean age of 4:7 and a standard deviation of 9 months; older cross-sex friends ranged in age from 8:0 to 8:8 with a mean of 8:3 and a standard deviation of 3 months.[3]

As one might expect from Rickelman's (1981) study, it was extremely difficult to fill the older cross-sex cell of this study. A research assistant spent one month going from door to door in two neighborhoods of Urbana, Illinois. Each of the five dyads that participated were cases of long-standing best friendships that had "gone underground." The children still played together in their homes, but they ignored one another at school. Later, I will supplement the quantitative analysis with a qualitative discussion of the friendships in this cell.

One child was randomly designated the host child, and all the audio recordings were made in that child's home. The mothers of the hosts and guests filled out a 33-item questionnaire that assessed the closeness of the best friendship. Items included information about whether the children often played together, called each other on the telephone, preferred each other to other playmates, were sad when parting, were happy when reunited, spontaneously spoke about each other, suggested visiting each other, ate at each other's homes, slept at each other's houses, and so on. Mothers also estimated the length of acquaintance of the dyad. The two mothers' scores were averaged to provide one index of the closeness of the friendship.

An adult female experimenter set up a tape recorder in the home of the host child. The major goal of the experimenter was to occupy the attention of the host's mother. There were two conditions. In one condition, the mother was the only adult present in the room in which the children normally played but was instructed not to interact with the children. In the other, the children were alone. Each session lasted approximately one-half hour. The order of the two conditions was randomized within cells. After the play session, each child was interviewed separately in a randomly determined order. Each child was asked for the names of three of his or her friends and asked with whom he or she would choose to play first, second, third, or fourth. A weighting scheme was then devised from the choice matrix, with a score of 100 for mutual first choices, 70 for mutual second choices, 50 for mutual third choices, 30 for mutual fourth choices, and 0 if the best friend was chosen by neither. Deviations from the diagonal of the choice matrix were weighted according to a fixed scheme.

Cronbach alpha generalizability coefficients were computed for each variable in the coding system shown in Table 4.4, as described by Gottman (1983), using point-for-point agreement (not collapsing over time). This is sufficient for sequential analysis. (The procedure is actually more stringent than is necessary; see Gottman, 1980.) The reliabilities were uniformly high, as follows: me, .980; feeling, .994; squabbles, 1.000; jokes, .989; question, .999; fantasy, 1.000; disagreement, 0.967; agreement, .960; clarifies message or gives a reason for disagreeing, .940; information, .965; we, .951; attention, .982; and weak demand, .844.

Sequential analysis was performed using dyad-by-dyad analysis. Sequential connection was determined by comparing conditional with unconditional probabilities using z-score statistics described in detail in Gottman (1983). Data were all converted to event sequential data, so that an event could not logically follow itself.

Results

Selecting a closeness criterion. To assess the overall effectiveness of potential criterion variables of the closeness of the children, a set of

Table 4.5. *Partial correlations of the mothers' questionnaire, the child interview controlling the sex composition of the dyad, age and acquaintanceship of the children with the potential criterion variables*

Potential criteria	Mother's questionnaire	Child interview
Agreement and disagreement proportions		
Host agreement [HAG]	.150	−.008
Host disagreement [HDG]	−.025	.052
Guest agreement [GAG]	.334*	.270[a]
Guest disagreement [GDG]	.146	.101
Relative climate of agreement		
HAG/HDG	.089	−.196
GAG/GDG	.047	.193
AV (5,6)	.080	.046
TOTAG/TOTDG	.202	.066
HAG−HDG	.113	−.031
GAG−GDG	.196	.167
Age	−.011	−.477**

[a]$p < .10$; *$p < .05$; **$p < .01$.

analyses were conducted that were parallel to those in the acquaintanceship studies reported in Gottman (1983). Partial correlations were computed (controlling age, acquaintanceship length, and sex composition of the dyad) between the mothers' questionnaire, the child interview data, and the 10 potential criterion variables considered in the acquaintanceship study (Table 4.5). The child interview data were suspect because of the restricted range of these variables; most younger friends tended to pick one another as first choices. The child interview data were strongly correlated with age; younger children tended to give one another the highest scores. The mothers' questionnaire showed no such bias. Unfortunately, because of these problems with the child interview data, they could not be employed as a criterion variable for indexing the closeness of the friendship.

Correlations were computed to assess the extent to which the mothers' questionnaire was similar to the mothers' questionnaire in the Gottman (1983) acquaintanceship studies. Gottman (1983) tested a behavioral criterion variable derived from the interaction. This variable indexed how well two unacquainted children "hit it off" and progressed toward friendship. The criterion had discriminated between friends and strangers in Study 1 [$F(1,12) = 6.65, p < .05$] of Gottman (1983) and correlated with a mothers' questionnaire assessment of the childrens' progress toward friendship in Study 2 ($r = .594, p < .01$). The criterion variable in the acquaintanceship studies was the proportion of guest agreement. In the present investigation the results of the mother questionnaires were identical to those in Gottman (1983); only guest agreement was significantly related to the mothers' questionnaire ($r = .334, p < .05$). Once again, it was denoted the "the criterion." However, because the correlation was lower than in the acquaintanceship study, relationships were presented between the social process variables and the criterion *and* the mothers' questionnaire.

Table 4.6 assesses the extent to which it is possible to generalize across the two repeated-measures conditions: mother present and mother absent. The results of a series of 2 × 2 × 3 repeated-measures analyses of variance are summarized in this table. There were two levels of sex and three levels for the sex composition of the dyad.

Fragile temporal structures. Table 4.6 shows that the mother's presence had a significant main effect on the criterion and on information exchange (HQ → GIN; GQ → HIN). It had significant interaction effects with age for information exchange (HQ → GIN) and exploration of similarity (HFE → GAG). It also had significant interaction effects with the sex composition of the dyad for the guest's squabbling (GS) and for the guest's conflict resolution (GWEA → HAG). It interacted significantly with both age and the sex composition of the dyad for criterion (GAG) and for disagreement chains (GDG → HDG).[4]

Thus, the interaction of friends was not robust. The main effects of the mother's presence or absence show that the mother's presence was entirely disruptive; *the children's interaction deteriorated in her presence.* The criterion was higher in her absence (.039) than in her presence (.029); information exchange was more successful in her absence (HQ → GIN, z-score 5.14; GQ → HIN, 7.39) than in her presence (HQ → GIN, 3.01; GQ → HIN, 5.09).[5] Therefore, the social processes studied might be aptly characterized as *fragile temporal structures.* They are observed only under certain conditions.

There is one methodological implication of these results. Researchers cannot assume that the presence of an adult observer does not seriously distort children's peer interaction with friends. Until now it has been

Table 4.6. *Effects of the mother's presence and absence (F ratios)*

| | Main effects | | | Interaction effects | | | |
| | Age | Males | Mother's presence | | | | |
Variables[b]	(X)	(M)	(G)	XM	GX	GM	GXM
Child interview	10.82**	2.78[a]	—	3.57	—	—	—
Criterion	0.01	1.55	20.67	1.34	2.81	2.29	8.86
Mothers' questionnaire	0.00	.33	—	2.03	—	—	—
Information exchange							
HATT	0.52	2.70[a]	2.66	2.06	2.91	0.28	0.24
GATT	0.13	0.85	2.89	2.69[a]	2.69	1.01	1.20
HIN	0.34	0.15	1.54	1.04	.39	2.25	2.44
GIN	0.58	0.45	0.93	0.80	0.27	1.35	0.06
HQ → GIN	1.91	0.24	21.26***	0.88	5.56*	0.14	2.02
GQ → HIN	11.69**	0.03	13.96***	1.52	0.00	0.49	0.83
Common-ground activity							
HWE → GAG	0.21	0.31	0.00	3.05[a]	0.29	0.28	0.17
GWE → HAG	3.09[a]	1.35	0.22	0.36	0.04	3.04[a]	1.60
HME	0.76	0.51	0.04	0.31	1.44	1.65	0.65
GME	1.38	0.91	1.83	0.23	0.04	0.59	0.66
Similarity/ differences							
HOAG → GAG	1.16	1.42	2.13	1.27	0.00	0.39	0.11
GQAG → HAG	0.20	0.04	3.92[a]	0.68	0.07	1.02	0.72
HFE → GAG	1.59	0.75	3.82[a]	0.11	4.68*	0.21	1.34
GFE → HAG	2.61	1.04	0.63	0.77	0.36	2.24	0.13
HFE → GDG	0.35	0.64	0.09	1.17	0.01	0.54	1.20
GFE → HDG	1.23	0.21	2.06	0.06	0.24	0.65	1.03
Conflict							
HDG → GDG	0.50	1.32	1.28	0.43	0.00	0.17	2.10
GDG → HDG	0.97	2.97[a]	1.14	1.94	3.36[a]	0.16	4.41*
HS	0.23	2.84[a]	0.07	1.34	0.28	1.04	0.01
GS	2.55	2.25	0.09	2.18	0.47	4.11*	0.18
Conflict resolution							
HDG → HCM	0.81	0.14	1.34	1.69	0.06	0.00	0.36
GDG → GCM	0.05	0.31	2.18	0.10	0.48	0.25	2.21
HWFA → GAG	0.51	1.48	1.38	0.12	0.58	0.32	2.62[a]
GWEA → HAG	0.66	0.18	1.40	0.27	0.84	4.91*	0.17

Table 4.6. *(Cont.)*

Variables[b]	Main effects			Interaction effects			
	Age	Males	Mother's presence				
	(X)	(M)	(G)	XM	GX	GM	GXM
Reciprocity							
HJ → GJ	2.77	0.40	0.13	0.31	0.53	0.76	0.32
GJ → HJ	1.62	0.55	0.30	0.58	3.07[a]	1.12	0.04
HG → GG	0.09	0.56	0.28	2.17	0.89	3.21[a]	1.31
GG → HG	0.40	3.33[a]	0.75	0.51	1.13	3.38[a]	0.98
HF → GF	0.41	0.33	1.07	0.32	0.69	0.54	1.08
GF → HF	0.32	1.04	0.62	0.21	0.92	0.38	0.89
Self-disclosure							
HQFE → GFE	0.28	0.57	0.44	0.70	1.48	0.86	0.53
GDFE → HFE	4.77*	1.64	1.55	4.03*	0.40	0.22	1.65
Communication clarity							
HQ → GCM	2.83	1.22	0.00	0.90	0.53	0.62	0.68
GQ → HCM	4.45*	0.79	1.34	0.54	0.74	1.78	0.91

[a] $p < .10$
[b] Abbreviations: H, host; G, guest; ATT, attention; IN, information; Q, question; WE, We; AG, agreement; ME, Me; QAG, question for agreement; FE, feelings; DG, disagreement; S, squabble; CM, clarifies message or gives a reason for disagreeing; WEA, weak form of demand; J, jokes; G, gossip; F, fantasy; QFE, question about feelings.
* $p < .05$; ** $p < .01$; *** $p < .001$.

considered a matter of choice as to whether live observers or tape recorders are used. However, without adequate checks on the generalizability of behavior across conditions of observation, this assumption must be considered questionable. Probably a wide range of factors, including obtrusive cameras and microphones, new places, and toys, decrease the social skillfulness and intimacy children display.

There were also significant interactions of the mother's presence or absence with age. As assessed by Scheffe's test, younger children's information exchange (HQ → GIN) was disrupted by the mother's presence, whereas older children's information exchange was not.[6] In the exploration of similarity, older children's interaction was disrupted by the mother's presence, whereas younger children's interaction was unaffected, although the means were not significantly different according to the Scheffe test.[7]

There were significant interactions of the mother's presence or absence with the sex composition of the dyad (see Table 4.6), but none of these differences were significant as assessed by the Scheffe test. There were two significant triple interactions, but once again, as judged by the Scheffe test, the only significant difference between means was that young cross-sex interaction was particularly disrupted by the mother's presence (for young children the criterion was .055 in the mother's absence and .027 in her presence).

To summarize, the presence of the mother had a powerful disruptive effect on the interaction of friends, particularly young friends.

Development and sex composition effects. Older friends were better than younger friends at message clarification (GQ → HCM); the z-score for younger friends was 1.38, whereas that for older friends was 2.34. Older friends were also better than younger friends at information exchange (GQ → HIN; HQ → GIN); the z-score for the younger friends was 5.15, whereas that for older friends was 6.34. Older friends were also more likely to engage in self-disclosure than younger friends (GQFE → HFE); the mean z-scores were 1.62 and 4.61 for younger and older friends, respectively.

There were several important negative results. There were no significant developmental changes in fantasy [by either the host, $F(1,24) = .48$, or the guest, $F(1,24) = .70$], in gossip [by either the host, $F(1,24) = .04$, or the guest, $F(1,24) = .31$]. There were also no significant developmental effects on the z-scores reflecting the reciprocity of fantasy, gossip, or humor.[8]

The absence of a developmental decline in fantasy in this study is not consistent with the results of Gottman and Parkhurst (1980). There were significant developmental main effects for humor. The older guest laughed and joked more (proportion, 4.9%) than the younger guest [proportion, 2.0%; $F(1,24) = 8.11, p < .01$]. This effect was marginal for the guest's joking [older proportion, 4.6%; younger, 2.4%; $F(1,24) = 3.66, p < .068$]. There was a significant interaction between age and the mother's presence or absence. For the host this effect was that older children joked more in the mother's presence (6.2%) than in her absence [2.9%; $F(1,24) = 9.27, p < .01$], whereas there were no differences for younger children (presence, 2.4%; absence, 2.5%). The interaction results for the guest paralleled those for the host. Older guests joked more in the mother's presence (proportion, 6.3%) than in her absence (proportion, 3.4%), whereas there was no difference for younger children [presence, 2.4%; absence, 1.6%; $F(1,24) = 4.41$, $p < .05$].

There was one significant interaction effect for age and the sex composition of the dyad. It occurred for self-disclosure (GQFE → HFE). At younger ages self-disclosure was greatest for cross-sex friends ($z = 2.84$) than for same-sex best friends ($z = 0.96$ for girls and $z = 1.04$ for boys). At older ages self-disclosure was greatest for same-sex rather than cross-sex best friends, and it was slightly (but not significantly) greater for girls than for boys (for older girls, $z = 8.70$; for older boys, $z = 4.10$; and for cross-sex older friends, $z = 1.03$).

The amount of self-disclosure of younger cross-sex friends was not significantly different from that of older boys and girls; however, the difference in the two same-sex self-disclosure z-scores does suggest that older girls self-disclose more than older boys. With a larger sample it is likely that a significant difference would be obtained.

This pattern of results implies that cross-sex friendship among preschool children has a uniquely intimate character, as discussed earlier in this chapter. The developmental change in cross-sex friendship is a mystery, but it has been noted repeatedly in the sociometric literature that cross-sex friendship choices decline dramatically in approximately the seventh year of life. For example, Epstein (1986) wrote:

> The literature suggests a curvilinear, developmental pattern of cross-sex choices of friends. Very young children make frequent cross-sex (sociometric) choices, children in elementary and middle school grades make almost no cross-sex choices, and adolescents increase their cross-sex choices of friends [p. 137].

One thing must be noted in the search for explanations of this phenomenon. The pattern of change in cross-sex friendships from early childhood through the early elementary school years is a step function; that is, it has essentially an on–off character. Explaining a step function requires another step function, one that goes on or off at an earlier age, that is, one that is what economists call a "lead indicator." As noted earlier, the most popular attempts at explanation have involved play preferences and the emergence of sex-role identity (see Rubenstein & Rubin, 1984) and rough-and-tumble play patterns. Explanations of this type do not have the necessary step-function character; instead, they invoke the presence of sex differences early in life and their gradual strengthening. Thus, they are not satisfactory explanations. The same is true of a hypothesis based on differential socialization of emotional expressiveness among the sexes. Initially this variable seemed to have the necessary step-function character, based on the reasoning of Buck (1975, 1977). However, more recent reports (Radke-Yarrow, 1985) suggest that, even when the child is 2, differential socialization of emotional expression has occurred in mother–child interaction. If these results are correct, differential socialization of emotional expression is also an unsatisfactory explanation.

Accounting for variation in closeness. Because we wished to generalize only to the mother-absent condition, we computed partial correlations of the process variables in the mother-absent condition with the mothers' questionnaire and the criterion, controlling age, the number of boys in the dyad, and the length of acquaintanceship of friends (see Table 4.7). Close friends were better (on the criterion) than distant friends at information exchange, conflict resolution, and self-disclosure. They also engaged in less squabbling than more distant friends. There were marginal effects. Common-ground activity was more likely, the exploration of differences was more likely, disagreement chains were less likely, and conflict resolution using weaker demands was more likely for close than for distant friends.

A similar pattern was obtained for the mothers' questionnaire. Close friends were better than distant friends at information exchange. Close friends squabbled less frequently and reciprocated humor more often than distant friends. Marginal effects were in the same direction. Close friends tended to exchange information more, establish common ground more, squabble less, and self-disclose more frequently than distant friends.

Table 4.8 summarizes the results of stepwise multiple regressions of the process variables with the criterion and with the mothers' questionnaire. With five process variables ($N/6$) it was possible to account for 51.8% of the variance in the criterion and 34% of the variance in the mothers' questionnaire.

Discussion

Several findings emerged from this study. First, to summarize the developmental results, the conversations of older friends were characterized by more information exchange, humor, self-disclosure, and message clarification (also an index of the interconnectedness of the

Table 4.7. *Partial correlations of the process variables with the criteria, controlling for age, number of males, and length of acquaintanceship, mother-absent condition*

Process variable	Mothers' questionnaire	Criterion
Communication clarity		
HQ → GCM	.229	−.035
GQ → HCM	.011	−.062
Information exchange		
HATT	.250	.362*
GATT	.226	.067
HIN	.320[a]	.549***
GIN	.352*	.243
H2 → GIN	.000	.412*
G2 → HIN	−.229	−.181
Common-ground activity		
HWE → GAG	.011	.036
GWE → HAG	.299[a]	.274
HME	−.005	−.091
GME	.090	−.036
Common ground: similarity and difference		
HQAG → GAG	.139	.176
GQAG → HAG	−.040	.068
HFE → GAG	.222	−.166
GFE → HAG	.148	−.084
HFE → GDG	−.006	.126
GFE → HDG	.128	.257[a]
Conflict		
HDG → GDG	.188	−.127
GDG → HDG	.057	−.268[a]
HS	−.377*	−.311[a]
GS	−.268[a]	−.382*
Conflict resolution		
HDG → HCM	.208	.370*
GDG → GCM	.182	.197
HWEA → GAG	−.109	.252
GWEA → HAG	−.058	.283[a]
Reciprocity		
HJ → GJ	.185	.117
GJ → HJ	.341*	.056
HG → GG	.137	.172

Table 4.7. *(Cont.)*

Process variable	Mothers' questionnaire	Criterion
GG → HG	.012	.202
HF → GF	.149	.118
GF → HF	.037	.123
Self-disclosure		
HQFE → GFE	.277[a]	.243
GQFE → HFE	.130	.393*

[a]$p < .10$.
*$p < .05$; **$p < .01$; ***$p < .001$.

Table 4.8. *Stepwise multiple regression analyses for friendship study, mother-absent condition*

Step and variable entered	Multiple R	R^2	F-Ratio
Criterion			
1. HIN	.520	.270	10.36**
2. HQ → GIN	.643	.414	9.53***
3. HDG → HCM	.686	.471	7.72***
4. GDG → HDG	.703	.494	6.11***
5. HATT	.719	.518	5.15**
Mothers' questionnaire			
1. GIN	.344	.119	3.77[a]
2. HQFE → GFE	.491	.241	4.28*
3. GWE → HAG	.533	.284	3.44*
4. GJ → HJ	.580	.337	3.18
5. HIN	.582	.340	2.47[a]

[a]$p < .10$.
*$p < .05$; **$p < .01$; ***$p < .001$.

dialogue; see Gottman, 1983) than the conversations of younger friends. Self-disclosure was most likely to occur among younger children in cross-sex friendships and among older children in same-sex friendships.

The behavioral criterion variable of the closeness of the friendship was the same as it was for the progress of unacquainted children toward friendship. It is the climate of agreement, particularly by guests, that best indexes closeness in this situation. This is encouraging, because similar results have been found in research on children's entry into peer groups and marital and family interaction (for a brief review see Gottman, 1983).

The mother's presence had a significant effect on the quality of the children's interaction (as indexed by the behavioral criterion variable) and on specific social processes; the children's performance deteriorated in the mother's presence. This suggests that children's interaction structures are fragile and require privacy to be displayed. As mentioned earlier, Corsaro (1981) proposed that preschoolers reject entering children to protect "interactive space"; young children have trouble maintaining complex dyadic interaction structures, and so they exclude others to maintain high-quality interaction.

Mothers disrupted younger–but not older–children's information exchange, and older–but not younger–children's exploration of similarity. These results are somewhat puzzling. Gottman (1983) found that information exchange is easier than establishing common ground (either by exploring similarity or by finding a common activity) in the sense that children return to information exchange when establishing common ground has failed. Information exchange is thus a kind of "home base" social process in play. Why is an easier social process (information exchange) disrupted among younger children, whereas a more complex process (the exploration of similarity) is not? A tentative answer has to do with the salience of the processes.

Gottman and Parkhurst (1980) reported that exploring similarity and building a "me too" climate of acceptance is more common among younger (below 6 years of age) than among older children (6 years or above). Older children can disagree and explore differences more comfortably and with less danger of escalation to conflict than younger children. These facts represent a trade-off in development. The climate of acceptance is probably a necessary foundation on which other social processes are based, particularly nonstereotyped fantasy (which requires continuous renegotiation of roles as the action unfolds). Fantasy declines dramatically from preschool to middle childhood. In contrast, conversational skills and the ability to resolve conflict increase with age. Hence, information exchange, a skill that is frequently used among preschoolers, may be more fragile because it represents the development of conversational skills. It is as if this were the area of conversation, as opposed to fantasy play, where development were taking place. For this reason information exchange, and not the exploration of similarity, may be most fragile among preschool friends.

Furthermore, I suggest that the exploration of similarity is most easily disrupted among older children because it is a different process among children of this group than it is among younger children. Whereas among younger children the exploration of similarity is related to building a climate of agreement, among older children it may be related to social comparison processes in general. That is, perhaps exploring similarity is related to exploring differences among older children, but not among younger children. It may be disrupted because there is a new process being developed of which it is a part – namely, social comparison. This is probably related to the emergence in force of the social process of gossip in children of this age.

Indeed, I believe that developmental changes in the function of exploring similarity is but one illustration of a general principle of social development, namely, that *the same social event may represent a different process at different points in development.* This is because social interaction is organized around different goals at different points in development, and the function of a social event cannot be understood apart from the goal of the period. As a result, although social processes can be identified and reliably scored across age groups, they are not really the same processes across development. Their relation to one another changes and so does their function.

In young childhood social processes function in the service of coordinated play. As I have suggested, coordinated play requires a high level of agreement relative to disagreement. Thus, social processes function *in the service of building a "me-too" climate of agreement and solidarity.* This can be illustrated in the manner depicted in Figure 4.1, where the 10 social processes and 2 affective states of the MACRO coding system (see Chapter 2) are shown relative to one another and the central goal of coordination of play.

Young children's cross-sex interaction is particularly disrupted by the mother's presence. This may be related to the finding that young friends' cross-sex interaction is high in self-disclosure. These friendships are very similar to many marriages: They are emotional and intimate, and they contain a wide range of both positive and negative affect. I would suggest, on the basis of these data, that the expression of feelings is most salient in younger cross-sex dyads. I do not mean to imply that it is unimportant to older or same-sex dyads, just that it is not as central. This is consistent with other research. For example, Sherman (1975) studied group "glee" among preschool children. Glee refers to the phenomenon of "joyful screaming, laughing and intense physical acts which occurred in simultaneous bursts or which spread in a contagious

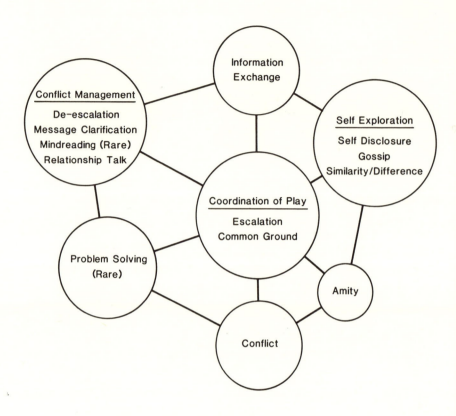

Figure 4.1. Organization of macrosocial processes among young friends (ages 3 to 7, approximately).

fashion from one child to another" (p. 53). What is important here is that glee among preschoolers was almost entirely a cross-sex phenomenon. It occurred 113 of 120 times in mixed-sex groups. Cross-sex relationships throughout the life span may be more intensely affective than same-sex relationships. Social events may also differ greatly between cross-sex and same-sex relationships. I have discussed some of these differences in this chapter (e.g., concerning risk, danger, and mastery of fear). These differences may also apply to social skills.

Whereas younger children were generally less skillful than older children, cross-sex friendship was an exception. This result is consistent with the well-known but poorly understood decline in cross-sex friendship in middle childhood discussed earlier. Nonetheless, this kind of volatile, intimate interaction is clearly likely to be the most fragile.

The social processes or skills studied can account for a sizable proportion of the variance in the closeness of friends. However, when compared with the results of Gottman (1983), these processes did not account for as much variance in the closeness of friends as they accounted for variance in the extent to which two unacquainted children would hit it off and progress toward friendship. Something is omitted from an inquiry limited to the set of social processes selected here. Thus, it is likely that these processes do not tell the whole story about the conversations of friends.

On the basis of this first exploratory study, it seems reasonable to suggest that different friendships may serve different functions at different developmental levels. For example, cross-sex friendships in preschool may have much to do with the expression and control of emotion, whereas same-sex friendships in middle childhood have much more to do with gossip and social comparison.

Older cross-sex friendships

The truly anomalous cell in this study was that comprising older cross-sex friends. These children had been friends for longer than those in any other cell. The average length of friendship for the other cells was 2.33 years, whereas that for older cross-sex friends was 5.67 years; the developmental main effect [$F(1,24) = 8.36$, $p < .01$] was due entirely to this cell. It is interesting that, even among younger children, cross-sex friends had been acquainted longer (2.71 years) than boy–boy pairs (1.62 years) or girl–girl pairs (2.06 years). For older children these means were 2.73 years among boy–boy pairs and 2.83 years among girl–girl pairs.

The lack of a developmental decline in fantasy in this study was puzzling, particularly because an earlier study has found evidence for such a decline (Gottman & Parkhurst, 1980). Gottman and Parkhurst (1980) analyzed the conversations of friends and strangers. They divided the tapes into two groups: those in which the host was under 5 years old (16 tapes) and those in which the host was 5 years or older (10 tapes).

They found no significant change in the connectedness of the conversation in this age range [coding collective monologue, $F(1,11) = 2.03$, n.s.; see Gottman & Parkhurst, p. 216]. However, they did find that the amount of conversation, relative to fantasy talk, activity-based talk, and collective monologue, increased significantly within this age range [$F(1,11) = 5.58$; $p < .05$]. They found only a marginally significant decrease in fantasy within this age range [$F(1,11) = 3.62$, $p < .10$]. However, when they employed a more restricted definition of fantasy that involved only speaking within a role, they obtained a large developmental change [$F(1,10) = 19.75$, $p < .01$; younger proportion, 3.9%; older proportion, 1.8%]. A decline was also observed in terms of how developed or extended the fantasies were; the fantasies of younger children were more extended. The findings were a bit complex, because the developmental decline in fantasy depended on the nature of the fantasy. Gottman and Parkhurst divided fantasies into domestic and adventure themes and found a developmental decline for domestic, but not adventure fantasies; in fact, fantasies in the latter category increased with age.

The discrepancies between the two studies can be explained, in part, by the fact that the present investigation included a much wider age range and particularly by the fact that the investigators went to great lengths to include older cross-sex friends. Older cross-sex friendships are extremely rare. In the present investigation, the conversations of cross-sex friends actually *increased* in fantasy with age. The results were as follows: for the host, $t(24) = 2.58$, with 1.5 and 8.8% proportions of fantasy for younger and older friends, respectively; for the guest, $t(24) = 2.19$, with 1.1 and 7.3% proportions of fantasy for younger and older friends, respectively. Older cross-sex friends also squabbled more often than other types of dyads. These differences were significant, however, only between cross-sex hosts and younger or older girls and between cross-sex guests and younger or older girls. *One of the purposes of the older cross-sex friendship may be to make it possible for children both to fantasize and to fight at high levels.*

Qualitative analysis of the transcripts of these friendship conversations supports this view. For example, one cross-sex friendship that involved 12.4% fantasy by the host also involved 7.6% squabbling by the host. The interaction of this dyad was filled with fantasy, but also with hostility. The boy nicknamed the girl "Sadness." She, for her part, said that she wished there would be a war so that the boy would get killed in it:

She: I wish there was a war and you were the center and you were one of the people in the war and you were playing like you were the dead one, on the bad team [*laughs*].
He: Don't worry, if I even get in the war I'll kill you.
She: What if I'm not in the war?
He: Ooh, you're smart [*sarcastic*].

Much of their interaction had a teasing, insulting quality similar to the ritual insult exchanges that can be found among young, preadolescent black children (see Labov, 1972).

She: David, would you stop?
He: No.
She: Would you stop humming?
He: No. You're so fat.
She: You are too, ha, ha, ha.
He: So are you. Hey, ugly down there, hah, hah.
She: David stop that.
He: Make me.
She: I don't make trash, I burn it.
He: Why ain't your momma burnt? Hah hah, smash that pile of trash.

Nonetheless, the pair showed a good deal of adventure and domestic fantasy. For example:

He: He comes, and then he uses a lot of fire. He turns around, that whole castle moves up in flames.
She: No, because the whole castle was metal.
He: So, metal catches on fire. Look, that NASA plane sitting there. He's just hanging on full blast, but he has the fire on full blast. The metal is melting and there is a step underneath. Da-da-da-da-da-da. Too bad NASA planes had guns.
She: Take over, take over, take over.

This adventure fantasy was quite extended, and both children were active participants in the war games. The following is part of a domestic (family trip) fantasy:

He: I think I'll have the son. Where's the son?
She: Ah, little boy, here's the son. Take one. You want a girl?
He: No.
She: For his sister, I mean.
He: Nope.
She: She has a twin sister.
He: No, I don't want a sister, because there's not enough room in the van.

Even though there is a great deal of squabbling on these tapes, there are also very high ratios of agreement to disagreement (5.83 and 7.50), which are necessary for fantasy.

Although hostility was fairly typical of these dyads, it had a fairly ritualized quality. An example from another dyad follows:

He: I think ya have a ugly face.
She: I've known that!
He: Oh, ya did?
She: Yea!
He: I know, I have one too [*giggles*].

These children are pretending to be television personalities and make fun of each other within that context.

We can see from these excerpts that cross-sex friendships that have persisted from young to middle childhood are very complex. We have no idea what functions such rare and special relationships serve.

In the spirit of hypothesis generating, it makes sense to end this chapter by describing Eric and Naomi's concept of a married couple. Eric and Naomi at times pretended they were a married couple called Bob and Claudia. Bob and Claudia always had things in need of repair. Much of their conversation involved trying to keep up with the continual state of decay and disrepair in their world:

N: Bob?
E: Ya, Claudia.
N: What?
E: That lights upstairs aren't working.
N: Oh, good, you know.
E: No, they're not.
N: I tried them yesterday and it wasn't working.
E: I know. All we need is a fix-it man, and you know what? I asked everyone in the world where there is a fix-it man. And I looked all over this room and there was no fix-it man. I looked all over the world. I looked at the moon, I looked almost by the side of the cat, and I looked everywhere.
N: But I know a man I saw, I called one yesterday and he said he'll come today.
E: Oh, good, what's his telephone number?
N: Ah, four-six-two-one.
E: OK, four-six-two-one.

Do not get the idea that Eric and Naomi think marriage is dull, because Bob and Claudia have very heroic jobs. For example, in the following excerpt Bob gives Claudia some very strange money:

E: OK, I'll give you some more money so you can buy some more things. Here's some more money.
N: *That's* strange money.
E: Yeah, of course, I have strange money. I like strange money. 'Cause I live on another planet. But I work on this planet.
N: Nah.

On the way to the store they make plans in case they have to deal with robbers.

N: OK and I'll go right away.
E: Well, yah, you go to the grocery store, right this minute.
N: And the flea store has this.

E: The frish store, the fresh store?
N: Yes.
E: I don't believe it, whop.
N: I'm buying it at a toy store, to buy Eric Fisher a record 'cause he doesn't has
   a . . .
E: What happened to his old one?
N: It's all broken.
E: How did it get all broken?
N: Ah, a robber stealed it, I think. That's what he said, a robber stealed it.
E: Did he see what the action was? You know my gun is in here, so could you
   go get my gun? It's right over there, back there, back there, not paper . . .
   did you get it?
N: Yes, I found the robbers right in the closet.
E: Good, kill 'em.
N: I killed em.
E: Already?
N: Yes, so quick they can't believe it.
E: Well, Claudia, you can call me Bob everytime, Claudia . . .

The world of cross-sex friendships is a very exciting world, indeed.

5. Speculations about social and affective development: friendship and acquaintanceship through adolescence

JOHN GOTTMAN AND GWENDOLYN METTETAL

This chapter presents a theory of social and affective development that spans the years from early childhood through later adolescence (approximately from years 3 to 17). This theory emerged from data-based speculations about the conversations of friends and the conversations of strangers becoming acquainted.

It is valuable to organize childhood in terms of the social processes that are salient at different ages. When this is done and the results are integrated with other developmental literature, three major developmental periods emerge. Each period is relatively homogeneous and stable in terms of the organization and function of its social processes.

It will be helpful to employ a visual image in the discussion that follows. Think of the set of salient social process as if it were the hub of a wheel; the rim of the wheel consists of the remaining social processes in the MACRO coding system, which are in the service of the hub. At each developmental period a different set of social processes occupies the hub. This metaphor will become clearer as the discussion proceeds. It implies that what is thought to be the same process at different ages (and is codable as the same process throughout the age span studied) turns out *not* to be the same process because its relations with other social processes changes. For example, gossip in early childhood, which is in the service of building solidarity, is not the same as gossip in adolescence, which is in the service of self-exploration, even though excerpts of gossip at different ages and stripped of context seem somewhat similar.

This visual metaphor also implies that each new developmental period entails a major reorganization of all the social processes and their relationships with one another (called "second-order" change), as well as the diminution of some processes and the addition or enhancement of others (called "first-order" change). There are specific reasons for the

192

centrality or salience of some processes within each period, which can be inferred by the content of the conversations.

Developmental *change* occurs because of changes in the affective competence demands of the ecological niches children are forced by our culture to occupy and to maneuver within. In middle childhood these demands are made by entrance into "real" elementary school (usually after kindergarten) and confrontation with the same-sex peer culture. There is some evidence that this peer culture has remained relatively intact in its games, norms, and rituals, many of which have existed, untouched, for centuries (Opie & Opie, 1959). In this peer culture the young child can no longer play only within the safety of the dyad. Corsaro (1981) has observed that it is normative for the preschool child to "protect the interactive space" of the dyad and reject a third child who tries to enter. We speculate that this is no longer adequate in elementary school; in fact, most teachers require that the young child manage in larger groupings. A second set of demands for social competence occurs at early adolescence and involves being able to interact with the cross-sex peer culture as well as the same-sex peer culture. Of course, these changes are accompanied by the powerful biological and emotional changes of puberty.

A significant bidirectional concomitant of these changes is, we believe, a qualitative change in cognitive competence. This change is reflected most obviously in changes in social competence. Thus, our hope is that we may be led to an integrated cognitive and social developmental theory.

Social development

As we have noted, three developmental periods emerge from our data. From the content of the conversations and the sources of high-intensity affect, one can infer the social concerns and social goals of each period. The first is from ages 3 through 7, the second from ages 8 through 12, and the third from ages 13 to 17. These ages are, of course, approximate. Clearly, individual differences cannot be ignored.

Early childhood. In young childhood the goal of peer interaction is coordinated play, by which we mean the coordination of interactive temporal play sequences between children (see Chapter 4). Coordinated play comprises a wide range of hierarchially organized social events. The hierarchy is organized by the amount of social involvement and attention the play requires of each child. At the lowest level of social involvement, coordinated but parallel play with accompanying activity talk offers conflict-free, peaceful companionship. An example is coloring side by side, but not coloring the same thing. Each child takes turns but does what he or she chooses to do. As the demand for attention, involvement, and coordination increases – for example, by coloring the same thing together – coordinated play offers both a greater potential for solidarity and amity (high levels of fun and other positive affects) and a greater opportunity for conflict and disagreement. Thus, two new kinds of social interaction have to be managed in the context of a greater demand for attention and involvement, namely, conflict and high levels of excitement. Both demand the ability to regulate one's emotional state to coordinate with another's; at a minimum, as we shall see, managing these social events requires behavioral inhibition. In moving from parallel play to a joint activity, the form of the conversation often shifts from connected "activity talk" (narrating one's actions: "I'm coloring mine green"; "I'm using red") to other kinds of conversation (e.g., demands followed by compliance of noncompliance: "Pass the green"; "Not till I'm done with it; here, try the blue"; "OK").

High levels of agreement and low levels of disagreement become increasingly necessary as the demand for involvement, attention, and coordination increases. Given the reasonable general principle that two unacquainted children will seek their highest level of common-ground activity and keep shifting (escalating and deescalating) this level of involvement to manage disagreement, the ratio of agreement to disagreement (AG/DG) is an important index of the overall social competence of the dyad. This appears to be a generally useful ratio. Among distressed married couples it is usually less than 1; among happily married couples it is generally greater than 1 (Riskin & Faunce, 1970).

At maximum AG/DG ratios between children, play can become high adventure. The highest level of coordinated play is nonstereotyped fantasy. It involves the continual negotiation of roles as children play out the action. To achieve this high level of coordination, high AG/DG ratios are essential. An interesting thing happens at these high ratios. The conversations become more metaphoric, more lyrical, less censored. In this context, dramatic play (taking the role of make-believe characters or parts of machines) becomes more common. We believe that this state of nonstereotyped fantasy play is very special for young children, who have limited representational abilities. Among friends, it is a vehicle for working out issues of major concern, such as plans, hopes, concerns, fears, anger, ambivalence about growing up, change, and transformation (see Chapter 4). When this happens, play activities and conversation are intricately interlaced.

For the first developmental period, then, the processes integral to coordinated play represent the hub of our imaginary wheel. The other social processes are in the service of maintaining the highest possible levels of coordinated play; they are at the rim, in service of the central process. The most obvious processes that serve the function of coordinating play are escalation and deescalation, message clarification, and conflict resolution. Young children have difficulty managing conflict once it has escalated, so they tend to avoid negative affect and other dangerous social events such as disagreement sequences (an example of a disagreement sequence is: "This is big," "Is not," "Is too," "Uh uh," "Uh huh," "Uh uh," "Uh huh," and so on indefinitely) and struggles for dominance. Less obvious are those processes that eventually come to be central to self-exploration, such as social comparison. This is so because a necessary condition for coordinated play is a "me too" climate of agreement (high AG/DG). Social comparison has a major role in this developmental period in building the "me too" climate. We think it likely that this climate is necessary for both children to feel emotionally safe enough to explore and create with the tool of nonstereotyped, coordinated fantasy play.

Why is fantasy play so important to this age group? It is important because young children do not have easy access to their problem-solving capabilities. They may be able to demonstrate these capabilities under specialized laboratory conditions, but in general they do not easily apply them to their central concerns. Fear of the dark is a good example.

Playing out one's fantasy of the successful resolution of a fear of the dark, rehearsing it repeatedly with occasional new solutions, and remembering the lot is perhaps not the optimal means for coping with fear. However, it works, and it does not demand high levels of abstract representation, generation of alternatives, comparison of alternatives in terms of some abstract standard. Thus, it is the tool of choice of this age group.

Middle childhood. The goal of children in the second period, which we refer to as middle childhood, is inclusion in the larger same-sex peer group. Cross-sex relations, though they exist, defer to the same-sex peer group. Groups in middle childhood are organized by same sex, and intergroup relations take on a special stereotyped character regulated by the same-sex group.

Thorne's (in press) anthropological work described differences between boys' and girls' groups in early and middle childhood. Her anecdotal observations suggested that boys played higher-energy games than girls on the playground and occupied an area about 10 times as great as girls. Girls played in smaller groups than boys, close to the school building and usually under closer adult supervision. In middle childhood, boys who moved into female spatial areas ran the risk of being teased, often with playful reference to sexual interest. Cross-sex interaction on the playground involved invasions, chases (usually with boys chasing girls), and what Thorne called "rituals of pollution." For example, girls' kisses had a secret power to contaminate ("transferring cooties"), which Thorne argued is probably vaguely connected to the threat of menstruation. The games and chants of girls more often involved heterosexual themes such as kissing than boys', and cross-sex interaction was filled with the danger of teasing. Thorne wrote that cross-sex interactions were fraught with the danger of being teased about "liking someone of the other sex. I learned of several close cross-sex friendships, formed and maintained in neighborhoods and church, which went underground during the school day." We discussed these "underground" cross-sex friendships in the previous chapter.

In our study girls in middle childhood discussed chasing boys. The following is an excerpt from the conversation of 10-year-old girls who "hit it off" well:

A: We chase boys.
B: We don't play shadow tag when it's sunny, which it rarely is.
A: We do. Except for chasing boys and playing chicken fights. Sometimes we play Kill the Guy.
B: Last year at our school they played Kill the Guy and one kid almost *did* get killed. He was knocked down and broke both of his legs and a hip and was out of school about half the year.
A: Oh well, we don't play Kill the Guy as rough. You know we don't use guns and ropes and sledgehammers.
B: They weren't using them neither.
A: We keep it down to hammers and chains.

This is a dramatic example of what Thorne discussed. Thorne also noted that in middle childhood cross-sex interactions, although rare, "introduced the heterosexual rituals of adolescence" (p. 22). In middle childhood (fourth and fifth grades), the boys' groups involved ritual insults and teasing. Fine (1981) pointed out that there are unstated, but clear limits to this teasing, which are rarely violated. Violations are recognized by everyone. For example, teasing a boy on the bus is acceptable, but throwing his baseball hat out of the window is not and is an embarrassment to his peers. As we shall see, embarrassment is to be avoided in middle childhood, and discussions about peer group norms often center around how to avoid embarrassment.

It has often been noted that children in middle childhood are creatures of rules and strict rituals and that they exhibit high levels of conformity (see Hartup, 1970, for a discussion). We suggest that *ritual during this period is in the service of providing a ceiling on emotional intensity.* This hypothesis ties social with emotional development, a theme that we develop in this chapter.

Ritual insults, put-downs, and teasing are not limited to boys. For example, in one school, preadolescent girls kept "slam books," in which they wrote nasty things about other girls (Giese-Davis, personal communication, 1985).

What is at the hub of our wheel for middle childhood? We suggest that *the most salient social process in middle childhood is successful negative-evaluation gossip.* Negative-evaluation gossip is the negative evaluation of some aspect of another person (or stereotype). It is successful if it is responded to with interest, more negative gossip, or (better yet) solidarity.

In middle childhood, children are very concerned with the norms of the same-sex peer group, figuring out which actions will lead to acceptance and inclusion and which to exclusion and rejection. Much of their conversation, which may at times occur in the context of coordinated play, has a "we against others" quality. The coordination of play is no longer the goal of the interaction. Not being rejected by the peer group is the goal.

The period of middle childhood can be summarized by reference to Figure 5.1. The hub of the wheel is *acceptance by peers.* The goal is to maximize acceptance and minimize rejection. The salient social processes are negative-evaluation gossip, support (amity), and common ground. These processes are in the service of acceptance and avoidance of rejection. We shall provide specific illustrations of this organization later in the chapter.

Adolescence. The concern during the third period (13 years to young adulthood) is that of understanding the self. Much of this understand-

Figure 5.1. Organization of macrosocial processes in middle childhood.

ing begins with establishing one's self in relation to distinctly different peer subgroups, each of which reflects differences in life goals, social class, philosophy of life, identity and life style, and ultimately different aspects of the self that must be recognized and accepted by the developing adolescent. The salient social processes are gossip and self-disclosure, with a heavy emphasis on problem solving and intense honesty. The most salient social process of adolescence involves the application of intense scrutiny and logic to the turbulent world of emotions and unstable personal relationships. Because of this fact, intense honesty can almost be "derived," in a mathematical sense, as a

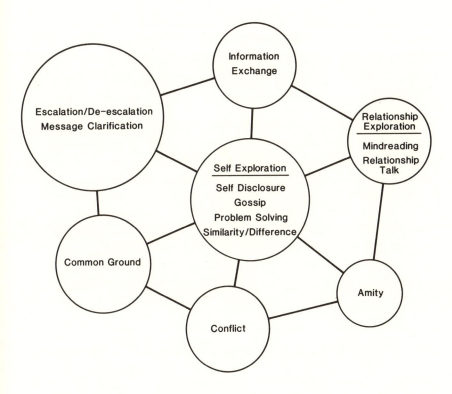

Figure 5.2. Organization of macrosocial process in adolescence.

necessary corollary concern of adolescence. In a climate of deceit none of this analysis is possible. Hence, the adolescent's great concern with loyalty and betrayal follows, for there can be no tolerance of lies and deceit from one's friends.

Figure 5.2 summarizes this characterization of adolescents' conversation with friends. At the hub of the wheel is *self-exploration*. The salient social processes connected with self-exploration are self-disclosure, gossip (both positive and negative evaluation), the exploration of similarity and differences, and problem solving. Other processes function essentially in service of the central goal. This will become clearer as our discussion proceeds.

Emotional development

Emotional development, we suggest, is the *theoretical* basis for social development. Here, "theoretical" refers to the explanation of the patterns of social development just outlined. We shall see that the three periods of childhood are quite distinct in terms of emotional development.

Early childhood. The first period is very emotional. Young children are highly labile emotionally, and the coordination of social interaction is a difficult accomplishment. Central to coordinating play are skills that have to do with learning emotional control. Our thinking here is consistent with that of Maccoby (1980), who described emotional control as the central theme of emotional socialization in young children. The concept of *affect regulation* has played a key role in writing about infant temperament and infant–caretaker relationships. It has played a key role in the theoretical writing on temperament of Buss and Plomin (1984) and of Rothbart and Derryberry (1981) (for a review see Goldsmith and Campos, 1982). Emotional regulation has also played a central role in neonatal assessment. The Brazelton test (Brazelton, 1973) includes such behavior as infants' self-quieting following distress. Brazelton has also written about infants' ability to organize themselves for social interaction (Brazelton, Koslowski, & Main, 1974). Rothbart and Derryberry's (1981) view of infant temperament is concerned with the reactivity of the nervous system and the self-regulation of reactivity. Examples of self-regulation in their theory are the channeling of attention and approach and avoidance.

Sroufe, Schork, Metti, Lawroski, and LaFreniere (1984) wrote about secure attachment and its consequence for preschool children. They emphasized the capacity for "maintaining organized behavior in the face of considerable arousal" (p. 293) and claimed that "regulation within the child-care giver dyad in infancy promotes the capacity for self-regulation in the preschooler" (p. 292). Sroufe emphasized the importance of affective regulation and control in the development of the child's social competence with peers (see also Sroufe, 1984). Furthermore, he argued that, if children do not learn emotional control, they will be unable to coordinate their play with another child, much in the same way that social-cognitive theorists (e.g., Selman, 1980) have suggested that mature perspective taking is a prerequisite of successful relationships. More specifically, in the context of friendship, emotional control is critical for the management of conflict, for without it coordinated play would be impossible. Thus, it is consistent with current speculation about social and affective development to suggest that the control of negative affect so that disagreements do not escalate is the major connection between the emotional and social realms. The control of negative affect must be learned in early childhood so that children will be able to engage in coordinated play with their peers. Much of this learning takes place in the peer friendship context, most of which is same sex. However, as we have observed (Chapter 4), the most emotionally laden interaction occurs in cross-sex friendship. In fact, differential emotional socialization of the sexes may be what splits cross-sex relationships at around the sixth year.

Middle childhood. The middle childhood period sees the rejection of sentiment and the overemphasis of reason and rationality. This aversion to sentimentality has often been attributed to boys. But we shall see, it need not be limited to boys. About three decades ago Stone and Church (1957) wrote that "no ten-year-old boy would be caught dead saying that he 'loved' anything" (p. 220). In Fine's (1981) discussion of the conversations of Little League middle childhood boys, he wrote that Stone and Church's quote was "confirmed by my observation that children who readily admit to affection become the objects of teasing or scorn" (p. 36). Fine noted that teasing and ritual insults (within informally established boundaries) characterized the boys' interaction and involved face saving and impression management.

The impression to be maintained is that of "being cool" – calm, unruffled, or always under emotional control. Most of children's humor during this period involves the appreciation of absurdity, puns, and delight over the irrational. McGhee (1979) noted that by the age of 7 children become fascinated by multiple meanings (as in puns or in jokes such as "Hey, did you take a bath?" "No. Why? Is one missing?") and riddle-type questions. McGhee wrote that middle childhood represents "the first sign of logic entering the humor process" (p. 77).

Technologies and organizational systems are very attractive to children of this age, and they have been described as rule-bound and rigid. Games, both organized and informal, become a major context for social interaction. The Opies' (e.g., Opie & Opie, 1959) work on organized games applies only to children in middle childhood.

Actually, it appears that not only the rules of the game but the very processes of negotiation are fascinating in middle childhood. Fine (1981) wrote that, between the ages of 7 and 10, children recognize that rules are regulators of others' behavior, but he noted that "although children claim that rules are absolute, in practice they are negotiated . . . by late preadolescence the negotiation of game rules provides almost as much interest as the game itself" (p. 38). Nonetheless, even if the picture of middle childhood's rigidity has been overdrawn, part of the appeal of games is their external structure, which is both absolute and permeable to modification within well-defined limits.

It seems reasonable to suggest, in building a theory of emotional development, that *the external structure becomes the substitute for the moment-by-moment management of emotion characteristic of young children, because the external structure is the vehicle for not being so controlled by the emotions.*

Adolescence. Adolescence witnesses the fusion of emotion and reason and the application of considerable cognitive powers, mainly toward figuring out the emotional world of interpersonal relationships. This emotional world has multiplied considerably in complexity since middle childhood through the new forms of cross-sex interaction that accompanies puberty. A significant change concerns gossip, which in adolescence can involve both positive and negative evaluations of the same thing. Adolescents can like parts of something and dislike other parts and still accept the whole. They are developing the same ability to like and dislike parts of themselves and still accept the whole. Social processes among adolescent friends involve endless reasoning about the world of emotions and personal relationships. Adolescents continually flirt with and play with the issues of loyalty and treachery, which in middle childhood were issues too complex to work with. Though the peer group is fluid, some friends of unquestioned loyalty are necessary for understanding change.

In adolescence the main goal of conversation is understanding the self in relation to others, and the tools for discussing this subject are considerable: (1) honesty among friends; (2) vulnerability in self-disclosures, that is, the sense of withholding nothing; (3) reciprocation of this risk in self-exploration; (4) being able and willing to solve problems, even if it requires being confronted by one's friend with "the brutal truth" about oneself and relentlessly carrying the personal reasoning to its ultimate conclusion (no matter how risky this may be).

We call this three-stage emotional view of childhood the "Star Trek theory," because one of the central themes of the television show was the fusion of rationality (the Vulcan side of Spock) and raw emotion (the emotional side of Spock and the great empathy and humanity of the doctor, Bones McCoy) into the balanced character of Captain Kirk.

One caution should be expressed. To characterize a period – for example, middle childhood – as concerned with gossip does not imply that gossip does not *occur* earlier or later, but simply that gossip is most salient during middle childhood and that other processes are in its service.

5.1. The salient social processes

In earlier chapters we gave a great deal of attention to the coordination of play in early childhood both among children becoming acquainted (Chapter 3) and among young friends (Chapter 4). Hence, we begin this section with a discussion of the middle childhood period, for which the salient social process is gossip.

Gossip

Gossip has a negative connotation in our society. It is usually associated with malicious intent and seen to be a social evil. There is no doubt that gossip has often been a social evil. This was certainly the case in post–Malleus Mallificarum Europe, in which neighbors bore witness to the Inquisition against witches, again in the New Salem witch trials, and most notably in such totalitarian regimes as Nazi Germany and Stalinist Russia, in which neighbor turned against neighbor in a reign of terror. However, Ting-Toomey (1979) noted that the term "gossip" actually derives from an old English contraction of "God plus sibb," implying a close relationship such as godparent. Only in the twentieth century has gossip taken on the connotation of small talk.

Gluckman (1971) viewed gossip as a social device for maintaining social boundaries between insiders and outsiders. It affirms the social norms and values of a particular network. However, the functions of gossip vary with developmental period. Gossip in early childhood usually has a "we against others" quality, so its major function is to build solidarity. For example, recall the conversation (Chapter 4) of two young friends, Matt and Jessica (ages 4 and 5 years), who expressed their anger at Jeffrey for putting a hole in Matt's cozy blanket and busting one of Jessica's pigeons.

In that conversation Matt and Jessica amplified and reflected one another's anger at Jeffrey, working themselves into a heated state, but very little happened beyond the solidarity implied by the "me too" climate. This is similar to the social process described in a film of Edward Mueller describing the social play of toddlers. As Mueller pointed out, for toddlers common ground is often literally that, namely, standing together in the same place or facing in the same direction. However, Matt and Jessica occupy the same *psychological* space, sharing the same affect directed at a third person, even finishing each other's sentences. Yet little else occurs.

To contrast the early childhood type of negative-evaluation gossip with the "same" process in middle childhood, we now present the conversation of a pair of 8-year-old best friends. This conversation illustrates the prevalence of gossip among children in middle childhood. It has the same "we against others" quality that exists to a small degree in conversations among young best friends. However, there is a crucial qualitative difference in gossip in middle childhood that is related to figuring out the norms of the group for peer acceptance. For example, it is important in the peer group of Erica and Mikaila not to be aggressive or bossy. To discuss this norm, these two girls use another girl, Katie, as the topic of negative-evaluation gossip:

E: Um, um Katie does lots of weird things. Like everytime she, we make a mistake, she says, "Well, *sorry*" [*sarcastic*].
M: I know.
E: And stuff like that.
M: She's mean. She beat me up once [*laughs*]. I could hardly breathe she hit me in the stomach so hard.
E: She acts like . . .
M: She's the boss.
E: "Now you do this." [Here we see fantasy as Katie is mimicked.]
M: "And I'll . . . "
E: "And Erica, you do this. And you substitute for the people that aren't here, Erica."
M: "And you do this, Mikaila. And you shouldn't do that, you shouldn't, you have to talk like this. You understand? Here, I'm the teacher here."
E: I know. She always acts like she's the boss.
M: So that's why we hid behind the sofa so she couldn't boss us around.

The gossip has a general shared negative evaluation that generalizes to Katie's character. This is important to note because it calls attention to the new *psychological* character of negative-evaluation gossip and the cross-situational generality of how one must act to avoid peer rejection. This developmental increase in psychological character has often been noted in research on social cognition (e.g., see Youniss, 1979).

M: She's mean.

E: No, she's mean.

M: Well, she is.

E: I know.

M: She says that she hates sugar and she eats it all the time. That's why she's so fat.

E: [*Laughter.*]

Their disapproval of Katie then moves to reestablishing their shared value of doing homework on time:

E: Katie said, "You better do your math assignment, guys."

M: Yeah, "Or else you're gonna get in trouble. What if there's a thunderstorm tomorrow? Or what if it snows?" And it can't snow in the summer.

E: I know. And, um, then she doesn't get *her* math done.

M: Yeah, and *she* gets in trouble.

E: Yeah, and she's the one that . . .

M: And she has to . . .

E: . . . says it.

M: Yeah, and she has to stay after school.

E: Yeah.

The two friends next enumerate a whole set of norms distinguished by their contempt for Katie's violation of these norms. We shall delineate these to dramatize the norm-setting function of negative-evaluation gossip.

1. *Not sharing*

    E: Oh, see, um, you know that tub she gave us for the spider?

    M: Yeah.

    E: She acts like she owns the whole thing.

    M: The whole spider.

    E: I know.

2. *Not taking responsibility for one's own actions*

    E: You know Elissa fed the spider two, two flies?

    M: Yeah. Katie let one out.

    E: She just went dunch and it went, and it buzzed out, you know?

    M: Yeah, she just . . .

    E: And she said . . .

    M: . . . she started . . .

    E: . . . "Katie, you left out one of the flies." And then she said, "Well, sooooory." Like she always does.

3. *Being a crybaby*

(a)   M: Yeah, and she always cries about little things. Right, Erica?

      E: Right, Mikaila?

      M: *Laughter.*

(b)   E: Katie at my birthday, Katie doesn't write very good.

      M: I know.

      E: She wrote this, um, thing to me and I couldn't read it so I gave it back to her and said I couldn't read it and she said, "Well, I can read yours" and she went off and cried just because I said I couldn't read her writing.

M: Yeah. She whines a lot.

E: And just because we won't eat with her because I wanna eat with you . . .

M: Yeah, she starts crying.

E: 'Cause she doesn't have anybody to eat with.

M: It's . . .

E: But there's thousands of people in the room to eat with.

M: Well she, she can eat with Charlotte but she just doesn't.

4. *Telling lies*

M: Katie said that her father child-abuses her . . .

E: And . . .

M: . . . and that she burned herself, that he burned her finger. This, this finger? This one right there? And, um, uh, about a week after I looked at her finger, this one? And it, and, and, there wasn't a burn. It was gone.

E: And remember she said that her father took a . . .

M: Hot . . .

E: . . . burning hot iron and put it on her . . .

M: back.

E: . . . and she said it was still there.

M: Yeah. And when she was wearing a one-piece bathing suit and she had to take it off, you, you looked on her back and there was nothing there.

E: No, it was just a plain back.

M: Yeah.

5. *Being a tattletale*

E: Katie's just a . . .

M: Tattletale.

E: Yeah, she tells on everything.

M: Yeah.

This conversation lasted about 45 minutes, and most of it consisted of negative-evaluation gossip and building solidarity. It was done light-heartedly and with ease. (The amount of ease and comfort with which any social process is performed at any age is indicative of competence.) The centrality of gossip is characteristic of the conversations of friends during middle childhood. The content of the gossip illustrates the relationship between this process and acceptance by peers. The objective seems to be to avoid being considered "weird."

The transition from fantasy to gossip

Fantasy has a characteristic shared by gossip. Fantasy makes it possible to project feelings that are difficult to admit onto another object. For example, the *doll* is afraid of the dark, not the child constructing the fantasy. This makes it easier to be distant from these feelings, *to avoid reexperiencing them* (we are indebted to P. Ekman for this suggestion), and perhaps even to assume a mastery role (the child can pretend to be the mommy comforting the frightened baby). It is then possible to explore a difficult feeling within a reasonably safe context. Gossip can play a similar role in terms of the projection of unacceptable feelings.

Gossip is especially likely to play this role during developmental transitions that witness a decline in fantasy play and the emergence of gossip on a grand scale. For example, in the following excerpt unacceptable sexual feelings are projected onto a third person through gossip and role playing:

M: Katie is gross, too. Once she went to my house.
E: Uh huh.
M: . . . to play and she says "Let's play Playboy" and I said, "No, that's too . . . " And I kept saying that and, and, and finally I don't know how she talked me into it and so she, she got undressed . . .
E: [*Laughs.*]
M: And I was a cameraman that pretended to take pictures like this [*pretends to roll a camera*].
E: Oh, gross [*laughs*].
M: And she went like [*plays with left breast*] feeling her . . . [*laughs*].
E: [*Laughs.*] And goes like this [*cheesecake pose*].
M: And she put her shirt above the toilet and it fell in [*laughs*].
E: [*Laughs.*] And then . . .
M: And then she wore it. And she said, "Ohh, [*inaudible*] peepers."
E: [*Laughs.*]
M: And then she goes like, she goes like this [*lifts leg and rubs her crotch*] [*laughs*].
E: [*Laughs.*] She goes like this [*rubs finger against side of nose*]. Ooooh, ooooh, ooooh, I got that itch.

It may be reasonable to hypothesize that *as new processes become salient developmentally, they temporarily serve the function of previously salient social processes*. This may ease the transition to a new developmental stage. We shall see this again in adolescence, when self-disclosure and problem solving are the salient social processes. In adolescence, self-disclosure performs some of the functions that gossip serves in middle childhood, namely, providing solidarity.

Self-disclosure and problem solving

Both gossip and self-disclosure among adolescents are in the service of relentless analysis and solving problems about emotional situations in personal relationships, all of which have to do with the goal of understanding the self. The following segment from the conversation of two 16-year-old friends illustrates that gossip is intricately tied with self-disclosure and followed by problem solving:

L: But the thing is, if my parents go to Panama in the middle of July, I won't; then I'll be missing the last two weeks of summer school. If I have to go . . .

R: Then, then, then you can't go.

L: I know that's the thing, that's what I been trying to. God, it's a hard decision. I don't know which would be better, going to Panama, I mean, 'cause I don't know when I'll get a chance to go to Panama again, or just to stay here and get away from my parents for a while because I really need to.

Next R does something that children almost never do in early or middle childhood. She asks some questions in an attempt to understand the nature of the problem:

R: If you went to Panama would you be, would you be around your parents more or less?

L: Oh, constantly.

R: When you go on vacations with them, do you get along with them very well?

L: I do, yeah; it's real amazing whenever we go on vacation . . .

R: It might be good for you.

L: That's what I was thinking, you know. I don't know.

The result is a real insight into the problem. R then explains her line of questioning in terms of her own experience with *her* parents. Notice that she is comfortable about being different from her friend, something difficult for young children in their need to establish a "me too" climate of agreement.

R: 'Cause, see, when I go on vacation with my parents, I do *not* get along with them.

L: Really?

R: 'Cause I feel stuck with them and I just feel more imprisoned than I ever do. And I just sit there [*laugh*].

L: It's so funny. You know, whenever my parents are away from everything, it's like, we all really have compatible personalities, you know. It's real nice when we go on trips, you know, 'cause I always feel so close to 'em. But like whenever, whenever I'm just at home, just because they just resent it a lot that I do lots of things outside the house and you know they just want me to stay home and I don't and I'm not going to either, you know, and it's not, it's not. The thing is they, they take it personally, you know. They think that I'm getting away from them. And I'm not and that's like the basis of like why we've been getting along so horribly lately. Just because they think I'm trying to get away from them.

R: I know, that's why I had to leave because I was never at home anyway 'cause I have a job and I go to school, and I never am at home period. And I just couldn't stay. But we went out for dinner the night before I left.

L: Did you?

R: Yeah.

L: Oh, that's nice. With your whole family?

R: Me and my mom and my dad. And surprisingly we had a *great time* [*laugh*].

L: Really? Where'd you go?

R: I was so surprised. We went to the Red Wheel.

L: Ooh, great.

The groundwork has been laid for this individuation in the context of friendship in middle childhood. We shall return to this point later. Notice that the self-disclosure, though in a sense reciprocal, is not temporally immediate, and, more important, it is in the service of the all-important analysis and problem solving.

Changing developmental functions of gossip

Although it is possible to code reliably a segment of conversation as gossip, this does not imply that it is, in effect, the same social process at different points in development. Indeed, it is contextualized by the functions it serves. We shall outline some hypotheses about this developmental trajectory for this important social process.

Functions of gossip in young childhood. As we have discussed, among young children gossip serves a primary role in promoting solidarity, a "we against others" climate of agreement that is necessary for the maintenance of coordinated play.

Functions of gossip in middle childhood. Among friends in middle childhood, *gossip is the thing.* Most gossip involves negative evaluation of specific people, and it leads to solidarity between friends of the "we against others" variety. As with Erica and Mikaila, it centers on norms and normative behavior and on behaviors to be avoided in order to be accepted by peers.

Acceptance is not the *stated* objective. Rather, the central objective of gossip-oriented discussions seems to be to avoid embarrassment. Embarrassment is often the main topic of self-disclosure in middle childhood. Embarrassing situations involve being noticed and exposed. They usually involve being "uncool" and stared at. They need *not* involve being seen as incompetent. Almost anything has the potential to become an embarrassing social event, such as spilling a soft drink, wearing the "wrong" clothes, sitting with the "wrong" person, or even being seen buying a bra. The goal in most situations is to give the impression of being in emotional control, unruffled, and even. Avoidance of embarrassment is thus concerned with appearing to be unemotional, which is consistent with the theory of social–emotional development we have been developing.

Concern with avoiding embarrassment is associated, in part, with the onset of puberty, which some children in this age group experience earlier than others, but which most are aware of:

A: You know what Mom did? . . . Everytime I go shopping with my mom and we're looking to a bra [*laughs*] she takes the bra rack and picks one of them. "Would this look good on you, Julie?" And everyone's staring at you [*laugh*]. So embarrassing.
B: My mom always pulls the rack and holds them up to me.

Related to the potential embarrassment of puberty's onset are cross-sex relationships during this period. These have progressed beyond the run, chase, and pollution games Thorne (1984) described, which are characteristic of 7- and 8-year-olds. Girls openly discuss boyfriends, often in ways that are intended to reveal how casual these relationships are. Teasing often involves cross-sex relationships. For example:

A: How's Lance [*giggle*]? Has he taken you to a movie yet?
B: No. Saw him today but I don't care.
A: Didn't he say anything to you?
B: Oh . . .
A: Lovers!
B: Shut up!
A: Lovers at first sight! [*Giggle.*]
B: [*Giggle.*] Quit it!

Some of the humor of this period involves ritual insults, some of which employ references to emerging sexual development. For example, two girls used the expression "titless tit" as an insult; Erica and Mikaila used "bosom" as an insult. In another interaction a girl teased her friend about having a baby with her boyfriend, which shows how the awareness of puberty is intricately connected to cross-sex relationships during this age span.

Even if friends do not tease one another about cross-sex relationships, they refer to them in gossip. In that context, these children rarely admit that they are intensely sentimental. For example, one girl discusses the note writing of the day:

A: I went note crazy today [*laughs*]. I must have written 20 notes today . . .

She then reads the notes to her friend, explaining the author and context of each note. In the process, she comes across a note in which a girl says that she likes B's boyfriend.

B: She likes him?
A: Yeah. Oh, I wasn't supposed to tell you that. So just forget it [*laugh*].
B: I wouldn't get mad. He likes Lucy.
A: He does? If he breaks up with you because of Lucy I will be so mad.

Whether boy-/girlfriend relationships are actually this casual is unclear. What is clear is that being openly emotional about these relationships is to be avoided.

Girlfriends however, endlessly discuss whether specific boys are cute. In these discussions one sees, at times, an emergence from the previous boy-hating period. For example, in the following excerpt two girls are discussing boys in their band:

A: Yeah. I don't, I don't, I hate being surrounded by guy drummers. It's just . . .
B: Guys are asses.
A: Unless they're cute. Well, you know . . .
B: [*Giggle.*]

Sometimes it is easier for children to talk about their sexual feelings if they make the conversation more abstract by discussing television, movie, or rock stars and their styles (speaking, dressing, acting). The safety provided by such a conversation is similar to that provided by projection in fantasy play (e.g., "The doll is afraid of the dark, not me"). We thus see that a new salient social process assumes some of the functions of the old one (fantasy). In adolescence one task is accepting diverse people, because it is related to the task of accepting diverse and contradictory parts of one's self. In middle childhood, children are generally unable to do this; they consider it a logical contradiction, hypocritical, and unacceptable. In adolescence this ability to see seemingly contradictory elements as parts of the same whole is related to the integration of logic with the emotions. Because middle childhood involves a denial of sentimentality, this integration is generally difficult.

As we have noted, gossip during middle childhood can assume some of the functions of fantasy. This seems to be a principle of developmental transitions – namely, *salient social processes do not disappear; rather, they are reorganized in the service of new salient processes.* For example, in the following excerpt, middle childhood children are drawing, and both activity talk (narrating one's actions) and fantasy are enlisted in the service of gossip:

A: This is the way I draw Gale, as a fish 'cause I don't like Gale. So, do you?
B: I guess not.
A: And I think Gale is one of those ugly fish that go to the bottom of the sea and that's where they should stay.
B: Uh huh.
A: This is one of them, but this is the prettier one of them.
B: I think I know what you're doing but I'm not sure.
A: The big black hole's right here.
B: Is this kinda like what you're doing? I didn't do it very well, but is this like what you're doing?
A: Yay.

B: OK.
A: Here is the black hole in space. Gale's mouth.

This is not to suggest that fantasy never occurs during middle childhood, but its occurrence is rare and usually in the context of a game with well-defined rules. We know of two friends and a brother who consistently played a game of king, queen, and slave in 500 B.C. In this game, whenever anyone did anything wrong, he or she would be killed. In Chapter 4, we suggested that cross-sex interaction among friends in middle childhood may be in the service of prolonging fantasy play.

A concern with perfection and purity seems to be a corollary of the merciless application of logic and reason in this period. For example, children have become aware of hypocrisy and stereotyping and reject it in all forms. In the following excerpt two friends discuss a story one has been writing:

A: And they wear these flowing white garments, and they smile and they love and they're so perfect in every respect. Now I gotta do something because, I mean it's just like a paradise. What I mean is . . .
B: Well, I do . . .
A: . . . is this a paradise never to be touched by the world?

In discussing the book *The Diary of Anne Frank*, two friends explore the Germans' hatred of Jews and decide that this hatred was caused by impoverished Germans' envying the wealth of some Jews:

A: Well, not *all* Jews lived in these well-to-do families in these well-to-do houses in these beautiful mansions and everything.
B: So if just, if just one of them did, the Germans could say, "Look at them" and just . . .
A: Then he happens to be a Jew, he happens to be *different* from us, and he has this and that, so that means that *all* Jews. That was stereotyping.

In applying logical reasoning to human behavior these two have discovered culture, the relativism of mores, and the invention that creates culture.

A: So you know how for years cultures have invented religions and things and worshipped things and invented things to explain natural happenings.

With these discoveries come doubt and skepticism, which are also applied to the identification of self with particular peer subgroups:

A: I don't have the qualities that general Calvin Kleiners [children who wear jeans designed by Calvin Klein] do and I don't get any security from the label. I just wear them as a pair of pants that keep me warm, and it's very obscene to go nude.
B: [*Laughs.*]

Fortunately, with this unrelenting purity comes some self-reflection. We see here the beginnings of the adolescent's concern with self:

B: You are not classified as a Calvin Kleiner because you don't have any snooty, snobbish qualities.
A: [*Laughs.*]
B: [*Laughs.*] Even though you're sometimes, you are a little snobby.
A: I put on airs.

It is evident in this period that even self-disclosure is of a particular form, again in the service of gossip and solidarity. For example, in the following excerpt, Mom's lectures are the subject of self-disclosure.

A: Whenever my mom gets mad at me, like she says, "Jane." When she starts bawling me out, I mean, she doesn't do it very often, but once in a while she gets so, I don't know, she's in a bad mood and we haven't done our homework or something.
B: Oh, I know.
A: And she'll go through "What's gonna happen to you when you get older?"
B: [*Laughs.*]
A: And you don't, you don't have any good grades, college grades or anything. And that gets me so, makes me feel so guilty and everything.
B: I know. I hate when my mom goes crazy.
A: [*Laughs.*]
B: She does any little thing and she goes crazy, starts screaming and yelling. Oh, I hate it too. Once, um, I was setting the table and didn't set it just right . . . and she started screaming at me because I didn't put the fork on the napkin . . . God, [*laugh*] what a stupid reason to get mad.

The discussion here involved no problem solving, no exploration of the problem, or resolution. The topic was subsequently dropped, apparently having adequately been dealt with by the creation of solidarity. This is a difference between the conversations of middle childhood friends and those of adolescents.

Children's expression in middle childhood of their new-found awareness of cultural relativism and arbitrariness of all norms at times entails a mocking attitude toward the world of adults. Their insight puts them above it all. They feel they can choose how to act; they need not be trapped by arbitrary, trivial standards the way adults are. In conversation we see the early childhood social process of *shared deviance* (see Gottman & Parkhurst, 1980) taking on a new function. In addition to the excitement and solidarity, as well as the license to be naughty and risk-taking, that it gives to young children, in middle childhood shared deviance has new power. In this period, children's logic allows them choice; they can remain unruffled by the relative, arbitrary, and trivial world of adults.

Gossip among strangers in middle childhood. Gossip is so important during middle childhood that its success may determine whether two strangers "hit it off." It is remarkable that two people who do not know each other and know no people in common can *base* their interaction on gossip. This fact is extremely revealing about this period of development. Gossiping involves shared negative evaluations of stereotypes – for example, about teachers:

A: If they could teach what they wanted to teach, they'd teach how to sleep.
B: [*Giggle.*]
A: They're really bored with school.
B: Hum um.

This negative evaluation of stereotypes is pervasive. Consider the following humorous excerpt:

B: My class is a turnoff; talk about the same things every day. I sit next to a creep.
A: Don't we all.

An example of a stereotype that children gossip about is a physical education teacher who is a "male chauvinist pig." Through shared negative-evaluation gossip, similarity and solidarity are established, as shown by the following excerpt:

A: I have a dumb teacher. She goes, "Well, I'd like to try your muffins but I have no sense of taste." I'm going [*makes a disgusted face*].
B: [*Giggle.*]
A: I mean you could tell by her clothes that she had no sense of taste . . . [*Later.*] Yeah, my teacher she shows the dumbest movies. We, Friday we saw a movie about how bread gets moldy. She wants to teach us all about, um, calories and stuff and she's so fat you can tell she needs to learn more than us.
B: [*Giggle.*]
A: There's not a fat person in the class, except for the teacher.
B: [*Giggle.*] About the most sophisticated foreign language teacher we have is our French teacher.
A: I can't stand it.
B: Oh, and she's always going, I say, "Hi, Miss Rickey" and she goes, "Bonjour" [giggles].
A: [*Giggle.*]
B: I was walking down steps and I almost fell. I was cracking up. I was going, "OK, whatever you say."
A: Ours is a mean French teacher and she goes, OK I was, I was writing a note to my friend, and she goes, "Are you doing your homework?" And I go, "No" and she goes, "Ah, ah, ah." You know, I mean I can't take this little kid stuff.
B: It's so pitiful to see the teachers.
A: Uh huh.

In successful acquaintanceship there is a continual exchange of tales of shared deviance that might be called "weird stories" (e.g., a tale of one boy who said, "Cheetos make you fart"), which leave the two acquaintances convulsed by laughter. They share a vision of the nearly absolute absurdity of social situations they encounter. The sense of the absurd develops in this period of life. J. Dunn (personal communication, 1979) has suggested that a sense of the absurd should be one of the major goals of development.

Self-disclosure comes on the heels of this stereotyped negative-evaluation gossip. For example:

A: We went to Florida for spring break and it's pretty nice down there now.
B: So did my sister's friend. Oh, I hate her so much; she acts like she's something hot.

Even information exchange is reorganized to serve the function of solidarity in the face of adverse conditions; for example, one pair of children discussed the fact that they both had cockroaches in their classes.

Gossip is often a precursor of self-disclosure, as the following excerpt of a conversation between two female strangers who know the same boy, Chip Buckley, illustrates:

A: Is Chip Buckley still short?
B: Yes, he is, very short.
A: [*Giggle.*]
B: Everybody says he comes out of a jar.
A: Oh.
B: It's because . . .
A: We used to call him Cookie Buckley. Don't tell him this, but I kinda miss him.
B: You, did you used to like him?
A: No, but you know it's boring without him.
B: Hmm.

Functions of gossip and self-disclosure in adolescence. In adolescence the exploration of self becomes the primary goal, and the process of self-disclosure is at the hub of our imaginary wheel.

Among friends. Adolescents' conversations with friends are characterized by the application of logic and psychological analysis to interpersonal events. The concern is with emotional self-understanding and self-disclosure. Honesty is a necessary concomitant of these discussions. Intimacy is only a secondary goal among close friends; intimacy is maintained in the service of self-exploration. Self-disclosure does not have to be immediately reciprocated, as demonstrated by the conversation cited earlier in this chapter in which R muses over a possible trip to Panama with her parents. In that conversation self-disclosure was reciprocated only in the service of problem solving (explaining a line of questioning). Dindia's (1982) work on the absence of temporal reciprocity of self-disclosure supports this observation.

Two friends may analyze a social interaction and employ relationship-talk statements, self-disclosure, similarities, amity, and mindreading all for the purpose of analyzing self. In the following excerpt two friends discuss how *both* of them typically overreact.

A: You know, and the way I reacted, I go, *"What?"* You know, *"What!"* I was getting mad, you know, and I was like, I mean, it didn't matter or anything, but I really don't do that usually.

B: Uh huh.

A: I usually ask a question, "Oh, really?" Or ask why . . . and you do that sometimes.

B: [*Laughs.*]

A: You do that really.

B: What, really?

A: You just like, "Oh, my God," you know, and I mean it's not bad . . .

B: Panic.

A: Yah, kind of a panic kind of a thing, exactly. Not that you are . . .

B: Uh huh.

A: But I do that too.

B: Probably one of the things you've picked up. You know, isn't it weird how you pick up things though?

This interaction is so intricate that an attempt to characterize it in terms of the MACRO coding system with a few sequences would be hopelessly foiled.

Much of the conversation involves comparison and analysis of interpersonal styles in the context of amity. Gossip still plays a vital role in this self-analysis, but its function has been reorganized. The purpose of middle childhood gossip is managing the same-sex group's norms about inclusion and exclusion. It promotes solidarity (we against others). Although similar in adolescence, gossip is only the appetizer on the menu; the main course is psychological exploration of the self. Two friends discuss this point:

A: But also, like, we were, remember in the park we saying how it's good to just talk about people, because then you can find out whether you want to be like that . . .

B: Right, right.

A: At least I can think, "Well, boy, I know I do not want to be that." And so . . .

B: Right, that's true . . . I'll listen to people on the bus and they'll be talking about . . . Oh, God, what jerks.

A: Ya, why are they just talking about other people?

B: I hate them.

A: Why don't they just talk about their own lives, you know?

B: Right, right. But then it's true everybody does it, and it is because you learn so much by talking about other people.

A: Yah, plus it's fun just to find out, plus find out what the other person thinks.

B: Really.
A: That's how you get your values too.

Once again we see that the same social process serves two very different objectives at two different points in development.

There are a number of social implications of solving problems about emotions that imply different functions of friendship in adolescence. For example, adolescent friends look to one another for help in getting over bad moods. This is a new function of the friendship and a by-product of being able to solve problems about affect. One friend confided that she had been feeling "lost" for several weeks, apparently because she had broken up with her boyfriend:

A: Throw the phone down and run back to John. I don't know about that. I've been wandering around sort of feeling kinda lost.
B: [*Giggle.*] Yeah.
A: People look at me, "What's the matter, Judy?" Oh, I don't know [*resignedly*] . . .
B: You are coping with things much better than I did, though [*giggle*], I must say.

The friends then discussed knowing that the breakup was inevitable and that the aftereffect would not last forever. The conversation provided a way of coping with loss and sadness.

In adolescence, friends also seem capable of confronting one another. They do this by mindreading, and it demonstrates an intimate caring. For example:

A: You missed two weeks of school.
B: I know. That's what Dad said. He said, "I guess London didn't help your grades," and I said . . .
A: No, and then you came back and were depressed and that didn't help school too much either. I mean, not wanting to be there doesn't help things at all . . .
B: I've got to get my grades up . . .
A: You're allowed only one B this quarter.
B: Yep . . .
A: You work your tail off in English.
B: Yeah. I'll get an A in English now.
A: OK.
A: [That bad grade] was your fault.
B: [*Giggle.*]
A: Because you were a stubborn little twit [*jokingly*].

The very confrontation and honesty represent a communication of intimacy among adolescent friends.

There is also concern in adolescence with maintaining the intimacy of friendship, and this becomes a legitimate *topic* of conversation. Whereas young children can at times metacommunicate (comment about the processes of interaction), it is in the service of conflict management, which is in the service of maintaining coordinated play. Recall the 4-year-old who said she was being bossy and that she would not be bossy anymore. This served to deescalate conflict. In adolescence, metacommunication maintains intimacy, which is partly in the service of the goal of self-exploration in the context of a relationship. In turn, the intimacy of friendship in adolescence is a safe base for self-exploration. For example:

A: I feel kinda icky about the past two weeks . . .
B: What? What in the past two weeks do you feel icky about?
A: It was like "Hi, Jane," "Hi, Suzie" [*giggle*], you know [*giggle*].
B: Yeah.
A: "Hi, Jane," "Hi, Suzie."
B: We didn't communicate. I haven't been communicating with much of anybody . . .
A: I understand that, but I felt like, you know, Janet was . . .
B: Janet had taken your place.
A: Yeah, that's what I felt like.
B: Janet's not gonna take your place, kiddo [*sigh*]. How many times do I have to tell you that?
A: I'm insecure, you know.
B: I know.

The issue is raised and explored, and reassurance is offered, after self-disclosure. However, it is important to recall that the major function of friendship in adolescence is self-exploration. There is a great deal of discussion of self in the context of gossip and self-disclosure. For example, in the following excerpt about a former boyfriend, the topic becomes one's morality and the processes are self-disclosure and social comparison:

A: [*joking*]: I think you should take Randy to court for statutory rape.
B: I don't. I'm to the point of wondering what "that kind of girl" . . . I don't know about the whole scene.
A: The thing is . . .
B: It depends on the reasoning. And how long you've been going out with somebody.
A: Yeah. I'm satisfied with my morals.
B: As long as you're satisfied with your morals, that's cool.
A: Yeah, but other people . . .
B: And I'm pretty, I'm pretty sturdy in mine.
A: Yeah [*giggle*], I know that. Mine tend to bend too easily.

In adolescence, friends help each other deal with anxiety about future plans by approaching the issue philosophically:

A: I don't know. Gosh, I have no idea what I want to do. And it really doesn't bother me that much that I don't have my future planned [*laughs*].
B: [*Laughs.*]

A: [*Laughs.*] Like, it bothers my dad a lot, but it doesn't bother me.
B: Just tell your dad what I always tell my dad: "Dad, I *am.*"
A: [*Laughs.*] Exactly.
B: "And whatever happens tomorrow, I *still* will be!"

There is also an ability to reflect on relationships themselves and the social processes involved. Although even young children can metacommunicate in the service of resolving conflict and maintaining coordinated play, they actually do this quite rarely. This is not the case for adolescents. They discuss relationships often and with great enthusiasm. In the following excerpt two friends joke about the enterprise of getting to know a new boyfriend:

A: I can't handle any more [boyfriends].
B: Yes, you can.
A: [*Laugh.*] OK, I'll try.
B: Five more. I want that blondie.
A: He's cute, but he could be a real jerk. You never know.
B: You have to find out.
A: You better find out.
B: "Hi. Are you a jerk?"

Friends in adolescence discuss their feelings about dating relationships. For example, one girl talked about a dinner date she had had:

A: Dinner was fun. We just sat there and talked and, um, we have a *whole* lot in common. That's the only thing. I mean, it'd be better if we were just friends; we get along so well. The only time we don't get along is when we're being like girlfriend and boyfriend relationship, like when we're talking on the phone, and like "Well, who else are you gonna go out with?"
B: [*Laughs.*]
A: And stuff like that.
B: "Oh, five other guys."
A: Which we haven't . . . mentioned since that very first time.

The concern that adolescent friends have with the processes of their relationships is apparent in their relentless examination of the friendship itself. For example:

A: I mean I play mother enough on you [*giggle*] . . . I mean you got back from England and you were upset.
B: Yeah . . .
A: . . . You needed it.
B: Yeah, I guess that makes sense.

Negative-evaluation gossip has a different function in adolescence than in middle childhood. At the outset, it is considerably more psychological. Moreover, it is in the service of self-exploration.

A: I can't stand the way she just plays games so bad with all her boyfriends.
B: And they take it.
A: Uh, they play 'em right back. That's the thing. "I wanna see other people." "Oh no, please don't see other people. I love you, I love you."

B: [*Laughs.*]
A: . . . and then the other one does it next week.

Because adolescents are reflective, they discuss social processes directly, which demonstrates a high level of abstract reasoning about social events.

Among strangers. When adolescent strangers hit it off, several types of social events occur. Foremost among these is self-exploration. Various social processes in adolescence are organized around this event. For example, in the following information exchange the purpose is self-exploration. The discussion is ostensibly about jobs the strangers have had, but note how the theme of L's impatience emerges:

R: I worked last summer in a camp for kids with muscular dystrophy.
L: Oh, really?
R: [*Nods.*] And that was real neat.
L: Oh – hmm . . .
R: So I don't know if Special Ed with physically handicapped or what, but I want to work with kids.
L: Oh huh . . .
R: I think it's fun.
L: That's good, that's really good. I think, I don't know, I'm not very patient.
R: [*Giggle.*]
L: I would not be good at that I think.

Exploration of the theme of L's impatience continues as the strangers discuss being aunts and their sisters' pregnancies. L talks about her baby niece:

L: She's so spoiled and gets her way. That's another one that I get impatient with, you know; she's so sweet and everything.
R: Uh huh.
L: I love to hold her. And then when she starts crying, I just can't . . .
R: You want to give her back.
L: I know. I wanna, humm, I would give her to my sisters and stuff whenever she cried. I'm very impatient. But one of these days I'll have to learn my lesson [*giggle*].
R: [*Giggle.*]
L: Either that or never have kids.
R: [*Giggle.*]

In many discussions, defining self is a "hidden agenda." For example, a discussion between two strangers about their older siblings was actually a discussion of their difficulties defining themselves as individuals; a discussion of territory (separate bedrooms) was a veiled discussion of individuality.

Another change since middle childhood is the fair amount of *positive-*evaluation gossip, unlike middle childhood's disdain for practically everything. Only some of this change is accounted for by the new appropriateness of admitting sexual attraction, which in middle child-hood is the subject of relentless teasing. Much of the change involves an attempt to have a balanced view of people.

Nonetheless, some of the shift to positive-evaluation gossip involves the admission and frank discussion of interest in the opposite sex. This is particularly evident in adolescent girls' discussions of boys and rock musicians. In the following excerpt two girls discuss a boy whom one of them finds sexually attractive.

R: He's cute.
L: Yeah, my friend likes him.
R: Really?
L: Yeah, she has the hots for him. Saw him last night. She's like "hmmm."
R: So do I.

Discussing sexual interests is a good way for adolescent female strangers to hit it off. In the following excerpt two girls discuss a local, successful rock group and a television documentary that appeared about the group:

R: They just talked to the four guys. I don't know that one of the guys is twenty-four. They're all real old, I think, like twenty-four or something, you know . . .
L: Is Gregory Ware cute? . . .
R: He looks cute in the, um, movie . . .
L: documentary but I really like him . . .
R: I know when I first saw him . . . 'cause he asked my friend out . . .
L: What was he like?
R: And they were going out and then he was really cute. We were all going, "God, who is that guy?" 'Cause he, you know, he's asking her what, asking us what our phone numbers are and we're all going, "God, he is so cute." Why, I don't know. He's OK.
L: He's turned punk now.
R: Yeah.
L: Yeah, I heard.

This is positive-evaluation gossip of a stereotyped figure.

Even negative-evaluation gossip at times has a positive ending. The beginning of the following excerpt is reminiscent of middle childhood's negative-evaluation gossip. Note, however, how the conversation even-tually changes (see asterisk). The universal middle childhood theme of embarrassment opens this adolescent conversation:

L: I told his sister . . . Oh, your brother's cute . . . and he came into the shop and they say, "Oh yeah, this is Nadine. She's your admirer" and every-thing. And I was sitting there.
R: That [was] not the guy?
L: That [was] not the guy. And I couldn't say it. I said, "Oh, yeah, I went to your street dance" and everything. And I was so embarrassed. And I wish I hadn't said I was his admirer.

R: While you were standing right there. That's mean, to say *that*.
L: I know.
R: I hate people who do that.
L: You're like, "Shut up."
R: I know, and you *don't* wanna say, "No, I'm not." So you go, "Thanks a lot" [*giggle*].
*L: [*Giggle.*] But I thought that was embarrassing. But then I started thinking he was kinda cute.
R: Well he's really nice though. He's real nice.
L: He's funny.
R: Yeah.

The following excerpt shows the same pattern of gossip about a stereotype group; once again, the asterisk marks a change from negative to positive evaluations of people:

R: Paula's kinda husky and short, and, you know . . .
L: Really. But, um, she's real moody.
R: Really.
L: Like, you know, you'll think she's mad at you, you know, she'll change.
R: Yeah.
L: And she's not really mad, mad at you or something.
R: [*Giggle.*]
L: And it's really weird. And she smokes cigarettes weird. I mean she smokes in the shop and she kinda I don't know, she [*blows*].
R: Yeah, they're all like that. They're kinda, they're all kinda weird.
*L: Yeah, I know but they're nice.
R: Yeah.
L: You know, when you talk to them.
R: Yeah, they're nice [*giggle*].
L: [*Giggle.*]

This presentation of two sides of someone or a group is not to imply that negative-evaluation gossip does not still play a role in acquaintance-ship in adolescence. In the following excerpt two girls discuss the current girlfriend of a boy one of them (L) is attracted to. What is slightly different about this excerpt is the vague psychological musing of L at the end:

R: We don't like her . . .
L: Oh [*giggle*].
R: [*Giggle.*]
L: I heard, Marsha says, she goes, "Well, it's hard. She's different. She's unique."
R: Yeah.
L: That's what she said about her.
R: She's real; she acts like they're in love and everything. Like she'll go around and kiss him at times, you know, when you would not kiss . . .
L: She's older than him, right?
R: She's older than him . . .
L: What does he see in her?
R: I don't know [*giggle*].

L: [*Giggle.*] That's a question, you know, when you see a guy, what does he see in her?

This philosophical musing does not accompany all negative-evaluation gossip of adolescents. We do not mean to suggest that there is any diminution of negative-evaluation gossip. For example, the following excerpt could have come from the conversation of two middle childhood girls:

L: Yeah, it was a fun game, except for, ah, we had all these old people sitting behind us, kept telling us to sit down.
R: Oh, man.
L: And it was like "Fine, find your seat" [*giggle*].
R: I know. Our, our games, it's always like sit down.
L: I know.
R: I can't see.
L: It's like sit, sit down [*giggle*]. I mean, damn! We only go to high school four years.
R: Yeah.
L: We might as well enjoy it [*giggle*].

Sensitivity and empathy are characteristic of the conversations of adolescent strangers who hit it off. For example, one of the girls in the following excerpt does not have a date for an important dance. She asks the other girl if *she* has a date.

L: Yeah [*giggle*]. I'm one of the last-minute ones. I don't even know if I'll like him or not, but that's . . .
R: Oh well, you'll have a good time.
L: It's all right though. He's not exactly let's get serious or anything.

This is quite typical. In fact, this empathy often accompanies *low-intimacy* self-disclosure. In the following excerpt two cheerleaders commiserate with one another because one is in a group that is not very cohesive; cheerleaders in her group often fight and several have quit:

L: You're kidding, they quit?
R: Yeah. They just wanted to do other things.
L: I haven't heard of people quitting. I didn't think, we never had anyone quit.
R: Really?
L: Ever.
R: It was weird, because each game we lost girls cheerleading.
L: That would be weird. Really?
R: It was weird.

This empathy leads R to a self-disclosure that involves what, for her, is a disappointment:

R: One thing about our school. It's a dud.
L: Really.
R: It's totally dead because I don't know . . . nobody ever.
L: Nobody responds.
R: No, huh uh.

L: I kinda noticed that.

A climate of intimacy is created in this conversation that leads to a self-disclosure when L discusses her large family:

L: I'm the youngest. It's a big family. Catholics [*giggle*], those Catholics, you know, reproductive . . .
R: I couldn't handle it myself, if I was the mother [*giggle*].
L: I know I couldn't. I don't know how I could. I think, you know, my mom's insane. She should be insane.

We would fail to convey the spirit of acquaintanceship in adolescents if we did not mention the occasional exaggerated affect of incredulous amazement. As embarrassment was a stylistic theme of middle childhood, surprise is a theme of adolescence. To write a script of adolescent acquaintanceship, one would have to include occasional excerpts such as the following. The topic is not sensationally intimate, but the overacted affect that accompanies it is. In order for surprise to work in acquaintanceship, it must be mirrored by the listener. In this conversation, R and L are discussing older friends who have left for college.

R: It's hard to get used to when they leave. It's really weird.
L: I know. I know it. I, just about two days ago one of 'em called me. She goes to Kentucky.
R: Oh really?
L: Uh huh. I mean she was like my sister, you know, another sister to me 'cause, you know . . .
R: [*Giggle.*]
L: She was so much older and we must have talked an hour long.
R: Oh really?
L: Oh gosh, I thought I was gonna die it was so long. Man, the bill's probably gonna be a million dollars.

Although the words themselves cannot entirely capture this characteristic of adolescent conversation, they do convey something of the flavor.

5.2. Relationship of model to cognitive and social-cognitive literatures

Relationship to cognitive development

Keating (1980) reviewed research on adolescent thinking in terms of the development of formal operational thought. He highlighted four categories of formal thought: (1) thinking about possibilities (as opposed to realities in the here and now); (2) thinking through hypotheses, particularly the interpropositional thinking of formal logic; (3) thinking ahead; and (4) thinking about the process of thinking. Keating also added a broad category he called "thinking beyond old limits," which included attempts "to make sense of all aspects of experience" (p. 215).

> Perhaps the best way to characterize this change is as a general broadening of horizons on all dimensions. Issues that have never or rarely been considered by the adolescent will take on enlarged significance and meaning. Topics of identity, society, existence, religion, justice, morality, friendship, and so on, are examined in detail and are contemplated with high emotion as well as increased cognitive capacity [p. 215].

We can see from this passage that to convey the spirit of adolescence, it is not enough to characterize thought in terms of formal operations. It is necessary to enter the realm of affect. It appears to be virtually impossible to describe adolescents in any other way. The question is one of emphasis. In writings about adolescent cognition, the awareness of thinking is the basis for "deriving" the adolescent's preoccupation with understanding the self. For example, Elkind (1981) employed Flavell's (e.g., see Flavell, 1977) notions of metacognitive processes to derive the increased introspection of adolescents.

We find it somewhat a strain to make a clear conceptual bridge from the standard Piagetian tasks that measure formal operational thought to the problem solving we have seen in these conversations. Nonetheless, our observations are reasonably consistent with the cognitive developmental literature.

The fascination with logic and the denial of sentimentality by which we characterized middle childhood is a new characterization (or perhaps a shift in emphasis) of that period. However, it is consistent with research on middle childhood. For example, Hartup (1970) described one Piagetian stage of social development, from about 5 to 8 years, in terms of "increasingly explicit and rigid conformity to social norms" (p. 407). Hartup wrote that a

> . . . marked change in the child's orientation to rules begins to occur at about age 10. He begins to perceive rules as human artifacts, emanating from a variety of persons. . . . Further, rules are no longer external and coercive [p. 407].

These observations are, in broad outline, consistent with our discussion.

We will not discuss here whether research evidence supports Piaget's theory or these general observations. It has become popular to devise research paradigms demonstrating that children have competencies much earlier than Piaget suspected. However, R. Parke observed (1984, personal communication) that notions of children's competence should be based on the ease of performance of a skill and its integration into the child's entire repertoire. He noted that in some ways research in cognitive development has become a science based on counterexample studies. These studies often show that a child is capable of demonstrating a particular competence earlier than Piaget suspected, if special laboratory conditions are set up so that the child's familiarity, comfort, or pretrain requisite subskills are maximized. Parke noted that one cannot base a theory of development on counterexample studies. One cannot conclude that qualitative changes in competence do not occur. In many ways, Parke argued for what Patterson (1982) termed a *performance* theory. We are interested in the child's focal concerns, what the child does characteristically, with ease, and how this is organized with respect to other processes in the child's repertoire.

We must be very careful not to assume that we are describing biological maturation here. It is quite easy to see the fallacy of this assumption by remembering that the kind of reasoning that Piaget suggested characterizes the mature adolescent is essentially reasoning with the scientific method. However, the scientific method is not very old. The idealized experiment invented by Galileo was a major revolution against Scholasticism. The "experiment crucis" that compared two hypotheses was invented by Newton. The contemporaries of Galileo and Newton had a great deal of trouble following the reasoning of these men. What, then, were the cognitive capabilities of the mature adult in pre-Newtonian or pre-Galilean times? Was Aristotle not "mature" cognitively because he formulated the law of gravitation incorrectly and in a logically circular fashion in terms of "natural place"? No, this cannot be the case.

It is thus to be absurd and ignorant of the history of ideas to characterize *development* in terms of the way we think in our era. For example, causal reasoning as we know it today was arrived at through centuries of dialectic by the greatest minds in the world. Even the number zero is a relatively recent invention.

If we had to search for universality in development that spanned history and culture, we suggest that the place to look would be the expression, control, and regulation of affect, particularly the interpersonal arenas that have the most impact on defining the self. Thus, we propose that affect should have theoretical preeminence over cognition. The dichotomy between affect and cognition, as we have already seen, is not easy to maintain, nor is it productive in the long run. Nonetheless, it seems reasonable to suggest that children respond to the problems put before them by the ecological niches in which they have to live and, hence, that cognitive development is driven by social and affective demands for competence. Exactly how this occurs must still be specified. Our goal has been to describe what we have observed and to organize it into a theoretically interesting picture.

Relationship to social-cognitive development

Most of the research on children's social cognitions related to friendship has employed interview methods. There are problems with an interview methodology, especially for young children, who may be at a particular disadvantage in articulating the processes of friendship formation and maintenance.

Nonetheless, the results of a wide range of these interview studies suggest a reasonably clear picture that is not inconsistent with the theory we have presented in this chapter. Table 5.1 summarizes some of the major studies to date. Each of these studies revealed a trend toward more psychologically oriented descriptions of friendship with increasing age. For example, Bigelow and LaGaipa (1975) concluded that young children describe a friend as someone who is rewarding to be with, whereas older children describe a friend as someone who empathizes with them and understands them. Berndt (1978) found that young children describe a friend as someone who participates in shared activities, whereas older children describe a friend as someone with whom they trust and with whom they are intimate. Youniss and Volpe (1978) found that young children describe a friend as someone with whom they share *things*, whereas older children emphasize sharing thoughts and feelings. This is consistent with the notion that, among young children, friendship is based on the coordination of play (and all that it entails). According to Selman (1981), young children think of a friend as someone to play with (Stages 0 and 1), whereas older children think of a friend as someone who provides mutual intimacy and support (Stages 3 and 4). Thus, children's concepts about friendship clearly become more psychological as age increases.

In early childhood a friend is described as a playmate. In the next phase, children's descriptions of their friends could be characterized entirely in terms of social support. This corresponds to Bigelow's empathetic stage and Selman's Stage 3 (intimate and mutually shared) and Stage 4 (autonomous interdependence), and it is supported by the findings of other researchers (e.g., Berndt, 1978; Gamer, 1977). This

Table 5.1. *Summary of research on concepts of friendship*

Study	5	6	7	8	9	10	11	12	13
Bigelow (1977)			(---reward–cost---)		(--normative--)		(--empathetic---)		
Berndt (1978)	(shared activity)						(intimacy, trust)		
Gamer (1977)		(helps/defends you)						(understands feelings)	
Youniss and Volpe (1978)		(share/play-----)					(share thoughts feelings)		
Selman (1981)	(momentary)	(one-way assistance)		(fairweather cooperation)		(---intimate-----)		(--autonomous---)	
Damon (1977)	(----fun/nice-----)				(reciprocal trust/intimacy)			(share secrets/talk)	

view is entirely consistent with our description of what we have called middle childhood, in which negative-evaluation gossip and social support play central roles.

It is more difficult to create a coherent picture of adolescent social cognition from the literature. The scant evidence would seem to point to the importance of the confidant aspects of friendship (see Bell, 1981; Brenton, 1975; Komarovsky, 1976). Once again, this viewpoint is entirely consistent with the picture we have presented.

Obviously, these brief reviews of cognitive and social-cognitive development are not meant to be exhaustive, but merely to suggest that existing literatures are reasonably consistent with our suggestions. We hope that grounding our views in a particular context will make our hypotheses concrete and testable, and we now turn toward the beginnings of that task.

5.3. Quantitative analysis of the data

We conducted a study that employed a 3 × 3 factorial design. There were three age groups: 6- to 7-year-olds, 11- to 12-year-olds, and 16- to 17-year-olds. There were three levels of acquaintance: strangers, acquaintances, and best friends. It was *not* a repeated-measures design. Mettetal's (1982) thesis presented only the results involving the comparison of acquaintances and friends. For the purposes of this book, the data were recoded with the MACRO system for only four cells of the original study: best friends and strangers at the 11 to 12 and 16 to 17 age levels. The youngest group was not recoded with MACRO because audiotape recordings made at home (of two best friend dyads per age group) showed that the laboratory tapes were similar to the home tapes only for the two oldest groups. For the 6- to 7-year-old group there was a great deal of shared fantasy play at home, but very little of it in the laboratory; most of the interaction in the laboratory was activity talk. Thus, the laboratory tapes were not representative of the home tapes for the youngest group. Mettetal's thesis presented an analysis of friends and acquaintances for all three age groups. As we shall see, and as Mettetal suggested, activity talk can be thought of as an index variable of coordinated play (see Gottman, 1983) for the youngest group. Thus, although the conversations on the laboratory tapes are not generalizable across settings for the youngest group, they are still useful. This is because of the great degree of covariation of activity talk and coordinated fantasy play due to the social processes of escalation and deescala-

Table 5.2. *Design of the study*

| Age | Aquaintanceship level | | |
	Strangers (n)	Acquaintances (n)	Best friends (n)
6–7	6	5	10
11–12	9[a]	5	10[a]
16–17	7[a]	6	10[a]

[a]Cells recoded with MACRO for this chapter.

tion (for a detailed discussion of these processes and of the concept of an index variable see Gottman, 1983).

There were 68 dyads in the study; all the subjects were female (see Table 5.2). Our conclusions thus apply to only one sex.

Procedure

Strangers arrived at the laboratory separately. Friends and acquaintances were also asked to arrive separately and to refrain from talking all day. Because the laboratory setting was unfamiliar, it was necessary to devise a procedure that made it possible for the children to be themselves, a procedure that minimized reactivity. To accomplish this for acquainted pairs, Mettetal employed an analogue of procedures used with married couples (see Gottman, 1979). First a play-by-play description of a previous conversation was elicited. The interviewer asked about the last (or most recent) memorable times the children were together and what they talked about. After the interview, the final instructions were the same for all dyads:

> I want you to try to forget that I'm here. Just imagine that you're [at lunch, school, scene from play-by-play] and you just started talking to each other. Talk just as you would if you were alone together. You don't have to explain to me what you're talking about. Just say what you normally would to the other person. You can talk about anything you want to. It's OK if you talk about lots of different things or just about one thing the whole time.

Confidentiality was ensured and then the conversation was videotaped for 30 minutes. All children sat at a table facing one another. Only crayons and paper for drawing were available to them. The children were

Table 5.3. *Coding system employed by Mettetal (1982) with reliabilities*

Category	Definition	Cronbach alpha
Fantasy (FA)	Make-believe play, mimicking others	.89
Activity talk (AT)	Discussion of present activity	.81
Gossip (G)	Any discussion of third party	.87
Same	Discussion of someone they both know	
Informational (GIS)	Neutral information	.83
Positive (GPS)	Positive information	.74
Negative (GNS)	Negative information	.85
Different	Discussion of someone only one knows	
Informational (GID)	Neutral information	.49
Positive (GPD)	Positive information	1.00
Negative (GND)	Negative information	.10
Disclosure (D)	Personal information or revelation	
Low intimacy (LID)	Nonthreatening facts, opinions, feelings	.80
High intimacy (HID)	Threatening facts, opinions, feelings	.58
Miscellaneous (MI)	General information, jokes and riddles, games, and anything not in other categories	.71
Evaluation codes		
Positive (+)	Conversation progressing smoothly, relaxed, or excited	.74
Negative (−)	Conversation that is angry or tense	.50

Note: Cohen's kappas were .81 for all content codes, .85 when all gossip categories were combined, and .74 when the evaluation codes were added.

shown the unobtrusive cameras and microphones. Remote-control cameras silently tracked each child, and the two pictures were merged in a split screen with a visible time code that advanced for each frame of the videotape.

Mettetal (1982) employed a 14-category coding system with a large interaction unit, the vignette. A vignette was a "section of conversation consisting of only *one* content category, such as fantasy" (Mettetal, 1982, p. 71). The length of each vignette was measured by the number of smallest meaningful speech units. A speech unit could be a sentence, a phrase, or even a speech fragment (e.g., "going there"). Table 5.3

summarizes the coding categories, their definitions, and their reliabilities. Low reliabilities for some codes (GID, GND, negative evaluation) led to the extension of MACRO for age groups in this study and recoding of the data with the revised MACRO system.

Results of the Mettetal coding system

Some results are immediately apparent from the very design of Mettetal's coding system. Foremost among these is that fantasy takes the form of role playing among young children, but of mimicking someone in the context of gossip among middle childhood and adolescent groups.

Mettetal (1982) analyzed her data in terms of the number of vignettes and the average length of the speech units in each vignette. The number of vignettes was the number of separate episodes of a category, whereas the number of speech units per vignette estimated the *duration* of each type of vignette. These variables were called *episodes* and *duration*, respectively.

Sudden decline of and the functions of coordinated play. It was expected that coordinated play, indexed by activity talk, would be highest for the youngest group, declining sharply for the two older groups. Both episodes and duration declined significantly with increasing age. For episodes, the pattern was $F(2,39) = 37.5$, $p < .001$, with mean proportions of .57 for the young group, .19 for the middle group, and .02 for adolescents. For duration, a similar pattern was observed [$F(2,39) = 29.3$, $p < .001$], with a young group mean of 21.06, a middle group mean of 8.73, and an adolescent group mean of 8.48. These data show a dramatic drop in the index of coordinated play in the two older groups.

Fantasy, which was rare (occurring only in 12% of the vignettes for the youngest group), showed no significant decline in terms of number of episodes [$F(2,39) = .01$]. This is because mimicking another person in the context of gossip was included in this category. However, mimicking tends to be brief, whereas fantasy role play tends to be extended, so the duration data should pick up the developmental dropoff that indexes the decline in the importance of coordinated play with increasing age. In fact, for duration of fantasy per vignette the younger group had a mean of 10 units per vignette, the middle group a mean of 3.7, and the adolescent group a mean of 1.9 [$F(2,39) = 13.3$, $p < .001$].

Only for the youngest group did the length of coordinated play, assessed by the duration of activity talk, discriminate between acquaintances and best friends [main effect $F(1,39) = 10.8$, $p < .001$; friends, mean 16.1; acquaintances, mean 11.8; interaction effect $F(2,39)$ = 6.1, $p < .01$, with the longest vignettes in the young friends' group, mean 25.6]. Thus, the extension of coordinated play for the youngest group is an index of the intimacy of friendship. This is not the case for middle childhood or adolescence. This effect measures the rise of conversation itself as a focus of interaction with development. For younger children coordinated play is the focus of interaction. Mettetal (1982) noted:

> During the play-by-play interview preceding taping, the interviewer would ask for details of the last time the two girls had talked together. The girls in the youngest group would often be puzzled by the question until the interviewer continued by asking when they had last spent time together. At that prompt most of the girls would mention a specific activity, such as playing house or going to Brownie Scouts, *and then recall what they had talked about* [p. 101, italics added].

Gossip. Gossip would be expected to increase in middle childhood and remain high in adolescence. The episode data showed this effect [$F(2,39)$ = 29.6; $p < .001$; young, .08; middle, .29; adolescent, .42] as did the duration data [$F(2,39)$ = 5.2, $p < .01$; young, 6.9; middle, 11.4; adolescent, 13.1]. However, at all ages the amount of gossip among friends and acquaintances did not differ significantly, as assessed by the Scheffe test.

Many of our hypotheses about middle childhood and adolescence concerned negative- and positive-evaluation gossip. Negative-evaluation gossip should be high beginning in middle childhood. Positive evaluation gossip should be highest for adolescents. Negative gossip about a person both girls know (GNS) showed an age effect [$F(2,39)$ = 9.3, $p < .001$], with the amount of GNS increasing with age (young, .02, middle, .19, adolescent, .17). About half of all gossip consisted of negative evaluation of a person both children knew. Note the sudden increase in GNS in middle childhood. This is as predicted. Positive gossip about a person also showed a significant age effect [$F(2,39)$ = 9.3, $p < .001$], with the following proportions: young, .00, middle, .02, adolescent, .05]. A similar pattern held for informational gossip [$F(2,39)$ = 7.5, $p < .001$, with the following proportions: young, .02, middle, .07, adolescent, .12].

Only negative gossip about a person whom only one person knew distinguished friends from acquaintances [$F(2,39)$ = 6.8, $p < .001$, with mean proportions of .00 for friends and .02 for acquaintances].

Self-disclosure. Low-intimacy self-disclosure showed a strong age effect only for the duration variable. This tells us something about the *way* it occurs: rarely and for a reasonably long duration [$F(2,39) = 7.8$, $p <$ .001; young, 11.1; middle, 13.6; adolescent, 17.8]. The adolescent mean differs from the two younger group means, which are not significantly different from one another. This supports the contention that self-exploration is important only for adolescents. There were no significant differences in low-intimacy self-disclosure between acquaintances and friends or significant interaction effects.

High-intimacy self-disclosure showed no significant episode age effects [$F(2,39) = 1.9$], but there were significant duration effects by age [$F(2,39) = 3.4$, $p < .05$; young, 4.3; middle, 10.6, adolescent, 28.1]. High-intimacy self-disclosures were frequent and brief for adolescents. However, as judged by the Scheffe test these differences were not significant. Nonetheless, the trend of these data is consistent with our contention that self-disclosure is most important among adolescents.

The episode data showed a significant main effect for acquaintance-ship [$F(1,39) = 4.8$, $p < .05$; friends, .04; acquaintances, .01]. Thus, friends disclosed high-intimacy information more often, but there were no significant differences in the duration of each disclosure.

MACRO coding

Tapes of the subjects in the four cells of the larger experimental design were recoded using the MACRO coding system described in Chapter 2. These cells were 11- to 12-year-old friends, 11- to 12-year-old strangers, 16- to 17-year-old friends, and 16- to 17-year-old strangers. In addition, two coders, using a four-point scale, independently rated whether the strangers hit it off or did not hit it off. The correlation between their ratings was quite high ($r = .89$). However, only three dyads in each of the four possible cells of this design (Hit It Off/Did Not × Age Group) clearly hit it off or did not. Hence, there were two designs: an Age × Acquaintanceship (Friend or Stranger) design and a breakdown among strangers of both age groups in terms of hitting it off or not. Because there were so few subjects in these designs and because some of the codes were relatively rare for a dyad-by-dyad analysis, data were often combined across subjects for nonparametric analysis. When cell sizes were unequal, frequencies of codes were adjusted downward to conform to the smallest cell size. Chi squares in these instances were asymptotic statistics.

The validity of the ratings of hitting it off was checked by comparing the amount of amity success (high levels of reciprocated positive affect) for strangers who did and did not hit it off. There was more amity success for 11- to 12-year-old strangers who hit it off ($\chi^2 = 9.1$, $p < .001$) and 16- to 17-year-old strangers who hit it off ($\chi^2 = 47.0$, $p < .001$) than for those who did not hit it off. Amity failure (unreciprocated humor and affection, usually) and conflict should negatively index hitting it off. This was so for 11- to 12-year-olds ($\chi^2 = 4.5$, $p < .05$) but not for 16- to 17-year-olds ($\chi^2 = 1.3$, n.s.). This implies that, by adolescence, children have learned to avoid conflict and to reciprocate positive affect with strangers regardless of whether the interaction as a whole is going well.

Specific predictions

We made several specific predictions for specific social processes. We shall discuss each process in turn.

Negative-evaluation gossip. We predicted that this process would discriminate between strangers who did and did not hit it off in middle childhood. For 11- to 12-year-olds, negative-evaluation gossip was indeed much more frequent among dyads that hit it off than among those that did not ($\chi^2 = 67.6$, $p < .001$). We also thought that this process would be so prevalent among strangers that sequences indexing continuance in this state would be as high among strangers as among friends. For this analysis we employed z-scores of the codes, with the data analyzed so that codes could follow themselves. This allowed evaluation of the extent to which negative evaluation gossip is an absorbing state, in the language of Markov processes. We found that these chains were actually more likely for strangers than for friends in middle childhood [$t(32) = 2.87$, $p < .05$; we used the mean square error (MSE) term from the analysis of variance (Age × Friend/Stranger) and the degrees of freedom for the MSE as well; see Myers, 1966]. The z-scores were 15.60 for strangers and 10.99 for friends.

We made no prediction about negative-evaluation gossip for adolescents but thought that the effect of this process in making friends would diminish with increasing age. This was not the case. Negative-evaluation gossip still discriminated between adolescent strangers who did and did not hit it off ($\chi^2 = 26.2$, $p < .001$).

We thought that negative-evaluation gossip would decline from middle childhood to adolescence, but we were wrong. It increased (χ^2

= 9.3, $p < .01$). Our prediction was probably affected by our observation that *positive*-evaluation gossip seemed to increase from middle childhood to adolescence.

Positive-evaluation gossip. The amount of positive-evaluation gossip did, as we predicted, increase dramatically from middle childhood to adolescence ($\chi^2 = 32.0$, $p < .001$). Also, z-scores indexing staying in this state showed significant developmental effects [$t(32) = 2.25$, $p < .05$]. Once again, we employed the MSE from the analysis of variance for this contrast. The mean z-scores were 10.77 for the adolescents and 6.24 for the 11- to 12-year-olds.

We also hypothesized that positive-evaluation gossip would discriminate between strangers who hit it off and those who did not, but only among adolescents. This was the case. [For middle childhood, $\chi^2 = 2.3$, n.s.; for adolescents, $\chi^2 = 24.0$, $p < .001$.]

Self-disclosure. We thought that high-intimacy self-disclosure would increase developmentally among friends. It did ($\chi^2 = 55.2$, $p < .001$). This was also true for low-intimacy self-disclosure ($\chi^2 = 55.2$, $p < .001$).

We also thought that self-disclosure among adolescents, but not in middle childhood, would discriminate between strangers who did and did not hit it off. This was the case for low-intimacy self-disclosure; it did not discriminate among 11- to 12-year-olds ($\chi^2 = 2.1$, n.s.), but it did discriminate among 16- to 17-year-olds ($\chi^2 = 7.4$, $p < .01$). High-intimacy self-disclosure was extremely rare among strangers in both age groups, and neither chi square was significant (11- to 12-year-olds, $\chi^2 = 1.3$, n.s.; 16- to 17-year-olds, $\chi^2 = 0.3$, n.s.).

Mindreading. Our mindreading code indexes psychological interpretations of the *other* person's character. We predicted that this would increase with age among friends. It did ($\chi^2 = 4.9$, $p < .05$). Not surprisingly, there was no mindreading among strangers.

Relationship talk. We expected that, among friends, comments about the relationship or the processes of communication would increase from middle childhood to adolescence. This did not occur; in fact, relationship talk declined with increasing age ($\chi^2 = 11.1$, $p < .01$). We do not understand this effect. It could be due to the relatively low reliabilities that accompany rare events. A conservative guess is that mindreading and relationship talk are part of the same process of psychological

Table 5.4. *Summary of characteristics of developmental periods*

Characteristic	Developmental period		
	Early childhood	Middle childhood	Adolescence
Goals, concerns	Coordination of play	Inclusion by peers, avoiding rejection	Self-exploration
Salient social processes	Common-ground escalation, deescalation, conflict management "Me too" climate	Negative evaluation gossip, amity, social support	Self-disclosure, gossip, problem solving
Supporting social processes	Fantasy, amity	Information exchange	Relationship exploration
Emotional tasks	Affect regulation	Avoiding embarrassment; rejection of sentiment, logic	Fusion of logic and emotion
Ecological niche	Dyad	Same-sex peer group	Same- and cross-sex peer group

mindedness, in which case they should be summed and we would find no developmental effect ($\chi^2 = 0.2$, n.s.). Not surprisingly, relationship talk did not occur at all among strangers.

We also analyzed these MACRO code data as event sequential data, in which a code cannot follow itself. Probabilities here gave the number of episodes of a particular MACRO code, independent of its length. These analyses paralleled those in Mettetal's thesis. The results of this reanalysis of the data generally paralleled those already presented.

5.4. Summary

Our coding systems and quantitative analyses of these data support our speculations and our qualitative analyses. What we have achieved, then, is a theoretical view of social and affective development that has a reasonable degree of internal consistency. Table 5.4 summarizes many of the major themes we have discussed about the nature of social and emotional development.

IV. Extensions

6. Conversations of college roommates: similarities and differences in male and female friendship

DOROTHY GINSBERG AND JOHN GOTTMAN

Journalistic psychological writing is replete with strong statements about the quality of male and female friendships. Some writers are convinced of the inferiority of male friendships. Two of these writers are Fasteau (1975) and Bell (1981).

Fasteau's book *The Male Machine* is typical of a genre of books by men (see also Goldberg's [1976] *The Hazards of Being Male*) that decry the hollowness, competitiveness, and lack of emotionality in men's relationships. Often these books are gratefully dedicated to a woman, as Fasteau's is to "Brenda, who showed me what it means to love another person." Fasteau describes men as incompetent in personal relationships (p. 3), afraid of experiencing emotions (p. 4), and insensitive (p. 4). He asserts that friendships between men are "shallow and unsatisfying" (p. 6). Moreover, their relationships supposedly contain a "stifling ban on self-disclosure" (p. 10), are void of any dependence of one friend on the other (pp. 11–12), and are characterized by "the inability to admit to being vulnerable" (p. 12); men are supposedly unable to express affection (p. 15) without fear of being labeled homosexual (p. 15). Affection between men, Fasteau claims, must "be disguised in gruff 'you old son-of-a-bitch' style" (p. 15). Men supposedly prefer to see each other in groups, in which talk is minimized and there is "safety in numbers." This makes personal communication, which requires a level of trust and mutual understanding not generally shared by all members of a group, more difficult and offers an excuse for avoiding "dangerous territory" (p. 17).

Fasteau wants to help men find a better way of life. For him,

> the process started when I began to understand, at least with Brenda, a more open, less self-protective relationship was possible. . . . I began to see . . . the level of intimacy that women, especially women active in the movement, shared with each other.

241

The contrast between this and the friendships I had with men was striking [pp. 17–18].

It is, of course, wonderful that Fasteau found happiness and a new way of life with Brenda. However, how accurate is his characterization of male and female friendships? Bell (1981) agreed with him:

Men interact with others in terms of roles . . . men often see persons not as complete human beings but as persons filling particular roles. . . . But women more often see the total person. This is reflected in the fact that women have fewer segmented, or specialized, friendships than do men [p. 69].

Bell wrote that "women can usually form friendships easier than men" (p. 61), that "female patterns of friendship are much more revealing and intimate than those found among men" (p. 62). We learn in his book that there is more reciprocity of self-disclosure among women (p. 65), that their friendships are "richer in spontaneity and confidences than males'" (p. 65), and that their friendships are stronger, closer, and longer lasting than men's (p. 68). Bell wrote that often "men get together in groups for various kinds of games, and the game is the reason for getting together," whereas for women "the real interest may be in communication rather than the game itself" (p. 79). The only acceptable conversation for men in Bell's own poker group "was brief kidding or needling exchanges. Any attempt at serious conversation was quickly ended by several of the players" (p. 79).

Are these the mournful yearnings of men rejected by same-sex peers, or is there some truth in all these assertions? Not all male writers share these viewpoints. We have already quoted from Brenton's (1974) study of friendship (Chapter 1) in which he found that blue-collar men's reports of their own friendships differed dramatically according to whether the interview was formal or informal. Brain's (1977) anthropological essay on friendship highlighted the great emotional power and intensity of male friendships among the Bangwa, even though friends are assigned and not chosen in this culture and the rights and obligations of both same- and cross-sex friendship are clearly specified.

Some of the most interesting writing about the worlds of men and women is based on archeological and anthropological speculations about our early hominid ancestors, diverse human cultures, and societies of nonhuman primates. It is reasonably clear that hunting has always been a male activity, whereas gathering has been female. What is perhaps not as well known is that the evidence suggests that hunting was always a highly organized and cooperative activity (see Leakey, 1982) and the notion of the solitary male killer was never a valid concept (except perhaps after the invention of powerful long-distance weapons such as the bow and arrow about eleven thousand years ago; see Ardrey, 1970, p. 345). Hunting was a social act requiring a high level of sensitivity, organization, communication, and cooperation. Tiger and Fox (1971) speculated about the historical origins of female–female versus male–male bonds:

> There is the crucial set of male–male bonds that underlie politics, defense, the conduct of war, and a host of other activities vital to the broad self-interest of the community; and the set of female–female bonds important in maintaining social coherence [p. 85].

They elaborated these differences by pointing out the male role in defense and the female role in child care. Within these roles they discussed the social dominance hierarchy that controlled competition and aggression within a community and its implications for cross-sex relations.

Stephenson's (personal communication) observations of free-ranging Japanese macaques documented the fact that the male dominance hierarchy depends on who the male's mother is. Status within the female social group is reflected within the male group, independent of the weight or strength of males. Dominant males carefully pick a time when they can call their friends for assistance in fighting subordinates.

To return to humans, within the separate male and female societies, Tiger and Fox suggest that specific types of male relationships emerge. Their historical discussion of Crow Indian practices suggests that male solidarity is often affirmed "by degrading the male–female bond . . . what they are saying is that, in some circumstances (before warfare), no woman is as important to any man as men are to one another" (p. 93).

> They also discuss the prewedding all-female bridal showers, in which towels, fish forks, sheets, glasses, or money represent her female associates' commitment to the mating bond and in turn enmesh her in a web of female-centered obligations [p. 93].

This ritual contrasts with the all-male stag party, which centers on sex, humor, and pornography and in which

> an "anti-female" tradition is often involved. Pornographic films may be shown, strippers may dance – in any case the potential tenderness between the man and wife is mocked by his friends' provision of squalid entertainment, perceived by them to be manly [p. 94].

These differences in ritual lead Tiger and Fox to discuss the existence of formal or informal male associations, "each with its emblems and secrets" (p. 94). All this is symbolic of the male–male bond. At one time "the lone male was probably a dead male – at least a male less likely to contribute effectively to the gene pool" (p. 95).

Today, however, male associations fulfill functions of socializing young males, engaging them in a variety of cooperative enterprises.

> It is a way of taking up the time and effort of the young by assimilating them into the schemes of the old . . . deciding which of the young men will be leaders . . . instructing them, testing them, thwarting carefully their impetuous drive to dominate. . . . This process offers them seniority in return for consent [p. 97].

All this controversy suggests that we have a "chaos of opinion," to quote Terman et al. (1938). The truth must lie somewhere in the chaos, and it probably is not be found in the single dimension of "superiority" of either male or female friendships. There are probably some fairly universal stylistic differences between the sexes, even among nonhuman primates, for example, with respect to their preference for rough-and-tumble play (see diPietro, 1981), and these differences are only a part of the picture. A scientific investigation of this issue must be prepared to find them. The challenge is to understand them.

Problems with self-reports

Many of our notions of sex differences are based on self-report data – data that are notoriously sensitive to artifacts of data collection. In Chapter 2 we cited Brenton's (1984) study of friendship, in which he found that blue-collar men's reports of their own friendships differed dramatically depending on whether the interview was formal or informal. The problem is even more widespread. For example, it is generally acknowledged that men are more likely to express anger than women. Yet when Averill (1983) employed a daily diary procedure, he found no sex differences in the expression and experience of anger. In fact, the structure of the experience antecedents, consequents, and phenomenology was strikingly similar for men and women.

A similar story is emerging for depression. Although depression is generally acknowledged to be primarily a female problem, when men and women are asked about the recent past (e.g., the past two weeks) there are no sex differences in their responses (D. Reiss, personal communication).

This is not to say that self-report data are not valid, but to caution against the general tendency of men to minimize their complaints and underreport difficulties. This is a well-known part of sex differences in socialization; boys are trained to complain less frequently than girls (see Block, 1983). These differences even exist on the Cornell Medical Inventory (e.g., see Ryle & Hamilton, 1962) despite the well-known worldwide superiority of women over men in health across the life span (e.g., Hoyenga & Hoyenga, 1979).

The problem has serious implications for the comparison of male and female relationships. A self-report measure of closeness or relationship satisfaction must be developed and validated that makes it possible to compare men's with women's friendships.

Social processes in adult friendships

Although few studies have systematically investigated the developmental nature of a relationship, there is an extensive literature in social psychology on interpersonal attraction (for review see Berscheid & Walster, 1969; Byrne, 1969; Lott & Lott, 1965; Secord & Backman, 1964). Many of the empirical findings on attraction support the principles of reinforcement theory and suggest that individuals evaluate one another in terms of their perceived reward potential.

For example, the possession of culturally valued attributes, such as physical beauty (Byrne, Ervin & Lamberth, 1970; Dion, Berschied, & Walster, 1972), cooperativeness (Deutsch, 1960; Solomon, 1960), and similarity of personality (Cattell & Nesselroade, 1967; Izard, 1960), social background (Festinger, 1950; Goodnow & Taguiri, 1952), and attitudes (Brewer & Brewer, 1968; Byrne & Clore, 1966; Veitch & Griffitt, 1973), leads to attraction. Other factors, such as propinquity, that is, the likelihood that individuals will come into contact and intereact with each other, also come into play. Interaction makes it possible for individuals to learn about the characteristics of others that make them attractive. This is supported by evidence from field studies (e.g., Byrne, & Buehler, 1955; Festinger, Schachter, & Back, 1950).

Little research, however, has been directed toward determining the stage of a relationship at which most of these and other factors are rewarding. For example, factors that lead to initial attraction may not be the same factors that sustain interest at later stages of acquaintance.

Furthermore, most of this research concerns only the earliest stages of a relationship. There has been a tendency to narrow the study of friendship formation to self-report measures of social attraction that were obtained after brief contacts between individuals who were not likely to meet again. These studies are most relevant to stages of "awareness" and "surface contact" in which individuals have not interacted or in which interactions are relatively superficial.

The determinants of liking in brief encounters may well operate to different effect in the context of ongoing relationships. There is evidence that findings based on brief encounters in which there is no anticipation of future contact cannot be generalized to relationships with a future. For example, Darley and Berscheid (1967) found that female college students were more attracted to a female student with whom interaction was anticipated than to a female student with whom interaction was not anticipated. This suggests that understanding friendship requires the study of relevant social processes in ongoing relationships rather than in ephemeral encounters created in the laboratory.

Although a few studies have investigated attraction in ongoing relationships, they are limited to the attitudinal rather than behavioral components of attraction. Longitudinal studies have investigated the connection between attraction and similarity, complementary in needs, and personality "fit" in friends (Newcomb, 1961) and dating couples (Kerckhoff & Davis, 1962; Levinger, Senn & Jorgensen, 1970). *Most of these studies have used self-report measures of attraction and variables that affect it rather than behavioral indices of attraction.* Although theories about relationship development attempt to describe interaction and communication patterns that characterize various stages of relatedness, little research has been done on this. Thus, although social psychologists *theorize* about interaction, they generally do not observe or measure interaction directly. Little is known about the relationship between attraction and interaction processes in ongoing relationships. Understanding how relationships develop might best be advanced by approaches that relate attraction or other indices of relationship development to actual interaction sequences.

Research that does examine interaction processes and communication patterns is found in three areas of theory and research. The first area deals with the formation of relationships and has focused largely on the growth of intimacy or acquaintance through self-disclosure. The second area deals with established social systems, such as marriages and families. Here, the focus is on comparisons of distressed and nondistressed marriages or family communication patterns. These two areas of research study relationships at different stages of relatedness. It is difficult, however, to compare findings based on marriages and families with the research on developing relationships, because different aspects of communication have been studied.

Marital and family research has often focused on the exchange of affective or evaluative messages such as pleasurable and displeasurable behavior (Wills, Weiss, & Patterson, 1974), supportiveness or defensiveness (Alexander, 1973), and negative and positive problem-solving behaviors (Billings, 1979). Without a means of relating different aspects of communication, we will have only incomplete knowledge about interrelationships among responses and patterns of behavior.

The third area, the province of sociologists and anthropologists, describes communication patterns that occur in field settings. It focuses on types of communication that experimentalists have tended to disregard. Gossip is an example of this. Unfortunately, as discussed in a later section, much of this research is nonquantitative and does not operationalize stages of relationships. Also, it focuses on only one or two types of communication. In order to explore the complexity of social conversation adequately, we need a broad-based and comprehensive system for measuring different aspects of communication. In our college roommate study, we attempted to use a coding system that served this purpose.

It should be pointed out that factors in addition to attraction affect whether an individual will actually choose to affiliate or maintain an interaction. For example, the accessibility of another individual and the perceived likelihood that the other will respond favorably are also important (Berscheid, Dion, Walster, & Walster, 1971; Shanteau & Nagy, 1976). Thus, a distinction must be made between liking and affiliative behavior. Most studies of attraction do not make this distinction. Furthermore, the fact that we can experimentally affect attraction between two strangers does not imply that these are the same factors that account for natural variation in the formation of relationships. To determine this, naturalistic observation of social interaction is required.

Even if studies of interpersonal attraction have added to our knowledge of how people become initially attracted to each other and subsequently form a relationship, we know little about friendship itself.

In summary, three shortcomings in the literature have been described: (1) the failure to examine social processes in established rather than superficial relationships; (2) the paucity of research that employs measures of interaction processes, as opposed to self-report measures; and

(3) the dearth of studies that investigate interaction in natural settings, in contrast to the laboratory.

A brief survey of theory and research dealing with interaction process revealed other limitations. First, research in various disciplines has focused on discrete and nonoverlapping social processes. Second, various disciplines have focused on different stages of relationships or have failed to specify adequately the stage of relationship to which their findings apply.

The study to be described here addressed these shortcomings. Thus, we used a broad-based and comprehensive coding system for measuring different social interaction processes that bridge across different disciplines. In addition, we employed both observational and self-report measures of relationships. We observed unstructured interaction in a natural setting in the context of established and ongoing relationships.

6.1. Preliminary Studies

Selection of a Measurement Instrument

The selection of an instrument for measuring closeness among friends evolved from previous unpublished work by Gottman. On the basis of the work of Schutz (1958), Gottman constructed a 72-item questionnaire to distinguish among friendships of different levels of closeness. The items in Gottman's friendship questionnaire were constructed to correspond to three dimensions that Schutz concluded account for what happens in an interpersonal relationship. According to Schutz, these dimensions manifest themselves in needs for affection, inclusion, and control. He stated that every person has a need to receive from others and a need to extend to others differing degrees of each of these dimensions. Similar dimensions have been found by other researchers (Bales, 1970; Foa, 1961; Leary, 1957).

The friendship questionnaire measured the concept of closeness by the degree of agreement with such statements as "My friend is someone I tell I like," and "My friend expresses liking for me." Half of the items were worded from the point of view of the subject as initiator of the interaction, and half were worded from the point of view of the subject as target of the interaction.

Each of the randomly ordered items were classified into nine general scales corresponding to the dimensions of affection, inclusion, control, and shared fantasy (Table 6.1). Affection refers to the need for mutual

Table 6.1. *Gottman's friendship questionnaire*

Scale	Item order	Item
Receives positive affect from friend	1	Is someone who makes me feel needed
	16	Expresses liking for me
	24	Is empathetic toward me
	33	Cares about me
	42	Expresses affection toward me
	50	Is someone who sees my faults but likes me anyhow
Expression of positive affect toward friend	2	Is someone to whom I can feel empathetic
	7	Is someone who brings out my deepest emotions
	20	Is someone who doesn't make me feel embarrassed to show my feelings
	21	Is someone I tell I like
	38	Is someone who makes me laugh
	45	Is someone who is always there when I need help
	54	Is someone who is interested in what I think
	68	Is someone to whom I can express affection
	70	Is someone I care about
Receives negative affect from friend	9	Lets me know when he or she is mad at me
	19	Tells me about his or her anxieties
	25	Is someone who starts fights with me
	56	Is willing to tell me about my faults
	71	Can be very nasty to me
Expression of negative affect toward friend	10	Is someone I can argue with about ideas
	28	Is someone to whom I can express anger
	31	Is someone I can be very nasty to
	44	Is someone I can easily start a fight with
	52	Is someone with whom I don't have to be polite
	62	Is someone I can confide in when I'm in trouble
	67	Is someone to whom I can express my fears and worries
Influences friend	14	Has accepted my views on several issues

Table 6.1. *(Cont.)*

Scale	Item order	Item
	27	Recognizes my capabilities
	30	Makes me feel smart
	48	Respects my thoughts and ideas
	58	Makes me feel competent
	63	Treats me like an important person
	65	Asks me for advice
	69	Has changed his or her views on some things as a result of my influence
Is influenced by friend	5	Is a capable individual
	8	Is someone I often turn to for advice
	35	Has my admiration
	41	Is someone whose thoughts and ideas I respect
	55	Has my respect
	72	Has changed my opinions on some things
Is responsive to friend	11	Is someone I can easily respond to
	22	Is someone I do things with
	23	Is someone I can share things with
	32	Is someone I find easy to pay attention to
	36	Is someone who feels good when with me
	41	Is someone I often include in things
	51	Is someone I can be sensitive to
	57	Is someone whose moods I can easily read
	61	Is someone to whom I can feel empathetic toward
Is responded to by friend	3	Is someone who understands what I mean without a lot of explanation
	12	Is usually attentive to me when I'm talking
	13	Is aware of me and attentive to me when we're together
	15	Is someone who feels sad when I feel sad
	17	Is someone who relates to me well
	18	Is someone with whom I can communicate
	26	Is someone who always has time for me
	34	Is someone who is like me
	40	Will help me out when I'm in a bind
	43	Is sensitive to my feelings
	46	Often includes me in things

Table 6.1. *(Cont.)*

Scale	Item order	Item
	53	Can read my moods
	59	Shares things with me
	60	Shares my interests
	64	Responds to me
Shared fantasy	4	Is someone I can just play with
	6	Is someone with whom I can be completely silly
	29	Shares innermost thoughts with me
	37	Is someone with whom I discuss my dreams
	39	Tells me about his or her dreams
	47	Is someone with whom I can talk about plans for the future
	66	Is someone with whom I can pretend and explore fantasies

caring, love, and affection with others and is related to becoming emotionally close. It involves confiding intimate anxieties, wishes, and feelings. Four scales correspond to the dimension of affection: (1) receives positive affect from friend, (2) expresses positive affect toward friend, (3) receives negative affect from friend, and (4) expresses negative affect toward friend. Inclusion involves wanting to be attended to, to attract attention, and to attract interest. According to Schutz, this leads to behavior related to becoming part of a group. Two scales correspond to the dimension of inclusion: (1) is responsive to friend and (2) is responded to by friend. The need for control involves the desire for power and influence. It is associated with attempts to establish and maintain mutual respect with others. Two scales correspond to the dimension of control: (1) influences friend and (2) is influenced by friend. The ninth scale includes items related to shared fantasy – for example, "My friend shares innermost thoughts with me." Shared fantasy was included because it was found by Gottman and Parkhurst (1980) to play a significant role in the friendships of young children.

Construct validity of Gottman's friendship questionnaire

Two studies were conducted to determine whether the questionnaire could distinguish among relationships of different levels of closeness.

The first study, conducted by J. Gottman (unpublished), utilized a within-subjects design and the second study, conducted by M. Glickman and D. Ginsberg (unpublished), utilized a between-subjects design.

Within-subjects design. Subjects were 107 undergraduates at Indiana University: 65 female students and 42 male students. A 2 × 2 (Sex × Level of Friendship) repeated-measures design was used. Subjects were asked to complete three questionnaires, one each to describe their relationship with an acquaintance, a friend, and a best friend. Subjects were asked to indicate the names of the people they were describing to ensure responses based on actual interpersonal experiences. The order of these questionnaires was counterbalanced.

For relationships of greater degrees of closeness, a greater amount of mutual affect, mutual responsiveness, mutual influence, and shared fantasy was expressed (Table 6.2). All nine scales had significant main effects of level of friendship. All the *F*-ratios were significant; the smallest was 81.67. A significant sex effect was found for five scales, with female students demonstrating higher mean scale scores than male students on the following scales: is influenced by friend, receives positive affect from friend, expresses positive affect toward friend, is responsive to friend, and is responded to by friend. All *F*-ratios were significant; the smallest was 6.21. There were also significant Sex × Level of Friendship interactions on the following four scales: receives positive affect from friend, expresses positive affect toward friend, is responsive to friend, and is responded to by friend. These *F*-ratios were all significant; the smallest was 3.08.

The findings indicated that each scale operated in the same way to distinguish among relationships of different levels of closeness. The closer the relationship, the higher was the score on every scale. This suggested that a total score could be used as a measure of relationship satisfaction.

Although the order of questionnaires was counterbalanced, it is possible that subjects' responses were influenced by the order in which the questionnaires were administered. Since there were three questionnaires, there were six different orders of presentation. One-way analyses of variance of order effects were employed for questionnaires of three levels of closeness for each of the nine scales. Of the 27 analyses (nine scales × three levels of friendship), only 5 indicated significant order effects. Four of the five significant order effects involved the best-friend questionnaire. Best friends were evaluated higher if they

Table 6.2. *Mean scale scores and F-ratios for friends of different levels of closeness (Within-subjects design)*

Group	Receives positive affect from friend	Expression of positive affect toward friend	Receives negative affect from friend	Expression of negative affect toward friend	Is responded to by friend	Is responsive to friend	Influences friend	Is influenced by friend	Shared fantasy
Females									
Acquaintances	18.22	27.60	12.09	18.91	44.80	27.88	24.92	19.82	18.60
Friends	25.29	37.26	15.83	23.98	62.85	37.85	31.89	25.55	27.31
Best friends	27.85	41.54	17.55	26.15	69.78	42.82	35.54	28.15	32.15
Males									
Acquaintances	17.19	26.67	13.12	20.21	45.14	27.21	25.10	18.43	18.64
Friends	21.60	33.05	15.12	23.74	57.95	34.31	30.02	23.91	25.29
Best friends	24.93	39.00	17.19	25.76	66.26	40.36	34.29	26.86	30.38
F-Ratios									
Friendship (F)	196.96**	216.95**	81.67**	93.23**	356.63**	331.96**	220.77**	172.71**	313.47**
Sex (S)	27.81**	15.89**	0.001	0.167	6.22*	10.93*	2.75	10.08**	3.40
F×S	3.08*	3.08*	2.67	1.75	4.36*	3.23*	2.24	0.08	2.26

*p < .05; **p < .001.

were last, after friends and acquaintances, for the following scales: shared fantasy [$F(5,101) = 2.32$, $p < .05$]; expresses positive affect to friend [$F(5,101) = 2.73$, $p < .03$]; receives positive affect from friend [$F(5,101) = 4.19$, $p < .01$]; and is responded to by friend [$F(5,101) = 2.92$, $p < .02$]. The other significant order effect involved the acquaintance questionnaire. Acquaintances were given a lower evaluation if they were last, after friends and best friends, for the scale influences friend [$F(5,101) = 2.60$, $p < .03$]. An artifact of the within-subjects design appeared to be that subjects' responses were influenced by their responses to the previous questionnaires. To control for effects of repeated measures, the next study utilized a between-subjects design.

Between-subjects design. In this study, rather than completing three questionnaires about three different people, subjects were asked to complete one questionnaire each. We also decided to test the application of our measure to a specific relationship. The subjects were asked to describe their relationship with their same-sex roommate. Roommates were selected because, with "round-the-clock" contact, they provide the most interesting possibilities for looking at conversation, which was the primary goal of this investigation. Two items were added to the questionnaire to assess the closeness of the relationship. These items were chosen to reflect two of the elements commonly used to describe close relationships. One element is affiliation or joint belongingness, and the other is liking or favorable attitude (see Huston & Levinger, 1978; Levinger & Snoek, 1972). The affiliation item asked the subject to rate how close a friend his or her roommate was on a seven-point scale ranging from *somebody I feel very positive toward* to *somebody I feel very negative toward.*

The subjects were 101 undergraduates – 50 female students and 51 male students – from introductory psychology courses at the University of Illinois. A 2 × 2 (Sex × Level of Friendship) factorial design was used. Since a subject's score on the affiliation item was strongly correlated with his or her score on the liking item (for females $r = .76$ and for males $r = .80$), the average of the scores for each subject was taken as a single friendship score. The range of friendship scores for male and female subjects was examined separately to determine cutoff points for each of three general levels of friendship. A trichotomous division of scores was made for each sex at cutoff points that appeared to correspond to natural breaks between groups. The number of subjects in each cell of the 2 × 3 design was as follows: 8 female acquaintances,

20 female friends, 22 female best friends, 11 male acquaintances, 15 male friends, and 25 male best friends.

There was a positive relationship between the level of friendship and the amount of mutual responsiveness, mutual affect expressed, mutual influence, and shared fantasy (Table 6.3). For all nine scales, there were significant main effects of level of friendship. The closer a subject was to his or her roommate, the more mutually expressive the roommates were in the nine interpersonal areas tapped by the questionnaire.

The results of the between-subjects study were very similar to the results of the within-subjects study. In both studies, all scales of the questionnaire significantly distinguished among relationships of different levels of closeness for both male and female subjects. In all cases, the closer a relationship, the higher was the score in the nine interpersonal areas tapped by the questionnaire. Again, each scale operated in the same way, and thus only a total score of relationship satisfaction was used.

In general, as we expected, female subjects reported higher mean scale scores than male subjects. There were two significant sex effects in the areas of shared fantasy [$F(1,95) = 7.94, p < .005$] and receives positive affect from friend [$F(1,95) = 5.79, p < .02$]. There were no significant Sex × Level of Friendship interactions.

On both the within-subjects and between-subjects designs, the higher group means for females is consistent with other self-report research (see Booth, 1972; Douvan & Adelson, 1966; Rubin, 1973). We must be careful, however, in concluding that these differences reflect genuine differences in the *behavior* of the sexes in their closest friendships; it is possible that both self-report methods and interview methods (e.g., Komarovsky, 1976; Rubin, 1976) tap differences in public presentation, which is a function of sex-role stereotypes. It is necessary to supplement self-report methods with observational methods to address this rival hypothesis. The fact that more extensive sex differences were observed in the within-subjects design may be a result of a sample bias. Another possibility is that the inconsistencies are due to differences in the nature of the relationships tapped by the two studies. In the within-subjects design, the subjects described relationships with an acquaintance, friend, and best friend of their choice. In the between-subjects design, the subjects were asked to describe their relationship with their roommate. There may be commonalities inherent in roommate relationships that minimize sex differences. This is fortunate, given the problem of sex differences in self-report data, as previously discussed. Nonetheless, it

Table 6.3. *Mean scale scores and F-ratios for friends of different levels of closeness (between-subjects design)*

Group	Receives positive affect from friend	Expression of positive affect toward friend	Receives negative affect from friend	Expression of negative affect toward friend	Is responded to by friend	Is responsive to friend	Influences friend	Is influenced by friend	Shared fantasy
Females									
Acquaintances	14.38	22.63	14.75	21.75	41.63	25.63	25.25	18.38	19.00
Friends	22.65	33.35	14.75	21.80	54.30	34.15	29.40	22.30	25.15
Best friends	27.32	40.14	17.77	27.91	68.45	41.59	35.36	26.45	32.41
Males									
Acquaintances	14.45	22.45	13.73	20.36	40.91	24.91	24.18	18.09	17.73
Friends	20.13	31.93	15.53	23.67	54.67	32.40	29.60	23.80	22.67
Best friends	24.20	35.88	17.48	26.24	64.40	39.08	33.24	26.08	27.88
F-Ratios									
Friendship (F)	73.69**	65.94**	6.77	15.21**	71.31**	61.31**	27.61**	38.95**	48.23**
Sex (S)	5.79*	3.04	0.05	0.19	0.73	2.23	0.90	0.14	7.94*
F×S	1.63	1.18	0.45	2.52	0.60	0.22	0.41	0.67	0.94

*p < .05; **p < .001.

will be necessary in future studies to control for sex differences in the selection of subjects so that relationships are matched for closeness and relationship satisfaction.

Selection of a setting and procedure

In the design of an observational methodology, the method of recording behavior and the social and physical context in which it is to be observed must be considered.

In order to observe reliable and representative behavior, we chose a physical setting that was as familiar and natural as possible – the subjects' dormitory room. In order to assess the effects of the social context on the subjects' behavior, we pilot-tested several interactional tasks.

Thirteen roommate pairs were recruited by telephone from a dormitory roster to participate in a study investigating roommate interactions. Arrangements were made for the experimenter to go to the subjects' dormitory room to administer Gottman's friendship questionnaire and to videotape the roommates interacting. Each roommate pair was asked to participate in two of the following interactional tasks: a NASA task, in which the subjects were asked to discuss and reach agreement about the supplies they would bring with them on a trip to the moon (Hall, 1971; Hall & Williams, 1966); an Improvised Conflict Method, in which each subject was given a different version of a conflict situation between roommates and asked to come to a consensus as to who would be most at fault (based on the Olson and Ryder Inventory of Marital Conflicts; see Olson & Ryder, 1970); a Conflict Inventory, in which each subject individually rank-ordered the severity of the most problematic of 10 roommate situations, which were then discussed by both roommates (the Conflict Inventory was based on Gottman's Problem Inventory for married couples [Gottman, 1979]); an Incomplete Sentences Blank, in which roommates were asked to discuss their responses to open-ended questions about their hopes and expectations for the future; and a semistructured interview in which roommates were asked to discuss with each other different aspects of their relationship. On the basis of data from this pilot work and subject reports in follow-up interviews, we discovered that the subjects' behavior was heavily influenced by the interactional task and the presence of a third person. The subjects' conversations appeared to be very stilted and superficial. In addition, the subjects often reported never having talked about these topics before and feeling unnatural in the presence of the experimenter.

In an effort to create a more ecologically valid environment, we tested a less reactive procedure. M. Putallaz (personal communication) suggested leaving a tape recorder with the roommates rather than videotaping them participating in an artificially created interaction task. On the basis of this suggestion, 10 new roommate pairs were recruited by telephone to participate in a study investigating roommate interactions. The experimenter left a tape recorder with them with instructions to record their conversations after the experimenter left. The subjects were instructed to go about their daily activities as usual, without doing anything differently except to turn on the tape recorder when they spoke to each other. The tape recorder was picked up a week later.

Audiotape recording was used instead of videotaping because, even though important nonverbal channels of communication are lost, audiotaping provides several important advantages: (1) An experimenter need not be present to operate the equipment; (2) the equipment can be left with the subjects so that conversation is recorded when it occurs naturally rather than in an artificially induced experimental session; (3) the equipment is less obtrusive; and (4) the subjects can turn the tape recorder on or off to protect their privacy.

The only indication on the pilot tapes that the conversations were not completely natural were comments about the tape recorder, such as "Is the tape recorder on?" and, after a long period of silence, "You can turn it off." There was no indication that the tape recorder was being turned off during private conversations. In order to assess the number of references to the experimental procedure, a reactivity category was added to the coding system. This code was used for any references to the tape recorder, experimenter, or experimental procedure. On the basis of our observations and subjects' reports, the experimental procedure appeared to be ecologically valid, and conversations between roommates sounded natural.

6.2. Methods

Subjects

Gottman's friendship questionnaire was administered to 200 introductory psychology students. They were instructed to respond to the questionnaire according to their feelings about their relationship with their same-sex roommate. Students without roommates, with more than one roommate, or with a cross-sex roommate were not included.

Subjects were recruited for the study on the basis of their scores on the friendship questionnaire.

The selection process involved rank-ordering all scores for each sex. Within each sex, the subjects recruited were those whose scores spanned the range on the friendship questionnaire. The subjects were contacted by telephone and asked to participate in a study of roommate relationships. Only subjects whose roommates agreed to participate were included. A same-sex experimenter made arrangements to meet the roommates in their dormitory room in order to administer the friendship questionnaire and several other questionnaires to both roommates and to provide audiotape recording equipment. After the experimental procedure was completed, two dyads were discarded from analysis either because their audiotaped conversations were inaudible or because a third person was present. Of those remaining, four female subjects and their roommates were above the median in their friendship score. These four dyads were selected to represent the upper range of the friendship score for females. The other 10 female subjects were in dyads in which both were below the median or one was above and one below. Four female subjects were chosen to represent the lower range of the friendship score. The subjects chosen were those with the lowest mean scores per dyad. The same method was used to select four male dyads representing the upper range of the friendship score and four male dyads representing the lower range. In total, 16 dyads were selected for analysis. They were selected so that there were no sex differences on the friendship questionnaire *within* condition (close or distant).

Procedure

The experimenter came to each subject's dormitory room and asked roommates to complete five additional questionnaires, including Gottman's friendship questionnaire. The results of the questionnaire data are not described in this chapter. The experimenter set up the equipment in the dormitory room and instructed subjects in its use. The experimenter tape-recorded each subject stating his or her name and a few brief comments in order to provide a means of identifying the subjects' voices later. The tape recorder was placed where it was visible and easily accessible to the roommates. They were instructed to turn the tape recorder on whenever the two of them were in the room talking. They were asked to turn the recorder off in the presence of other people.

They were requested not to interrupt their daily activities or make conversation for the purpose of filling up the tape, but to carry on as normally as possible. The tape recording equipment was picked up by the experimenter a week later. Although it was hoped that subjects would fill up at least one 45-minute side of the cassette, this was not always the case. There was a great deal of variability among dyads in the amount of conversation recorded. Typewritten transcripts varied in length from 4 to 30 pages.

The tapes were transcribed verbatim by at least two transcribers before analysis. The second transcriber checked and corrected the transcripts. Sections of the transcript with third persons present were not coded.

Selection of a coding system

The development of a classification or coding system is a selective process that always results in the loss of some information. Although no coding system is completely satisfactory, it is important that the system chosen serve the relevant research issues. In this case, the goal was to examine those aspects of social conversation that have the most implications for friendship. The system should also be sufficiently detailed for the application of sequential analysis. All too frequently in social psychological research, only one or two behaviors are selected for coding. This can lead to incomplete knowledge about interrelationships among responses and about patterns of behavior. Since the present investigation was part of a larger project on the description of friendship in children and adults, a coding system that could be applied to both age groups was needed.

The children's MICRO coding system (see Chapter 2) was revised (in collaboration with Deborah N. Mauger) for use in the roommate study. It was essentially the same coding system, except that categories and examples relevant to adult conversation were added. These categories added were the content codes, opinion, and the reactivity code. Numerous examples from adult conversations were included in a code manual, which made fine distinctions between the codes.

Lumping scheme

Since one of the goals of this investigation was to examine disclosure reciprocity as a function of intimacy of information exchanged, some

Table 6.4a. *Generalizability coefficients for content codes*

Code	Frequency[a]	Mean square subjects (transcripts)	Mean square residual	Cronbach alpha
Me	632	99.28	1.57	.969
Feeling	694	274.26	3.79	.973
Mindreading	70	11.59	0.15	.974
Sympathy	2	0.14	0.00	1.000
Offer	5	0.45	0.00	1.000
Rule	2	0.14	0.00	1.000
Information	1407	455.69	3.57	.984
Clarifies message	290	42.94	0.83	.962
Failure to clarify message	38	5.01	0.24	.908
Agreement	548	102.61	3.28	.938
Disagreement	142	45.17	1.29	.944
Command	27	3.95	0.11	.944
Attention getter	166	27.22	0.08	.994
Polite request	2	0.14	0.00	1.000
Suggestion	37	2.98	0.01	.992
Asks permission	1	0.07	0.00	1.000
Demand as question for information	0	—	—	—
Wanna	0	—	—	—
We'll have to	4	0.21	0.02	.842
Let's	9	0.64	0.02	.946
Roles to both	0	—	—	—
We both	3	0.15	0.02	.787
Me too	20	1.30	0.03	.949
We against others	1	0.07	0.00	1.000
Repetition	26	1.85	0.10	.897
Joining in	0	—	—	—
Opinion	16	1.22	0.16	.766
Reactive	67	41.09	0.00	1.000
Disagreement with clarification	4	0.24	0.03	.747

[a]Frequency refers to how often this code was noted in the sample by one or both coders and is thus the diagonal plus off-diagonal total in the Cohen kappa matrix over all 28 transcripts.

modifications (i.e., lumping and splitting) of the coding system were necessary to distinguish different levels of intimacy. The feeling (FE) code was split to distinguish between superficial feelings (FE1) and intimate feelings (FE2). The me (ME) code was divided into exclamations (ME1), simple self-statements, (ME2), and personally revealing self-statements (ME3). Two summary codes that represent two different

Table 6.4b. *Generalizability coefficients for content codes*

Code	Frequency[a]	Mean square subjects (transcripts)	Mean square residual	Cronbach alpha
Fantasy	44	8.49	0.23	.947
Squabble	35	8.37	1.02	.784
Joke	400	88.17	7.38	.845
Question	641	145.72	1.23	.983
Gossip	788	414.31	1.91	.991

[a]Frequency refers to how often this code was noted in the sample by one or both coders and is thus the diagonal plus off-diagonal total in the Cohen kappa matrix over all 28 transcripts.

levels of intimacy were created from the feeling (FE1, FE2), me (ME2, ME3), and opinion (OP) codes. They were high-intimacy self-disclosure (HSD), composed of the FE2 and ME3 subcodes; and low-intimacy self-disclosure (LSD), composed of the FE1, ME2, and OP subcodes. Exclamations (ME1) remained a separate coding category. In addition, the agreement (AG) code was split to distinguish between mere acknowledgment (AG1) and praise (AG2).

All the other codes either remained the same or were lumped into the summary codes presented in Chapter 2. Lumping decisions were made on a logical basis. Because many of the demand codes were infrequent, the various types of demands (COM, ATT, Q/PRE, SUG, Q/SUG, QASK, Q/IND, WA, HWA, Q/WA, LTS, RV, AH, Q/LTS, and ROL) were lumped into a summary code labeled controlling statements (CONT).

Not all double-code combinations are logically possible. Squabbles and jokes cannot logically co-occur. An analysis of the frequencies of occurrence and co-occurrence of the double codes with the content codes showed that, except for the question (Q) and joke (J) double codes, the other double codes, fantasy (F), squabble (S), and gossip (G), were relatively independent. Fantasy, squabbles, jokes, questions, and gossip took precedence over all content codes and over one another. Squabbles, an infrequent double code, was absorbed by the disagreement content code and collectively labeled negativity (NEG). We both (WE) and we against others, (WEG), both infrequent codes, were absorbed by the me too (TOO) code and collectively labeled you and me

(YM). Clarifies message (CM) was absorbed by the information (IN) code. Sympathy (SY) and offers (OF), two infrequent codes, were combined into one category called support (SUP). This lumping scheme resulted in 19 mutually exclusive and exhaustive coding categories. Generalizability coefficients for the content codes are listed in Table 6.4a; those for the double codes are in Table 6.4b.

Dominance and asymmetric relationship satisfaction

In our sequential analyses we consistently designated the person with the higher friendship score Person 1 and the person with the lower friendship score Person 2. Bernard (1972), in his book on marriage, noted that husbands in our society tend to score *higher* in marital satisfaction than their wives. Although this is not a consistently obtained result, husbands in our society also tend to be dominant in their marriages (but see Strodtbeck, 1951, for a cross-cultural analysis). For the purposes of our analysis, we reasoned that the person in a relationship with the highest relationship satisfaction ought to be getting the most rewards from the relationship and should probably have the most power in the relationship. To test this hypothesis, we reasoned that Person 1 should be issuing a higher proportion of demands of all types than Person 2. A correlated t-test on the proportions of demands of all types supported this contention [$t(15) = 1.85$, $p < .05$, one-tailed]. This asymmetry is related to Kelley's (1979) suggestion that an asymmetry in dependence "sets the stage for the less dependent person to exercise more influence in the relationship" (p. 45).

We should clarify that the terms "subordinate" and "dominant" refer to a dimension that is usually orthogonal to the intimacy of the relationship. The subordinate person is often an emotional caretaker of the relationship. We have anecdotally observed that in young friends this asymmetry can be a function of an asymmetry in social skillfulness; the subordinate person does most of the work of message clarification, conflict resolution, and general maintenance and repair of the relationship. The subordinate member need not be doing this work out of tension, fear, or worry; negative affect enters into this asymmetry only when relationships are distressed.

We shall continue this analogy with roommates and refer to Person 1 as the *dominant* person in the dyad (i.e., in Kelley's terminology the less dependent person) and to Person 2 as the *subordinate* person in the dyad.

6.3. Results

The reactivity of the experimental procedure was assessed by the proportion of the utterances made by each member of the dyad that were coded with the reactivity code. The reactivity of the experimental procedure was independent of closeness (for the dominant person, $r = .19$, n.s.; for the subordinate person, $r = .15$, n.s.) and the sex of the dyad (for the dominant person, $r = -.21$, n.s.; for the subordinate person, $r = -.15$, n.s.).

There was no relationship between sex and the closeness score (the average of the two friendship scores, $r = -.18$, n.s.). Thus, the experimental procedure was successful in selecting for analysis 16 dyads matched for closeness. Thus, in this study female dyads were similar to male dyads. The length of acquaintanceship was strongly related to closeness ($r = .81$, $p < .001$). These two constructs, thus, could not be disentangled. This makes sense; it implies that only those roommates who are close continue to live together.

A series of 2×2 analyses of variance, with two levels of closeness and two levels of sex (male/female), found no significant interactions between the sex composition of the dyad and relationship satisfaction for any process variable under investigation. The results that follow will be presented as correlations with closeness and sex. We are aware of the issues of using correlations with an extreme groups design. However, all the analyses are consistent with the analyses of variance, and we believe that the results are easier to understand as correlations.

The pattern that popular psychology literature describes must involve *both* sex differences in a social process and a correlation between that process and closeness. For example, Bell would say that self-disclosure is both more characteristic of close than distant relationships and more characteristic of women than men. If it is more characteristic of one sex than the other, it must be described as a *stylistic* difference, that is, not one meaningfully related to closeness.

Self-disclosure. Table 6.5 shows that there was no significant relationship between the amounts of either low-intimacy or high-intimacy self-disclosure and closeness (the average friendship score of the dyad). However, there was one significant sex difference. The subordinate female roommate in the dyad was more likely to self-disclose (HSD2) than the subordinate male roommate. The probability of high-intimacy self-disclosure was thus a *stylistic* difference between the sexes, but it

Table 6.5. *Correlations of closeness and sex with amounts and type of self-disclosure*

Self-disclosure[a]	Closeness	Sex[b]
HSD1	.246	−.245
LSD1	−.330	−.138
HSD2	−.068	−.446*
LSD2	−.069	.325

[a] HSD, High-intimacy self-disclosure; LSD, low-intimacy self-disclosure.
[b] 0 = Female; 1 = male. A negative correlation implies that this behavior is more characteristic of female dyads than of male dyads.
*p < .05.

Table 6.6. *Self-disclosure sequences*

Sequence[a]	Closeness	Sex[b]
Reciprocity HSD1 → HSD2	.300	.180
Reciprocity HSD2 → HSD1	−.113	.040
Reciprocity LSD1 → LSD2	.003	.220
Reciprocity LSD2 → LSD1	−.572**	.036
Deescalation HSD1 → LSD2	−.387	.026
Deescalation HSD2 → LSD1	.009	.438*
Escalation LSD1 → HSD2	−.477*	.386
Escalation LSD2 → HSD1	.261	−.411

*p < .05; **p < .01.

was not related to closeness. This is an important distinction. It means that male and female roommates differ in how much they self-disclose. The subordinate female roommate discloses more than the subordinate male roommate; dominant male roommates and dominant female roommates are not different. However, none of these differences is related to closeness. Thus, the assertions about women disclosing more than men in their close relationships do not hold up once we control for the amount of closeness in the relationships of the two sexes.

Sequential analysis makes it possible to examine the other popular hypothesis about self-disclosure, namely, that women reciprocate self-disclosure more often than men. Table 6.6 summarizes the correlation of sex and closeness with the z-scores for *reciprocity sequences*, sequences in which the intimacy of the consequent self-disclosure matches the intimacy of the antecedent self-disclosure. Table 6.6 also summarizes the correlations for *escalation sequences*, sequences in which the intimacy of the consequent self-disclosure is higher than the intimacy of the antecedent self-disclosures, and for *deescalation sequences*, sequences in which the intimacy of the consequent self-disclosure is lower than the intimacy of the antecedent self-disclosure. The reciprocity of high-intimacy self-disclosure was not related to closeness or sex. Thus, reciprocating self-disclosures of high intimacy were neither more characteristic of one sex nor related to closeness. In contrast, the reciprocity of *low*-intimacy self-disclosure by the dominant partner was significantly related to closeness, although it was negatively related ($-.57$, $p.<, 01$). This was true for both sexes. Escalation of the dominant person's self-disclosure by the subordinate person was negatively related to closeness for both male and female dyads.

Three conclusions emerge. First, reciprocity of high-intimacy self-disclosure is independent of closeness. Second, it is more characteristic of distant than of close dyads for the subordinate person to attempt to escalate the intimacy of the self-disclosure. Third, deescalation of a high-intimacy self-disclosure by the dominant person is characteristic of male dyads, but it is independent of closeness. Once again we have a stylistic difference between the sexes, but one unrelated to closeness.

These results present an incomplete picture, in part because of the narrowness of the behaviors under investigation. So many other things naturally occur in a clip of conversation containing a self-disclosure that we must broaden the range of behaviors we consider to understand the social processes related to closeness and to sex difference. Table 6.7 presents the correlations of the z-scores of eight social processes that are consequences of self-disclosure with closeness and sex. Only information exchange and joking were positively related to closeness. It is interesting that the question had to be asked by the dominant roommate (in response to a low-intimacy disclosure) and that humor was the tactic of the subordinate roommate (in response to a high-intimacy disclosure). This was true for both sexes. Several sequences were characteristic of roommate pairs who were *not* close, including giving information and topic shifts. This was true for both males and females.

Negative affect by the subordinate person in response to a low-intimacy self-disclosure by the dominant person was more characteristic of female than of male dyads, although once again this was a stylistic difference between the sexes that was independent of closeness. How-

Table 6.7. *Consequences of self-disclosure*

Social process	Closeness	Sex
Acknowledgment		
HSD1 → ACK2	.318	−.325
HSD2 → ACK1	−.093	.344
LSD1 → ACK2	.250	−.158
LSD2 → ACK1	.351	.238
Information exchange		
HSD1 → QS2	.092	.100
HSD2 → QS1	−.351	.375
LSD1 → QS2	.240	−.238
LSD2 → QS1	.546*	−.022
HSD1 → IN1	.108	−.185
HSD2 → IN2	−.490*	.380
LSD1 → IN2	−.021	−.323
LSD2 → IN1	−.575**	.111
Topic shift (non sequitur)		
HSD1 → NCM2	−.513*	.159
HSD2 → NCM1	.257	−.249
LSD1 → NCM2	−.584**	−.025
LSD2 → NCM1	−.248	−.043
Negative affect		
HSD1 → NEG2	−.311	.385
HSD2 → NEG1	.053	−.239
LSD1 → NEG2	.319	−.654**
LSD2 → NEG1	−.337	−.098
Directives		
HSD1 → CNT2	.393	−.168
HSD2 → CNT1	−.007	−.145
LSD1 → CNT2	.108	.397
LSD2 → CNT1	.173	−.393
Mindreading		
HSD1 → YOU2	.271	−.201
HSD2 → YOU1	.065	−.086
LSD1 → YOU2	−.594**	.442*
LSD2 → YOU1	−.163	.034
Gossip		
HSD1 → GOS2	−.120	−.233
HSD2 → GOS1	.124	.335
LSD1 → GOS2	.169	−.344
LSD2 → GOS1	.373	.061

Table 6.7. *(Cont.)*

Social process	Closeness	Sex
Joking		
HSD1 → JK2	.446*	.211
HSD2 → JK1	−.263	.248
LSD1 → JK2	−.002	−.318
LSD2 → JK1	.369	−.274

*$p < .05$;** $p < .01$.

ever, mindreading by the subordinate person following a low-intimacy disclosure by the dominant person was both negatively related to closeness and significantly more characteristic of male roommates. This is the kind of pattern of correlations that Fasteau and Bell wrote about. Note that it is the *only* such pattern among the 88 correlations in Tables 6.6 and 6.7. It was certainly not predicted theoretically, and it is thus difficult to interpret.

In general, mindreading by the dominant roommate was unrelated to closeness ($r = .02$) or sex ($r = .06$). In contrast, the probability of mindreading by the subordinate person was related to closeness ($r = .49$, $p<.05$), though it was not more characteristic of male than female roommates ($r = −.10$). The correlations with closeness were positive only if humor ($r = .43$, $p < .05$) or gossip ($r = .47$, $p < .05$) by the subordinate roommate preceded the subordinate roommate's mindreading. The importance of this pattern in Table 6.7 remains a mystery.

Mindreading. Table 6.8 presents the consequences of mindreading (which was a characteristic consequent of low-intimacy self-disclosure in distant dyads and in male dyads) and the correlation of the z-scores for these sequences with closeness and sex. Nearly all the consequents were negatively correlated with closeness, except for direct acknowledgment. This was true independent of the sex of the dyad. Negative affect as a consequence of mindreading by the dominant person was more characteristic of female than of male dyads, but once again this was a stylistic difference unrelated to closeness. Mindreading involves psychological interpretations of the other person's behavior or attributions of feelings or motives to the other person. For example, "You just can't tolerate deviance" followed by acknowledgment: "Maybe you're right."

Table 6.8. *Consequences of mindreading and their correlations with closeness and sex*

Social process	Closeness	Sex
Acknowledgment		
YOU1 → ACK2	.434*	.131
YOU2 → ACK1	.271	−.235
Information exchange		
YOU1 → QS2	−.563*	.015
YOU2 → QS1	−.234	.258
YOU1 → IN2	−.392	.235
YOU2 → IN1	−.457	.282
Topic shift		
YOU1 → NCM2	−.457*	.026
YOU2 → NCM1	−.378	.296
Negative affect		
YOU1 → NEG2	−.039	−.430*
YOU2 → NEG1	+.098	−.187
Directives		
YOU1 → CNT2	−.702***	.338
YOU2 → CNT1	.134	−.268
Mindreading		
YOU1 → YOU2	−.514*	.145
YOU2 → YOU1	−.631**	.238
Gossip		
YOU1 → GOS2	.049	.262
YOU2 → GOS1	−.382	.268
Joking		
YOU1 → JK2	−.049	.132
YOU2 → JK1	−.265	.255
Self-disclosure		
YOU1 → HSD2	−.289	.327
YOU2 → HSD1	.028	−.144
YOU1 → LSD2	−.499*	−.021
YOU2 → LSD1	−.089	−.045

*p < .05; **p < .01.

Table 6.9. Consequences of gossip and their relationship
to closeness and sex

Social process	Closeness	Sex
Acknowledgment		
GOS1 → ACK2	.432*	−.130
GOS2 → ACK1	.067	.146
Information exchange		
GOS1 → QS2	.123	.299
GOS2 → QS1	−.361	−.138
GOS1 → IN2	−.284	−.256
GOS2 → IN1	−.397	−.050
Topic shift		
GOS1 → NCM2	−.456*	−.103
GOS2 → NCM1	−.339	−.008
Negative affect		
GOS1 → NEG2	−.621**	.080
GOS2 → NEG1	−.460*	.212
Directives		
GOS1 → CNT2	.286	−.083
GOS2 → CNT1	.099	−.503*
Mindreading		
GOS1 → YOU2	.317	−.230
GOS2 → YOU1	.060	−.176
Gossip		
GOS1 → GOS2	.417	.291
GOS2 → GOS1	−.004	−.053
Joking		
GOS1 → JK2	.319	.338
GOS2 → JK1	−.164	.155
Self-disclosure		
GOS1 → HSD2	.035	−.458*
GOS2 → HSD1	−.015	.119
GOS1 → LSD2	−.023	.168
GOS2 → LSD1	−.223	.038

*$p < .05$; **$p < .01$.

Gossip. Table 6.9 presents the relationships between the eight social processes and gossip. One of our hypotheses was that gossip is a precursor of self-disclosure in close dyads (see Chapter 2). This hypothesis was not supported. However, gossip by the dominant person was a precursor of self-disclosure in *female* dyads, although this was a stylistic difference independent of closeness.

The reciprocity of gossip was not significantly related to closeness. The amount of gossip by either person was also unrelated to closeness (GOS1, $r = .10$; GOS2, $r = -.24$) or to sex (GOS1, $r = .14$; GOS2, $r = .11$). However, we cannot conclude that gossiping was unrelated to closeness. It was important for the subordinate person, independent of sex, to acknowledge the dominant roommate's gossip ($r = .43, p < .05$). Furthermore, topic shifts and negative affect following gossip by subordinate partners were consequents characteristic of distant dyads of both sexes. Another stylistic consequent of female dyads was the use of directives by the dominant roommate in response to the subordinate roommate's gossiping; this sequence was, once again, unrelated to closeness. Female dyads were more likely to use all forms of directives (CONT) than male dyads (CNT1, $r = -.54, p < .05$; CNT2, $r = -.41$, $p < .10$). The probability of use of directives was related to closeness (CNT1, $r = .38, p < .10$; CNT2, $r = .53, p < .05$).

Similarities and differences. Table 6.10 presents the relationships between the exploration of similarities and differences and the dyad's closeness and sex. The exploration of similarities and differences was unrelated to closeness, although there was a purely sex-related stylistic difference. Female dyads were more likely than male dyads to explore differences. This occurred asymmetrically, when the subordinate person expressed a difference in response to the dominant person's self-disclosure.

Conflict and humor. Table 6.10 also shows that both extended conflict and extended humor were *positively* related to closeness, as suggested by Hinde (1979). In both cases the reciprocation was asymmetric; it was performed by the subordinate person in the dyad.

Affect. Table 6.11 presents the results of the analysis of the probabilities of affective and informational interaction. Only the amount of negative affect expressed by the dominant person was positively related to closeness. This display of negative affect was more likely for female than for male roommates. *The interactions of women were more likely than the*

Table 6.10. *Similarity and difference exploration, extended conflict, and extended humor sequences and their correlations with closeness and sex*

Social process	Closeness	Sex
Similarity		
HSD1 → ACK2	.396	−.325
HSD2 → ACK1	−.143	.344
LSD1 → ACK2	.329	.238
LSD2 → ACK1	.250	−.158
Difference		
HSD1 → NEG2	−.314	.385
HSD2 → NEG1	.110	−.239
LSD1 → NEG2	.323	−.654**
LSD2 → NEG1	−.337	−.089
Extended conflict		
NEG1 → NEG2	.452*	−.411
NEG2 → NEG1	−.023	−.227
Extended humor		
JK1 → JK2	.438*	−.105
JK2 → JK1	.226	−.227

*$p < .05$; **$p < .01$.

Table 6.11. *Amount of affect and its relation to closeness and sex of the dyad*

	Correlation with	
Social process	Closeness	Sex
Negative affect		
NEG1	.587**	−.491*
NEG2	.225	−.508*
Humor		
JK1	.147	−.685**
JK2	.396	−.434
Information		
IN1	−.080	.664**
IN2	−.118	.335

Table 6.12. *Consequences of negative affect expressed by the dominant member of the dyad (NEG1)*

	Correlation with relationship satisfaction	
Sequence	Females	Males
NEG1 → NEG2	.722*	−.022
NEG1 → QS2	.666*	.083
NEG1 → ACK2	.633*	.078
NEG1 → EXC2	−.621*	.289
NEG1 → NCM2	−.667*	−.838**
NEG1 → HSD2	.045	−.757*
NEG1 → YOU2	.110	−.719*
NEG1 → CNT2	−.147	−.835**

$*p < .05$; $**p < .01$.

Table 6.13. *Stepwise regression of process variables with friends' relationship satisfaction*

Process variable	Step	Multiple R	R^2	F-Ratio
YOU1 → CNT2	1	.702	.492	13.57**
LSD1 → YOU2	2	.801	.641	11.62***
GOS1 → GOS2	3	.876	.768	13.22***
LSD2 → IN1	4	.895	.800	11.06***
GOS1 → NEG2	5	.911	.830	9.79***

$**p < .01$; $***p < .001$.

interactions of men to be affective and less informational. For most variables these were stylistic differences unrelated to closeness. However, negative affect by the dominant roommate was both more characteristic of close roommates and more characteristic of female roommates. This was not the case for positive affect, although humor was more characteristic of women than men. Men's interaction was more informational and, hence, affectively neutral than women's, though these relationships were unrelated to closeness.

Table 6.12 presents the consequences of negative affect by the dominant roommate (NEG1). Note that *not a single consequence of negative affect is positively related to closeness for male roommates, whereas three such sequences exist for female roommates.*

Collinearity. To assess the degree of collinearity in the social process variables, a stepwise regression was performed using all process variables that correlated significantly with closeness. Because there were only 16 dyads, the regression was cut off at $N/3$, or five variables. Table 6.13 summarizes the results of this regression. The major result is that five variables are capable of accounting for 83% of the variance in closeness among friends. Thus, although one must be cautious about this conclusion, there is a relatively low level of collinearity among these variables with regard to closeness.

6.4. Discussion

Amount and intimacy of self-disclosure

The amount of low- and high-intimacy self-disclosure was investigated as a function of the closeness of the relationship. No support was found for Altman and Taylor's view that individuals tend to disclose more information about themselves or disclose at greater levels of intimacy as a relationship develops. We did not find significantly greater amounts of either low-intimacy or high-intimacy self-disclosure in relationships characterized by greater levels of closeness.

Only two observational studies were found in the literature that examined the intimacy level of self-disclosure as a function of acquaintance. Davis (1978) observed same-sex stranger dyads alternately take turns disclosing information about themselves from a list of preselected intimacy-scaled topics. The intimacy of the disclosures of both partners increased over the course of 12 trials. The other study examined the intimacy of self-disclosure as a function of the topic of conversation as well as acquaintance. Morton (1978) compared the intimacy level and topic of self-disclosure of stranger dyads and marital dyads. Married couples communicated with more descriptive intimacy (i.e., private facts) but not with more evaluative intimacy (i.e., personal feelings or opinions) than stranger dyads.

In these two studies the composition of the dyads and the stages of acquaintance they represented were not comparable to the dyads in the present investigation. In the Davis study, the dyads were composed of same-sex strangers who became acquainted during a single encounter. In the Morton study the interactions of opposite-sex strangers and married couples were compared. The low acquaintance groups in both studies were composed of strangers and were therefore less committed to maintaining a relationship than even the most distant roommates in the present investigation. The failure to find greater intimacy in close than in distant roommates in the current study may be due to the fact that all subjects were involved in established and ongoing relationships with their roommates. Perhaps the level of intimacy is a salient dimension in relationship development only in, or in comparison with, the earliest stages of acquaintance and not in ongoing relationships with a future.

A related possibility is that, because roommates live together, they have access to private information about each other, independent of closeness, that may minimize differences in the level or intimacy of self-disclosure. Investigating relationships where private information is not publicly available in a shared living environment may result in greater differences between close and casual friends than those found in the present investigation.

Our investigation also allowed dyads to interact naturally whereas the Davis and Morton studies interrupted the natural flow of conversation and restricted subjects' interaction to the selection and discussion of preselected intimacy-scaled topics. The artificial salience of intimacy level in these studies may have exaggerated the relationship between intimacy and acquaintance. When subjects are allowed to respond freely, other types of interaction or "contents" of conversation may be more salient.

If the level of intimacy of self-disclosure is not the factor that promotes closeness between people who are already acquainted and share basic information, what is?

Disclosure reciprocity

Reciprocity of self-disclosure was investigated as a function of the intimacy of the information disclosed and the closeness of the relationship. No support was found for Altman's (1973) view that mutual reciprocity plays a greater role in the early stages of a relationship than in later stages. Mutually contingent reciprocity of high-intimacy and low-intimacy self-disclosure was not related to the closeness of the relationship.

Although mutually contingent reciprocity was unrelated to acquaintance in our study, asymmetric reciprocity was significantly more characteristic of distant than of close relationships for (1) the subordinate partner to escalate the intimacy of the self-disclosure and (2) the dominant partner to reciprocate low-intimacy self-disclosure. In other words, one member of the dyad assumed the reciprocating role, and the other member of the dyad escalated the level of intimacy. Neither of these behaviors was predictably reciprocated by the other.

How do the findings on disclosure reciprocity in this study compare with the results of other studies? Only one observational study has adequately tested for mutually contingent reciprocity. Dindia (1983) used sequential analysis to test for mutually contingent reciprocity in unstructured dyadic interactions between strangers who became acquainted over the course of three sessions. In examining the consequences of self-disclosure for both members of the dyad through five lags, she found no evidence of mutual reciprocity. Together these findings disconfirm the view that self-disclosure is mutually reciprocated.

The results on asymmetric or "one-way" reciprocity are not as clear-cut. In the present investigation asymmetric reciprocity was related to acquaintance and to the role (i.e., dominant or subordinate) each member of the dyad assumed relative to the other. In the Dindia study no evidence of asymmetric reciprocity was found. Because of the lack of significant findings, the effects of acquaintance, personal factors, and dyadic composition on reciprocity of self-disclosure were not assessed.

One study that examined the effects of dyadic composition on reciprocity in stranger dyads revealed a pattern similar to that found in the present investigation. Davis (1978) attempted to test for mutual reciprocity by computing the rank-order correlation between the intimacy levels of each subject's self-disclosure and the antecedent disclosure of each subject's partner, and vice versa. He found no evidence of mutual reciprocity but did report that self-disclosure was reciprocated in an asymmetric manner. One partner assumed the reciprocating role, whereas the other behaved independently in selecting the intimacy levels. The reciprocating partner tended to be the less disclosing member of the dyad, whereas the more disclosing partner assumed primary responsibility for increasing the level of intimacy. Unfortunately, the statistical methods used in the Davis study did not rule out the rival hypothesis that the level of intimacy could have resulted from two independent trends toward greater intimacy over time (as discussed by Dindia, 1983). Despite the fact that Davis did not use sequential analytic techniques that controlled for base rates, his findings are not inconsistent with the hypothesis that distant relationships are characterized by asymmetric reciprocity. Furthermore, the direction of reciprocity may be related to the role differentiation in the relationships.

Taken together, these studies suggest that, although early stages of relationships may be characterized by asymmetric temporal linkage of self-disclosure, mutual reciprocity of self-disclosure does not characterize close relationships. In fact, Murstein et al. (1977) found that endorsement of a reciprocal exchange orientation regarding interpersonal relationships was positively correlated with relationship satisfaction among roommates but negatively correlated with relationship satisfaction among married couples. Although Murstein et al.'s methods were not observational, their findings suggest that well-functioning close relationships (happy marriages) are not characterized by mutual reciprocity. Clark and Mills (1979) found that an exchange orientation may actually have the effect of impairing close relationships. They manipulated the basis on which interpersonal rewards were exchanged and whether an attractive confederate seemed receptive to future interaction. It was found that, when strangers had an opportunity for future contact, a reciprocal exchange orientation reduced interpersonal attraction.

Much has been written in the self-disclosure literature about the importance of reciprocating self-disclosure to show one's liking and trust of another person. The present findings suggest that disclosure reciprocity is not the process by which this occurs. Nonetheless, it is intuitively appealing to assume that the way an intimate disclosure is responded to will have an impact on the quality of the relationship. Unfortunately, few studies have investigated consequences of self-disclosure other than more self-disclosure. Many studies limit subjects' responses to disclosure of information from a list of preselected intimacy-scaled topics. This prevents a subject from responding to or initiating an interaction with anything but self-disclosure at various levels of intimacy.

Other consequences of self-disclosure

Reisman and Yamokoski (1974) conducted one of the few observational studies that used a multiple-category coding system for interpersonal responses rather than a unidimensional rating scale. Although they did not focus on the consequences of self-disclosure in particular, they did observe the way college students responded to a friend's discussion of a personal problem. Although some individuals responded with self-disclosure, friends were more likely to respond with either expository statements (an analysis or explanation of their friend's problem) or questions. Moreover, when subjects were asked how they would *like* their friends to respond to them when they were discussing a personal problem, the communication most favored was expository.

In the Reisman and Yamokoski study, the stated goal of the interaction was for one subject (who was assigned the role of "helper") to aid his or her friend in solving a personal problem. Thus, it is not surprising that the most frequently observed response and the response most preferred by subjects was an explanation or analysis of the problem. Undoubtedly the manipulated goal of the interaction influenced the response to the disclosure.

In comparing our results with those of other studies, it became obvious that demand characteristics specific to various experimental settings influence the way self-disclosure is responded to. Most experimental studies of self-disclosure instruct subjects to respond so that the other person will form an accurate impression of them. Berg and Archer (1982) pointed out that such studies emphasize the need to exchange information (i.e., private facts) and focus almost exclusively on the intimacy of the facts revealed. Conversation in real-life settings, however, does not require that the goal of interaction be restricted to impression formation. A person may strive for other goals in an interaction, such as obtaining support, being entertained, or increasing their attractiveness.

Berg and Archer (1982) experimentally manipulated the goal of an interaction to investigate its impact on responses to the low-intimacy and high-intimacy self-disclosure of a confederate. They examined only three types of response: descriptive intimacy ("the extent to which intimate facts are revealed"), evaluative intimacy ("the extent to which strong emotions or judgments are expressed"), and topical reciprocity ("the extent to which the response addresses the same subject matter as the initial disclosure"). It should be noted that "topical reciprocity" is an inappropriate use of the term "reciprocity" because it refers only to a one-way contingency. Nonetheless, these findings have relevance to the present investigation.

Berg and Archer employed a condition with no stipulation to exchange information; rather they asked subjects to bring to mind a real-life conversation when they replied. In this condition subjects responded with less descriptive intimacy (private facts) and more topical reciprocity (responses that addressed the same topic as the initial disclosure). Thus, in conditions that were more natural than others, subjects were more likely to address the same topic as the discloser *without necessarily revealing self-information or expressing affect*. This occurred when the confederate's input was either a high-intimacy or a low-intimacy self-disclosure.

Berg and Archer also found that when subjects were motivated to create a favorable impression, while at the same time keeping in mind a real-life conversation when they replied, they responded with more evaluative intimacy (affective statements or judgments) than they did in the other conditions. Furthermore, this response was more likely to occur following high-intimacy rather than low-intimacy self-disclosure.

These findings suggest that, in a natural setting in which there is also little motivation to be liked, individuals will respond to self-disclosure by addressing the same topic as the initial disclosure without necessarily revealing self-information or expressing affect. This hypothesis is consistent with our results. In a natural setting in which individuals wish to be liked by each other, there is more affective responsiveness, particularly in reaction to high-intimacy self-disclosure.

Although differences in the coding systems used make direct comparisons between the present investigation and that of Archer and Berg difficult, some parallels can be drawn. Our category of information exchange as a consequence of self-disclosure was similar to topical reciprocity because it addressed the same topic as the initial disclosure (otherwise it would have been coded as a topic shift) and was devoid of self-information or affective expression. We found that information exchange by both partners as a consequence of self-disclosure was more likely to occur in distant relationships than in close relationships. Being liked in distant relationships may be viewed as being less important than being liked by a close friend.

In the present investigation, subordinate partners in close relationships were more likely than those in distant relationships to respond to their dominant partners' high-intimacy self-disclosure with positive affect (joking and laughter). Thus, in close relationships where concern about being liked may be great, a certain amount of positive affective responsiveness seems important as a consequence of self-disclosure, at least by the subordinate partner.

Other studies have suggested that the affect expressed in a response and the extent to which it addresses the same topic as the initial disclosure have a positive influence on attraction for the respondent (Berg & Archer, 1980; Davis & Perkowitz, 1979).

In the present study topic shifts by the subordinate as a consequence of self-disclosure were more characteristic of distant relationships. This suggests that responsiveness, in terms of addressing the same topic as the person disclosing, has an impact on closeness. Apparently, it is important for the subordinate to respond to the disclosure, while the affective quality of the response may determine whether it will enhance closeness. Perhaps, as will be discussed later, topic shifts serve as a means of avoiding conflict with which a distant relationship is not equipped to cope.

It may be that to be truly responsive the *subordinate* partner not only must respond to the dominant partner's self-disclosure, but must do so with positive affect. The following example illustrates this point. The dominant roommate has just returned from the student health center, where she was given birth control pills for medical rather than contraceptive purposes. The subordinate partner responds to her roommate's high-intimacy self-disclosure with little verbal content but very playful and supportive laughter:

Dominant partner: I was just embarrassed that I could know somebody, you know. Six people can't even . . .
Subordinate partner: [*Laughs.*]
D: At least I wasn't there for birth control. She was though. You know what . . . weird though. Feels strange sitting in there. You know, talking about it in relation to you. So is it . . . were . . . , you know. It's always the older people that things happen to. You know, it's like we're now the older people and here they are talking to me about birth control. I've always been younger and always heard about it, you know?
S: Yeah.
D: Older ladies take the pill . . .
S: [*Laughs.*]
D: . . . and here they are talking to us. Strange to see all these girls around the room.

In another example, involving male roommates, the subordinate partner responds to his roommate's high-intimacy self-disclosure with good-natured teasing:

D: I got pretty messed up at your party.
S: [*Laughs.*] I don't know what you guys did; you guys put away an entire keg of beer.

In order to be truly responsive, it seems important for the *dominant* partner to respond to the subordinate's self-disclosure with a question. Perhaps a question communicates liking or an interest in what the other person has to say. Vondracek (1969) found that a "probing" technique used by an interviewer resulted in a greater amount of self-disclosure than "reflecting" or "revealing." The roles of interviewer and interviewee may be analogous to the roles of the dominant and subordinate partners in the present study (with regard to the balance of power in the relationship). The following examples illustrate this process. The first dyad is male:

S: . . . and Wednesday I got two big exams.
D: Exams in what?

The second dyad is female:

S: God, when I woke up this morning and it was twelve o'clock, I practically jumped through the roof, I was so surprised.
D: What time'd you think it was?

Another way to interpret our results on the consequences of self-disclosure is based on social pentration theory. In distant relationships, interpersonal behaviors are assumed to be relatively superficial and stereotyped according to cultural prescriptions. In close relationships, interpersonal behaviors are relatively unique to the dyad rather than culturally stereotyped and are described as "freewheeling" and spontaneous.

In examining the consequences of self-disclosure in distant relationships we find that both partners predictably respond with information exchange. This may be a culturally stereotyped response that occurs in distant relationships regardless of the intimacy level of the original disclosure or the person's role in the relationship. Perhaps it is a low-risk response. In contrast, the consequences of self-disclosure in close relationships are differentiated to a greater extent by the roles the roommates have assumed in the relationship. The dominant partner responds to self-disclosure with a question, whereas the subordinate partner responds with humor. Thus, the partners' interpersonal behavior is individualized and unique to the roles assumed by members of the dyad.

Mindreading

Previous research by Gottman (1979) demonstrated that mindreading can be functional or dysfunctional, depending on the affect with which it is delivered. Mindreading delivered with positive or neutral affect characterizes nondistressed marital relationships. Gottman noted that mindreading in that context seems to function as a sensitive probe or exploration of the other's experience. It is responded to with agreement and further elaboration. In the present investigation, the amount of mindreading by the subordinate partner was positively related to satisfaction. The social contexts (i.e., antecedents) in which this predictably occurred were characterized by positive affect (joking and laughter) or were at least neutral with regard to the dominant partner because they focused on other people (gossip).

Examples of the gossip followed by mindreading sequences (GOS2→MR2) of the subordinate roommate taken from written transcripts illustrate this point. Mindreading in the context of gossip seemed a way to personalize the discussion by including or reminding the other person of the way she or he fit into the situation being discussed. Occasionally it seemed to serve as a psychological interpretation. We present some examples to show how the mindreading code functions differently, depending on its sequential context.

In the following example the subordinate female roommate is gossiping about the costume a friend wore to a Halloween party. She then describes where her roommate (the dominant partner) was when the situation occurred. Her roommate acknowledges the scenario.

S: And when Sue came out in the pink wig and blacked out her tooth . . .
D: You're putting me on.
S: Oh, God! It was so funny. I got a picture of her. You were sleeping. That's right. It was like at one o'clock or twelve-thirty in the morning. It was where Greg from the Phi Delt house came over. She told you he came over.
D: Oh, Ok. Yes, she told me.

In another conversation between female roommates, mindreading seems to function as a psychological interpretation. The dominant partner is gossiping about her feelings toward a friend (Joe). The subordinate partner joins in the gossip and in the process offers an interpretation of her roommate's feelings. The dominant roommate agrees with this interpretation and elaborates on it.

D: I just hope Joe isn't mad at me. I'd be really bummed if he was. I think I'll still feel bad about it.
S: Umhm. But Joe does that a lot. You know what I mean? You might . . . sometimes it bugs me. I don't know. It bugs me when he does it to you, but it doesn't bug me. It doesn't bug you so it doesn't matter, really.
D: It doesn't bug me 'cause I'm not worried about John at all. You know?

In contrast, mindreading sequences preceded by self-disclosure (LSD1→MR2) seemed to convey or were responded to as a more critical message and were negatively related to satisfaction. The subordinate partner seemed to use the dominant partner's low-intimacy self-disclosure as a basis to admonish or question the partner rather than make a neutral attribution. In the following example, female roommates start by establishing a similarity between them. The subordinate partner then makes a somewhat critical mindreading statement in response to the dominant partner's low-intimacy self-disclosure. This is followed by disagreement on the part of the dominant partner.

D: I'd much rather sit here and figure out my tax than do my math.
S: Me too. My math is simple.
D: Half the things I do, they don't have to do with things I have to do.
S: And you wonder why you stay up 'till three o'clock in the morning.
D: No, I don't wonder. I know.

In another example, involving male roommates, the dominant partner is expressing a feeling about the hosts at a fraternity party. The subordinate partner responds to his roommate's low-intimacy self-disclosure by mindreading; that is, he makes an attribution about his roommate's feelings concerning the way a party crasher was dealt with. In this context mindreading by the partner is questioning the validity of the dominant partner's position. After a brief discussion, the dominant partner ends up disagreeing with the original attribution and discounting his roommate's statement.

D: They got me so ticked last night. I don't know.
S: You were sayin', you know, how you were sayin' that you were pissed off 'cause they kicked John [out].
D: Yeah.
S: I don't know . . . that's . . . I just think that if somebody was at one party, you know, and you don't know him . . .
D: Uhhuh.
S: . . . and [he] starts drinking beer . . .
D: Nobody even cared about that! It didn't matter. They just answered to Peterson and then they left. There was no hassle. [I'm] not really mad.

Although differences in the coding systems used in Gottman's earlier research and the present investigation make direct comparisons difficult, there appear to be some parallels. Gottman found that mindreading delivered with negative affect was responded to as if it were a criticism; it was disagreed with, and a self-defensive elaboration followed. This pattern was found to characterize distressed marital relationships. In the present investigation, mindreading by the subordinate partner in response to the low-intimacy self-disclosure of the dominant partner was negatively related to closeness. Mindreading in this context seemed to function as a criticism directed at the dominant partner's disclosure. Thus, it appears to be important for the subordinate partner to mindread, but only in certain social contexts. We propose the hypothesis that mindreading in response to the other person's self-disclosure may impede closeness, whereas mindreading in the context of laughter, joking, and gossip may promote it.

Gossip

Anthropological research suggests that gossip may be an indication of a certain degree of familiarity and trust between individuals. Although in the present investigation the amount of gossip was unrelated to closeness, the way it was responded to was related to closeness. Topic shifts and negative affect by subordinate partners may impair closeness. Perhaps gossiping has to be received in a more receptive social climate to promote trust and liking. Acknowledgment of the dominant partner's gossip by the subordinate partner is related to closeness and thus serves this function.

Contrary to predictions, gossip in our investigation was not an antecedent of self-disclosure in close relationships. Although this emerged logically from the assumptions of incremental exchange theory, we could not make precise predictions from this theory. In the area of social relationships there is a gap in our knowledge between the content-free principles of social exchange and the content of actual interpersonal interaction. It is a problem for the researcher to identify and measure specific behaviors that function according to theory. This is difficult when the theory is not content specific.

Extended conflict and extended humor

In their description of the stages of the social penetration process, Altman and Taylor (1973) addressed the role of evaluation in developing relationships. They theorized that, as relationships develop, people become more willing to communicate positive and negative affective statements. "People become more willing to criticize and to praise one another, to demonstrate positive and negative feelings, and to be less inhibited in evaluating one another" (p. 135). It may be helpful to use their framework to interpret the present results on extended conflict and extended humor.

Altman and Taylor (1973) characterized the beginning stages of relationships in the following way:

> At this stage people also tend not to evaluate one another openly, especially in a negative manner. There is a general reluctance to criticize and, if done, it is usually in a gentle, culturally approved and nonemotional fashion. If anything, silence is maintained or conversational direction altered rather than subjecting the other person to direct criticism. This is not only evidenced in verbal behavior, but also at nonverbal levels, with a general holding back

of negative reactions such as frowns, signs of anger, and negative head nods. If anything, one is apt to see indirect techniques of conflict avoidance, such as facing away, attempting to break off eye contact, moving out of the conversation, or attempting to change the conversation [p. 137].

This suggests that distant relationships are characterized by little negative evaluation and conflict. Conflicts or open expressions of negative affect are likely to be avoided by a tactic such as changing the topic of conversation. This may help to explain our finding that topic shifts by the subordinate partner following self-disclosure and gossip are more likely to occur in distant relationships. This may, in fact, be a successful strategy in avoiding open conflict, because we found that casual relationships were characterized by less negative affect, at least on the part of the dominant partner. When gossip was responded to with negative affect by the subordinate partner, it was negatively related to satisfaction. Thus, our results support Altman and Taylor's theory.

Altman and Taylor (1973) also theorized that closer relationships are characterized by "affective exchange," which they described as

a readiness to make positive or negative evaluations of the other. Criticism or praise, hostility or love, and approval or disapproval at outer layers are done easily and without any thought of threat to the relationship as a whole [p. 139].

This suggests that close relationships are characterized by both negative and positive affective exchange. This view was supported by the present investigation. Both extended conflict and extended humor were more likely to occur in close relationships than in distant relationships. But we found that it was the subordinate partner who assumed the role involving reciprocating affect. The following example illustrates extended conflict between close female roommates:

S: I hate this when I don't have a whole lot of homework and then other times I just get killed and swamped with it.
D: Yeah, but it seems like you have more days when you don't have that much.
S: Yeah.
D: Every so often you sit and you say that you don't have any.
S: No.
D: And I always, I always have so much it makes me sick.
S: No, I was thinking it was the opposite.
D: You got to be kidding.
S: No, 'cause like all last week and stuff, no I think it was the week before when you were saying that you don't like to do homework and stuff like that.
D: But I had it.

S: Yeah, but you weren't doing it and I thought, "gosh, am I always overstudying or . . . "
D: You can't overstudy at this school, impossible.
S: You know, that's true.

The extended conflict in this excerpt may be viewed as functional because it is positively related to closeness. However, the roommates actually reached a point of agreement after both expressed contradictory viewpoints. Once again, the context in which negative affect or conflict is expressed determines whether it is functional or dysfunctional. For example, negative affect expressed by the subordinate roommate in response to the other's gossip is dysfunctional (negatively related to closeness). The way distant roommates deal with conflict may be to avoid it or to insert it at times that are disruptive or counterproductive. It seems most productive for the subordinate partner to express negative affect after the dominant partner has already done so. Perhaps this is when the dominant partner is most receptive to discussing a conflict. The dominant partner's reciprocation of the subordinate partner's negative affect is unrelated to closeness. Therefore, the burden may lie on the subordinate to choose the appropriate time to express conflict. Apparently, subordinate partners in close relationships do this, whereas those in distant relationships are less likely to do so.

In the present study, humor in an extended chain was positively related to satisfaction. The following example demonstrates extended humor between close female roommates (who are discussing what to wear to a Halloween party):

D: I'll be a crayon. It's something unique.
S: What should I be?
D: How many crayons have you seen walking around [laughs]?
S: I know what. Don can be a kangaroo and I'll be his baby.
D: Ooh!
S: He'd have to carry me around. What a load!
D: [Laughs.]
S: I'm not that fat!
D: [Laughs.]
S: [to tape recorder] . . . You may think I'm a huge monster.
D: [to tape recorder] . . . She only wears a size five junior petite. She could use the fat, I'll tell you that.

This example of extended humor seems to convey a certain amount of familiarity and trust between the roommates. It demonstrates shared knowledge about another person (Don), as well as comfort derived from teasing the subordinate roommate about her weight. Personalized humor that was unique to each particular dyad typified the examples we found.

In summary, our results on extended conflict and extended humor support the view that positive and negative affective exchanges are more likely to occur in close relationships. Furthermore, there may be an active attempt to avoid negative affect in distant relationships as evidenced by (1) topic shifts by the subordinate as a consequence of self-disclosure and gossip, and (2) a lesser amount of negative affect expressed by the dominant partner.

6.5. A second look at sex differences in relationships

We opened this chapter with a look at some popular theories about presumed sex differences in relationships. To close, we shall take a second, closer look at this issue. First we shall discuss stylistic differences between the sexes that are unrelated to satisfaction.

Jourard and Lasakow (1955) were the first to report sex differences in self-disclosure; women had higher scores than men. Subsequently, numerous studies found similar results (e.g., Jourard & Landsman, 1960; Jourard & Richman, 1963; Pederson & Breglio, 1968; Pederson & Highbee, 1969). These results were certainly not conclusive, since a number of other studies failed to find sex differences in self-disclosure (e.g., Dimond & Hellkamp, 1969; Doster & Strickland, 1969; Vondracek & Marshall, 1971). In reviewing the literature, Cozby (1973) noted that no study has shown that men actually disclose more than women regardless of the disclosure variable used. Whether men actually disclose less or merely report disclosing less (most of these studies used self-report measures) is unclear. Further findings on factors affecting self-disclosure such as interactional contexts and modes of self-disclosure must be more carefully examined. In one study, for example, Pederson and Breglio (1968) reported that women (using written self-descriptions) did not use more words to describe themselves than men, but they disclosed more intimate information about themselves than men did. Morton (1978) found that, although men in a structured interaction disclosed very private facts at a rate equal to women, the latter communicated more intimately than men when an evaluative component (i.e., feelings and judgments) was involved.

The present investigation was the first to examine multiple types of disclosure in unstructured interactions. Our findings suggest that many sex differences in self-disclosure are only stylistic (i.e., unrelated to closeness) or vary as a function of dominance in the relationship.

Gossip among close male roommates was common and not very

different from that among female roommates, except for the qualities we note anecdotally: (1) It tended to be brief, and (2) it had an objective. For example, in the following example the dominant partner is trying to persuade his roommate to visit a depressed friend:

D: I went, I went up and talked to Jack.
S: What?
D: On the fourth floor.
S: Oh, yeah! How's he doing?
D: He's doin' all right. He, uh, he's a little bit, depressed. He's got schoolwork, you know, it's always on his mind.
S: Maybe I should go over and see him sometime.
D: If you're gonna be there, that would be very good.

Self-disclosure among close male roommates occurred regularly. For example:

S: The book opens my heart probably more than anything.
D: Yeah.
S: That's why I don't know, I'm a little leery of life [*laughs*].
D: How do you mean it opens your heart?
S: This is Christ's . . . his attitudes toward the world he knew, a view for himself. This is really neat.
D: You mean like it's, mean like a magical world?
S: Uh, I guess.

At times the disclosure involved discussing relationships:

D: You're not giving up on that, are you?
S: I'm just gonna have to, Joe.
D: Why?
S: What am I supposed to do now? She lied. Get her down in a corner somewhere?
D: Man, I mean, after all [*long pause*]. I got a new sweatshirt this weekend.
D: Did you?
S: It's just a sweatshirt, you know. Nothing spectacular.

Tiger and Fox (1970) noted that some self-disclosure between close males had a particularly antifemale quality, which was a way of asserting closeness between the males. In one case A and N discussed A's forthcoming wedding. First N noted how his roommate's fiancée thought about the wedding all the time:

A (dominant): She's got the whole wedding planned and . . .
N: I know.
A: And I haven't done a damn thing.
N: She spends, I bet, she spends twenty-two hours a day thinking about that wedding.
A: [*Laughs.*]

Later, when A discussed the wedding positively, he took some kidding from his roommate.

A: Yeah, we really, there's some cool things that are going to happen, that are kind of a surprise-type thing, you know. We are going to do some things that are different, that I think . . .

N: A unique wedding, huh?

A: Yeah, that *she's* thought of, or, I don't know, if she, if she thought of 'em or heard of them or what, but there, I think might turn out to be cool. I hope [*laughs*] but . . .

N: [*Hums "Here Comes the Bride."*]

A: Shut up, Jesus.

N: [*Laughs.*]

A: I don't, God!

N: Well, I won't say a word if you want to be a bad boy for a little while down here before she gets down here.

A: Well, if the opportunity arises.

This continued with A actively discussing his interest in other women:

A: I wish Marla didn't have a boyfriend.

N: Yeah, he's pretty steady.

A: I think so. He *lives* here; his car is always here [*laughs*]. He is! Everytime I went down there and Marla's there, he's there. I don't know when he studies . . .

N: I don't know when *she* studies.

The fact that the interactions of women were more likely to be affective and less informational than the interactions of men was the most stylistic sex difference we found. Another sex difference was associated with dominance. As subordinate partners, female roommates displayed more high-intimacy self-disclosure than male roommates. In all cases, female dyads were more likely to engage in the following sequences: LSD1 → NEG2, YOU1 → NEG2, GOS2 → CONT1, and GOS1 → HSD2.

For only three variables was there a significant correlation with both relationship satisfaction and sex: low self-disclosure by the dominant partner followed by mindreading by the less satisfied partner (LSD1 → YOU2), the probability of negative affect being expressed by the dominant partner (NEG1), and the probability of both partners using directives (CONT1 and CONT2). Male dyads were more likely to engage in the first sequence, as were distant dyads. Negative affect was more likely to be expressed by the dominant person among female dyads and among close dyads. Female dyads were more likely to use directives, as were closer dyads.

It may be extremely important to explore the second social process, negative affect expressed by the dominant partner. Gottman (1979) reported an interesting sex difference in marriages with respect to negative affect. Husbands were as likely to reciprocate negative affect in high-conflict interaction whether they were happily or unhappily married. Happily married husbands deescalated negative affect only in low-conflict interaction. In high-conflict interaction affect was deescalated only by wives, and then only if they were happily married.

To explore this social process purely for the purpose of generating hypotheses, correlations with closeness were computed separately for male and female roommates for the consequences of negative affect expressed by the dominant member of the dyad (NEG1). For both sexes NEG1 was correlated positively with closeness (for female roommates $r = .58$, $p < .10$; for male roommates, $r = .60$, $p < .10$). People tend to express negative affect only in close relationships. Table 6.12 presented correlations with sequences that follow NEG1. For female roommates, five correlations were significant (see Table 6.9). Three of these correlations were positively correlated with closeness: reciprocating with negative affect, asking a question, and acknowledgment. For male roommates, four correlations were significant and *none* of these was positive. For men, there are no positive consequences of negative affect, but for females it may be an opportunity for closeness. This may account, in part, for the great difficulty married couples have with negative affect. Wives often complain that their husbands withdraw from arguments, whereas husbands often complain that their wives are too emotional and quarrelsome. We suggest that *men apparently do not view intense negative affect as an opportunity for closeness, whereas women do.*

The Gottman–Levenson hypothesis

J. Gottman and R. Levenson (unpublished) reviewed the literature on sex differences in marital interaction. They noted that even the earliest studies on marriage revealed sex differences in marital grievances. In unhappy marriages, wives complain about their husbands' emotional withdrawal and husbands complain that their wives are too critical and complaining. Komarovsky's (1962) data suggest that husbands do not withdraw in happy marriages; in fact, they self-disclose as much as their wives. The evidence is that husbands withdraw in the face of intense negative affect.

Observational studies of marital interaction have found the following consistent sex differences: (1) Men are more likely to avoid conflict and are more reconciling and conciliatory than their wives; (2) women more often engage in conflict and are more coercive than their husbands; (3) women express more negative affect than men; (4) men are "overly rational" in resolving disagreements, whereas women are "overly emotional."

Gottman and Levenson reviewed physiological data that supported the following hypothesis: There are sex differences in the autonomic nervous system (ANS). Men have higher ANS base rates, greater ANS response to stress, and slower recovery than women. Gottman and Levenson proposed that strong negative affect is more upsetting to men than to women and that many of the sex differences in marital interaction are probably related to men's attempts to prevent the level of conflict from escalating. If it does escalate, ANS arousal bodes ill for marital conflict resolution. It is likely to lead to overlearned and more automatic cognitive and behavioral responses and to make openness and creative problem solving unlikely.

This hypothesis is consistent with our results about sex differences in negative affect. Apparently in their friendships both men and women express negative affect only to the friends they feel closest to. However, women are far more capable of handling negative affect than men.

7. Toward a model of peer acceptance

MARTHA PUTALLAZ AND ANNE HOPE HEFLIN

The ability to establish satisfactory peer relationships appears to be a critical skill for children to master. Evidence has indicated low levels of peer acceptance (as measured by sociometric questionnaires) to be predictive of a wide variety of maladaptive outcomes in later life (Asher, Oden & Gottman, 1977; Hartup, 1983). Given its apparent importance, it is not surprising that the process of peer acceptance has drawn much research attention, particularly in recent years. In fact, Rubin (1983) reported that in one journal the number of publications concerned with this issue had doubled in 10 years.

Described in this chapter is a line of research, begun in 1977, the goal of which has been to develop a model of children's social acceptance by peers. To understand the focus of this research, an appreciation of the historical context in which the work was undertaken is necessary. The "state of the art" of the field of peer acceptance in 1977 was considerably different than it is today. The research has become more sophisticated, both methodologically and conceptually. Until the late 1970's, however, this research was marked primarily by a global correlates approach to detecting behavioral differences between children of high and low social status. Investigators, lacking a theory to guide them in their efforts, examined the relationship between a series of relatively unrelated global variables, such as positiveness (Hartup, Glazer & Charlesworth, 1967), dependence (Moore & Updegraff, 1964), and aggression (McGuire, 1973), and sociometric status. Given their global, disparate nature, it was difficult to integrate these findings into a satisfactory, cohesive explanation of peer acceptance. Moreover, interventions aimed at in-

The authors acknowledge the support of a William T. Grant Faculty Scholar Award to the first author and thank Blair Sheppard for his comments on an earlier version of this chapter.

creasing the acceptance of low-status children had to be designed on the basis of these global correlate findings (without any guidance for translating the results into specific teachable skills) or the authors' own logic, armchair speculation, and intuition. It is not surprising, therefore, that generally the results of these well-intentioned interventions were quite disappointing (Asher et al., 1977).

What the field seemed to require at that time was a richer, more descriptive and theoretical understanding of how children went about the business of making friends and what resulted in their being accepted, rejected, or ignored by peers. Toward this end, a detailed observational research approach was undertaken, through which specific, concrete differences in behavior between high- and low-status children could be detected. Such a microanalytic observational approach also permitted analysis of the children's interaction in terms of sequential patterns of behavior rather than just the simple frequencies of occurrence of particular behaviors. Thus, this research approach allowed the analysis not only of the behaviors characterizing children of high and low peer acceptance, but of the patterns of interaction as well.

Furthermore, to be useful for intervention, the results of this research had to be phrased in a manner permitting their translation into relatively easily learned skills and strategies. In addition, the identification of general strategies was clearly preferable to the identification of highly situationally specific strategies. In other words, it was hoped that the data base developed from such detailed coding and analysis of children's behavior would permit the development of a model of social acceptance that contained both *general principles* of interaction and *explicit trainable behavioral strategies* for meeting these principles. Such a model would be helpful for developing the general goals of an intervention program in addition to the specific skills or strategies to be taught in order to meet these goals.

The final principle guiding this research was that observations of children in situations involving friendship making would be relevant to the design of interventions. Two appropriate situations were selected: a dyadic play situation and a situation requiring children to enter groups of their peers. The latter situation was considered crucial since the implicit goal of intervention programs was to help low-social-status children to enter and become integrated into existing peer groups. Yet empirical information as to how children did this was lacking.

In summary, the aim of the research described in this chapter was to develop a model of peer acceptance that was thoroughly grounded in a detailed understanding of children's entry and interactive behavior and that would be useful for the development of effective interventions with socially unaccepted children. Thus far, three major studies have been conducted that suggest some major elements to be contained in such a model. These three studies are described in turn, and the implications of the studies are considered together.

7.1. Study 1: a first look at entry

Procedure

Second and third graders participated in the research. In all, 20 dyads were formed: 10 popular pairs and 10 unpopular pairs, homogeneous by sex and sociometric status. In addition, 20 children were selected to attempt to enter these dyads, thus creating four conditions. These conditions involved the entry of a popular or unpopular child into either a popular or an unpopular dyad. Each dyad was videotaped playing a word-naming game for 10 minutes. This game involved spinning a needle, which landed on one of three categories: first names, animals, or jobs. The player then had to select a letter from a box and think of a word that began with the letter and fit the given category. If a word was correctly named, the player picked a card that indicated the number of spaces the playing piece could be moved on the game board. Fifteen minutes of additional videotaped data were then obtained on the attempts of a third child to enter the group. Verbatim transcripts were made from the videotapes and were coded using the interaction coding system developed by Gottman and Parkhurst (1980). Basically, this system consisted of 4 double codes (i.e., codes that can co-occur with all other codes) and 16 content codes. It was designed to describe children's conversations exhaustively and to facilitate the study of the social processes thought to be relevant to friendship. Four new double codes were added to describe the entry sequence, specifically, one entry code (bid for entry) and three group-response codes (accept, reject, ignore).

Dyadic interaction results

To explore whether the styles of dyadic interaction before the entry of a third child differed as a function of the popularity composition of the dyad, the ratio of agreement to disagreement was assessed for each dyad. Unpopular dyads had a lower ratio than popular dyads (1.28 vs.

2.86), a finding also characteristic of distressed families (Riskin & Faunce, 1970) and distressed couples (Gottman, Markman & Notarius, 1977). The difference in this agreement-to-disagreement ratio appeared to be a result of unpopular children disagreeing more frequently than popular dyads. Furthermore, the use of sequential analysis and a reexamination of the context of the transcripts revealed that popular and unpopular children differed in the manner in which they disagreed. When popular children disagreed, they tended to cite a general rule as the basis of their disagreement and then provide an acceptable alternative action for the other child. For example:

> No, you ain't. You ain't supposed . . . you ain't supposed to use this first. You're supposed to pick one of these.

In contrast, unpopular children typically expressed their disagreement by stating a very specific prohibition of the other child's act without providing an alternative action for the child:

> No. Can't say "bank" again [after the child had used the word "bank" in a previous turn during the game].

Entry results

Popular and unpopular children differed in the ways they attempted to enter groups. Consistent with the dyadic results, unpopular entering children had a lower agreement-to-disagreement ratio than popular entering children (.89 versus 2.17). In addition, they were more likely to use four entry bids than popular children. Specifically, when entering groups, unpopular children were more likely than popular children to disagree, ask informational questions, say something about themselves, and state their feelings and opinions. These four entry behaviors all seemed to be attempts to call the group's attention to the entering child. That is, unpopular children seemed to try to exert control and divert the group's attention to themselves rather than attempt to integrate themselves into the ongoing conversation of the group. These strategies had a high probability of resulting in the group's ignoring or rejecting them. This point can best be illustrated by several excerpts from the transcripts. The following portion illustrates one unpopular child's attempts to call attention to herself repeatedly by stating her feelings and the manner in which she was continually ignored by the group. The name of the entering child is italicized.

Janet: Ok, I want this one again.
Terry: This is fun, ain't it?
Janet [*to Vera*]: Do you want this one again?

Vera: I want this one.
Terry: This is a nice room, ain't it?
Janet [*to Vera*]:   You can have this one. Here.
Terry: This is a nice table, ain't it?

This unpopular child repeatedly tried to divert the group from their ongoing activity of choosing playing pieces, to no avail. The group members simply continued to ignore her.

The following excerpt is another example of an unpopular child's attempts to join the group's conversation by drawing attention to himself. Rather than talk about the game the group members were engaged in, he tried to redirect the conversation to an incident that involved only himself during recess. Again, however, this strategy resulted in the child being ignored by the group.

Tom: *M.* Um . . . um . . .
Eric: Oh, you know . . . [*David makes a face and they laugh.*] You know I was playing with Glen. I hope you don't get mad at me. We're playing out there and Glen, he started to wrestle. I told him no, so . . .
Tom: Monkey, Monkey. Hey, um monkey. Monkey, Um, "Move ahead three spaces." It's your turn, dumdum.
David: Hey, um, *M.* Monkey.
Eric: Uh, Glen . . . I poked his eye. I accidently poked Glen's eye and then he . . . said he wouldn't take my apology, so Brian started getting mad at me so . . . and there I . . . Glen can see now . . . he said he couldn't see. Now he could see.
David: I like this game.
Tom: Ok. Ok.

In contrast, popular children seemed to employ the more effective entry strategy of attempting to determine the "frame of reference" (Phillips, Shenker, & Revitz, 1951) common to the group members (i.e., activities, goals) and then establishing themselves as sharing in this frame of reference. The following excerpt provides an illustration of this strategy, which in this case proved quite successful, since the child was not only accepted but finally invited to join in the play of the game:

Sam: "Animals."
Craig: What'd you get . . . *B*?
Matt: What'd you go and pick?
Sam: Take another turn.
Matt: Bear.
Sam: Gorilla. Thank you. Matt.
Matt: Let's see . . .
Sam: Move ahead . . . [*inaudible*]
Matt: Your turn.
Craig: "Animals." Bear.
Matt: Hey, mix these up.
Craig: I know. Ok, hold it. Yeah, do that. I got "Move ahead three." Ooh. How lucky can you get. One, two, three. Your turn, Matt.

Thus, popular children may be better able to determine the prevailing norms or expectations in a given situation and to act in accordance with those norms than unpopular children. (For a more detailed presentation of this study, see Putallaz and Gottman, 1981a, b.)

7.2. Study 2: test of a principle of entry

The results of Study 1 suggested one important principle of successful entry behavior (i.e., fitting in with the group's frame of reference) and several key entry behaviors. However, the study had four limitations. Therefore, a second study (1983) was conducted to test the frame of reference hypothesis while controlling for the four limitations. To control the first limitation, two child confederates were enlisted to serve as the dyad that all subjects attempted to enter. The use of confederates ensured that all subjects confronted a similar entry situation and permitted the group's activity or frame of reference to be changed several times. Thus, it provided a controlled test of children's abilities to detect such a change and to change their behavior accordingly.

The use of unfamiliar confederates further ensured that no history of interaction with the group members would influence a subject's behavior. Asher and Hymel (1981) suggested that using familiar peers, as in the earlier study, makes it impossible to examine whether a child's behavior caused the low status or whether the child's low status caused the dysfunctional behavior to occur in response to being ignored or treated poorly by classmates. This entry context also permitted an examination of the earlier study's findings in a situation requiring children to enter groups of unfamiliar rather than familiar peers.

In addition, the children's entry behavior was assessed during the summer *before* their entry into first grade, and the results of this assessment were used to predict later sociometric status in first grade. Positive results with this younger age group would have important clinical implications in terms of prevention. Any differences found to predict social status in first grade would allow intervention at an early age. Furthermore, the predictive nature of the study would provide a stronger test of the role of dysfunctional behavior in determining social status than would a study collecting behavioral and sociometric data at the same time.

A fourth limitation of the earlier study was that it included only a behavioral assessment of the children's entry skills. Because the children's knowledge regarding the entry situation was not assessed, it was impossible to determine whether observed behavioral differences were due to a behavior skills deficit, a perceptual deficit (i.e., an inaccurate or incomplete perception of social situations), or simply a failure to perform known skills for a variety of reasons (e.g., excessive anxiety and lack of confidence [Asher & Hymel, 1981]). Thus, in order to distinguish a performance or perceptual deficit from a skills deficit, a variation of an interview procedure introduced by Forbes and Lubin (1979) was adopted in this study. All subjects were shown their video-tapes after their sessions and interviewed to assess the extent to which they were aware of the different activities of the group. Thus, the children's perceptions of the situation could be compared with the group's actual behavior, so that a measure of the accuracy of the children's perceptions could be obtained. It was predicted that the relationship between a demonstrated tendency to fit in with the group and future social status would be strongest among those children who accurately perceived the group's behavior. This hypothesis was based on the assumption that the ability to fit into the group's frame of reference would be facilitated by an ability to perceive accurately what the group was doing. Demonstration of this skill would thus require both having the skill and accurately perceiving when and in what form to use the skill.

Procedure

Twenty-two boys participated in this second study. Again, verbatim transcripts of the children's speech were made from the videotapes and coded using the system developed by Gottman and Parkhurst (1980). Three additional double codes were added so that the proportion of relevant comments contributed by each subject during the session could be determined. All thought units were double-coded for relevance with the following codes: (1) *relevant:* coded whenever the subject made a statement directly related to the group members' discussion (e.g., group members are trying to think of words that rhyme with "sandal" and subject says, "How about candle?"); (2) *irrelevant:* coded whenever the subject made a statement not related to the ongoing discussion (e.g., group members trying to think of words that rhyme with "sandal" and subject says, "I'm going to be in first grade"); and (3) *tangential:* coded whenever the subject made a statement indirectly related to the ongoing discussion but not pertinent to it (e.g., group members are thinking of words that rhyme with "sandal" and subject says, "That's what I'm wearing").

Replication of the behavioral findings of Study 1

As mentioned previously, the use of an entry situation allowed an examination of the earlier study's findings in a situation requiring children to enter groups of unfamiliar rather than familiar peers. Thus, it was possible to examine whether the aspects of children's entry behavior identified earlier as differentiating popular and unpopular children were similarly predictive of social status in this entry context. All of the correlations between the proportions of these behaviors displayed and social status were, with one exception (i.e., the use of feeling statements), in the predicted direction, thus offering support for the earlier findings. The children who would be less socially accepted in first grade were more apt to disagree, ask questions for information, and talk about themselves and less likely to agree with the group members than were their higher-status counterparts.

The following sequence illustrates the nature of this negative relationship between these entry behaviors and social acceptance. It was chosen to highlight the unsuccessful entry strategy of one subject who would be socially unaccepted four months later in first grade. His attempts are marked by a high usage of informational questions, self-statements, and disagreement:

Subject: [*upon walking in*] Where's mine? [*referring to playing piece*]?
Child 1:   Wait 'till we're done.
Subject: Where's the start? Start's over there.
Child 2:   Yeah, we played it before.
Subject: I'll tell you the best way to play it. This is the start. [*Returns their pieces to start.*] Remember?
Child 2:   [*Moves the piece back.*] Yeah, but we're playing it now and we want to finish before we start over.
Subject: Where's mine?
Child 1:   Wait 'till we're done.
Subject: That's not the way to play it.
Child 1:   You don't even know how to play it.
Subject: Yes, I do. I know how to play every game.
Child 2:   Do you know how to play poker?
Subject: No, I do not. But I do know how to play chess.

This style of entry is quite similar to that typical of the unpopular children in the first study.

Test of the relevance hypothesis

Beyond a simple replication of the earlier findings, this study was also conducted to test the notion that fitting in with, or being relevant to, the group's ongoing activity was critical to successful entry behavior. Recall that all subject behaviors were coded according to their relevance. As a first test of the relevance hypothesis, the proportion of relevant behaviors was correlated with each individual entry behavior and with sociometric status. As expected, when usage of the entry behaviors predictive of sociometric status was correlated with the relevance code, the resulting correlations were in the same direction as those obtained with sociometric status and generally revealed stronger relationships. Thus, it is possible that relevance is a mediating factor in the relationship between behavior and sociometric status. In other words, the critical determinant of a behavior's relationship with sociometric status may not simply be whether it calls attention to the entering child, which was the hypothesis suggested in the earlier study, but rather whether the behavior is used in a relevant manner. Calling attention to oneself may be problematic only if it diverts the group from its ongoing activity or conversation. In support of this contention, the children whose behaviors and conversations were generally relevant to the ongoing activities of the group were more socially accepted in the first grade than were the children whose behaviors were not relevant ($r = .45$, $p < .05$).

It is interesting that the children who would be socially accepted in first grade were not more likely than those who would not be accepted to conform directly to the group's activities (i.e., actually play the games). Instead, they were simply less likely to act in a manner that redirected the group's attention, and they were more likely to act in a manner related to what the group was doing. In addition, the relationship between this type of behavior and sociometric status was strongest for those entering children who accurately perceived the norms of the group, as indicated by the postsession interview results. Therefore, the ability to monitor or read the ongoing flow of interaction and respond to feedback may be necessary for fitting in with the group.

Although sequential analyses could not be performed due to the scripted nature of much of the confederates' behavior, the transcripts were reviewed in order to understand the relationship between relevance and social acceptance. Consistent with the earlier study, irrelevant comments were often ignored by the group members, as shown by the following excerpt. Note that this subject seems unaware of his lack of impact on the group.

Child 2 [*to subject*]:   Ok, you got "move ahead seven spaces."
Subject: I'm ahead of you two, aren't I? One time I beat, um . . . I um, um got
     one right on Mastermind when I didn't even notice it and I um . . . I did

not . . . I got everything right except everything else. I didn't 'cause I beat Donna at backgammon yesterday.

Child 2:   N.

Subject: I beat Donna the whole game. She . . .

Child 2:   Three, four, five, six. Oops.

Sometimes it was clear that the irrelevancy and its diversion were annoying to the group members, as illustrated by the following excerpt. Again, the subject does not seem to read the group's response to his behavior and does not adapt his behavior accordingly.

Subject: Well, I got a little gun that's like a pistol at home and it's missing a crocket that's supposed to go on the spring and stay there 'till it shoots.

Child 2 [*to Child 1*]:   Come on, go. Would you just go?

Child 1:   OK.

Subject: I probably had either one yesterday which I know how to do now.

Child 2 [*to subject*]:   OK, go!

Child 1 [*to subject*]:   Just go!

Children often persisted in being irrelevant despite the group members' increased annoyance and irritability. Occasionally, the group members became involved in the irrelevant conversation and became even more frustrated with the subject's irrelevance:

Subject: I wonder whose the trailer?

Child 2:   It is.

Child 1:   This is a trailer.

Subject: I know. It must be a van trailer.

Child 2:   What?

Child 1 [*trying to return to script*]:   Um . . .

Subject: It's a semi trailer or something?

Child 2:   This is what?

Child 1 [*returning to script*]:   I am Darth Vader.

Subject [*inaudible*]:   . . . whatever.

Child 2:   What?

Subject: What trailer is it?

Child 2:   A plain old trailer.

Subject: How'd it get here? Semi driver or something?

Child 2:   Someone drove it here.

Child 1:   Somebody got a truck and drove it here, that's how.

Subject: Was it a semi?

Child 1:   What?

Subject: Was it a semi?

Child 2:   Semi?

Subject: Was it a semi?

Child 2:   What's a semi?

Subject: A semi.

Child 2:   No such thing.

Subject: Yes, there is.

Child 2 [*to Child*]:   Was it?

Child 1:   How should I know?

Subject: My grandpa's gots one. Was it a semi?

Child 2:   I . . .
Child 1:   I don't know who drove it here or what kind of thing they drove it in
           'cause I didn't see it!
Child 2 [*returning to script*]:   I am . . .
Child 1 [*returning to script*]:   I'm Darth Vader.

Summary

The model of peer acceptance emerging from this research includes at least two general principles concerning behaviors that lead to social acceptance. To be accepted by peers, children must behave in a manner consistent with the ongoing activity or frame of reference of the children with whom they would like to interact. They should also be positive or agreeable in their interactional style. In addition, from this research we can derive some relatively explicit suggestions regarding how these general principles can be achieved. First, positiveness or agreeableness is determined at least partially by children's capacities to avoid escalation of conflict through careful explanation of their disagreement and by provision of an alternative action or possible compromise for the other children. Second, children have to learn to detect the prevalent norms within a group and to exhibit behavior that is relevant to those norms. It does not seem necessary, however, that they conform actively to the group's behavior, but rather that they not interfere or attempt to redirect the group's behavior until firmly established as a member of that group. Specific suggestions about how to become a member or be accepted by a group of children include the following: waiting to determine the activity or conversational topic of the group before acting, not talking too frequently, agreeing and exchanging relevant information with the group members, and orienting oneself toward the group in terms of eye contact, proximity, and body position. In other words, it is important that entering children demonstrate their similarities to the group by establishing synchrony with the members in terms of their behavior, conversation, and affect.

7.3. Study 3: origins of peer acceptance

One of the most striking findings of the study just described is that before children enter first grade they display behavioral differences that are predictive of their later sociometric status. Other investigators have reported this apparent relationship between sociometric status and social behavior in children as young as preschool and kindergarten age (e.g.,

Hartup et al., 1967; Marshall & McCandless, 1957; McGuire, 1973; Moore & Updegraff, 1964). Given the very early appearance of this relationship, it seems reasonable to examine the role of parents in the development of their children's social competence and acceptance by peers. However, a review of the literature indicates that very little such research exists. Moreover, the few investigators who have examined this relationship (i.e., Elkins, 1958; Kolvin, Garside, Nicol, MacMillan, Walstenholme, & Leitch, 1977; Winder & Rau, 1962) used only questionnaire or interview data and did not employ behavioral data. The results of investigations of other forms of parental influence on children's behavior (e.g., Maccoby & Martin, 1983) suggest that focusing on parental behavior should prove fruitful. If such social behavior is learned, at least in part, through early family interaction, it may be possible to develop preventive interventions that can be implemented before children experience any negative consequences of social unacceptance. Furthermore, if parents do play an important role in the development and maintenance of children's social behavior related to peer acceptance, then any model of peer acceptance not incorporating parental influence would be incomplete. Similarly, the potential success of any intervention not including parents would most likely be compromised.

Thus, a major purpose of the third study to be described was to explore the potential link between the social behavior of mothers and their children. A second purpose was to examine the social behavior of the participating children interacting with their peers, in this case an unfamiliar agemate. In this manner, the children's interactional style with their mothers could be compared with their interactional behavior with peers. A similar pairing of the children's unacquainted mothers also allowed an initial examination of the mothers' own interactional style with their peers'. Thus, the mothers' behavior in a situation somewhat analogous to that of their children could be explored and compared. (For a complete and detailed report of this research see Putallaz, 1984.)

Procedure

Each session involved four participants: two unacquainted first-grade children of the same sex, race, and level of social status and their mothers. First, each mother–child pair was videotaped for 15 minutes while they played the same word-naming game used in the two earlier studies. In the second part of the study, the two children were videotaped playing together with a variety of toys for 15 minutes. Meanwhile, their mothers (in a separate room) were videotaped discussing, if they chose to, a suggested set of general issues related to children's social development. In total, 55 children and their mothers participated in this research. Verbatim transcripts were made of all videotaped interactions between mother–child, child–child, and mother–mother pairs and then coded using a system developed by Gottman, Parkhurst, and Bajjalieh (1982; see Chapter 2). This coding system was a revised version of the Gottman and Parkhurst (1980) system used previously and consisted of 41 content codes contained within the broader categories of demands, demands for the pair, inclusion, self-focus, emotive, social rules, and information and message clarification statements. The system also permitted these content codes to be double-coded as gossip, fantasy, joking, squabbling, or positive affective codes.

Mother–child interaction results

Child behavior. To examine the relationship between the behavior of the children during the mother–child interaction situation and their sociometric status, the proportion of each behavior for each child was correlated with the child's social status score. Applying two criteria (statistical significance and a mean frequency of at least once per session across the children), four behaviors exhibited by the children during their interactions with their mothers were related to their social status. Consistent with the earlier research, the use of self-statements or talking about oneself was associated negatively with social status. Talking about oneself in a squabbling tone of voice and, in fact, simply using a squabbling tone of voice were also correlated negatively with peer acceptance. Only disagreement accompanied by a rationale or explanation was related positively to social status, a finding again consistent with the earlier investigations.

Maternal behavior. To examine the relationship between the mother's behavior while interacting with their children and their children's social status, a similar procedure was followed. Considering only behaviors that correlated significantly with social status and occurred with a mean frequency of at least once per mother–child pair, 13 of the mothers' individual behaviors were related to the peer acceptance levels of their children. These appeared to cluster into four general types of maternal behavior. The first type was a commanding, demanding mode that was related negatively to children's status. The following transcript sample provides an example of a mother engaged in this type of interaction:

Mother: "Animals." This is mine. Animal that starts with a *G*. Goat. OK. "Move ahead seven spaces," One, two, three, four, five, six, seven. Go ahead. Put the things down. Just put it down flat. Now try to spin it. Just spin it.
Child: OK, I did. "First names."
Mother: OK.
Child: *L*.
Mother: That'll be easy.
Child: Hmmm.
Mother: Come on. A first name that starts with an *L*.
Child: Lori.
Mother: Right. Now pick one of these.

The second general type of maternal behavior was a feeling mode, including both stating one's own and questioning about the other's feelings, which was associated positively with social status:

Mother: Oh, me. Another *S*. A . . .
Child: Jobs.
Mother: No.
Child: I know one.
Mother: You can't tell me. It's an animal . . . animal. I can't think of an animal that starts with an *S*.
Child: I thought it said jobs.
Mother: No. Um . . . *S* . . . animal . . . a . . . No, a swordfish is a fish. I can't think of one. I'm going to have to lose my turn.
Child: No, swordfish is good.
Mother: You think that's OK? That's really a fish. That's not an animal.
Child: That *is* an animal.
Mother: You think I should take it? OK. "Move ahead one space." I don't think I did too good.
Child: You did! You did good.

The third general type of maternal behavior was an agreeable, positive mode and a disagreeable, squabbling mode, with the former being related positively and the latter related negatively to sociometric status. The following example is of a mother engaged in a disagreeable, squabbling form of interaction. She is angry with her son, who has been unable to name many words correctly:

Child: I don't know anything.
Mother: Think of it, Steven! Forget it. I ain't got time to worry with you. [*Skips his turn and takes her own turn.*] An *H* for an animal. It's a horse. I don't think you like this too much, do you? First names.
Child: *H* again.
Mother: All right, what's somebody's name with an *H*?

Child: Uh . . .
Mother: Do you know what Papa's first name is?
Child: Uh uh.
Mother: OK, is anybody in your class got an *H*?
Child [*whining*]: Nobody does.
Mother: You can't think of a first name for an *H*? You're not going anywhere if you don't think of something. You'll be staying right here in this spot the rest of the afternoon 'till we go home.
Child [*whining*]: Nobody in my class . . .

The final general type of maternal behavior was a clarification mode in which mothers of higher-status children appeared to request repetition from their children, whereas the mothers of lower-status children seemed more likely to fail to clarify their statements for their children. The next excerpt illustrates the failure of one such mother to clarify her statements upon her daughter's request:

Mother: "First names."
Child: How come I'm winning?
Mother: *T*. Tara. "Move ahead two spaces."
Child: Jobs. *T*. Typing.
Mother: Right.
Child: "Move ahead six spaces." One, two, three, four, five, six. Gosh, Ma! Look where I'm at!
Mother: What if you were to get "Move back a hundred places?"
Child: Huh?
Mother: *T*. "First names." Ted.

In order to reduce these 13 behaviors, a stepwise multiple-regression procedure was employed, predicting sociometric status from these 13 behaviors. Three behaviors entered the equation: disagreement, demands in the form of informational questions, and total positive statements expressed by mothers toward their children (multiple R = .64). Thus, maternal behaviors from two of the general clusters described earlier predicted children's social status quite well.

Child–child interaction results

The procedure for analyzing the dyadic interaction between the children was similar to that followed to analyze the mother–child interaction data, except that the dyad was treated as the unit of analysis. Fifteen behaviors exhibited by the children during the peer interaction situations were related significantly to their social status. However, these behaviors fell within three general types of child behavior. The first type was a demand mode, which was related positively to status. This is interesting since children of *higher* status were more apt to use demands (in the form of informational statements) with their peers, whereas it was the mothers of *lower* status children who were more apt to use demands (in the form of informational questions) with their children.

The second general type of behavior was an agreeable, positive mode and a disagreeable, squabbling mode of behavior, which were, respectively, related positively and negatively to social status. Three of the behaviors of this type (i.e., disagreement with rationale, squabble/self-statement, and total squabble statements) were related to social status in a like manner in the child portion of the mother–child results. In addition, several of these behaviors were similarly correlated to social status in the mother part of the mother–child interaction data (i.e., disagreement, total squabble statements, total positive statements, and agreement minus disagreement score). The one behavior that was related to social status in the reverse manner when used by mothers was question for agreement. Mothers of higher status were more apt to use this form of questioning with their children, whereas *lower* status children tended to use this behavior more often with peers.

Because of this puzzling relationship, the transcripts were reviewed to ascertain whether the code was used differently in the two settings. From inspection, this seemed to be the case. When mothers asked their children a question for agreement, it seemed to be to draw out agreement, thus avoiding conflict. The following excerpt illustrates this point (the question for agreement phrase is italicized):

Mother: Let's put our cards here, *OK?*
Child: All right.

In contrast, children seemed more likely to ask questions for agreement without pausing for their peer's affirmation and often while they were attempting to take some liberty with the rules during play. The following excerpt provides an example:

Child: Now we get two chances, *OK?* I got another chance. Whoops. I get another chance. I get another chance.

The third type of behavior related to peer acceptance during the child–child interaction was an information exchange mode. There were four significant behaviors of this type (i.e., question for information about the other, gossip/information, total gossip statements, and question for repetition), all related negatively to social status. To understand this negative relationship, the transcripts were again reviewed. It seemed from examination that the first of these behaviors, question for information about the other, often led to disagreement or establishment of a lack of similarity between the two children.

Child 1: *Have you ever been in the Girl Scouts?*

Child 2:   No.
Child 1:   Oh, I have and I'm going there again.

Exchanging gossip with the other child (i.e., gossip/information statement and total gossip statements) was also correlated negatively with social status. Typically, these were reactive statements to the situation (i.e., "They're taking pictures of us") or discussions concerning their mothers:

Child 1:   My momma's in there.
Child 2:   I know.
Child 1:   Not over there with them. There in that room. She's, she's . . .
Child 2:   Your momma, your momma's in there with my momma.

The final behavior included in the information exchange mode was question for repetition. Whereas this behavior was related positively to social status when used by mothers with their children it was related negatively to social status during peer play. Again, an examination of the transcripts revealed an apparently different use of this behavior by mothers and children. When used by mothers, it seemed to be a genuine attempt to improve communication between themselves and their children:

Child: a caa . . . a cafe . . . ateria.
Mother: *What?*
Child: A lady who works in the cafeteria.
Mother: No, that was . . . that starts with a C.

In contrast, when used by children with their peers, it seemed to be a marker for an episode of miscommunication, as illustrated by the following excerpt:

Child 1:   What are they doing in there?
Child 2:   See them two little girls?
Child 1:   *Huh?* What are they doing? Do you know?
Child 2:   *What?*
Child 1:   Those girls and my mommy.

At times this miscommunication seemed intentional:

Child 1:   You got any more gum?
Child 2:   *Huh?*
Child 1:   You got any more gum?
Child 2:   *Huh?*
Child 1:   You got any more gum?
Child 2:   Hey! I made one!

Mother–mother interaction results

The same procedure used to analyze the child–child data was used to examine the results of the mother–mother interaction situation. Seven behaviors were related significantly to the children's social acceptance scores and occurred with a frequency of at least once per mother dyad. First, mothers of higher-status children tended to talk more than mothers of lower-status children. Second, only the agreeable mode of behavior, and not the disagreeable mode, was related to the children's social status in this situation. However, it is not surprising that at an initial meeting two strange adults would not disagree very much with each other. Interestingly, agreement was related to social status positively (although marginally), whereas joking behavior was related negatively to social status. This result is in contrast to the child–child interaction results, in which joking was more characteristic of higher-status children than of lower-status children. A review of the transcripts indicated that joking among children was usually a reflection of their getting along well; it consisted primarily of laughing or joking around during play and a corresponding lack of disagreement or squabbling. In contrast, the laughter among the mothers often seemed to reflect nervousness or discomfort and sometimes seemed inappropriate. The following excerpt illustrates this point:

Mother [*talking about one of her older children*]:   He'll get so he can't get his breath
    and start coughing.
Mother 2:   Hmmm.
Mother 1:   And he's so thin for ten years old, so thin. He still can wear the same
    pants he wore when he was in first grade just about.
Mother 2:   [*Nervous laughter.*]

The third major finding was that the two forms of information seeking by the mothers in the mother–mother interaction situation were correlated negatively with their children's social status scores. The first of these, question for information about the other, was similarly associated negatively with social status during the child–child situation. From inspection of the transcripts, it appeared that mothers asking such questions were somewhat intrusive and perhaps premature in their questioning:

Mother 1:   Did you all live in_____when you were young?
Mother 2:   Well, I did when I was young. We lived around here.
Mother 1:   What was your name then?

The other form of information soliciting used by the mothers was gossip/question for information. This behavior disrupted the flow or direction of the other mother's conversation. Consider the following example in which a mother is attempting to explain her beliefs about the influence friends have on children:

Mother 1:   Most of the time, because that way it's easier for them to make
    friends in school too. They look forward to going to school.

Mother 2:   Hmmm Hmmm. What grade is your son in?
Mother 1:   First.

Thus, for the mother–mother interaction situation, agreement between mothers was related positively to their children's social status, whereas joking and information soliciting were associated negatively.

Discussion

The primary purpose of this last study was to examine the relationship between maternal behavior and children's sociometric status and social behavior. The results clearly suggest that such a relationship exists. Mothers of higher-status children appeared to be more positive and less disagreeable, more concerned with communication clarity, and less commanding and demanding when interacting with their children than mothers of lower-status children. When interacting with another adult, the mothers of higher-status children spoke more, agreed more, were less tense (displayed nervous laughter less), and asked fewer prying personal questions than did the mothers of less accepted children. Moreover, subsequent analyses showed that the behavior mothers exhibited with their children was highly related to the way their children acted, both with them and with peers (see Putallaz, 1984).

These results are consistent with (although clearly not a confirmation of) a model suggesting that children acquire at least some of their social behavior repertoire through interaction with their mothers, which in turn influences their sociometric status.

If indeed such a sequence does occur, it seems that the transfer of behavior from mother to child occurs at a relatively macro as opposed to micro level. In other words, children are more apt to adopt fairly general behavior strategies from interacting with their mothers than to model specific maternal behaviors directly. Two findings support this conclusion. First, the maternal behaviors that correlated with children's social status clustered into four general types representing four general themes (commanding, feeling, affective, and communication clarity). The themes underlying these types of individual maternal behaviors may exert a stronger influence on children's social behavior than the individual behaviors themselves. Second, in a subsequent analysis the three maternal behaviors that entered the regression equation predicting children's social status were more clearly related to the children's behavior than were the identical maternal behaviors. This suggests that, rather than there being a one-to-one transfer of specific behaviors, general themes are carried over to children's behavior.

Given such a global influence, this suggests at least two ways of testing the influence of maternal behavior on child behavior in future research. It is possible that mothers' general orientations in social interaction, such as a positive or negative disposition (i.e., agreeable, positive versus disagreeable, squabbling behaviors), are modeled by children and generalize to their interactions with peers. However, it is also possible that maternal behaviors evoke responses from children or induce complementary styles in children that later transfer to interactions with peers. For example, commanding mothers may develop disagreeable children, or questioning and clarifying mothers may produce children who clarify their disagreements.

The results of the third study are consistent with both kinds of effects. For example, the results are consistent with the notion of general thematic modeling in at least two instances. First, children in their social interactions with peers seemed to model their mothers' general affective dispositions. This notion is supported by the number and size of significant correlations between disagreement and total positive statements expressed by mothers during their interactions with their children and the affective codes their children subsequently displayed in the child–child situation. In addition, there is evidence, albeit incomplete, that both lower-status children and their mothers lacked an implicit notion of social contingency. In the transcript excerpts presented earlier, lower-status children were more apt to call attention to themselves and introduce irrelevant observations (e.g., "My momma's in there") than their higher-status peers, who appeared to clarify or contribute to ongoing conversations. Conversational relevance has been found previously to predict sociometric status (Putallaz, 1983), as has interaction disruptiveness (Coie & Kupersmidt, 1983; Dodge, 1983). Furthermore, behavior of low-status children seemed to emphasize their dissimilarity rather than similarity to peers (see Gottman, 1983, for a discussion of the importance of establishing similarity in the development of friendship). A similar tendency to interrupt the flow of discourse also characterized the interaction of the mothers of lower-status children with each other. As noted earlier, they often disrupted the direction of the other mother's conversation by exhibiting tension rather than support (e.g., nervous laughter) and by focusing on potentially irrelevant details (e.g., "What grade is your son in?" "What was your name then?") that were somewhat intrusive and diversionary. Thus, the results of the present study are consistent with the suggestion that two general thematic tendencies are modeled by children of lower social status, namely, a negative affective tone and a tendency toward disruptiveness and irrelevancy. Clearly, both possibilities require further study, especially the latter, since it was based on an examination of transcripts.

There is also evidence that the behavior of mothers evokes responses that induce a complementary interactional style in their children. This notion appears to be particularly true with respect to the demand dimension. As mentioned earlier, higher-status children were more apt to use demands with their peers, whereas the mothers of lower-status children were more likely to use demands with their children. This result suggests that children's autonomy or assertiveness may be an induced derivative of autonomy giving by mothers rather than a modeling of maternal behavior. Children may learn to adopt a role vis-à-vis power from their status in the mother–child relationship. On the basis of their maternal relationships, lower-status children may come to expect to have lower power status in their interactions with peers. Therefore, they are less apt to assert themselves or make demands on their peers, but more likely to disrupt the interaction by being irrelevant or calling attention to themselves and by being generally disagreeable and negative. Clearly, further research is needed to clarify the processes through which maternal behavior influences child behavior; both general modeling and response evocation or role induction are two likely possibilities.

7.4. Summary and conclusions

To summarize the implications of these three studies considered together, it is necessary to return to the initial purposes of this research. The first was to develop a richer, more descriptive and theoretical understanding of how children become accepted socially by their peers. Toward this end, a detailed, microanalytic observational approach was undertaken through which specific, concrete differences in behavior between children of high and low social status could be detected. Second, it was hoped that the data base developed from the detailed coding and analysis of children's behavior would permit the development of a model of peer acceptance that contained both general principles of interaction and explicit teachable behavioral strategies for meeting these principles. Such a model would contain both the general goals of an intervention program and the specific skills or strategies to be taught in order to meet these goals.

Clearly, this line of research has come a long way in fulfilling its intent. At least two general principles of behaviors that lead to social acceptance have been identified. As stated earlier, to be accepted by peers, children need to behave in a manner consistent with the ongoing activity or frame of reference of the children with whom they would like to interact, and they must be positive or agreeable in their interactional style. In addition, this research has suggested relatively explicit ways in which both principles can be achieved. First, positiveness or agreeableness is determined at least partially by children's ability to avoid escalation of conflict through careful explanation of their disagreement and by provision of an alternative action or possible compromise for the other child. Second, children must learn to detect the prevalent norms within a group and to exhibit behavior and conversation that is relevant to rather than disruptive of those norms.

There are at least four reasons for espousing these principles with some confidence. First, they were replicated across the three studies described in this chapter, each involving a somewhat different situation (i.e., interaction with familiar peers, unfamiliar peers, and mothers). Furthermore, in the second study described, these principles were found to be highly predictive of sociometric status four months later. Third, similar patterns of behavior were found to characterize the mothers of lower-status children when they interacted with other mothers as well as with their children. Finally, these principles are consistent with the results of other researchers engaged in careful observational research with socially accepted and unaccepted children, notably the results of Coie and Kupersmidt (1983), Dodge, (1983), and Dodge, Schlundt, Schocken, and Delugach (1983).

This line of research has begun to suggest how these general principles or behaviors can be acquired by children. The third study indicates that children acquire at least some of their social behavior repertoire through interaction with their mothers. Possible processes through which maternal behavior may influence child behavior include both general modeling and response evocation or role induction. However, it is important to note that the direction of influence is unclear from these data. It may indeed be that disagreeable mothers cause their children to squabble with them or that positive mothers model this behavior for their children and that these behaviors subsequently transfer to interactions with peers. However, it is equally likely that difficult, squabbling children cause their mothers to respond to them in a disagreeable, demanding manner, or, similarly, it may be easy for mothers to be positive with pleasant, relevant children. In any case there is a clear relationship between the behaviors mothers display when interacting with their children and the manner in which their children behave, both with their mothers and with peers.

Certainly, more research is needed to test such a causal linkage. If this relationship is demonstrated ultimately to hold, the results presented here have several implications for interventions designed to increase children's peer acceptance. First, mothers (and probably parents in general) should be an important consideration in the design of such programs. In addition, fairly explicit factors should be targeted in attempts to influence maternal behavior (i.e., the commanding, feeling, affective, and communication clarity modes). Moreover, this sort of data would be especially useful in the development of interventions with parents, because they indicate not only general parental tendencies associated with sociometric status, but also specific concrete suggestions concerning how parents might implement or avoid these tendencies. Perhaps the most important conclusion to be drawn, however, is that we are close enough to a sufficient understanding of children's peer acceptance that the next few studies should provide a strong basis for effective interventions with socially unaccepted children. In particular, research testing the proposed causal linkages is necessary and will likely yield interesting and fruitful results.

8. How young children get what they want

JENNIFER PARKHURST AND JOHN GOTTMAN

Linguists interested in pragmatics have been concerned with how intended meaning is conveyed by language. The problem has been to explain how listeners understand an enormous variety of linguistic forms and read them appropriately. What is critical in understanding this problem is that linguists have come to realize that the meaning of what people say cannot be arrived at simply *by study of language itself.* Language, it turns out, cannot be understood without an excursion into social interaction, and ultimately into culture. Understanding what people say requires an understanding of the social context, social mechanisms, and human motivations.

To understand how language *functions* is the goal of this work. As we shall see in this chapter, the most successful analysis of language from this perspective has involved trying to understand people's tactics for accomplishing their goals within stated interactive constraints. To explain the notion of an "interactive constraint," we shall discuss Brown and Levinson's (1978) theory of politeness in this chapter. They proposed that "face saving" is an interactive constraint in obtaining compliance with a request or demand. What one obtains from such an analysis is some understanding of how people within a speech community use language. Language can thus be a tool for understanding culture in an extremely parsimonious way, if one is a sociolinguist. However, our interest is not cultural, but developmental.

Our goal in this chapter is to understand the social structure of the ways in which children affect and influence one another in conversation. To do this we shall employ linguistic concepts. However, whereas the sociolinguist or the linguist interested in pragmatics is interested in language and in making only brief excursions into the social world, our interest is in the social world of childhood and in making only a brief excursion into the linguistic world.

To study how children affect and influence one another we shall limit our inquiry to directives and requests.[1] We begin with a discussion of how adults convey the fact that a message is a directive.

8.1. The literature on adult directives

Most of the linguistic literature on directives has been concerned with understanding how an indirect statement can be clearly received as an imperative. For example, "Turn up the heat" is a clearly stated imperative, but often "Is it cold in here?" will do just as well. How is it that statements that do not have the obvious imperative form and *appear* to be statements of information or requests for information can still be correctly perceived as requests for action?

There have been two approaches to answering this question. The first is based on an analysis of the language itself and the second on an analysis of context.

The language itself. The linguistic literature (Clark & Lucy, 1955; Cole, 1975; Danson, 1975; Fraser, 1975; Gordon & Lakoff, 1975; Green, 1975; Grice, 1975; Searle, 1975; Morgan, 1978) points out that nonimperative requests are of two forms: (1) statements or questions in which the imperative form of one's request is imbedded (e.g., "Could you pass the salt?") and (2) statements or questions in which there is no direct reference to the desired action, though the object of one's concern may be referred to (e.g., "Have you got the scissors?").

Statements and questions serving as directives have been taxonomized (e.g., Gordan & Lakoff, 1975; Searle, 1975) into (1) those that state the speaker's desire for some object or action ("I want . . . ," "I wish you would . . . "); (2) those related to the listener's ability to perform the desired action ("Can you . . . ?" "You could . . . ," "Do you have time to . . . ?"); (3) questions concerning the listener's performance of or intent to perform the desired action ("Were you going to?", "Did you . . . ?"); (4) questions concerning the listener's willingness to perform the action ("Do you want to . . . ?", "Would you mind . . . ?"); (5) utterances providing or questioning reasons for performing an action, including obligations ("The baby's crying," "Didn't you have to . . . ?" "You need to . . . "); (6) utterances questioning the listener's reasons for not performing an action ("Why not . . . ?"); and (7) implied requests, or *hints* that often refer directly or indirectly to rules or obligations (Ervin-Tripp, 1977) or to other reasons for doing something (e.g., "What's that I see on the floor?" "He got another one and I didn't," "Naptime!"). One problem with this taxonomy, however, it is that it does not, in itself, indicate how requests can be identified. None of the types of statements and questions used as requests are used only for that function.

Some researchers (e.g., Green, 1975) have pointed out that most indirect request forms and even inferred request forms (Newcombe & Zaslow, 1981) follow a limited number of specific formulas. These include such forms as "Would you . . . ?" "Could you . . . ?" "How about . . . ?", "Why not . . . ?" and "Have you got a . . . ?" The directive intent of indirect requests using these formulas is grasped as quickly as that of direct imperatives by adults and even more readily than their literal meaning when used in context (Gibbs, 1975). Many specific "inferred" requests or hints are used so routinely to convey directive intent in certain contexts that they are or come to be automatically interpreted as such (Green, 1975; Morgan, 1975). Among these are such requests as "Is your mother there?" (over the telephone or at the door), "Do you have the time?" or "It's dinnertime." Conventional usage helps to explain how requests are identified as such, but it is clearly not the only factor involved. Not all indirect or implied requests follow conventional formulas, and all the formulas used conventionally to convey requests are at times used successfully to convey other intent (e.g., "Why did the artist paint it blue? Why not paint the boat white?").

Even in cases where someone is not using a form or a statement that is conventionally used to convey a request, Green (1975) points out that distinctive intonation patterns distinguish directives from informative utterances. As a result, recognizing that the other is making a request should seldom be difficult in actual conversation. However, it is also true that requests are usually recognizable even in print. Clearly, none of the linguistic examinations of requests have managed to account fully for the way people recognize a request as a request.

The context. Context, of course, is the linguist's excursion into the social world. It refers to the conversational context in which requests are issued, the nature of the relationship between the listener and speaker, the social obligations and responsibilities of each, and the setting and circumstances. Linguists (Gordon & Lakoff, 1975; Grice, 1975; Searle, 1975) have attempted a logical analysis of the social conditions under which requests are reasonable and when people will assume that a statement or question is intended as a request. If a person makes a statement or asks a question in a context where, if taken literally, the utterance does not make sense, the listeners will look for some other, indirect meaning. If the statement or question can be seen to be concerned with the conditions under which a particular request would be reasonable, and if that request is in fact one that the person might reasonably make in that context, then the listener assumes that the statement is a request. This can be seen in the following example, where the listener is actually mistaken in making such an inference:

A [*at neighbor's kitchen door*]: Do you still have all that honey?
B: Sure. How much do you need?
A: Oh, I don't need any. My mother just gave me more than I can use and I wondered if you could use some.

Identifying the intended request is relatively easy when it is embedded in a question or statement. But with *hints*, the listener must rely more heavily on acquired cultural knowledge of such factors as the social obligations and responsibilities of each person in the context to infer the request.

Developmental implications. The analysis of context is relevant to understanding the development of children's social competence. Because we can expect children to change developmentally in their sensitivity to context, we would expect young children to have more difficulty anticipating how others will interpret or respond to their utterances than older children. For example, hints are probably more effectively directed to familiar peers, such as friends, than to strangers. This is because hints are easily misinterpreted by people who do not have the same set of assumptions or knowledge about a situation.

Interactive constraints

Some linguists have wondered why speakers bother to choose one request form over another. O'Keefe and Delia (1982) suggested that children choose specific communication strategies to overcome obstacles to their primary goals. Such aims can be thought of as secondary goals and can be viewed as constraints that accompany the context in which a person has a goal. Jacobs and Jackson (1980) recommended examining such interactive goals when studying request strategies. For example, they described "prerequests" as requests designed to create a cooperative stance in the listener (e.g., "Could you do me a favor?" "Do you have a moment?"). Weiser (1977) proposed an explanation of hints and other ambiguous statements in terms of secondary goals. She noted that there is an advantage to being ambiguous if a request is likely to be seen as improper or presumptuous. If the speaker's meaning is ambiguous, it is easier to disclaim any offensive intention if the listener gets angry. This type of reasoning leads us to a discussion of Brown and Levinson's (1978) theory.

Brown–Levinson theory of politeness

Brown and Levinson (1978) developed a theory to explain the existence not only of the variety of request forms, but of all those linguistic tactics that could be classed as polite. They noted that the patterns and devices of politeness are remarkably similar from language to language. Furthermore, the meaning of all polite forms is easily recognized in literal translation by speakers of other languages.

Brown and Levinson proposed that the reason for this universality is that all of these tactics are logical solutions to two universal, inherent problems of human interaction. First, attempts to influence others' behavior violate a basic motivation of all people not to be constrained or interfered with. They referred to this motivation as people's "negative face needs." Second, another basic human motivation is the desire to be envied, admired, approved of, or cared about. Brown and Levinson referred to this motivation as "positive face needs." These are interactive constraints. As we shall see, the Brown–Levinson theory is a strategic theory of interaction, in the tradition of Erving Goffman (1967).

According to Brown and Levinson, satisfaction of people's negative and positive face needs requires the cooperation of others. For this reason, if two people serve each other's face needs, they will both be better off than if they do not. However, people are presumed to be rationally self-interested and to respect others' face needs only to the extent that there is reason to fear resultant anger, withdrawal of love, loss of custom, punishment, refusal, or lack of concern for one's own face needs if they do not. The degree to which the other person has control over resources one desires or can retaliate in other ways will affect the extent to which one actually fears retaliation. However, fear of retaliation is also affected by one's perception of how much it would cost the other person to retaliate. The other's freedom to retaliate effectively is affected partly by one's own ability to counterretaliate. Two factors that affect people's ability to retaliate and to counterretaliate are their relative social status and the degree to which they have personal relationships with one another. Since uncertainty should increase people's tendency to "play it safe," politeness should also be a function of familiarity. This analysis is capable of explaining the normally greater politeness of social inferiors to social superiors, the greater politeness of strangers to one another than to friends, as well as the courtesy of salesclerks to customers.

Brown and Levinson also discussed the kinds of polite strategies people employ and the ways in which people choose an appropriate degree of politeness. The selection of an appropriate level of politeness depends on the likelihood of the listener's adverse reaction, for example, the listener's noncompliance. There are four strategies: (1) a "bald-on-record" approach, in which the request is blunt; (2) positive politeness (e.g., using flattery or suggesting common interests); (3) negative politeness (e.g., deference, minimizing the imposition, allowing the listener to refuse gracefully); and (4) an "off-record" approach, which involves being tactful and making a request only by implication (e.g., "Are you driving to the party tonight?" equals "Can I have a ride?").

Brown and Levinson's theory, not surprisingly, can account for existing data (e.g., Ervin-Tripp, 1977) on formal interactions between adults who differ in status. For example, Brown and Levinson predicted that less polite forms should occur most often towards others who are inferior or very familiar. Deferential forms should be used more frequently in addressing strangers and superiors and when the imposition is great. The same pattern might also be predicted for hints, except that one might also predict their use among familiar people rather than strangers because of the dangers of misunderstanding. A limitation of using Ervin-Tripp's data to test Brown and Levinson's theory is that all indirect requests are grouped together. This means that forms emphasizing obligation are included with deferential forms. The former should be used primarily in addressing inferiors. Ervin-Tripp found that need or desire statements and imperatives were directed primarily at subordinates or, in the latter case, toward familiar equals as well. Imbedded imperatives (indirect requests) were most often directed toward unfamiliar people and toward people differing in rank. Along with such deferential modifiers as "please" and tag questions, imbedded imperatives were also favored by people addressing others in their own territory and where there was a considerable imposition. Permission requests were most often directed at superiors. Hints were employed most often when both the speaker and those addressed were familiar with the rules of a highly structured situation or were familiar with one another's habits and motives.

Critique of the literature on adult directives

The adult sociolinguistic literature has a number of limitations. To begin with, linguists do not generally explain how they derive categories. Indeed, in many cases, authors appear to have derived their categories intuitively, without the benefit of a large body of examples of actual speech. As a result, the classification schemes of some published papers fail to include types of requests that appear in other papers.

Furthermore, authors have seldom taken the time to test the usefulness of their theories or particular classification system. It cannot be overemphasized that *similarly structured linguistic forms may represent different tactics and serve different strategies, whereas widely different structures and devices may serve the same strategy.* Classification systems must be designed with a particular research purpose in mind. It may be appropriate to place "I need to use your red pencil" and "I need you to lend me your red pencil" in different categories if one is concerned with how the listener infers intent, but from a strategic viewpoint, the two sentences probably function quite similarly. Conversely, "You need to use this one" and "Do you want to use this one?" may be similar in the the mechanism by which their intent is inferred, but the strategies they exemplify are quite different.[2]

Fortunately, these specific criticisms do not apply to Brown and Levinson's theorizing. But their work is not developmental. Furthermore, it could benefit greatly from quantitative sequential analysis of conversation. This would allow one to ask how various strategies influence the listener's compliance and how these vary contextually (e.g., as a function of relative status or familiarity).

Also Brown and Levinson did not catalogue strategies for increasing compliance and reducing the likelihood of conflict that are not described by the politeness dimension. An example of a nonpolite strategy is the use of threats or anger to coerce compliance (e.g., "If you don't let me use it, I'll tell your mother"). Status differentials may affect the use of threats (i.e., threats should be used more by hosts than guests). Another strategy is to state why the listener ought to comply. One can do so by invoking rules, placing emphasis on one's needs, or giving persuasive reasons. Examples of this strategy are "You have to put her head through first," "You'll tear it if you put it on that way," "I need that to finish my house," and "We're supposed to take turns." One can pursue the same strategy by appending a rationale after the request. One might predict that these strategies are used more often by speakers familiar with the situation and its rules than by speakers who are not. Neither threats nor statements of one's obligation are attempts to reduce the threat imposed by the request.

Finally, Brown and Levinson ignored Green's point about the importance of the interaction of linguistic forms with the paralinguistic features that accompany them. Orders, demands, suggestions, requests, and pleas also differ in their forcefulness and voice tone. It would be important to code not only the linguistic form of an utterance but also its paralinguistic features.

In the study to be described in Section 8.3, we address some of these specific criticisms of Brown and Levinson's theory and the literature on adult directives. Among other things, we examine requests issued by children during the course of naturalistic dyadic play. We vary children's relative status by varying their control over resources. This is accomplished by recording the children's conversations in the home of one of the pair of children (the "host"). In this situation hosts have more control over resources than do guests. We also examine the effects of familiarity by comparing pairs of friends and pairs of strangers.

8.2. The developmental literature

Brown and Levinson's theory is not a developmental theory. Nevertheless, it is possible to modify it to make it developmental and test the extent to which children's directive use conforms to its predictions. Among the competencies a child must develop before being able to behave as Brown and Levinson predict are the ability to recognize the intent of a range of directive forms, production of directive forms of various degrees of politeness, and knowledge of polite strategies. Each of these competencies is considered next.

Directive use in children

Children issue directives in a variety of forms at a very early age. Children first show directive intent before developing language, by Stage 5 of Piaget's stages of sensorimotor development (Bates, Camaioni, & Volterra, 1979). At this stage, they use gestures and vocalizations to convey their intent. Directives are common among children's early utterances (Ervin-Tripp, 1977), and after early childhood the proportion of utterances that are directives does not appear to change (Garvey, 1974; Levin & Rubin, 1983). Even at very early stages of language development, children use a sufficient range of directives to convey different levels of politeness. At the two-word stage, children have been observed to issue requests through imperatives, goal objects or locations ("More juice"), statements of possession ("That mine"), problem statements ("Carol hungry"), desire statements ("I want dolly") and interrogatives conveyed through rising intonation ("More juice?"). By 2½ years, many children are using "please," permission requests, and imbedded imperatives such as interrogatives, conditionals, requests for information, collective requests, and hints (Bates, 1976; Ervin-Tripp, 1977; Newcombe & Zaslow, 1981; Read & Cherry, 1978). And by 4 years, children's repertoire of request forms and modifications includes most adult forms and request tactics. But it is not necessary to possess all these forms in order to use all of Brown and Levinson's strategies. Children at the two-word stage already have the means to be deferential and go "off record."

Children respond at a very early age to a wide variety of interrogative and declarative utterances as if they were actually directives. In fact, young children appear to have a bias to respond to utterances as directives whether or not they are intended as such (Ervin-Tripp, 1977; Shatz, 1979). Shatz studied children whose mean length of utterance (see Brown, 1973) was 1.0 to 1.8, 2.0 to 2.7, and 3.2 to 4.0. All groups showed a strong bias to treat any utterance as a request, though this declined with age. Overall, the proportions of meaningful action responses by children to imperatives, interrogatives, and declaratives were extremely high (.98, .93, and .83, respectively). Children were also increasingly affected by the conversational context in interpreting interrogatives and declaratives requests. Ervin-Tripp (1977) reported similar findings with a child of 3 years and 3 months who tended to interpret problem statements as demanding a solution from him. Examples she cited included: (1) Mother: "I'm cold"; Child: "I already shut the window"; (2) Mother: "It's noisy in here"; Child: "Do you want me to shut the door?"

Development of children's directive strategies

Studies that identify developmental changes in children's usage of directive strategies fall into several groups: (1) studies of children's ability to recognize degrees of politeness and produce polite directives on request, (2) studies of developmental changes in the directive forms or strategies children favor in a given situation, (3) studies of the request forms children use after their initial request fails, and (4) studies of contextual effects such as the other person's relative age, status, or social distance and the nature of the situation. The last-named studies also provide evidence of the degree to which children are strategic.

Most children do not appear to recognize politeness or to be able to use it as a strategy before age 4 (e.g., Bates, 1976). An apparent exception is that, among very young children, the use of "please" begins as a result of parental reinforcement, and even 2½-year-old children remark that "you have to say please" (Read & Cherry, 1978). In fact, Read and Cherry found that 2½-year-olds actually use "please" more often than older children. However, those of their subjects who endorsed the use of "please" were no more apt to use "please" in their requests than the others, nor did they become more polite when their initial request failed.

Bates (1976) attempted to assess children's ability to recognize which request forms were more polite and to be more polite on request. When 2- to 4-year-old children were told that they had to be more polite to a puppet they were asking for candy, only half the children adopted a more polite way of asking; the rest either made no change or became less polite. Furthermore, the first polite form very young children shifted to was the interrogative, even though the interrogative was not generally viewed by children in this age range as "nicer." On the contrary, young children tended to regard the imperative as nicer than the interrogative, and the only characteristic the children could accurately distinguish as nicer at levels above chance was the use of "please."

In short, it would appear that before age 4 children are not well equipped to adjust their politeness strategically when making requests. Rather the ability to use politeness as a strategy seems to begin at about 4 years and continues to improve between 4 and 6 years. After 4 years, virtually all children can change to more polite forms on request and are more polite initially (Bates, 1978). Furthermore, the ability to identify a variety of polite tactics as nicer (e.g., ingratiating voice tone, use of the interrogative, and use of conditional voice) develops between 4 and 6 years.

A number of researchers have looked at developmental changes in the request forms or strategies children favor in a given situation, although in all cases these researchers have studied usage in only one situation.

Three studies have looked at directive usage (Garvey, 1974; Levin & Rubin, 1983; Read & Cherry, 1978). Read and Cherry (1978) studied children in the age range from 2½ to 4½ years but did not examine usage in a relatively natural situation, as when a child is interacting one to one with a familiar peer. Instead, they looked at the directives children produced when asked to make a request of a puppet. In this respect their study is not comparable to that of Garvey (1974), who studied children 3½ to 5½ years old, and Levin and Rubin (1983), who studied children ranging in school level from preschool to third grade.

Despite these differences, an overview of the findings of these studies suggests that the imperative is the directive approach most favored at all ages. The proportion of imperatives does not change after early childhood and is used for 80 to 90% of all directives in the naturalistic studies of children's interaction with peers. Otherwise, younger children rely more heavily on arguments that others ought of comply, whereas older children rely more on politeness. Read and Cherry recorded a drop in the proportion of want/need statements from 23% at 2½ years to 4% at 4½ years. Garvey found a drop in the number of need statements but not want statements. Garvey also reported a drop with age in the number of "You have to . . . " directives. However, interrogatives increase with age until first grade and then decline somewhat, and there is some indication that the use of inferred requests increases through third grade (Garvey, 1975; Levin & Rubin, 1983; Read & Garvey, 1978).

These changes may involve a shift from a strategy by which one tries to get the other to accept one's own stance to strategies that take account of the fact that others dislike being imposed on. A study by Clark and Delia (1976) of the development of children's persuasive strategies revealed that developmentally the first strategy children introduced after relying on direct requests was to explain their own desires. Somewhat older children tried to forestall counterarguments (fourth to sixth grade). Even older children tried to demonstrate how the other might benefit from compliance (seventh to ninth grades).

We know little about what children do after their initial request has failed. Most researchers report only on children's inflexibility or tendency to repeat the same tactics. However, Read and Cherry (1978) reported that children 2½ to 4½ years old become more explicit when they change their tactics. Similarly, Newcombe and Zaslow (1981) reported that 2½-year-olds become more direct.

Studies of the effects of relative status and other contextual factors on children's directive use (James, 1975, cited in Ervin-Tripp, 1977; Lawson,

1967; O'Connell, 1974) show that children over 4 years, and at least some younger children, use deference and hints. Mitchell-Kernan and Kernan (1977) suggest more specifically that, among children 7 to 12 years old, deference is used to increase the likelihood of compliance, whereas hints are used to avoid a negative reaction when an outright request would be contrary to etiquette. Also, direct forms may be used to gain or assert status. Furthermore, children are more likely to avoid making requests when a negative response is likely.

Taken together, studies of children's directive usage suggest that children under 4 years (1) make their intent more explicit after noncompliance and (2) attempt to justify their request to persuade others to comply. Children over 4 years use deferential tactics when refusal or retaliation is likely. At least after 7 years, and perhaps as young as 4 years, children use hints rather than direct requests when the latter might be considered out of line. They also use direct requests to manipulate their status relative to others. Children 10 years and older forestall the other person's objections; children 13 years and older attempt to make their requests attractive to the other person.

Young children as strategists

Being strategic implies being sensitive to contextual factors affecting the likelihood of compliance and the relative advantageousness of various strategies. Relatively few studies have investigated when children's use of directives begins to be strategic. Two dimensions are useful in discussing the development of children's strategic sense: their inflexibility and their awareness of context.

Inflexibility. Very young children show a strong tendency simply to repeat their tactics if their initial request is unsuccessful (Newcombe & Zaslow, 1981; Read & Cherry, 1978). Read and Cherry found little change in children's inflexibility between 2½ and 4½ years. However, Levin and Rubin (1983) reported an increasing tendency to shift to other request forms and a decreasing tendency simply to repeat failed requests between nursery school and second grade.

Awareness of context. There is considerable evidence that children over 4 years old adjust the form of their directives in response to the other person's age or status, the situation, or the nature of the request

(Ervin-Tripp, 1971; Mitchell-Kernan & Kernan, 1977). Imperatives tend to be addressed to persons of lower status; imperatives addressed to superiors are usually pleas or urgent warnings. It appears that by 4½ or 5 years, children vary their use of strategies in accordance with predictions made by Brown and Levinson.

Young children do not necessarily match their use of a strategy (in relative frequency) with its effectiveness. For example, in preschool pairs Garvey (1974) found that most requests were direct, although indirect requests were, in general, more successful than direct requests.

On the basis of the adult and developmental literature, what appears to be most needed is (1) to determine which request strategies children respond to and under what circumstances these are advantageous; (2) to identify the range of request strategies children employ, and how they develop, by examining children's use of different directive forms and modifications; (3) to determine when children begin to use request strategies strategically to pursue particular personal or social objectives by examining children's use of strategies in relation to their actual advantageousness; and (4) to develop a useful theoretical framework for studying children's development in this area. Earlier we proposed that Brown and Levinson's theory might form the basis for such a framework.

8.3. A study of children's directive strategies

In this section, we report several findings of a study addressed to the objectives previously listed. The study was based on the conversations of pairs of children playing at home. In light of the above-mentioned criticisms of previous studies, this study (1) examined children's directive use and strategies in the context of natural interaction with peers; (2) looked at behavior and response in several situations, permitting identification of the request forms that were used and that functioned similarly and differently in any given age group; (3) attempted an analysis of the different situations in terms of the power of each child to control the situation and to retaliate, as well as the child's certainty about the appropriateness of requests; (4) employed a relatively fine grained coding system for requests, allowing grouping of request forms on the basis of similar function; and (5) examined the effect of situational factors on children's response to different request forms, as well as their effect on children's usage.

Table 8.1. *Age characteristics of the subjects*

	Host		Guest		Mean age difference (range), months
	Age range	Mean age	Age range	Mean age	
Younger					
Best friends					
(8 dyads)	2:11–4:9	4:0	2:9–5:0	4:2	3.5 (1–9)
Strangers					
(8 dyads)	3:0–4:10	4:2	2:7–5:6	4:6	6 (1–11)
Older					
Best friends					
(5 dyads)	4:11–6:0	5:3	5:2–8:0	6:3	12 (0–37)
Strangers					
(5 dyads)	4:0–6:10	5:6	4:0–6:0	5:0	6.5 (1–10)

Methods

Subjects. The subjects comprised 13 pairs of children who were best friends and 13 pairs of strangers. The sample was described in Gottman and Parkhurst (1980). The host in each pair of best friends was also the host to an unfamiliar visitor, except in one case, where the host of a pair of friends was recorded on audiotape while visiting a stranger. Eight hosts ranged in age from 2 years and 11 months to 4 years and 9 months. Five hosts ranged in age from 4 years and 11 months to 6 years. The children were audiotaped as they played together in the host's house. Sixty to 90 minutes of conversation were audiotaped in most cases. In two pairs of younger strangers only 15 to 20 minutes were recorded before the visitor began to cry and was taken home. Kolmogorov–Smirnov tests showed no significant differences in age between hosts and either group of guests or between the two groups of visitors in each age group. Chi-square tests showed that the age of visitors was significantly related to that of their host among both friends and strangers [χ^2 (1) = 6.72, $p < .01$; χ^2 (1) = 25.44, $p < .001$, respectively]. A description of the subjects can be found in Tables 8.1 and 8.2. Data were pooled across dyads within each combination of age and acquaintanceship.

Coding system. The children's utterances were coded using a modification of the MICRO coding system described in Chapter 2. Twenty-two directive codes were defined using this system. The first four codes were defined on the basis of either the mode of interaction or the manner of delivery: (1) requests issued in the context of fantasy; (2) joking requests;

Table 8.2. *Sex composition of the subject pairs*

Other child	Primary subject			
	Younger girls	Younger boys	Older girls	Older boys
Best friend				
Girls	3	1	2	0
Boys	3	1	2	1
Stranger				
Girls	4	0	4	1
Boys	2	2	0	0

(3) threats and angry requests; and (4) requests uttered with loving or enthusiastic voice tone. All the remaining codes concerned requests that were intended literally and seriously and that were delivered neutrally. Some of these were coded in categories defined on the basis of function: (5) attempts to get the other's attention ("Lookit," "You know what?"); (6) requests for help ("Could you help me tie these?"); and (7) sympathetic gestures and other prosocial offers that were not the result of demand or obligation ("Let me fix that for you"). Serious literal requests for objects or actions were coded into 15 categories defined on the basis of form. Grouped on the basis of Brown and Levinson's strategies of politeness, these were as follows:

A. Bald-on-record (blunt) forms, where the speaker's wishes or attempts to constrain the other's behavior are expressed without modification: (8) imperatives ("Give me the red one"); (9) requirements of the other ("You hafta . . . ," "You need to . . . "); (10) want/need statements ("I wanna . . . ," "I hafta . . . ," "I need to . . . ")

B. Forms consistent with positive politeness tactics, emphasizing commonality or shared interest: (11) simultaneous suggestions for each child ("You be . . . and I'll be . . . "); (12) collective suggestions ("Let's . . . ," "We could . . . ")

C. Forms including elements consistent both with positive and with negative politeness tactics: (13) requirements for the pair, as if rules ("We gotta . . ."); (14) collective suggestions in interrogative form ("How about if we . . . ?"); (15) inquiries concerning the other's desires ("Do you want . . . ?" "Would you like . . . ?")

D. Forms consistent with negative politeness tactics, deferring to the other: (16) noninterrogative requests modified by "please" ("Please, give me . . . "); (17) interrogative requests ("Could you . . . ?" "Will you . . . ?"); (18) permission requests ("May I . . . ?" "Is it OK if I . . . ?"); (19) suggestions ("You could . . . "); (20) interrogative suggestions ("How about . . . ?" "Why don't you . . . ?")

E. Off-record forms, or hints: (21) interrogative hints ("Have you got . . . ?"); (22) declarative hints ("That goes upstairs").

None of these categories included negative requests. Requests for the other to stop doing something were coded as disagreements.

Reliability between coders for any given utterance was high. Cronbach's alpha was at least .90 for all but five request categories and higher than .75 for all but three categories. Reliability was lowest for hints: only .66 for declarative hints and .00 for interrogative hints. The low reliability of hints results in part from their infrequency; it also may reflect the fact that hints are by definition ambiguous in intent to coders as well as to other listeners. Offers were the only other group of requests with reliability less than .75.

Neither group used requests uttered with loving or enthusiastic voice tone. Otherwise, all other codes were used in both age groups.

Data analysis. The data were analyzed in two ways. One approach was to (1) determine theoretically what strategies children might use and when, (2) sort request forms according to the strategies they should serve, (3) predict children's response to and use of requests exemplifying different strategies, and (4) examine children's response to and usage of different requests to see if the data were consistent with predictions. This approach was designed to test Brown and Levinson's theory concerning the effects of the situation on children's request strategies. The results of this analysis are presented in this chapter. The second approach was to examine how children used and responded to various request forms to determine request forms with similar usages and functions. This approach allowed us to examine the extent to which Brown and Levinson's theoretical groupings of tactics are valid. In addition to being of theoretical interest, this latter analysis has implications for investigators interested in designing systems for coding children's requests. It provides empirical support for Brown and Levinson's strategies as the basis for classifying requests. Details of this analysis, its results, and the methodological issues related to it are not reported here. Readers interested in an account of these may write to the first author.

The following analyses are based entirely on literal requests for goods, actions, or permission. Requests for information, requests uttered in the context of fantasy, and requests for attention are not included.[3]

8.4. Testing Brown and Levinson's theory

We examined two general assertions of Brown and Levinson's theory: that the ability to command compliance without adverse consequences is a function of people's resources and capacity to retaliate, and that there is an optimum level of politeness which varies with the situation.

With regard to compliance, we expected on the basis of our reading of Brown and Levinson's theory that control over resources and capacity to retaliate would influence the patterns of compliance to requests and the likelihood of making requests. Findings of this sort would confirm that children are sensitive to power relations.

With regard to politeness, we sought answers to questions of the following types: Does children's compliance with requests vary as a function of the politeness of the request? If so, is the optimum level of politeness the same when one is talking to a stranger and when one is talking to a friend? Is it the same when one is talking to a host and guest? If there is an optimum level of politeness, are children sensitive to this fact; that is, do children use certain strategies more frequently when they appear to offer an advantage in gaining compliance? Answers to questions of this type can provide evidence for Brown and Levinson's assertion that people are polite out of self-interest.

Contextual influence on compliance with requests

Earlier it was proposed that the ability to gain others' cooperation is a function of one's control over desired resources and one's ability and willingness to retaliate if the other does not obey. In pairs of strangers, hosts presumably have more control and a greater capacity to retaliate without fear of counterretaliation than guests. A host can evict a guest, but a guest cannot evict a host. Thus, hosts should be less compliant than guests in pairs of strangers if children are sensitive to these factors. But among friends, the guest's capacity to retaliate should be closer to that of the host. If the host is attached to the guest, the guest can threaten to go home or sever the relationship. The host stands to lose if the threat is carried out. Therefore, hosts' likelihood of compliance should be close to that of guests in pairs of friends.

An examination of the nature of children's response to requests tended to confirm these expectations. The proportion of compliant responses [agreement/(agreement + disagreement)] is presented in Table 8.3. The pattern of responses among older children was as predicted, even though none of the differences were statistically significant. The main exception to the predictions was that younger children behaved with their friends as they did with strangers, guests being more

Table 8.3. *Compliance with and issuance of requests*

	Younger children				Older children			
	Best friends		Strangers		Best friends		Strangers	
	Hosts	Guests	Hosts	Guests	Hosts	Guests	Hosts	Guests
Compliance[a]	.66	.49	.55	.50	.58	.59	.62	.47
Issuance[b]	.058	.050	.073	.041	.055	.056	.067	.037

[a]Measured as agreement/(agreement + disagreement).
[b]Proportion of all utterances of a pair that were requests.

compliant with their hosts' requests than hosts with their guests' requests [$\chi^2(1) = 6.30$, $p < .02$].[4]

Contextual influence on issuance of requests

The sensitivity of children to their control over a situation and to their relative capacity to retaliate should also be seen in the number of requests they issue in different situations. Because of the hosts' greater control over the situation, guests are in the position of having to ask permission more often than hosts. On the other hand, fear of retaliation should make guests who are strangers particularly wary of making requests. This fear should be increased by the fact that guests of strangers should be in greatest uncertainty concerning the social appropriateness of their requests or the imposition they might involve. The guest of a friend should have knowledge about the rules at the friend's house and of the friend's likely response to particular requests. The visiting stranger's lack of knowledge about the situation also implies that the host has to direct the stranger to a greater extent than a visiting friend.

For these reasons, visiting strangers should issue fewer requests than their hosts. Among friends, if anything, guests should issue *more* requests than their hosts. Finally, hosts of strangers should issue more requests than hosts of friends and visiting friends more than visiting strangers.

Findings on the issuance of requests are presented in Table 8.3. Most of these predictions were confirmed. Among both younger and older strangers, hosts issued many more requests than their guests, this difference being highly significant [$\chi^2(1) = 39.52$, $p < .001$; $\chi^2(1) = 48.88$,

$p < .001$).[5] Also as predicted, hosts in both age groups issued significantly more requests when interacting with strangers than when interacting with friends [χ^2 (1) = 7.64, $p < .01$; χ^2 (1) =5.29, $p < .05$], and guests who were friends issued more requests than guests who were strangers [χ^2 (1) = 4.96, $p < .05$; χ^2 (1) = 15.26, $p < .001$]. Among friends, the number of requests issued by hosts and guests did not differ significantly. Among younger friends, hosts of friends issued slightly more requests than their guests. This finding was the only one that deviated from predictions. Among older friends, the proportions of requests issued by hosts and guests were essentially identical.

These results, together with the previous ones, are consistent with the hypothesis that the ability to command cooperation is a function of relative control and capacity for retaliation. Furthermore, our analysis of the power relations between friends and strangers was essentially correct. Finally, children are sensitive to contextual factors. The single exception is younger children, who either cannot rely on threats to walk out or are insensitive to guests' capacity to retaliate against friends by leaving.

Average optimum level of politeness

Is there an average optimum level of politeness in each of the four situations defined by host or guest status and acquaintanceship? Brown and Levinson argued that both liabilities and advantages are associated with politeness and that people should be no more polite than is necessary to obtain best results. This implies that, in a given context and for a given request, there is an optimum level of politeness.

The proportion of compliant responses to those requests in each politeness category receiving an overt reply was calculated for each age group (Table 8.4). The hypothesis that there is an optimum level of politeness in any situation was confirmed among older children but not among younger children. There was significant variation in response across the range of politeness for three of four conditions among older children: older hosts of friends [χ^2 (2) = 12.86, $p < .05$], older guests of friends [χ^2 (2) = 6.37, $p < .05$], and older hosts of strangers [χ^2 (1) = 4.66, $p < .05$].[6] The response was curvilinear as a function of politeness in all these three cases. The optimum level of politeness was highest for hosts of strangers (at the level of negative or mixed politeness) and lowest for hosts of friends (between positive politeness and no politeness at all). The optimum level for guests of friends was intermediate.

Table 8.4. *Compliance with requests of various degrees of politeness*

	Younger children				Older children			
	Best friends		Strangers		Best friends		Strangers	
Degree of politeness	Hosts	Guests	Hosts	Guests	Hosts	Guests	Hosts	Guests
No politeness	.64 (66)	.48 (46)	.60 (23)	.50 (23)	.60 (25)	.59 (35)	.59 (30)	.45 (24)
Positive politeness	.82 (11)	.60 (18)	.00 (3)	.50 (6)	.90 (19)	.79 (14)	.50 (8)	.60 (5)
Mixed politeness	.76 (21)	.50 (41)	.41 (17)	.62 (8)	.33 (6)	.83 (6)	1.00 (4)	.50 (4)
Deference	.68 (19)	.37 (19)	.60 (5)	.25 (4)	.25 (8)	.33 (6)	.86 (7)	.44 (9)
Hints	.67 (3)	.67 (3)	1.00 (1)	—	—	.00 (1)	—	.67 (3)

Note: Numbers in parentheses represent frequencies of requests to which there was verbal agreement or disagreement.

Table 8.5. *Proportion of requests employing politeness and other strategies*

| Strategy | Younger children | | | | Older children | | | |
| | Best friends | | Strangers | | Best friends | | Strangers | |
	Hosts	Guests	Hosts	Guests	Hosts	Guests	Hosts	Guests
No politeness	.595	.569	.580	.564	.642	.645	.644	.598
Positive politeness	.145	.165	.098	.198	.192	.195	.169	.158
Mixed politeness	.103	.095	.223	.140	.072	.053	.056	.042
Deference	.116	.119	.066	.081	.048	.064	.080	.122
Hints	.012	.018	.010	.000	.003	.001	.000	.048
Anger/ coercion	.037	.018	.006	.006	.003	.001	.030	.000
Humor	.008	.081	.016	.012	.038	.021	.021	.032

This suggests that in this age group the optimum increases as a function of lack of attachment and of guest as opposed to host status. In contrast, politeness had no significant affect on compliance with requests among younger children in any of the four conditions.

Although politeness affected older children's response to requests in any context, levels of politeness did not eliminate the effects of contextual factors on compliance across contexts. Examination of compliance at the level of politeness that was optimal for each group of older children shows that compliance was greatest to requests issued by hosts of strangers, followed by hosts of friends, guests of friends, and guests of strangers.

Children's use of politeness

The question of greatest interest was whether children used politeness strategically to increase the likelihood of compliance. Once it is known what degree of politeness is most advantageous in each situation, it is possible to see if children's use of polite forms parallels their advantageousness. Results on children's use of politeness are presented in Table 8.5. This table shows that children 5 to 6 years old used politeness strategically to obtain compliance but that children less than 5 years old did not. The use of strategies among older children reflected changes in their relative advantage or disadvantage in every case except those forms classified as incorporating both positive and negative politeness. Older children's use of hints and of deferential forms were greatest in situations where they were advantageous. One would predict that hints would be used primarily by guests of strangers. Deference would be used by all strangers, but especially by strange guests. This is precisely what was found. A significantly greater proportion of requests were conveyed through hints by guests of strangers than their hosts ($\chi^2 = 9.00$, $p < .001$), hosts of friends ($\chi^2 = 6.40$ $p < .05$), or guests of friends ($\chi^2 = 4.46$, $p < .05$). Older children were much more apt to be deferential in issuing requests to strangers than to friends [$\chi^2(1) = 17.29$, $p < .001$].[7] Among older strangers, guests were also more deferential than their hosts [$\chi^2(1) = 6.75$, $p < .02$].

It was predicted on the basis of advantageousness that older friends should use positive politeness more often than older strangers. This occurred, though variations in usage were not significant.

Predictions that requests combining positive and negative politeness should be used most often by guests of friends and hosts of strangers were not confirmed. Instead, these forms were used more often by hosts and friends among older children. This was consistent with both response to and usage of collective forms including only positive politeness tactics.

On the basis of patterns of compliance among older children, it would be predicted that bald-on-record requests are used more often by friends than strangers and more often by hosts than guests, especially among strangers. This pattern was found, though the only significant difference was between hosts of friends and guests of strangers [$\chi^2(1) = 4.16$, $p < .05$].

The conclusion to be drawn is that older children's use of and response to directives and to different degrees of politeness conform well to the predictions of Brown and Levinson's theory and that their use of different degrees of politeness is strategic. Only the use of requests incorporating elements of both positive and negative politeness did not conform to predictions based on response. However, the latter grouped together widely differing forms which one would expect to be used very differently. The use of some, such as collective requirements, might be expected to be governed by factors other than the degree of optimum politeness.

In contrast, younger children's use of politeness was not as predicted by its lack of effect on younger children's compliance with requests. On the basis of patterns of compliance, younger children should use politeness seldom or not at all. However, younger children were actually more polite than older children, especially hosts of friends [$\chi^2(1) = 7.33$, $p < .01$], guests of friends [$\chi^2(1) = 11.82$, $p < .01$], and hosts of strangers [$\chi^2(1) = 9.98$, $p < .001$].[8] Although context should have no effect on their politeness, younger children were more polite to their friends than to strangers. They were more deferential to their friends than to strangers [$\chi(1) = 4.07$, $p < .05$]. They also used hints more often in conveying requests to friends than to strangers. Their use of forms combining negative and positive politeness bore no relationship to patterns in the response to such requests. Although there was no reason to predict any such difference in usage, these forms were used more often by younger strangers than younger friends, a difference highly significant in the case of hosts [$\chi^2(1) = 22.06$, $p < .001$]. Guests of strangers issued a higher proportion of requests incorporating positive politeness than their hosts [$\chi^2(1) = 5.67$, $p < .05$]. There was no such difference among friends. The only variation in young children's usage of politeness that might be related to compliance, since it paralleled changes in absolute compliance to such requests, was in these children's use of positive politeness (Table 8.4).

Notwithstanding the fact that younger children used politeness in ways that were not predicted by patterns of compliance, one result was consistent with the finding that politeness made no difference to younger children's compliance with requests: Among younger children, there was no significant variation as a function of contextual factors in the proportion of requests that were bald on record.

The conclusion to be drawn is that younger children are polite and their use of politeness is, in a number of cases, affected by contextual factors. However, younger children do not appear to use politeness as a strategy to gain compliance.

Extent to which children use politeness strategically

Even though children 5 to 6 years old use strategies in ways that parallel their relative success, they are underpolite. Under all circumstances more than 60% of requests were bald on record. For instance, although the average optimum level of politeness among hosts of strangers was at the level of deference or some combination of deference and positive politeness tactics, only about 15% of requests incorporated tactics at these levels of politeness, and virtually all the rest were less polite. This is not in accord with predictions. If the average optimum level of compliance is at the level of deference or some combination of deference and positive politeness, the average level of politeness should also be between the two. The number of requests that are more polite than this should be the same as the number of requests that are less polite. However, this was not the case.

Success of Brown and Levinson's theory

A summary of the analysis based on prior classification of requests by strategy suggests that, to a large extent, Brown and Levinson's theory can account for variations in children's ability to command compliance as well as children's usage of different request forms, provided that one is dealing with children over 5 years old. Older, but not younger, children's compliance with requests is affected by their degree of politeness. In each condition studied, there was an average optimum level of politeness at which compliance peaked. This was higher for strangers and for guests than for hosts. Variations in older children's usage in different conditions could be accounted for largely in terms of the optimum level of politeness. However, Brown and Levinson's theory of politeness did not account entirely for older children's use of different request forms and, in particular, did not account for younger children's use of different request forms. The latter did not respond to politeness as predicted by the theory, nor was their use of politeness consistent with either the situational analysis or the relative advantage of polite strategies. Older children used deference, tact, and emphasis on commonality as strategies to increase compliance. The only strategy whose usage among younger children may have been affected by its success in gaining compliance was emphasis on commonality.

8.5. Other influence strategies

An alternative strategy that children use to make compliance to their requests more likely is to convince listeners that they ought to comply. We refer to this as "assertions of validity." A number of specific tactics are directed to this end, including statements of obligation and the assertion of rules and reasons. Examples are assertions concerning the other's requirement to act in a given way ("You have to . . . "), assertions of mutual requirement ("We have to . . . "), reasons ("This one fits her better"), assertions of need ("I need to . . ."), and assertions of desire ("I want to . . . "). Compliance using the ratio agreement/ (agreement + disagreement) following polite requests (tactful or deferential requests), assertions of validity, and imperatives is presented in Table 8.6. Among younger children, assertions of validity usually received a more favorable response than either polite requests or imperatives. Guests of friends were the only group for which this was not true. Consistent with this, guests of friends made proportionally fewer assertions of validity than other groups, although this difference was not statistically significant. Older children hosting friends were the only older group in which assertions of validity offered a clear advantage over polite tactics or imperatives. The use of such assertions among older children was greater when they were advantageous. Assertions of validity were used significantly more often by older children hosting friends than either their guests [$\chi^2(1) = 6.01, p < .02$] or children hosting strangers [$\chi^2(1) = 6.97, p < .01$].

Another strategy for increasing compliance is the use of anger or threats. One would predict coercion to be most effective when used by children hosting strangers and most ineffective when used by guests who are strangers. Among friends, host and guest should be more evenly matched in their ability to coerce compliance than among strangers. Children's compliance with angry or threatening requests could not be examined because the number of coercive requests was too small in several contexts. However, older children hosting strangers issued more angry or threatening requests than their guests or either group of friends. This difference was only marginally significant [$\chi^2(1) = 3.54, p < .10$]. Among younger children, friends used coercive tactics more often than strangers [$\chi^2(1) = 4.45, p < .05$]. This pattern might occur because friends can make more effective threats within the bond of affection.

Humorous requests, another strategy for increasing compliance, did not occur often enough to judge the effects of situational variables. The most common response to joking requests in all groups was a humorous or laughing answer. It was not possible to identify such responses as compliant or noncompliant. One might also question whether many joking requests were intended to be taken seriously as requests. It is possible that they served as a means of affecting the emotional climate. They may have served to avert or defuse anger, for example.

8.6. A developmental model of strategicness in children's requests

According to Brown and Levinson, if an individual is rationally self-interested and motivated by the desire to act without constraint and to

Table 8.6. *Relative advantage of alternative strategies for compliance*

	Best friends				Strangers			
	Hosts		Guests		Hosts		Guests	
	AG/(AG + DG)	Proportion of requests	AG/(AG + DG)	Proportion of requests	AG/(AG + DG)	Proportion of requests	AG/(AG + DG)	Proportion of requests
Younger children								
Polite requests	.67 (46)*	.231	.44 (36)	.231	.56 (23)	.387	.50 (12)	.221
Assertions of validity	.74 (38)	.217	.43 (28)	.211	1.00 (4)	.226	.67 (3)	.262
Imperatives	.62 (39)	.426	.59 (27)	.404	.57 (21)	.420	.50 (6)	.349
Older children								
Polite requests	.28 (14)	.124	.53 (13)	.128	.91 (11)	.136	.50 (16)	.222
Assertions of validity	.73 (11)	.237	.14 (7)	.177	.71 (7)	.175	.64 (11)	.206
Imperatives	.50 (16)	.454	.69 (29)	.500	.56 (25)	.493	.38 (16)	.423

*The number in parentheses represents the number of instances in which there was an overt response indicating compliance or noncompliance.

feel valued, admired, and loved by others, that individual should behave as the older children in our study did. Younger children appear to be self-interested. They act to get what they want. They also seem rational in some sense. However, they do not respond to politeness with greater compliance, nor do they use it to gain compliance as older children do. Thus, we are left to explain why Brown and Levinson's model fits children over 5 years old but not younger children. One explanation is that younger children do not make inferences about others' intent in formulating a request, whereas older children do.

This theory has a number of implications. If children do not make inferences about others' strategic intent, they will take an interrogative request to mean that they, in fact, have a choice. Thus, if they are asked if they want to do something, and do not want to, they will not. Interrogative requests *should* decrease the likelihood of compliance. On the other hand, arguments that the other ought to comply *should* increase the likelihood of compliance if anything. This is because understanding the implications of such arguments does not require inferring the intent that underlies the other's choice of directive form.

Another implication is that, although more constraining forms are generally more aversive, differences in tactics should not lead to differences among younger children's perceptions of the other child (e.g., as nice or bossy). Such perceptions and the gratitude or resentment that follows from them, are dependent on the ability to infer the intent underlying the other's choice of request form. Positive response to deferential requests requires that the child infer the other's intent, since positive response to deferential requests implies that children perceive that the other is being nice. Deferential requests make explicit what is wanted. Therefore, the child's problem in inferring intent is not in inferring that something is wanted or what it is. Rather, the child addressed must be able to recognize that the speaker is offering the freedom to choose, as a cooperative and considerate gesture.

If the listener is to respond with increased compliance to the realization that the other is being deliberately nice, an entirely self-interested individual must also recognize that, if the speaker receives no consideration in return, the speaker is likely to respond with resentment and stop being considerate. The listener must also recognize the benefit to be gained from the other's continued cooperation. This requires considerable role-taking ability beyond most 5-year-olds' capabilities. Thus, it seems unlikely that 5-year-olds' use of and compliance with requests is based only on rational self-interest.

The possibility should be considered that children become compliant toward others simply out of gratitude. This means that the child who infers that the other is being deliberately considerate will like the other and reciprocate. Although this requires some inference of the other's intent, it is not as advanced as that necessary to comply with politeness out of recognition that it is in one's self-interest to do so. If children are nicer toward children they believe are considerate to them, children should infer that, if they are polite to others, others will appreciate their consideration and therefore be more compliant in return. Once this is understood, children should infer that others are polite to them in order to gain their cooperation.

The development of young children's use of and response to deferential politeness might change in accordance with the following sequence:

1. Children are compliant if they feel they must comply, but dislike being constrained and are more apt to become angry when demands are made of them;
2. Children infer that others dislike having demands placed on them. If they fear making others angry, they avoid issuing blunt requests. Instead, they strategically use questions as a means of exploring whether a request is acceptable;
3. Children infer that others are asking questions to avoid upsetting them by requesting something unpalatable. In response, they show increased compliance;
4. Children infer that others will recognize their consideration and that this will lead to increased compliance if they are deferential. Therefore, they are deferential in order to obtain compliance. In fact, they come to view compliance as a proper and friendly response to their politeness. They feel resentment when others do not acknowledge their deference with increased compliance or other evidence of a desire to cooperate;
5. Children realize that others are nice to them to gain increased compliance. Therefore, they also recognize that, if they do not show cooperation in return, the others will be resentful and will retaliate by no longer being considerate of them if it is in their power. Children will then recognize when it is in their own self-interest to cooperate with others in exchanging consideration for one another's feelings and needs.

These stages should have different effects on children's behavior, given the power relations described earlier. At Stage 2, children should use polite forms when addressing those most likely to become angry. At Stage 3, politeness should make the greatest difference to the response of hosts of strangers since they are least constrained to comply. Thus, politeness should be most advantageous to guests of strangers. At Stage 4, children should recognize this, and guests of strangers should be most polite. Hosts of strangers should be least polite. The latter should also be particularly apt to retaliate if their own politeness does not lead to compliance. Finally, at Stage 5, children should recognize this, as well as the fact that politeness is used to seek compliance and so may indicate lack of social obligation to comply. At this stage politeness should be most advantageous to both hosts and guests in the stranger situation and least advantageous among friends.

Thus, it is possible to locate the younger and older groups of children in this study in this proposed sequence. The behavior of the younger children, who are most polite to their friends, is consistent with their having learned to make inferences about others' dislike of imposition and how this can lead to anger (Stage 2). Among younger children anger is most likely to exist between friends. Older children, among whom strangers, and especially strange guests, are most polite, mainly exemplify stages 4 to 5.

If these changes occur with advanced development, politeness will become increasingly necessary to obtain compliance. It should be noted that younger children, in spite of their lack of immediate response to politeness, are not significantly less likely than older children to comply with requests overall. Furthermore, in younger children's dealings with others of the same cognitive characteristics, the rationales they use to gain compliance are their most effective tactics. Therefore, it is possible to ask whether it is any improvement for children to respond to politeness and to use politeness strategically in modifying requests. Again, if older children respond to lack of politeness with resentment and lack of cooperation whereas younger children do not, does development represent improvement? Although younger children should not respond with resentment and retaliation to lack of politeness, being constrained to act in a particular way should still conflict their motives. If that is so, interaction should be less pleasant for each child in a situation where directives are presented in constraining forms than in a situation where they have the choice to refuse. Politeness, therefore, still has implications for the pleasantness of the interaction between children and the likelihood of quarrels whether or not it increases overall compliance.

The use of directives of different degrees of politeness is likely to have consequences other than the effect on immediate compliance examined in this investigation. These include greater reciprocal politeness by one's companion, which implies a correlation between the politeness of children and of their companions that is independent of any correlation of politeness with age or situational factors. They also include greater overall compliance by the other with all of one's requests – including less polite ones – as a function of one's overall politeness; and more agreeable interaction, including a greater likelihood of agreement with other kinds of utterances, fewer quarrels, and prolonged sequences of make-believe, conversation, and other activities.

None of these were examined in the present study because there were not enough pairs of children to perform the necessary statistical analyses. However, one suggestive observation that should stimulate further study is that younger children, who were more polite overall, were also generally more agreeable. The proportion of agreement (including acknowledgment of the other's statements, agreement, compliance, and compliments) was greater among the utterances of young children than among those of older children. Another suggestive observation is that the one group of children who were least polite (younger boys playing with boy strangers) stood out from the other groups because of the proportion of utterances in negative voice tone. Whether politeness decreased the risk of quarreling and led to more agreeable interaction or whether agreeableness, along with the use of polite request forms, was a function of some other factor requires further study. However, considering the greater risk that conflicts will lead to quarrels among younger children (Gottman & Parkhurst, 1980), the greater politeness of these children may, in fact, be designed to avert quarrels. This explanation is consistent with the developmental sequence proposed.

An appropriate way to end this chapter is to urge further research in a similar vein. It was suggested earlier that researchers interested in children's use of language in social situations ought to identify the strategies children employ in the pursuit of their goals and in their selection of language and to look at the extent to which children are strategic in selecting tactics. In order to do the latter we propose that researchers examine how children respond to various strategies. The usefulness of this approach is demonstrated by the finding that politeness has little effect on the compliance of a child under 5 years of age and that the level of politeness among children 5 to 6 years is suboptimal. We also propose that researchers pay much more attention to the kinds of interactional constraints that children face, and to analyze how the social context modifies those constraints. The value of doing so has been illustrated by the ways that host versus guest status and friendship bonds affect the power relations between children and the advantageousness or disadvantageousness of being polite. Finally, we urge greater concern for explaining developmental changes in children's use of language and the development of more theory capable of guiding research. Again, the usefulness of Brown and Levinson's theory of politeness as a framework for studying children's requests has been amply demonstrated. However, the present study is only one preliminary attempt to study a few strategies for modifying one kind of speech act in relation to one kind of social goal. Even politeness may have more aims than gaining immediate compliance. Any adequate examination of children's use of language in social interaction requires acknowledgment of the range of social functions that language can serve and of the fact that children do more than make demands of each other.

9. Friendship and postdivorce adjustment

DOROTHY GINSBERG

It is estimated that each year more than 2 million people are divorced (Glick & Norton, 1979). This figure is significant because of the growing body of evidence linking marital disruption to a wide variety of emotional and physical disorders. Divorce or separation has been associated with higher rates of suicide (Stack, 1980), depression (Pearlin & Johnson, 1977), dissatisfaction with the quality of life (Campbell, Converse, & Rodgers, 1976), alcoholism (Wechsler, Thum, Demone, & Dwinnel, 1972), psychiatric hospitalization (Bloom, 1975), acute and chronic physical illness (Verbrugge, 1979), and motor vehicle accidents (McMurray, 1970) than have other marital statuses.

The process underlying the link between major life changes and negative health consequences is not well understood. Although experiencing a major life change places individuals in a high-risk category, not all of them experience significant problems (Rabkin & Struening, 1976). Similarly, there is a great deal of variability in the amount of distress experienced by divorced individuals (Goode, 1956). Identifying what enables some individuals to remain resilient in the midst of marital disruption may increase our understanding of the factors that lead to effective coping. This may also have implications for the development of intervention strategies.

Social support has received a great deal of attention as a protective factor in the literature on stressful life events (Antonovsky, 1974; Caplan, 1974; Cassel, 1976). We have little information, however, about how support influences well-being or which types of influence are important. Methodological limitations of previous research have obscured information about social support processes. Social support should be viewed as a multidimensional concept and assessed with both observational and self-report methods. Such methods were employed in a study to be described in this chapter.

The goal of this research was to describe and analyze how social support is related to postdivorce adjustment. This study showed that postdivorce adjustment is greater when specific forms of social support are present. Although a number of components of social support were assessed, the confidant relationship was the primary focus. Interview and survey studies suggest that one of the most valued functions of friendship is the role of confidant (Crawford, 1977; Parlee, 1979; Phillips & Metzger, 1976; Reisman & Shorr, 1978).

The introductory material that follows is organized into three parts:

1. Postdivorce adjustment. The level of psychological adjustment was the dependent variable in this study.
2. Problems in conceptualizing and operationalizing social support. Previous research on social support has been limited by methodological problems of vagueness of definition, delayed recall rather than recent recall, and exclusive reliance on self-report data. The present study employed methods designed to overcome these problems
3. A multidimensional view of social support. Multiple dimensions of social support served as the independent variables in this study.

The relationship between social support and postdivorce adjustment was studied in a small sample of recently divorced women. Although divorce is stressful for both men and women (Weiss, 1975), divorced women were the focus of the present investigation because they face somewhat specialized problems. These include reduced economic resources (Brandwein, Brown, & Fox, 1974; Campbell et al., 1976), financial discrimination (Brandwein et al., 1974; Weitzman, 1975), and social isolation (Hetherington, Cox, & Cox, 1978; Raschke, 1977).

Postdivorce adjustment

Many authors conceptualize separation and divorce adjustment as a progression through several stages. Their theories often focus on different dimensions of the divorce process. Herrman (1974) and Froiland and Hozeman (1977), for example, focus on the cognitive and affective dimensions of adjustment. They describe the following five stages: (1) denial, (2) anger, (3) bargaining, (4) depression, and (5) acceptance. In contrast, Bohannon (1970) focuses on the major life areas that require readjustment in various stages of divorce: (1) emotional divorce, (2) legal divorce, (3) economic divorce, (4) co-parental divorce, (5) community divorce, and (6) psychic divorce.

In reviewing the conceptualizations of divorce adjustment, Price-Bonham and Balswick (1980) concluded that some of the difficulties in conceptualization stem from the fact that the stages of adjustment are cyclical and overlapping. They pointed out that stage theories have yet to be empirically validated. Not surprisingly, there has been a lack of consistency in the operationalization of divorce adjustment.

In the study described here, postdivorce adjustment was operationalized with multiple measures that reflect the symptoms that bring divorced individuals to the attention of clinicians. Since the clinical picture seems to reflect a range of emotions (Johnson, 1977; Weiss, 1975), the most appropriate way to operationalize postdivorce adjustment (or its absence) may be to measure several salient mood states. Accordingly, three measures were the Revised UCLA Loneliness Scale (Russell, Peplau, & Ferguson, 1978), the Center for Epidemiologic Studies Depression Scale (Radloff, 1977), and the Profile of Mood States (McNair, Lorr, & Droppleman, 1971). These instruments are described in more detail in Section 9.1.

Problems in conceptualizing and operationalizing social support

Although fairly recent studies have shown a relationship between social support and postdivorce adjustment (e.g., Raschke, 1977; Spanier & Casto, 1979), most studies suffer from at least one of the following methodological problems:

Vagueness. The concept of social support is often very global or vaguely defined. For example, in one study investigating correlates of divorce adjustment, support was defined as "interviewees' statements that their friends, relatives, and other acquaintances were generally supportive" (Spanier & Casto, 1979). This leaves us with very little information about the quality of support that is protective or lowers the risk of psychological problems. Even if it can be demonstrated that the presence of supportive relationships influences healthy functioning, the process by which this operates is not understood. Little is known about what "significant others" talk about or do together, or what the function of various activities may be, or how mutually satisfying relationships are maintained or fail to be maintained, and so on. The present study attempted to delineate more clearly the important characteristics of social support.

Retrospective character. Many studies of the postdivorce period rely on retrospective self-reports of social activity and affective state (e.g., Goode, 1956; Spanier & Casto, 1979). Since retrospective reports may be distorted, a self-monitoring methodology that reduces the length of recall time may provide more accurate reporting. In the present study a daily diary record was used for this purpose. A diary record provides an "in vivo" description of social activity and corresponding mood state.

Self-report data. Finally, many studies of social support rely exclusively on self-report data for information about the availability or adequacy of social support (e.g., Chiriboga, Roberts, & Stein, 1978; Rache, 1977). Self-report procedures are used to measure social support without a clear understanding of how they overlap with measures of psychological adjustment. Since self-report measures are often used to assess psychological adjustment, it is possible that the correlations between social support and psychological adjustment reflect common-method variance. If people do not feel well in general, they may be more likely to report adjustment problems as well as underestimate the actual quantity or quality of their social interactions with others. Self-report measures must be used in combination with observational methods to tap both the subjective and objective realities of relationships. It would be desirable in future research to include behavioral observations of social interaction. If we use measures that clearly distinguish between objective characteristics of the individual's social support and the individual's perception of them, we are in a better position to make inferences that can guide further work. The study to be described here used both observational and self-report methods to assess social support.

The following four methods were used to assess social support: (1) interview, (2) questionnaire, (3) observation of social interaction, and (4) daily diary record. Interview and questionnaire methods were used to collect retrospective self-report data. Observation of social interaction and the diary record were used to minimize problems of common-method variance and recall error. These procedures are described in more detail in Section 9.1.

Multidimensional view of social support

Thoits (1982) argues that such dimensions as the amount of support, the types of support (e.g., practical assistance, cognitive guidance, companionship), and the sources of support (e.g., friends, family, co-workers) may be important in determining the impact of social relationships on well-being. She reviews evidence that "not all sources or types of social support are equally effective in reducing distress" (p. 147). This suggests that a multidimensional approach to the assessment of social support is necessary to understand how social relationships facilitate coping and what aspects of social relationships account for this.

Four dimensions through which social support may be available to divorced women were assessed in the study described in this chapter:

1. *Social network.* This includes one's ties with a group of people and the associations within the group (Leavy, 1983). Measurement of social network is divided into structural variables (number of people and pattern of dyadic relationships within the network) and content variables (qualitative nature of dyadic interactions within the network).
2. *Subjective evaluation of support.* This category encompasses divorced women's satisfaction with their social interactions.
3. *Level of social participation.* This refers to the level of activity of divorced women in formal and informal social groups.
4. *Confiding relationships.* A confidant has been defined as someone with whom one's most personal difficulties can be discussed (Miller & Ingham, 1976). In the present study a detailed description of the confidant relationship was provided through observational and self-report methods.

The social support variables of interest are defined in Table 9.1. Although other researchers have examined social correlates of postdivorce adjustment, few have attempted to assess the social support system with such a diversity of variables.

Summary

The research to be described in the following pages considered concepts derived from the social support and life event literature to examine postdivorce adjustment. The limitations of previous research include the failure to describe adequately the characteristics of an individual's social relationships, possible distortions in reporting due to recall errors, and the exclusive use of self-report measures.

The present study used self-report and observational methods to describe the confidant relationship, supplemented retrospective reports of social activity with data from diary records, and was based on a multidimensional assessment of social support. It provides a description and analysis of how social support is related to psychological well-being during the postdivorce period.

9.1. Method

Subjects

Subjects were recruited through public courthouse records available in Champaign and Cook Counties in the state of Illinois. Potential subjects

Table 9.1. *Social support variables*

Variable	Method of assessment	Operational definition
Structural variables of the social network		
Network size	Interview	Total number of persons with whom subjects engage in five specific activities (i.e., financial aid, practical assistance, cognitive guidance, emotional support, and social companionship) or whom subjects consider important
Multiplexity	Interview	Number of network members with whom subjects engage in more than one type of activity
Reciprocity	Interview	Proportion of relationships with members of the network in which there is an equal exchange of supportive activities
Marital density	Interview	Number of network members who know the former spouse divided by the total number of persons in the network
Proportion divorced	Interview	Number of network members who are divorced divided by the total number of persons in the network
Content variables of the social network		
Practical assistance	Interview	Proportion of network members who provide practical assistance (e.g., running errands, helping with household tasks, house sitting)
Cognitive guidance	Interview	Proportion of network members who provide cognitive guidance (e.g., information, advice)
Emotional support	Interview	Proportion of network members who provide emotional support (e.g., caring)
Social companionship	Interview	Proportion of network members who provide social companionship (e.g., going to movies, having over for dinner)
Financial assistance	Interview	Proportion of network members who provide financial assistance

Table 9.1. *(Cont.)*

Variable	Method of assessment	Operational definition
Subjective evaluation of support		
Social mood	Diary record	Mean mood rating per hour of social contact based on a 7-point rating scale
Support from relatives	Interview	"How did your relatives react to news of your divorce; were they supportive or nonsupportive or what?" "Nonsupportive" was coded zero; "supportive" was coded 1
Support from friends	Interview	"How did your friends react to news of your divorce; were they supportive or nonsupportive or what?" "Nonsupportive" was coded zero; "supportive" was coded 1
Dating satisfaction	Interview	"Are you satisfied with your present dating situation?" "Not satisfied" was coded 2; "mixed feelings" or "satisfied" was coded 1
Level of social participation		
Duration of social contact	Diary record	Total number of hours spent per week socializing with others
Organizational participation	Interview	Number of organizations and clubs in which there is participation
Characteristics of the confidant relationship		
Closeness to confidant	Questionnaire	Miller Social Intimacy Scale (MSIS)
Verbal responses of confidant	Observation of social interaction	Coding system developed by Reisman and Yamokoski (1974)

were women who had been granted divorce decrees within the previous year and who did not have children. Women without children were selected to reduce the complexity of the analyses. Women who were under 20 years of age or who had been married for less than one year were excluded from the subject population. Two divorced women who were referred to the investigator by other subjects were also recruited for the study. They had been granted divorces in other states but were living in Champaign County and otherwise fit the selection criteria.

Including the two referrals, 304 divorced women were sent personal letters informing them of the study. The letters asked potential subjects to contact the investigator by telephone or by returning a prestamped, self-addressed postcard to indicate their interest in participating. Up to two follow-up letters were sent, if necessary, to women who failed to respond. Potential subjects failing to respond were not telephoned because it was stipulated by the circuit judge that subjects indicate an interest in participating before being contacted by the investigator. For those responding affirmatively, appointments were made for interviews in the subjects' homes or the project offices, depending on subject preferences.

Letters sent to 64 potential subjects were returned because the addressees were unknown or had moved and forwarding addresses were unavailable. Of the 240 women whose letters were apparently delivered, 187 (78%) declined participation or failed to respond and 53 (22%) agreed to participate. Fifteen of the volunteers had to be excluded from the study because they had moved too far away to be interviewed or had children from previous marriages. Children from previous marriages were not documented in court records. Appointments were made with the remaining 38 women (16% of those who received letters) for interviews. Thirteen subjects did not complete all phases of the study. Only the 25 subjects (10% of those receiving letters) who completed all phases of the study were included in the final analyses.

The women in the final sample ranged in age from 21 to 66 years, with a mean age of 29.92. The length of marriage varied from 16 months to 472 months, with a mean length of 86.64 months. The length of time from date of the divorce decree to initial contact by the investigator ranged from 1 to 13 months, with a mean length of 6.48 months. The majority of women had divorced on grounds of mental cruelty (80%), had been married only once (92%), had petitioned for divorce themselves (62%), were Caucasian (96%), and were Protestant (72%). The educational level ranged from 12 to 20 years in school, with a mean of 16.16 years.[1]

After divorce, the yearly income was less than $5,000 for 8% of the sample. Sixteen percent of the divorced women had a yearly income of between $5,000 and $9,999, whereas 28% had an income range of $10,000 to $14,999. Twenty percent reported an income between $15,000 and $19,999, and the remaining 28% of the sample had incomes of greater than $20,000 per year after the divorce. The mean income per year was in the $10,000 to $14,999 range.

Table 9.2. *Descriptive statistics for the postdivorce adjustment measures (N = 25)*

Parameter	Profile of Mood States	Revised UCLA Loneliness Scale	Center for Epidemiologic Studies Depression Scale
Mean	68.96	36.75	11.84
Standard deviation	26.61	9.07	6.69
Maximum	113	58	27
Minimum	18	21	1

The mean network size of the sample was 17.17 persons. According to Phillips (1981), a social network of that size falls within the modal range for a normal population. The subjects spent a mean of 39.92 hours per week in the company of others. This did not include interpersonal contacts during working hours. Thus, the women comprising this sample were not socially isolated.

Table 9.2 presents descriptive statistics for the three measures of postdivorce adjustment. The mean loneliness and depression scores show that this sample was similar to various normal samples (Radloff, 1977; Russell et al., 1979) but markedly less depressed than hospitalized psychiatric patients (Radloff, 1977).

In an effort to determine differences between divorced women who did and did not participate in the study, sociodemographic information available in the courthouse records were examined. This information was age, grounds for divorce, identity of the petitioner, length of marriage, number of marriages, and time since divorce. On the basis of two-tailed *t*-tests, there was no evidence that the 38 divorced women who participated in the study differed from the 266 divorced women who did not participate.

Procedures

The procedures of the present study consisted of four phases: one 1½ hour structured interview, a self-administered questionnaire battery, a diary record, and an audiotaped conversation with a close friend. These procedures are described below.

Structured interview. Subjects were interviewed to assess the structural and content variables of the social network. The social network assessment was a modification of the method described by Phillips (1981). Subjects were asked to give the first names of people with whom they engaged in specific types of exchanges. The types of exchange were organized into five categories: (1) financial assistance, (2) practical assistance, (3) cognitive guidance, (4) emotional support, and (5) social companionship. The proportion of network members in each of the five areas was calculated to measure the content of available support. After anyone else the individual considered important was included, the list comprising members of the social network was considered complete. Additional information about each person was then obtained. The structural network variables that were derived from this assessment were marital density, multiplexity, reciprocity, network size, and proportion divorced.

Another purpose of the interview was to assess the amount of participation in social groups and organizations, support of the divorce from relatives, support of the divorce from friends, and dating satisfaction. All interviews were tape-recorded.

Most of this interview was developed through pilot testing, although certain items were derived from the interviews of Lopata (1973) and Campbell et al. (1976). At the end of the interview, subjects were given a questionnaire battery and diary record to be completed during the week. At that time, they were also informed of the third phase of the study, the audiotaped conversation with a friend. The interviewer explained the procedure and discussed some of the plans designed for the protection of confidentiality (e.g., removing all identifying information from the tapes, freedom to discontinue experimental participation at any time). On the basis of the social network assessment, a confidant (or if there was no confidant available, the closest available friend or relative) was chosen for the audiotaped conversation.

Self-administered questionnaire battery

Confidant questionnaire. The Miller Social Intimacy Scale (MSIS, Miller, 1979) was used to assess the intimacy of the relationship with the friend who participated in the audiotaping session. This 17-item scale has been shown to have reasonable construct validity in marital relationships and friendships. Furthermore, MSIS scores have shown a negative relationship to mood disturbance (Miller, 1979).

Psychological functioning. Measures of psychological functioning were selected that would tap areas frequently described in clinical literature as problematic for divorced individuals: loneliness, emotional turmoil, and depression (Johnson, 1977; Weiss, 1976). It was also considered desirable to use standard measures that can be readily compared across studies and populations. The measures selected were those that would reflect transient mood states rather than stable personality traits, since the postdivorce adjustment period is characterized as cyclical. The following questionnaires were used:

1. Loneliness: Revised UCLA Loneliness Scale. This 20-item measure of loneliness has been shown to be related to reports of limited social activities and was able to discriminate between a group of students attending a loneliness workshop and a group of students in an introductory psychology course (Russell et al., 1979).
2. Emotional turmoil: Profile of Mood States. This test consists of 65 items that are factored into six mood scores: tension-anxiety, depression-dejection, anger-hostility, vigor-activity, fatigue-inertia, and confusion-bewilderment (McNair, Lorr, & Droppleman, 1971). Subjects were asked to rate adjectives according to "how they have been feeling during the past week including today" on a five-point scale ranging from *not at all* to *extremely*. All items were keyed in the same direction, except for those in the vigor-activity scale and two other items – *relaxed* in the tension-anxiety scale and *efficient* in the confusion scale. To score these items, the direction of the rating scales was reversed. A total score of emotional disturbance was derived for use in the present investigation.
3. Depression: Center for Epidemiologic Studies Depression (CES-D) Scale. This 20-item measure has been shown to be related to clinical ratings of depression and to other scales designed to measure depression (Radloff, 1977).

General information. Included on this form were questions about sociodemographic variables that could influence adjustment: age, length of marriage, time since divorce, income, religion, and education.

Diary record. Each woman was asked to complete a diary record every day for one week. The diary record was divided into five columns labeled "Time," "Place," "Activity," "People," and "Mood." The mood category was a seven-point affective rating scale from *very low spirits* to *very high spirits*. Each woman was instructed to write the time, where she was, what she was doing, who she was with, and how she was feeling on the mood scale from the time she got up in the morning until she went to bed. She was given a list of places, activities, and people to choose from. Each woman was encouraged to make recordings throughout the day, but if she found that impossible, to make recordings at the end of the day. This method allowed the *"in vivo"* description of mood along with a description of whom the individual was with (if anyone) and what they were doing. Two variables that were derived from the diary record for further analyses were social mood and duration of social contact.

Audiotaped conversation with a friend. Subjects were provided with a cassette tape recorder and a tape. They were asked to meet with their "closest available friend" at home or another place that was mutually convenient and afforded some privacy. Subjects were asked to discuss a personal problem or uncertainty with their friend. The problem was to be of their own choosing. The divorced women were asked to present the problem and their friends were designated "helpers." After the session was over, the divorced women were asked to rate the helpfulness of the conversation, the supportiveness of their friends, and the degree of comfort they felt during the discussion on three 7-point rating scales. In order to assess the ecological validity of the conversation, subjects were also asked to rate how typical this conversation was in comparison with previous conversations they had had with the same friend. Again, a 7-point rating scale was used.

Of the 25 audiotaped conversations slated for inclusion in the final sample, one had to be excluded because it was inaudible. Thus, analyses of the audiotaped conversations were based on 24 rather than 25 subjects.

The coding system. The goal of the audiotaped portion of the study was to examine the way friends respond to the disclosure of a personal problem. A coding system was needed to describe the friends' responses exhaustively, as well as to facilitate the identification of the types of communication that promote coping.

Reisman and Yamokoski (1974) developed a coding system to describe the types of communication used to help a friend deal with a personal problem. Their system was modified during pilot testing for use with the present subject population. The modified coding system used to categorize the verbal responses is described in Table 9.3. In defining the coding categories, the friend with a problem is referred to as A, and the helping friend as B.

Generalizability study. Two codes independently coded four pages of each transcript, which were selected from a table of random numbers. Interobserver agreement was tied to specific behavior units according to the method developed by Gottman (1979). The generalizability claim being made in the present investigation was that the variance due to subjects was greater than the variance due to coders or coder-by-subject interaction. Thus, generalization was across coders. The design for the

Table 9.3. *Verbal responses of friends*

Code	Definition	Example
Empathetic	B communicates understanding of what A seems to be saying, feeling, or thinking.	"I know how you must feel."
Responsive	B communicates receiving A's message and seems to understand it.	"Um hm, yes, I see."
Expository feedback	B communicates expert analysis or explanation of A's problem, behavior, or possible course of action.	"He probably hasn't called you because he doesn't think you want to hear from him."
Interrogative	B asks A for clarification or for more information about A.	"What did you say to him?"
Self-disclosure	B communicates information about B.	"I used to be that way."
Suggestion	B tells A what to do; B gives advice or specific directions.	"Just tell her that you deserve a raise."
Positive evaluation	B comments on the goodness, intelligence, or value of what A has said or done.	"You did a great job."
Criticism	B disagrees or corrects A's reasoning or behavior.	"There's a problem you're not seeing."
Social	B refers to a third person for the purpose of comparing or contrasting some aspect of the problem A is discussing.	"C had the same problem you do and it cost him an extra semester in school."
Joking	B responds with laughter, silliness, or kidding to what A is saying.	"I wonder what you'd look like in a peg-leg. Put a little inflatable parrot on your shoulder."
Incomplete thought unit	B makes statements that are incomplete or fragmented to the extent that it is not possible to judge their communicative functions, usually because of an interruption by A.	"I think. . ."
Reactive	B refers to the tape recorder.	"Is the tape recorder on?"
Other	B makes statements that do not seem to fit the above; for example, B responds by changing the subject.	

Table 9.4. *Generalizability coefficients for verbal response codes*

Code	Frequency[a]	Mean square subjects (transcripts)	Residual	Cronbach alpha
Empathetic	5	.389	.067	.706
Responsive	228	59.369	.121	.996
Exposition	203	35.512	1.012	.945
Interrogative	126	43.304	.211	.990
Self-disclosure	59	15.110	.048	.994
Suggestion	50	11.119	.947	.843
Positive evaluation	10	.653	.017	.949
Criticism	19	1.946	.246	.776
Social comparison	14	3.655	.069	.963
Joking	60	9.036	.097	.979
Incomplete thought unit	30	3.660	.017	.991
Reactive	5	.389	.000	1.000
Other	5	.335	.000	1.000

[a]Frequency refers to how often this code was noted in the sample by one or both coders and is thus the diagonal plus off-diagonal total in the Cohen kappa matrix over all transcripts.

generalizability study was a within-subjects analysis of variance repeated over independent coders for each code.

Table 9.4 presents the generalizability coefficients for the verbal response codes. The coefficients are very high, except when codes occurred infrequently. Cohen's kappa was computed for the verbal response codes. A statistic was computed across all verbal response codes, summed across all transcripts. Cohen's kappa was .878.

9.2. Statistical Analysis

In the present investigation, correlational analyses were employed to assess the relationships between the independent and dependent variables. Because of the multivariate nature of the issues, multiple-regression analyses were also employed.

Sociodemographic variables

The variance accounted for by religion and education was partialed out in all analyses, because these variables were significantly related to depression (CES-D) and/or emotional turmoil (Profile of Mood States).[2]

Social support as correlates of postdivorce adjustment

In order to test the hypothesis that social support is related to postdivorce adjustment, partial correlations (controlling for religion and education) were calculated. This was done for each social support variable taken separately and also by a single regression equation to show the incremental effect of entering each variable in turn. Multiple-regression analyses were employed to determine the contribution of the social resources to the variance in each of the adjustment measures.

Analysis of the confidant relationship

Next, the way friends helped divorced women deal with a personal problem was analyzed. The correlation of each type of communication with the divorced women's perceptions of the conversation was assessed. The proportions of responses of friends in each of the nine coding categories served as independent variables. Ratings of the perceived supportiveness, comfort, and helpfulness of the conversation served as the dependent variables.

9.3. Results and Discussion

Correlations among measures of postdivorce adjustment

Emotional turmoil (Profile of Mood States) and depression (CES-D) scores were highly related.[3] Both were unrelated to the level of loneliness (Revised UCLA Loneliness Scale). These results suggest that postdivorce adjustment is at least a two-dimensional construct. Loneliness measures one domain, emotional turmoil and depression together measure another domain. Previous research has demonstrated that loneliness is independent of other dysphoric mood states (Russell et al., 1979). On the basis of these findings, loneliness was assessed in the present study as a separate variable. Emotional turmoil and depression scores were combined to form another variable called dysphoria. Dysphoria was derived from the mean of the emotional turmoil and depression z-scores.

Social support and postdivorce adjustment

The relationships among the social support variables and the two postdivorce adjustment variables are summarized in Table 9.5.

Table 9.5. *Zero-order* (r) *and multiple correlation statistics for selected social support variables with loneliness and dysphoria (controlling for education and religion)*

Social support variables (df)[a]	Revised UCLA Loneliness Scale		Dysphoria	
	r	Beta[b]	r	Beta[b]
Social network: structure				
Multiplexity (20)	−.164		.255	
Reciprocity (20)	−.070		−.122	
Marital density (20)	.061		.254	
Proportion divorced (20)	.488*	.296**	.310	
Network size (20)	−.244		.383*	
Social network: content				
Practical assistance (20)	−.330		−.198	
Cognitive guidance (20)	−.350		−.159	
Emotional support (19)	−.267		−.266	
Social companionship (20)	−.172		.001	
Financial aid (20)	.009		.158	
Subjective evaluation				
Support of the divorce from relatives (21)	−.101		−.466*	−.488*
Support of the divorce from friends (21)	−.437*	−.244*	−.193	
Social mood (21)	−.407*	−.350***	−.325	
Dating satisfaction (21)	−.635***	−.478***	.222	
Social participation				
Organizational participation (20)	−.072		.028	
Duration of social contact (21)	−.332		.052	
Confidant relationship				
MSIS (21)	−.146		−.255	
Empathetic (20)	−.095		.166	
Responsive (20)	−.090		−.147	
Exposition (20)	.040		−.138	
Interrogative (20)	.374*		−.098	
Self-disclosure (20)	−.166		.224	
Suggestion (20)	−.111		−.023	
Positive evaluation (20)	−.244		−.109	
Criticism (20)	.020		−.105	
Social comparison	−.109		.269	
Joking (20)	−.053		−.016	
Incomplete thought unit (20)	−.028		−.180	

Table 9.5. *(Cont.)*

Social support variables (df)[a]	Revised UCLA Loneliness Scale		Dysphoria	
	r	Beta[b]	r	Beta[b]
Reactive (20)	.178		.249	
Other (20)	−.118		.094	
Summary regression statistics				
Multiple R		.836		.470
R^2		.700		.221
Adjusted R^2		.636		.186
Standard error		5.467		.853
F Value		11.067***		6.247*
df		4, 19		1, 22
N		24		24

Note: Positive correlations indicate more of the social resource and greater psychological distress.

[a]Degrees of freedom (df) vary due to missing data.

[b]Standardized regression coefficient for each social resource when all predictors (with F-to-enter at the .05 level) have been entered into the regression.

*$p < .05$; **$p < .01$; ***$p < .0001$.

Structure of the social network. None of the structural social network variables were significantly correlated with the postdivorce adjustment variables except for proportion divorced and network size. The higher the proportion of divorced individuals in the women's social network (proportion divorced), the greater the loneliness. The larger the social network (network size), the more dysphoria.

Thus, in terms of *whom* divorced women interacted with, the marital status of network members was a better predictor of loneliness than was associating with acquaintances of one's former husband (marital density). Women who associated with a greater proportion of divorced persons were lonelier. This is surprising because one might expect divorced women to seek out and derive comfort from others who have had similar experiences. Perhaps a high proportion of divorced individuals in the social network reflects rejection from married friends and isolation from a mainstream social life. Several divorced women in the study reported losing married friends with whom they had socialized as a couple. Their high loneliness scores showed that women with a large proportion of divorced friends felt cut off socially. Socializing with predominantly divorced people apparently reinforced their sense of alienation.

The findings also indicated that having a large number of acquaintances did not ease the distress of the early postdivorce period. It was quite the contrary. Larger social networks were associated with greater dysphoria. Although social relationships presumably provide benefits, this result shows that they may incur costs as well. Many of the stresses people experience in their daily lives are engendered by the demands, constraints, and conflicts associated with social relationships. High levels of social activity create more obligations to reciprocate and may conflict with other responsibilities. For example, one of the divorced women in this study complained that, even though she had more friends than she had ever had before, she found this to be very demanding of her time and energy. Furthermore, even though one may have many acquaintances, these relationships are not necessarily satisfying. A flurry of social activity during the early postdivorce period may reflect a search for more fulfilling relationships. Frenzied social activity with a large number of superficial contacts may be motivated by ambivalence or fear of intimacy.

Content of the social network. None of the content types of interaction (practical assistance, cognitive guidance, emotional support, social companionship, or financial assistance) was significantly related to either of the postdivorce adjustment measures. It is possible that recently divorced women are more sensitive to the reactions of others to the divorce than they are to the availability of general social resources. Findings that bear on this interpretation are presented next.

Subjective evaluation

All the variables assessing satisfaction with social interactions were positively related to some aspect of postdivorce adjustment. The more positive the affect during daily social encounters (social mood), the lower was the loneliness score. Social mood was assessed by diary record. Thus, immediate recall of the affective quality of social interactions was a better predictor of current loneliness than was delayed recall of specific types of interaction.

Perceived support of the divorce from relatives was significantly related to a lower level of dysphoria. This finding suggests that specific reactions of relatives to the divorce rather than more generally focused support may be paramount during the early postdivorce period.

Themes of approval and disapproval frequently arose during the interviews when women described relatives' reactions to news of the divorce. This is not surprising since the period following divorce is usually characterized by self-doubt and heightened sensitivity to evaluations by others.

Some women seemed to seek reassurance from their relatives that they were making the right decision. For example, one woman stated, "Because I didn't have self-confidence, I needed to be told that what I was doing was for the best." Others were concerned that they would be blamed for the breakup or that negative judgments would be made about their moral character. One woman was so apprehensive about her parents' reaction that she still had not told them about her divorce two months after it had taken place. Sometimes the approval of relatives helped the women deal with their self-accusations: "My sister knows what I'm like so she helps me not blame myself." In general, these results show that, during the early postdivorce period, women are very vulnerable to family criticism and approval. Perceived support of the divorce from relatives appears to assuage self-recriminations and the agony of ambivalence.

Similarly, women who perceived their friends as supporting the divorce were significantly less lonely than women who did not. The same themes of approval and disapproval came up in discussing friends' responses to divorce. Thus, support from outside the family circle was also important. One woman said, "I needed to know someone cared besides my mother and father." Another woman said, "The most help I got in feeling better was talking to people with similar problems. It was reassuring. I felt I was a terrible person. The most valuable thing that I got out of it was that I wasn't a terrible person."

Here again, specific reactions to the divorce (in contrast to more generally focused types of support) were significant predictors of either loneliness or dysphoria. This was true for both relatives and friends. These findings indicate that an accepting, nonjudgmental attitude toward the woman's role in the divorce may be the primary task of significant others during the early postdivorce period.

Women who were satisfied with their present dating situation were significantly less lonely than dissatisfied women. Although acceptance from friends and relatives and affectively positive social interactions were important, no factor was a stronger predictor of loneliness than dating satisfaction.

Level of social participation

Psychological adjustment was independent of the level of social participation. The total number of hours spent socializing during a week-long period (duration of social contact) and participation in clubs and organizations (organizational participation) were unrelated to both measures of adjustment.

A consistent pattern throughout this study was that the *amount* of social activity (duration of social contact, participation in clubs and organizations) or, as previously discussed, the *number* of acquaintances (network size, multiplexity) was either unrelated to adjustment or associated with greater dysphoria. In contrast, variables that measured the affective *quality* of social relationships (social mood, dating satisfaction, perceived support of the divorce from friends and relatives) were positively related to some aspect of adjustment. Thus, it seems that the quality is more important than the quantity of interpersonal relationships.

Characteristics of the confidant relationship

None of the characteristics of the confidant relationship were significantly related to an adjustment variable except for the proportion of interrogative statements. Women who were asked more questions by the confidant were lonelier.

The relationship between the proportion of questions asked and loneliness is somewhat surprising. One would expect requests for clarification or for more information to improve the quality or accuracy of communication and understanding between individuals.

Questions are cited below in the context of verbatim transcripts to clarify their social function. Two examples follow:

1. Divorced woman: And his comment was that "Well, I would come over and visit my friend."
   Friend: Was that including you?
2. Divorced woman: And he told me he would be calling me this week to ask me out for lunch.
   Friend: He had told you that once before?
   Divorced woman: Last week.

Although these questions may seem fairly neutral, they could be viewed as challenges or reflections of a lack of understanding. Another possibility is that friends who frequently ask questions may be dominating the conversation and less likely to allow the divorced woman to be heard. Transcripts of friends who asked the most questions supported this. In the following example, the divorced woman is trying to decide if she will be better off leaving the city of Champaign and finding a new job elsewhere. Her friend seems to be dominating the conversation with her questions.

Friend [*interrupting*]:   Have you been looking in the paper for apartments in Champaign?

Divorced woman: No, I haven't. I don't know what to do about that either . . . you know . . . My lease's up in October . . . Guess I should decide . . .

Friend: Have you decided you're moving out yet though?

Divorced woman: No, I haven't decided . . . well . . .

Friend [*interrupting*]:   Great [*sarcastically*].

Divorced woman [*interrupting*]:   I know I have to move from my building. Well, I told you, you know, like . . .

Friend [*interrupting*]:   Yeah, yeah.

Divorced woman [*interrupting*]:   Yeah [*laughs*]. So if I move out . . . [*laughs*] . . .if I [*laughing*] . . . if I moved out, I really like, you know, building J which is . . .

Friend: Which one's that?

Divorced woman: It's, you know, that drive that's . . .

Friend: The old way you used to go in?

Divorced woman: Yeah, the old way you used to . . .

Friend [*interrupting*]:   Yes.

Divorced woman [*continuing*]:   . . . go in, it's at the very end.

Friend: Oh, on the corner?

Divorced woman: Yeah.

Friend: That corner back there?

Divorced woman: That one's G and the other one is F, I think.

Friend: Yeah.

Divorced woman: [*Laughs.*]

Friend: Yeah . . .

Divorced woman [*interrupting*]:   So that would . . .

Friend [*interrupting*]:   Well, why? Is it nicer or do you just like it 'cause its quiet or something?

In this example the friend seems to be controlling the direction of the conversation with her questions. The two women seem to be side-tracked rather than dealing with the original problem.

In another dyad, the friend seems to be attending to her own concerns rather than being responsive to the divorced woman. The divorced woman has been trying to decide what to do about her relationship with her boyfriend, Paul. She has already stated that, although she does not want to be involved with him, she does not want to hurt him, either. Her friend refocuses the discussion with a question about the divorced woman's former husband, Bruce.

Divorced woman: Well, you know, I think you have to define the terms of any relationship. I mean, I guess maybe that's why I thought . . .

Friend [*interrupting*]: What would you want in a husband if you were getting married again? Different than what Bruce was?

Divorced woman: Well, I would want someone who was certainly more sensitive to me.

Friend: Well, somebody who supported you, too.

Divorced woman: Financially?

Friend: Yeah?

Divorced woman: No.

Friend: No?

Divorced woman: Not at all. That doesn't bother me in the slightest. But, you know, the reverse is true, though. I don't want to have to support anyone else.

Friend: Yeah, but you wouldn't want, you wouldn't want to have to make your own living, too. Say you were married and he had a real good job, wouldn't you want to live on his money or what?

Divorced woman: No.

Friend: If you were going to keep house and be a real wife?

Divorced woman: No. See, I

Friend [*interrupting*]: Let him foot the bill?

Divorced woman: I don't believe that that would be being a real wife anymore than someone working. I mean you can only clean house so much. No, I simply detest housework. If I had children, I'd want to stay home and I would hope that . . .

Clearly, the issues of concern to the divorced woman were not being addressed by her friend. Although the task of the discussion was to help the divorced woman, her friend seemed more concerned about promoting her own beliefs about relationships. Fisher, Nadler, and Whitcher-Alagna (1982) assert that it is threatening to accept help from someone who is viewed as having ulterior motives. They suggest that "helping" behavior in such a situation is not viewed as an expression of caring or concern. Rather, it may raise fear about the possibility of manipulation or exploitation.

In the previous examples, frequent questioning dominated the conversation. Furthermore, the directions in which the questions led did not seem related to the central issues. This may raise doubts about the sincerity or good will of the help giver. Rather than providing support, this type of "help" may threaten the recipient.

Regression analyses

Stepwise regression analyses were employed to determine the contribution of all social support variables to variance in the two measures of psychological functioning (see Table 9.5).

Four variables (proportion divorced, perceived support of the divorce from friends, social mood, and dating satisfaction) accounted for 70% of the variance in loneliness. The best predictor of dysphoria was support of the divorce from relatives. It explained 22.1% of the variance in dysphoria.

These regression analyses show that several sources of support (or failure thereof) must be taken into consideration in predicting postdivorce adjustment. No *one* interpersonal relationship, including the confidant relationship, can accurately predict how well a divorced woman will do. Support of the divorce from relatives was the only social support variable that explained unique portions of variance in dysphoria. Four sources of support (or sources of interpersonal costs) explained unique portions of variance in loneliness. Dating satisfaction was the best predictor of loneliness (or its absence), but we would lose predictive ability by not taking into account whether a divorced woman also reported receiving support from her friends. The affective quality of daily social encounters and the proportion of divorced individuals in the social network must also be considered. One source of support could not be substituted for another. They were additive in increasing our ability to explain individual differences in postdivorce adjustment.

Summary of the social correlates of postdivorce adjustment

Dimensions of postdivorce adjustment were positively related to dating satisfaction, support of the divorce from relatives, support of the divorce from friends, and positive affect during daily social encounters. All these variables dealt with the importance of intimacy, caring, approval, and acceptance. They were in sharp contrast to the variables that were negatively associated with aspects of adjustment.

The negative correlates were network size, proportion of divorced persons in the social network, and questions. The latter variables represented the *number* of people divorced women interacted with (network size), *whom* they interacted with (proportion divorced), and a social process that was characterized by domination (questioning). Thus, dimensions of positive affective support versus disapproval were most salient in explaining variations in well-being after a divorce.

Various types of social support were associated differently with the two measures of psychological adjustment. The source of support (whether a relative or a friend) showed the clearest pattern. Support of the divorce from relatives was associated with less dysphoria but was unrelated to loneliness. In contrast, the quality of relationships outside the family circle (dating satisfaction and support of the divorce from friends) was associated with less loneliness but was unrelated to dysphoria. Loneliness was more completely accounted for by social factors than was dysphoria (70% compared with 22.1%).

The regression analyses showed that no single social relationship can accurately predict postdivorce adjustment. Nonetheless, one must examine social support processes in an interpersonal context to understand how they function. In the next section, the confidant interaction provides an interpersonal context in which social support processes can be observed. The confidant interaction merits special attention because it is the most natural vehicle through which intimacy, caring, approval, and emotional support can be expressed.

The verbal responses of the confidants were the independent variables, and the divorced woman's perceptions of the interaction were the dependent variables. This contrasts with a previous section that examined the verbal responses of confidants in relation to postdivorce adjustment. Examining the divorced women's perception of the confidant interaction reveals which interpersonal behaviors are supportive, helpful, and comforting. Excerpts from the conversations are, again, presented to help clarify the social functions of various interpersonal behaviors.

Description of the confidant relationship

The results concerning specific behavioral processes within confiding relationships are summarized in Table 9.6. The way a confidant responds to the disclosure of a personal problem is shown in the first column. The second column lists the mean proportion of responses in each coding category. The remaining columns give the zero-order correlations and multiple correlation statistics between each type of response and the divorced woman's report of how supportive, helpful, and comfortable she perceived the discussion to be.

The most frequent types of response (in descending order) were responsive, exposition, interrogative, and self-disclosure. These were followed by suggestion, incomplete thought units, criticism, social comparison, joking, positive evaluation, other, reactive and empathetic.

Confidants who provided more analysis or explanation of the divorced woman's problem, behavior, or possible course of action (expository feedback) were perceived as more supportive. This included attempts by the friend to summarize, define, elaborate, or analyze in a neutral or supportive way what the divorced woman had said or done.

Table 9.6. Zero-order (r) and multiple correlation statistics for the verbal responses with perceptions of the conversation (controlling for education and religion)

	Mean proportion of responses in each coding category ($n = 24$)	Perceptions of the conversation					
		Support		Helpfulness		Comfort	
Verbal response		r	Beta[a]	r	Beta[a]	r	Beta[a]
Empathetic	.006	.043		.201		.362*	
Responsive	.313	-.407*	-.433*	-.249		-.219	
Exposition	.221	.402*		.296		-.312	
Interrogative	.150	-.075		-.273		-.256	
Self-disclosure	.081	.040	-.010	.144		.459*	.467*
Suggestion	.048	.233		.033		.055	
Positive evaluation	.014	.361*		.037		.406*	
Criticism	.018	.174		.089		.032	
Social comparison	.016	.182				.234	
Joking	.016	-.141		-.143		.005	
Incomplete thought unit	.038	.190		.237		-.363*	
Reactive	.007	-.084		.015		.143	
Other	.009	-.179		-.104		.151	
Summary regression statistics							
Multiple R			.433				.467
R^2			.187				.218
Adjusted R^2			.150				.183
Standard error			1.054				.633
F Value			5.063*				6.140*
df			1, 22				1, 22

[a] Standardized regression coefficient for each social resource when all predictors (with F-to-enter at the .05 level) have been entered into the regression.

*$p < .05$.

Two examples follow:

1. Divorced woman: . . . So, I'll find out when I talk to him face to face.
   Friend: So, in other words, you felt it was something that he didn't really feel comfortable talking about over the phone. And that's why he was asking you out to lunch.

2. Divorced woman: Not having a choice in the courses I'm going to take is driving me bananas.
   Friend: Because you don't want to make any mistakes.

Each of these friends demonstrates that she understood how the divorced woman felt. Although this type of expository feedback was not significantly related to perceived help in solving the problem, it was viewed as supportive. The caring and concern communicated through expository feedback appears to be more important than the problem-solving function it may be intended to serve.

Positive evaluation was positively related to perceived support and perceived comfort. Positive evaluation includes the confidant's comments on the goodness, competence, or value of either the divorced woman herself or her statements, actions, or reasoning. This hypothesis was confirmed. Three examples follow:

1. Friend: I think that it's generous of you to realize all the pain that he's probably gone through. And I think that it's nice that you accepted and listened to him after everything that's happened.

2. Friend: I think I give you credit for being smart enough to know when you felt like it was getting serious.

3. Divorced woman: I think I'll try to talk to her about it tomorrow.
   Friend: That's a good idea.

These responses by the confidants may be seen as bolstering the divorced woman's positive feelings about herself. They offer support and approval of her current coping efforts.

Here again, although positive evaluation was viewed as supportive, it was not associated with helpfulness in solving the problem.

Empathy was positively related to perceived comfort. Empathetic responses communicated understanding or agreement with what the speaker was saying, feeling, or thinking. Often the tone of voice, indicating emphatic support rather than neutrality, was what distinguished empathy from merely responsive communications. Two examples of empathy follow:

1. Divorced woman: It's almost easier when you have to do certain things. Do you understand what I'm saying?
   Friend: Oh, of course, I do. I know exactly what you're saying.

2. Divorced woman: Every portion of your life is a phase as far as I am concerned.

   Friend: Exactly!

Instances of empathy were infrequent (0.6% of responses), but they were important in communicating a receptivity to what the divorced women were saying. Reisman and Yamokoski's (1974) research suggested that a large proportion of empathy is acceptable only in professional helping relationships. Thus, there may be a ceiling on the proportion of empathy that is desirable between friends.

The present data suggest that a small proportion of empathy may be of value in informal helping relationships by increasing the comfort of the person to which empathy is directed.

Divorced women felt more comfortable when their friends shared their own experiences by self-disclosing. Three examples of self-disclosure follow:

1. Friend: Sometimes I get real confused, too. I had a date last night where I told this person intimate things about myself.

2. Friend: I went through the same thing. But I was really rushed into it.

3. Friend: I think I used to have a fear of being bored. I grew up always feeling as though I was bored.

Even though these discussions were supposed to revolve around the divorced woman's problems, the friends disclosed personal information about themselves as well. These self-disclosures seem to communicate to the divorced woman that she is not alone with her problem. Apparently, this kind of sharing creates a more comfortable situation in which to discuss a personal problem. Seeking help about a personal problem may put a person in a dependent or inferior position. When the help seeker also becomes a recipient of self-disclosure, she may feel that she is being treated as a friend, an equal, and as a person who has something to offer. This may reassure the divorced woman that she is not being judged, pitied, or patronized. Self-disclosure was related to how comfortable the divorced woman felt and not to how helpful the discussion was. Thus, the supportive (as opposed to helping) function of self-disclosure predominated.

In contrast to the previous response categories, the proportion of responsive statements was negatively related to support. Friends who spent more time merely acknowledging what the divorced women were saying were viewed as less supportive. Three examples follow:

1. Divorced woman: When he comes home he's here for her.
   Friend: Oh.

2. Divorced woman: Do you know what I mean?
  Friend: Yes.
3. Divorced woman: No, I mean the one he is serious about?
  Friend: Hmmm.

Perhaps women desire more substantive feedback and active involvement in the conversation than is reflected in a responsive statement.

Incomplete thought units were negatively related to perceived comfort. They included responses of the confidant that were so incomplete or fragmented that it was not possible to judge their communicative function. They seemed to occur for such reasons as an interruption by the divorced woman or a lost thought.

The multiple-regression statistics show that there was a high degree of collinearity among verbal responses in predicting support and comfort. The best predictor of perceived support was the responsive code. The best predictor of perceived comfort was self-disclosure.

Ecological validity. Two variables were examined to assess the ecological validity of the tape-recorded conversation: the proportion of the use of the reactive code and self-reports about how typical the conversation was perceived to be.

Only 0.7% of the responses were coded as reactive (see Table 9.6). Thus, a very small proportion of responses were references to the tape recorder, the interviewer, or the experimental procedure. This indicates that the content of the conversation did not revolve around the women's participation in the study. Furthermore, the reactivity of the experimental procedure was independent of how supportive, helpful, and comfortable the conversation was perceived to be (see Table 9.6).

Women were also asked to rate how typical the tape-recorded conversation was in comparison with previous conversations they had had with the same friend. A scale of 1 to 7 corresponding to *very typical* to *not at all typical* was utilized. The ratings ranged from 1 to 6 with a mean of 2. Most of the women (23 of 25) rated the conversation as 3 or less. Thus, the majority of women in the sample considered the conversation to have been relatively typical.

Summary of the confidant relationship

In this section the nature of the confidant relationship is described. Several specific behavioral responses of confidants were significantly related to how supported and comfortable the divorced women felt during a problem-solving discussion. Thus, the behavioral data presented in this section helped to clarify the nature of emotional support.

Emotional support (perceived support and/or comfort) was positively associated with expressions of approval, empathy, the confidant's willingness to share their personal experiences and problems, and expository feedback (information or explanation of the problem, behavior, or possible course of action). Emotional support was negatively associated with behaviors that seemed to reflect emotional detachment or lack of involvement. Those behaviors were responsive statements (superficial acknowledgments) and incomplete thought units.

Although several behaviors were associated with emotional support, none were significantly related to how helpful the confidant was perceived to be in resolving the problem. Thus, the affective dimensions of problem-solving behaviors had more impact on the divorced women than the instrumental (helping) functions of the very same behaviors. In this study, both self-report and behavioral data suggested that emotional support and acceptance are the most important functions of the social network during the early postdivorce period.

9.4. Conclusions

This study assessed the social correlates of postdivorce adjustment with both self-report and observational methods. Not all sources or types of social support were equally effective in reducing distress in this population. Furthermore, different types of distress (i.e., loneliness or dysphoria) were associated with different aspects of social relationships. Since other studies have used only one or two measures of social support, this kind of differentiation has not been demonstrated before. At least four specific conclusions can be drawn from this study.

First, women in the first year after divorce benefit most from acceptance, intimacy, and emotional support rather than tangible assistance. Women in the early postdivorce period are especially vulnerable to expressions of approval or disapproval. Supportive, nonjudgmental reactions of the social network to the woman's role in the divorce are especially important factors. This suggests that effective supporters must make it clear that any help extended is an expression of love and respect for the needs of the recipient and not an attempt to manipulate, criticize, or control.

Second, in evaluating the well-being of divorced women, the quality of interpersonal relationships in at least three areas must be considered. These include heterosexual relationships, friendships, and family relationships. For example, even if a woman reports good support from friends and satisfaction with her dating situations, disapproval of the divorce by important family members may jeopardize the adjustment process. Divorce may, in part, be a family affair, and the perceived impact on the divorced woman's family and its reactions to her may have to be dealt with. Similarly, difficulties in establishing satisfying heterosexual relationships may hinder the adjustment process. Divorced women may need to work through problems contributing to dissatisfaction in their relationships with men. They may also need encouragement or guidance on where and how to start dating again. Likewise, the presence of a supportive and accepting peer group contributes to well-being in ways that family and dating relationships do not. Having satisfying relationships in all three areas appears to be most beneficial.

Third, simply increasing social activity does not compensate for a lack of emotional support and intimacy. The quality rather than quantity of interpersonal contacts determines their psychological value.

Fourth, divorced women should maintain social ties or make new ones with those of a different marital status. Isolating themselves in the world of the divorced reinforces their sense of alienation.

Several limitations of the present research should be mentioned. The results are limited by the nature of the sample, primarily well-educated young women without children. The sample was further restricted to women who had been divorced for a year or less. Women in other socioeconomic groups may prefer different types of support. Older women with children may have greater need for tangible assistance such as baby sitting and financial support. It is also possible that emotional support and acceptance are replaced by other forms of support at other stages in the separation and divorce process.

The coding system in the present study was selected on an a priori basis without knowledge of the aspects of interpersonal behaviors that would be perceived as supportive and/or associated with postdivorce adjustment. Utilizing a coding system is a selective process that always results in a loss of some information. The transcripts had to be examined to understand how questions, for example, contributed to loneliness. Transcripts revealed that the confidants' behaviors that contributed to the well-being of divorced women reflected responsiveness to their concerns, acceptance, and understanding. The behaviors that detracted from well-being reflected domination or emotional detachment. This suggests that future studies would benefit by employing coding systems that more directly assess issues of interpersonal control and the support–disapproval dimension of interpersonal behaviors.

Although several behavioral responses of confidants (empathy, self-disclosure, expository feedback, positive evaluation) were perceived as supportive, they were not significantly related to postdivorce adjustment. The most likely explanation for this inconsistency is the fact that behavioral processes were observed in only one relationship. The regression analyses showed that a single relationship does not accurately predict postdivorce adjustment, because adjustment is associated with social support from a number of sources. Future research should assess the quality of relationships in three important spheres of influence: the family, friends, and the dating relationship.

Finally, this study focused on the availability and impact of social resources on coping with divorce. It did not focus on the personal or psychological resources available to cultivate supportive relationships. There is little doubt that social competence, for example, influences the availability and adequacy of supportive relationships. For example, having a confidant requires certain social skills to develop and maintain intimacy. This research assessed specifically the confidant's "competence" in providing support. A promising direction for future research would be to analyze the confidant interaction bidirectionally. In this way the divorced woman's competence in eliciting support could also be assessed.

References

Abrahams, R. D. (1970), A performance centered approach to gossip. *Man, 5,* 290–301.

Achenback, T. M., & Edelbrook, C. S. (1981). Behavioral problems and competencies reported by parents of normal and disturbed children aged four through 16. *Monographs of the Society for Research in Child Development, 46* (Serial No. 188).

Alexander, J. F. (1973). Defensive and supportive communication in normal and deviant families. *Journal of Consulting and Clinical Psychology, 40,* 223–31.

Allen, V. L. (Ed.), (1976). *Children as teachers.* New York: Academic Press.

Allison, P. D., & Liker, J. K. (1982). Analyzing sequential data on dyadic interaction. *Psychological Bulletin, 91,* 393–403.

Altman, I. (1972). *Reciprocity of interpersonal exchange.* Paper presented at the 80th Annual Meeting of the American Psychological Association, August.

Altman, I. (1973). Reciprocity of interpersonal exchange. *Journal of the Theory of Social Behavior, 3,* 249–61.

Altman, I., & Haythorn, W. W. (1967). The ecology of isolated groups. *Behavioral Science, 12,* 169–82.

Altman, I., & Taylor, D. A. (1973). *Social penetration: The development of interpersonal relationships.* New York: Holt.

Amble, B. R. (1967). Teacher evaluations of student behavior and school dropouts. *Journal of Educational Research, 60,* 53–8.

Andrews, G., Tennant, D., Hewson, D. M., & Valliant, G. E. (1978). Life event stress, social support, coping style, and risk of psychological impairment. *Journal of Nervous and Mental Disease, 166,* 307–16.

Angst, J. & Dobler-Mikola, A. (1983, December). *Do the diagnostic criteria determine the sex ratio in depression?* Paper presented at the 22nd Annual Meeting of the American College of Neuropsychopharmacology, San Juan, Puerto Rico.

Antonovsky, A. (1974). Conceptual and methodological problems in the study of resistance resources and stressful life events. In B. S. Dohrenwend & B. P. Dohrenwend (Eds.), *Stressful life events: Their nature and effects* (pp. 245–58). New York: Wiley.

Argyle, M. (1969). *Social interaction.* London: Methuen.

Argyle, M., Furnham, A., & Graham, J. A. (1981). *Social situations.* London: Cambridge University Press.

Arnetz, B. B., Theorell, R., Levi, L., Kallner, A., & Enroth, P. (1983). An experimental study of social isolation of elderly people: Psychoendocrine and metabolic effect. *Psychosomatic Medicine, 45,* 395–406.

Asher, S. R. (1978a). Children's peer relations. In M. E. Lamb (Ed.), *Social and personality development.* New York: Holt, Rinehart, & Winston.

Asher, S. R. (1978b). Some kids are nobody's best friend. *Today's Education, 71*(1), 23–9.

Asher, S. R. (1979). Referential communication. In G. Whitehurst & B. Zimmerman (Eds.), *The functions of language and communication.* New York: Academic Press.

Asher, S. R., & Gottman, J. M. (Eds.). (1981). *The development of children's friendships.* Cambridge University Press.

Asher, S. R., & Hymel, S. (1981). Children's social competence in peer relations: Sociometric and behavioral assessment. In J. D. Wine & M. D. Smye (Eds.), *Social competence.* New York: Guilford.

Asher, S. R., Hymel, S., & Renshaw, P. D. (1984). Loneliness in children. *Child Development, 55,* 1456–64.

Asher, S. R., Oden, S. L., & Gottman, J. M. (1977). Children's friendships in school settings. In L. G. Katz (Ed.), *Current topics in early childhood education* (Vol. 1). Norwood, NJ: Ablex.

Asher, S. R., & Renshaw, P. D. (1981). Children without friends: Social knowledge and social-skill training. In S. R. Asher & J. M. Gottman (Eds.), *The development of children's friendships.* Cambridge University Press.

Asher, S. R., Renshaw, P. D., Geraci, R., & Dor, A. (1979, April). *Peer acceptance and social skill training: The selection of program content.* Paper presented at the biennial meeting of the Society for Research in Child Development, San Francisco.

Asher, S. R., & Wigfield, A. (1981). Training referential communication skills. In W. P. Dickson (Ed.), *Children's oral communication skills.* New York: Academic Press.

Bakeman, R. (1978). Untangling streams of behavior: Sequential analysis of observational data. In G. P. Sackett (Ed.), *Observing behavior: Vol. 2. Data collection and analysis methods.* Baltimore: University Park Press.

Bakeman, R., & Gottman, J. M. (1986). *Observing interaction: An introduction to sequential analysis.* Cambridge University Press.

Bales, R. F. (1950). *Interaction process analysis.* Cambridge, MA: Addison-Wesley.

Barclay, J. R. (1966). Sociometric choices and teacher ratings as predictors of school dropout. *Journal of Social Psychology, 4,* 40–5.

Barthell, C. N., & Holmes, D. S. (1968). High school yearbooks: A non-reactive measure of social isolation in graduates who eventually become schizophrenic. *Journal of Abnormal Psychology, 4,* 313–16.

Bates, E. (1975). Peer relations and the acquisition of language. In M. Lewis & L. A. Rosenblum (Eds.), *Friendship and peer relations* (pp. 259–91). New York: Wiley.

Bates, E. (1976). *Language and context: The acquisition of pragmatics.* New York: Academic Press.

Bates, E., Camaioni, L., & Volterra, U. (1979). The acquisition of performatives prior to speech. In E. Ochs & B. Schieffelin (Eds.), *Developmental pragmatics.* New York: Academic Press.

Bell, R. R. (1981). *Worlds of friendship.* Beverly Hills CA: Sage.

Bell, W. (1961). The utility of the Shevky typology for the design of urban subarea field studies. In G. Theordorson (Ed.), *Studies in human ecology.* Evanston, IL: Row & Peterson.

Berg, J. H., & Archer, R. (1980, August). *The nature of disclosure reciprocity: Three forms of reciprocation.* Paper presented at the American Psychological Association, Montreal, Canada.

Berg, J. H., & Archer, R. L. (1982). Responses to self-disclosure and interaction goals. *Journal of Experimental Social Psychology, 18,* 501–12.

Berkman, L. F., & Syme, S. L. (1979). Social networks, host resistance, and mortality: A nine-year follow-up study of Alameda County residents. *American Journal of Epidemiology, 109,* 186–204.

Berndt, T. J. (1978). *Children's conceptions of friendship and the behavior expected of friends.* Unpublished manuscript, Yale University, New Haven, CT.

Berndt, T. J. (1981). The effects on friendship of prosocial intentions and behavior. *Child Development, 52,* 636–43.

Berndt, T. J. (1982). The features and effects of friendship in early adolescence. *Child Development, 53,* 1447–60.

Berndt, T. J. (1986). Sharing between friends: Contexts and consequences. In E. C. Mueller & C. R. Cooper (Eds.), *Process and outcome in peer relationships* (pp. 105–28). New York: Academic Press.

Berndt, T. J., Caparulo, B. K., McCartney, K., & Moore, A. (1980). *Process and outcomes of social influence in children's peer groups.* Unpublished manuscript, Yale University, New Haven, CT.

Berscheid, E., Dion, K. K., Walster, E., & Walster, G. W. (1971). Physical attractiveness and dating choice: A test of the matching hypotheses. *Journal of Experimental Social Psychology, 7,* 173–89.

Berscheid, E., & Walster, E. H. (1969). *Interpersonal attraction.* Cambridge, MA: Addison-Wesley.

Bianchi, B. D., & Bakeman, R. (1978). Sex-typed affiliation preferences observed in preschoolers: Traditional and open school differences. *Child Development, 49,* 910–12.

Bigelow, B. J. (1977). Children's friendship expectations: A cognitive-developmental study. *Child Development, 48,* 246–53.

Bigelow, B. J., & LaGaipa, J. J. (1975). Children's written description of friendship: A multidimensional analysis. *Developmental Psychology, 11,* 857–8.

Billings, A. (1979). Conflict resolution in distressed and nondistressed married couples. *Journal of Consulting and Clinical Psychology, 47,* 365–76.

Birchler, G., Weiss, R., & Vincent, J. (1975). Multimethod analysis of social reinforcement exchange between maritally distressed and nondistressed spouse and stranger dyads. *Journal of Personality and Social Psychology, 31,* 349–60.

Birren, J. C. (1944). Psychology examinations of children who later became psychotic. *Journal of Abnormal and Social Psychology, 39,* 84–96.

Bishop, Y. M. M., Fienberg, S. E., & Holland, P. W. (1975). *Discrete multivariate analysis: Theory and practice.* Cambridge, MA: MIT Press.

Blau, Z. S. (1961). Structural constraints on friendships in old age. *American Sociological Review, 26,* 429–39.

Block, J. H. (1979). Another look at sex differentiation in the socialization of mothers and fathers. In J. Sherman & F. L. Denmark (Eds.), *Psychology of women: Future directions of research.* New York: Psychological Dimensions.

Bloom, B. L. (1975). *Changing patterns of psychiatric care.* New York: Human Sciences Press.

Bloom, B. L., Asher, S. J., & White S. W. (1978). Marital disruption as a stressor: A review and analysis. *Psychological Bulletin, 85,* 867–94.

Booth, A. (1972). Sex and social participation. *American Sociological Review, 37*, 183–92.

Booth, A., & Hess, C. (1947). Cross-sex friendship. *Journal of Marriage and the Family, 36*, 38–47.

Bott, E. (1971). *Family and social network*. (2nd ed). London: Tavistock.

Bower, E. M., & Lambert, N. M. (1965). In-school screening of children with emotional handicaps. In N. Long, W. Morse, & R. G. Newman (Eds.), *Conflicts in the classroom*. Belmont, CA: Wadsworth.

Bower, E. M., Shellhammer, T. A., & Daley, J. M. (1960). School characteristics of male adolescents who later become schizophrenic. *American Journal of Orthopsychiatry, 30*, 712–29.

Bowman, D. H., & Matthews, C. V. (1960). *Motivations of youth for leaving school* (Project 200). Washington, D.C.: U.S. Office of Education Cooperative Research Program.

Bowman, K. M. (1934). A study of the pre-psychotic personality in certain psychoses. *American Journal of Orthopsychiatry, 4*, 473–98.

Brain, R. (1977). *Friends and lovers*. New York: Pocket Books.

Brandewien, R. A., Brown, C. A., & Fox, E. M. (1974). Women and children last: The social situation of divorced mothers and their families. *Journal of Marriage and the Family, 36*, 498–514.

Brazelton, T. B. (1973) *Neonatal behavioral assessment scale* (National Spastics Society Monograph). Philadelphia: Lippincott.

Brazelton, T. B., Koslowski, B., & Main, M. (1974). The origin of reciprocity: The early mother–infant interaction. In M. Lewis & L. Rosenblum (Eds.), *The effect of the infant on its caregiver*. New York: Wiley.

Brenneis, D., & Liens, L. (1977) "You fruithead": A sociolinguistic approach to children's dispute settlement. In S. E. Ervin-Tripp & C. Mitchell-Kernan (Eds.), *Child discourse*. New York: Academic Press.

Brenton, M. (1974). *Friendship*. New York: Stein & Day.

Brewer, R. E., & Brewer, M. B. (1968). Attraction and accuracy in perception in dyads. *Journal of Personality and Social Psychology, 8*, 188–93.

Brickman, P., Meyer, P., & Fredd, S. (1975). Effects of varying exposure to another person with familiar or unfamiliar thought processes. *Journal of Experimental and Social Psychology, 11*, 261–70.

Brown, G. S., Bhrolchain, M. N., & Harris, T. (1975). Social class and psychiatric disturbance among women in an urban population. *Sociology, 9*, 223–54.

Brown, G. W., Harris, T., & Copeland, J. R. (1977). Depression and loss. *British Journal of Psychiatry, 130*, 1–18.

Brown, P., & Levinson, S. (1978). Universals in language usage: Politeness phenomena. In E. N. Goody (Ed.), *Questions and politeness: Strategies in social interaction*. Cambridge University Press.

Brown, R. (1973). *A first language*. Cambridge, MA: Harvard University Press.

Buck, R. W. (1975). Nonverbal communication of affect in children. *Journal of Personality and Social Psychology, 31*, 644–53.

Buck, R. W. (1977). Nonverbal communication of affect in preschool children: Relationships with personality and skin conductance. *Journal of Personality and Social Psychology, 35*, 225–36.

Bugenthal, D. E., Love, L. R., & Gianetto, R. M. (1971). Perfidious feminine faces. *Journal of Personality and Social Psychology, 17*, 314–18.

Bukowski, W. M., & Newcomb, A. F. (1984). Stability and determinants of sociometric status and friendship choice: A longitudinal perspective. *Developmental Psychology, 20*, 941–52.

Burchard, J. D. (1979). Competitive youth sports and social competence. In M. W. Kent & J. E. Rolf (Eds.), *Primary prevention of psychopathology: Vol. 3. Social competence in children.* (pp. 171–96). Hanover, N.H: University of Vermont Press.

Burgess, E. W., Locke, H. J., & Thomes, M. M. (1971). *The family.* New York: Van Nostrand Reinhold.

Busk, P. L., Ford, R. C., & Schulman, J. L. (1973). Stability of sociometric responses in classrooms. *Journal of Genetic Psychology, 123,* 69–84.

Byrne, D. (1969). Attitudes and attraction. In L. Berkowitz (Ed.), *Advances in experimental social psychology* (Vol. 4). New York: Academic Press.

Byrne, D. (1971). *The attraction paradigm.* New York: Academic Press.

Byrne, D., & Buehler, J. A. (1955). A note of the influence of propinquity upon acquaintanships. *Journal of Abnormal and Social Psychology, 51,* 147–8.

Byrne, D., & Clore, G. L. (1966). Predicting interpersonal attraction toward strangers presented in three different stimulus modes. *Psychonomic Science, 4,* 239–40.

Byrne, D., Ervin, C. R., & Lamberth, J. (1970). Continuity between the experimental study of attraction and real-life computer dating. *Journal of Personality and Social Psychology, 16,* 157–65.

Campbell, A., Converse, P. E., & Rodgers, W. L. (1976). *The quality of American life.* New York: Russell Sage Foundation.

Caplan, G. (1974). *Support systems and community mental health.* New York: Behavioral Publications.

Cassel, J. (1976). The contribution of the social environment to host resistance. *American Journal of Epidemiology, 104,* 107–23.

Cattell, R. B., & Nesselroade, J. T. (1967). Likeness and completeness theories examined by 16 personality factor measures on stably and unstably married couples. *Journal of Personality and Social Psychology, 1,* 351–61.

Chaikin, A. L., & Derlega, V. J. (1976). Self-disclosure. In J. W. Thibaut, J. T. Spence, & R. C. Carson (Eds.), *Contemporary topics in social psychology.* Morristown, NJ: General Learning Press.

Chance, M. R. A., & Larsen, R. (Eds.). (1976). *The social structure of attention.* London: Wiley.

Chandler, M. (1973). Egocentrism and anti-social behavior: The assessment and training of social perspective-taking skills. *Developmental Psychology, 9,* 326–32.

Cheek, F. E. (1964). The "schizopherenogenic" mother in word and deed. *Family Process, 3,* 155–77.

Chiriboga, D. A., Roberts, J., & Stein, J. A. (1978). Psychological well-being during marital separation. *Journal of Divorce, 2,* 21–36.

Clark, M. S., & Mills, J. (1979). Interpersonal attraction in exchange and communal relationships. *Journal of Personality and Social Psychology, 37,* 12–24.

Clark, H. H., & Lucy, P. (1975). Understanding what is meant from what is said: A study in conversationally conveyed requests. *Journal of Verbal Learning and Verbal Behavior, 14,* 56–72.

Clark, M. S. (1984). A distinction between two types of relationships and its implications for development. In J. C. Masters & K. Yarkin-Levin (Eds.), *Boundary areas in social and developmental psychology.* New York: Academic Press.

Clark, R. A., & Delia, J. G. (1976). The development of functional persuasive skills in childhood and early adolescence. *Child Development, 47,* 1008–14.

Cobb, S. (1976). Social support as a moderator of life stress. *Psychosomatic Medicine, 38*, 300–15.

Cohen, J. J., D'Heurle, A., & Widmark-Petersson, V. (1980). Cross-sex friendships in children: Gender patterns and cultural perspectives. *Psychology in the Schools, 17*, 523–9.

Cohn, D. A., Lohrmann, B. C. & Patterson, C. J. (1985, April). *Social networks and loneliness in children.* Paper presented at the biennial meeting of the Society for Research in Child Development, Toronto.

Coie, J. D., & Dodge, K. A. (1983). Continuities and changes in children's social status: A five-year longitudinal study. *Merrill-Palmer Quarterly, 29*, 261–82.

Coie, J. D., Dodge, K. A. & Coppetelli, H. (1982). Dimensions and types of social status: A cross-age perspective. *Developmental Psychology, 18*, 557–64.

Coie, J. D., & Kupersmidt, J. B. (1983). A behavioral analysis of emerging social status in boys' groups. *Child Development, 54*, 1400–16.

Cole, P. (1975). The synchronic and diachronic status of conversational implicature. In P. Cole and J. L. Morgan (Eds.), *Syntax and semantics* (Vol. 4). New York: Academic Press.

Conger, J. C., & Keane, S. P. (1981). Social skills intervention in the treatment of isolated or withdrawn children. *Psychological Bulletin, 90*, 478–95.

Conger, J. J., & Miller, W. C. (1966). *Personality, social class, and delinquency.* New York: Wiley.

Conger, J. J., Sawrey, W., Turrell, E. S. (1958). The role of social experience in the production of gastric ulcers in hooded rats placed in a conflict situation. *Journal of Abnormal Psychology, 57*, 214–20.

Cooper, C. R., Marquis, A., & Ayers-Lopez, S. (1982). Peer learning in the classroom: Tracing developmental patterns and consequences of children's spontaneous interactions. In L. C. Wilkinson (Ed.), *Communicating in the classroom.* New York: Academic Press.

Corsaro, W. A. (1981). Friendship in the nursery school: Social organization in a peer environment. In S. R. Asher & J. M. Gottman (Eds.), *The development of children's friendships.* New York: Cambridge University Press.

Coulthard, M. (1977). *An introduction to discourse analysis.* London: Longman.

Cowen, E. L., Pederson, A., Babijian, H., Izzo, L. D., & Trost, M. A. (1973). Long-term follow-up of early detected vulnerable children. *Journal of Consulting and Clinical Psychology, 41*, 438–46.

Cozby, P. C. (1972). Self-disclosure, reciprocity and liking. *Sociometry, 35*, 151–60.

Cozby, P. C. (1973). Self-disclosure: A literature review. *Psychological Bulletin, 79*, 73–91.

Crawford, M. (1977). What is a friend? *New Society, 42*, 116–77.

Cronbach, L. J., Glaser, G. C., Nanda, H., & Rajaratnam, N. (1972). *The dependability of behavioral measurements: Theory of generalizability for scores and profiles.* New York: Wiley.

Curry, T. J., & Kenny, D. A. (1974). The effects of perceived and actual similarity in values and personality in the process of interpersonal attraction. *Quality and Quantity, 8*, 27–44.

Cutrona, C. E., & Peplau, L. A. (1979, April). *A longitudinal study of loneliness.* Paper presented at the annual meeting of the Western Psychological Association, San Diego, CA.

Daher, D. M., & Banikiotes, P. G. (1976). Interpersonal attraction and rewarding aspects of disclosure content and level. *Journal of Personality and Social Psychology, 33*, 492–6.

Damon, W. (1977). *The social world of the child*. San Francisco: Jossey-Bass.

Darley, J. M., & Berscheid, E. (1967). Increased liking as a result of the anticipation of personal contact. *Human Relations, 20,* 29–40.

Davis, J. (1976). Self-disclosure in an acquaintance exercise: Responsibility for level of intimacy. *Journal of Personality and Social Psychology, 33,* 787–92.

Davis, J. (1978). When boy meets girl: Sex roles and the negotiation of intimacy in an acquaintance exercise. *Journal of Social Psychology, 36,* 684–92.

Davison, A. (1975). Indirect speech acts and what to do with them. In P. Cole & J. L. Morgan (Eds.), *Syntax and semantics* (Vol. 3). New York: Academic Press.

Dean, A., & Lin, N. (1977). The stress-buffering role of social support. *Journal of Nervous and Mental Diseases, 165*(6).

Derlega, V. J., Wilson, M., & Chaikin, A. L. (1976). Friendship and disclosure reciprocity. *Journal of Personality and Social Psychology, 34,* 578–82.

Deutsch, M. (1960). The effects of cooperation and competition upon group process. In D. Cartwright & A. Zander (Eds.), *Group dynamics: Research and theory* (2nd ed., pp. 414–48). Evanston, IL.: Row & Peterson.

De Vries, R. (1970). The development of role-taking as reflected by the behavior of bright, average, and retarded children in a social guessing game. *Child Development, 41,* 759–70.

Diaz, R. M., & Berndt, T. J. (1981). Children's knowledge of a best friend: Fact or fiction. *Developmental Psychology, 18,* 787–94.

Dimond, R. E., & Hellkamp, D. T. (1969). Race, sex, ordinal position or birth, and self-disclosure in high school students. *Psychological Reports, 25,* 235–8.

Dion, K., Berscheid, E., & Walster, E. (1972). What is beautiful is good. *Journal of Personality and Social Psychology, 24,* 285–90.

DiPietro, J. (1982). Rough and tumble play: A function of gender. *Developmental Psychology, 17,* 50–8.

Dodge, K. A. (1983). Behavioral antecedents of peer social status. *Child Development, 54,* 1386–9.

Dodge, K. A., Schlundt, D. C., Schocken, I., & Delugach, J. D. (1983). Social competence and children's sociometric status: The role of peer group entry strategies. *Merrill–Palmer Quarterly, 29,* 309–36.

Dohrenwend, B. S., & Dohrenwend, B. P. (1974). *Stressful life events: Their nature and effects*. New York: Wiley.

Dore, J. (1977). Children's illocutionary acts. In R.O. Freedle (Ed.), *Discourse production and comprehension*. Norwood, NJ: Ablex.

Dore, J., Gearhart, M., & Newman, D. (1978). The structure of nursery school conversation. In K. E. Nelson (Ed.), *Children's language* (Vol. 1). New York: Gardner Press.

Doster, J. A., & Strickland, B. R. (1969). Perceived child-rearing and self-disclosure patterns. *Journal of Consulting and Clinical Psychology, 33,* 382.

Douvan, E., & Adelson, J. (1966). *The adolescent experience*. New York: Wiley.

Doyle, A., Connolly, J., & Rivest, L. (1980). The effect of playmate familiarity on the social interactions of young children. *Child Development, 51,* 217–23.

Duck, S. W. (1973). *Personal relationships and personal constructs: A study of friendship formation*. New York: Wiley.

Duck, S. W. (1976). Interpersonal communication in developing acquaintance. In G. R. Miller (Ed.), *Explorations in interpersonal communication*. Beverly Hills, CA: Sage.

Duck, S. W. (1984). *Friends for life: The psychology of close relationships*. New York: St. Martin's Press.

Duck, S. W., Miell, D. K., & Gaebler, H. C. (1980). Attraction and communication in children's interactions. In H. C. Foot, A. J. Chapman, and J. R. Smith (Eds.), *Friendship and social relations in children*. New York: Wiley & Sons.

Duncan, S. (1972). Some signals and rules for taking speaking turns in conversation. *Journal of Personality and Social Psychology, 23*, 283–92.

Duncan, S., & Fiske, D. (1977). *Face-to-face interaction: Research, method, and theory*. Hillsdale, NJ: Erlbaum.

Eder, D., & Hallinan, M. T. (1978). Sex differences in children's friendships. *American Sociological Review, 43*, 237–50.

Edwards, A. S., & Langley, L. D. (1936). Childhood manifestation and adult psychosis. *American Journal of Orthopsychiatry, 6*, 103–9.

Elkind, D. (1980). Strategic interactions in early adolescence. In J. Adelson (Ed.), *Handbook of adolescent psychology*. New York: Wiley.

Elkind, D. (1984). *Children and adolescents: Interpretive essays on Jean Piaget*. New York: Oxford University Press.

Elkins, D. (1958). Some factors related to the friendship choices of ninety eighth-grade children in a school society. *Genetic Psychology Monographs, 58*, 207–72.

Epstein, J. L. (1986). Friendship selection: Developmental and environmental influences. In E. Mueller & C. Cooper (Eds.), *Process and outcome in peer relationships*. New York: Academic Press.

Epstein, J. L., & Karweit, N. (Eds.). (1983). *Friends in school: patterns of selection and influence in secondary schools*. New York: Academic Press.

Ervin-Tripp, S. (1977). Wait for me, roller skate! In S. Ervin-Tripp & C. Mitchell-Kernan (Eds.), *Child discourse*. New York: Academic Press.

Fagot, B. I. (1977). Consequences of moderate cross-gender behavior in preschool children. *Developmental Psychology, 13*, 166–7.

Fasteau, N. D. (1975). *The male machine*. New York: Delta.

Feshbeck, N. D., & Sones, G. (1971). Sex differences in adolescents' reactions toward newcomers. *Developmental Psychology, 4*, 381–6.

Festinger, L. (1950). Laboratory experiments: The role of group belongingness. In J. G. Miller (Ed.), *Experiments in social process* (pp. 31–46). New York: McGraw-Hill.

Festinger, L. (1954). A theory of social comparison processes. *Human Relations, 7*, 117–40.

Festinger, L., Schachter, S., & Back, S. (1950). *Social pressures in informal groups: A study of human factors in housing*. New York: Harper.

Fine, G. A. (1980). The natural history of preadolescent male friendship groups. In H. C. Foot, A. J. Chapman, & J. R. Smith (Eds.), *Friendship and social relations in children* (pp. 243–320). New York: Wiley.

Fine, G. A. (1981). Friends, impression management, and preadolescent behavior. In S. R. Asher & J. M. Gottman (Eds.), *The development of children's friendships*. Cambridge University Press.

Fischer, C. S., & Phillips, S. L. (1979). *Who is alone? Social characteristics of people with small networks*. Paper presented at a conference on loneliness, University of California, Los Angeles.

Fisher, J. D., Nadler, A., & Whitcher-Alagana, S. (1982). Recipient reactions to aid. *Psychological Bulletin, 91*(1), 27–54.

Flavell, J. H. (1977). Metacognition and cognitive monitoring: A new area of cognitive-development inquiry. *American Psychologist, 34*, 906–11.

Fleming, D., & Ricks, D. F. (1970). Emotions of children before schizophrenia and before character disorder. In M. Roff & D. F. Ricks (Eds.), *Life history research in psychopathology* (Vol. 1, pp. 240–64). Minneapolis: University of Minnesota Press.

Foa, V. G. (1961). Convergences in the analysis of the structure of interpersonal behavior. *Psychological Review, 61,* 341–53.

Foot, H. C., Chapman, A. J., & Smith, J. R. (1977). Friendship and social responsiveness in boys and girls. *Journal of Personality and Social Psychology, 35,* 401–11.

Foot, H. C., Chapman, A. J., & Smith, J. R. (Eds.) (1980). *Friendships and social relations in children.* New York: Wiley.

Forbes, D., Katz, M. M., & Paul, B. (1982). *Dinosaurs don't like rain: A dramatic analysis of children's fantasy play.* Unpublished manuscript, Harvard University, Cambridge, MA.

Forbes, D., & Lubin, D. (1979). *Reasoning and behavior in children's interactions.* Paper presented at the meeting of the American Psychological Association, New York, August.

Forbes, D., & Lubin, D. (1983). *Verbal social reasoning and observed persuasion strategies in children's peer interactions.* Unpublished manuscript, Harvard University, Cambridge, MA.

Fraser, B. (1975). Hedged performatives. In P. Cole & J. L. Morgan (Eds.), *Syntax and semantics* (Vol. 3). New York: Academic Press.

Frazee, H. E. (1954). Children who later become schizophrenic. *Smith College Studies in Social Work, 23,* 125–49.

Freud, A., & Dann, S. (1951). An experiment in group upbringing. In R. Eisler (Ed.), *The psychoanalytic study of the child* (Vol. 6). New York: International Universities Press.

Friedlander, D. (1945). Personality development of twenty-seven children who later became psychotic. *Journal of Abnormal Social Psychology, 40,* 330–5.

Froiland, D. J., & Hozeman, T. L. (1977). Counseling for constructive divorce. *Personnel and Guidance Journal, 55,* 525–9.

Furman, W. (1984). Some observations on the study of personal relationships. In J. C. Masters & K. Yarkin-Levin (Eds.), *Boundary areas in social and developmental psychology.* New York: Academic Press.

Furman, W. (1982). Children's friendships. In T. Field (Ed.), *Review of human development.* (pp. 18–33). New York: Wiley.

Furman, W., & Bierman, K. L. (1981). *Children's conceptions of friendship.* Unpublished manuscript, University of Denver, Denver, CO.

Furman, W., & Childs, M. K. (1981, April) *A temporal perspective on children's friendships.* Paper presented at the biennial meeting of the Society for Research in Child Development, Boston.

Gamer, E. (1977). *Children's reports of friendship criteria.* Paper presented at the Massachusetts Psychological Association, Boston.

Garmezy, N. (1974). Children at risk: The search for antecedents of schizophrenia: Part 1. Conceptual models and research methods. *Schizophrenia Bulletin, 1,* 14–89.

Garvey, C. (1974). Some properties of social play. *Merrill–Palmer Quarterly, 20,* 163–80.

Garvey, C. (1975). Requests and responses in children's speech. *Journal of Child Language, 2,* 41–63.

Garvey, C. (1977). The contingent query: A dependent act in conversation. In M.

Lewis & L. A. Rosenblum (Eds.), *Interaction, conversation, and the development of language*. New York: Wiley.

Garvey, C., & Ben Debba, M. (1974). Effects of age, sex, and partner on children's dyadic speech. *Child Development, 46,* 1159–61.

Garvey, C., & Berndt, R. (1975). *The organization of pretend play.* Paper presented at the annual meeting of the American Psychological Association, Chicago, August.

Garvey, C., & Hogan, R. (1973). Social speech and social interaction: Egocentrism revisited. *Child Development, 44,* 562–8.

Genishi, C., & DiPaolo, M. (1983). Learning through argument in a preschool. In L. C. Wilkinson (Ed.), *Communicating in the classroom.* New York: Academic Press.

George, S. W., & Krantz, M. (1981). The effects of preferred play partnership on communication adequacy. *Journal of Psychology, 109,* 245–53.

Gessell, A., & Ilg, F. L. (1946). *The child from five to ten.* New York: Harper Bros.

Gibbs, R. W., Jr. (1979). Contextual effects in understanding indirect requests. *Discourse Processes, 2,* 1–10.

Ginsberg, D. (1980). *Friendship and mental health.* Unpublished manuscript, University of Illinois, Champaign.

Glick, P. C., & Norton, A. J. (1979). Marrying, divorcing, and living together in the U.S. today. *Population Bulletin,* No. 32. Washington, D.C.: Population Reference Bureau.

Gluckman, M. (1963). Gossip and scandal. *Current Anthropology, 4,* 307–16.

Gluckman, M. (1983). Psychological, sociological, and anthropological explanations of witchcraft and gossip. *Man, 3,* 20–34.

Glucksberg, S., & Krauss, R. (1967). What do people say after they have learned to talk? Studies of the development of referential communications. *Merrill–Palmer Quarterly, 13,* 309–16.

Goldberg, H. (1976). *The hazards of being male.* New York: Signet.

Goncu, A., & Kessel, F. (1983). *"Are we pretending?": An observational study of imaginative play communication.* Paper presented at the annual meetings of the American Educational Research Association, Montreal.

Goode, W. J. (1956). *After divorce.* New York: Free Press.

Goodnow, R. E., & Tagiuri, R. (1952). Religious ethnocentrism and its recognition among adolescent boys. *Journal of Abnormal and Social Psychology, 47,* 316–20.

Goody, E. N. (1978). Toward a theory of questions. In E. N. Goody (Ed.), *Questions and politeness: Strategies in social interaction.* Cambridge University Press.

Gordon, E., & Lakoff, G. (1975). Conversational postulates. In P. Cole & J. L. Morgan (Eds.), *Syntax and semantics* (Vol. 3). New York: Academic Press.

Gordon, S. (1976). *Lonely in America.* New York: Simon & Schuster.

Gottman, J. M. (1979). *Marital interaction: Experimental investigations.* New York: Academic Press.

Gottman, J. M. (1980). Analyzing for sequential connection and assessing interobserver reliability for the sequential analysis of observational data. *Behavioral Assessment, 2,* 361–8.

Gottman, J. M. (1983). How children become friends. *Monographs of the Society for Research in Child Development, 48* (3, Serial No. 201).

Gottman, J. M. & Bakeman, R. (1979). The sequential analysis of observational data. In M. Lamb, S. Soumi, & G. Stephenson (Eds.), *Methodological problems in the study of social interaction.* Madison: University of Wisconsin Press.

Gottman, J., & Notarius, C. (1978). Sequential analysis of observational data using Markov chains. In T. Kratochwill (Ed.), *Strategies to evaluate change in single subject research*. New York: Academic Press.

Gottman, J. M., Gonso, J., & Rasmussen, B. (1975). Social interaction, social competence, and friendship in children. *Child Development, 46*, 709–18.

Gottman, J. M. Markman, H., & Notarius, C. (1977). The topography of marital conflict: A sequential analysis of verbal and nonverbal behavior. *Journal of Marriage and the Family, 39*, 461–77.

Gottman, J. M., & Parkhurst, J. T. (1980). A developmental theory of friendship and acquaintanceship processes. In W. A. Collins (Eds.), *Minnesota symposia on child psychology* (Vol. 13). Hillsdale, NJ: Erlbaum.

Gottman, J. M., Parkhurst, J., & Bajjalieh, S. (1982). *Children's social speech during play: A coding manual*. Unpublished manuscript, University of Illinois, Champaign.

Green, G. M. (1975). How to get people to do things with words: The imperative question. In P. Cole & J. L. Mortgan (Eds.), *Syntax and semantics* (Vol. 3). New York: Academic Press.

Greenberg, M. T., Siegel, J. M., & Leitch, C. J. (1983). The nature and importance of attachment relationships to parents and peers during adolescence. *Journal of Youth and Adolescence, 12*, 373–86.

Grice, H. P. (1975). Logic and conversation. In P. Cole & J. L. Morgan (Eds.), *Syntax and semantics* (Vol. 3). New York: Academic Press.

Griffin, H. (1985). The coordination of meaning in the creation of a shared make-believe reality. In I. Bretherton (Ed.), *Symbolic play: The representation of social understanding*. New York: Academic Press.

Gronlund, N. E., & Holmlund, W. S. (1958). The value of elementary school sociometric status scores for predicting pupils' adjustment in high school. *Educational Administration and Supervision, 44*, 225–60.

Haley, J. (1964). Research on family patterns: An instrument measurement. *Family Process, 3*, 41–65.

Hall, G. S. (1904). *Adolescence* (Vol. 2). New York: Appleton.

Hall, J. A. (1979). Gender, gender roles, and nonverbal communication skills. In R. Rosenthal (Ed.), *Skill in nonverbal communication: Individual differences*. Cambridge, MA: Oelgeschlager, Gunn, & Haig.

Hall, J., & Williams, M. S. (1966). A comparison of decision-making performances in established and ad hoc groups. *Journal of Personality and Social Psychology, 3*, 214–22.

Hallinan, M. T. (1977). *The development of children's friendship cliques*. Paper presented at the American Sociological Convention, Chicago.

Hallinan, M. T., & Tuma, N. B. (1978). Classroom effects on change in children's friendships. *Sociology of Education, 51*, 270–82.

Hannerz, U. (1967). Gossip, networks, culture in a black American ghetto. *Ethnos, 32*, 35–60.

Harper, R. G., Wiens, A. N., & Matarazzo, J. D. (1978). *Nonverbal communication: The state of the art*. New York: Wiley.

Harter, S. (1983). Developmental perspectives on the self system. In P. H. Mussen (Ed.), *Handbook of child psychology: Vol. 4. Socialization, personality, and social development*. New York: Wiley.

Hartup, W. W. (1970). Peer interaction and social organization. In P. H. Mussen (Ed.), *Carmichael's manual of child psychology*. New York: Wiley.

Hartup, W. W. (1975). The origins of friendship. In M. Lewis & L. Rosenblum, (Eds.), *Friendships and peer relations*. New York: Wiley.

Hartup, W. W. (1978). Children and their friends. In H. McGurk (Ed.), *Issues in childhood social development*. London: Methuen.

Hartup, W. W. (1979). Peer relations and the growth of social competence. In M. W. Kent & J. E. Rolf (Eds.), *Primary prevention of psychopathology*. (Vol. 3). Hanover, NH: University of Vermont Press.

Hartup, W. W. (1983). Peer relations. In E. M. Hetherington (Ed.), *Handbook of child psychology: Vol. 4. Socialization, personality, and social development*. New York: Wiley.

Hartup, W. W., Glazer, J. A., & Charlesworth, R. (1967). Peer reinforcement and sociometric status. *Child Development, 38,* 1017–24.

Hayes, D. S. (1978). Cognitive bases for liking and disliking among preschool children. *Child Development, 49,* 906–9.

Hayes, D. S., Gershman, E., & Bolin, L. J. (1980). Friends and enemies: Cognitive bases for preschool children's unilateral and reciprocal relationships. *Child Development, 67,* 1276–9.

Henderson, S., Byrne, D. G., Duncan-Jones, P., Adcock, S., Scott, R., & Steele, G. P. (1978). Social bonds in the epidemiology of neurosis: A preliminary communication. *British Journal of Psychiatry, 132.*

Herrman, S. J., (1974). Divorce: A grief process. *Perspectives in Psychiatric Care, 12,* 108–12.

Hetherington, E. M. (1972). Effects of father absence on personality development in adolescent daughters. *Developmental Psychology, 7,* 313–26.

Hetherington, E. M., Cox, M., & Cox R. (1977). The aftermath of divorce. In J. H. Stevens, Jr., & M. Matthews (Eds.), *Mother–child, father–child relations*. Washington, D.C.: National Association for the Education of Young Children.

Hetherington, E. M., Cox, M., & Cox, R. (1978). Stress and coping in divorce: A focus on women. In J. Gullahorn (Ed.), *Psychology and transition* (pp. 40–65). New York: Winston.

Hinde, R. A. (1979). *Towards understanding relationships*. New York: Academic Press.

Hirsch, B. J. (1981). Coping and adaptation in high-risk populations: Toward an integrative model. *Schizophrenia Bulletin, 7,* 164–71.

Hockenbury, D., Jones, W. H., Kranau, E., & Hobbs, S. A. (1978, March). *Verbal and interactional correlates of loneliness*. In W. H. Jones (Chair), Empirical studies of loneliness. Symposium presented at the annual meeting of the Southwestern Psychological Association, New Orleans, LA.

Holmes, T. H., & Masuda, M. (1974). Life change and illness susceptibility. In B. S. Dohrenwend & B. P. Dohrenwend (Eds.), *Stressful life events: Their nature and effects* (pp. 45–72). New York: Wiley.

Homans, G. C. (1961). *Social behavior: Its elementary forms*. New York: Harcourt Brace & World.

Hops, M. (1982). Social skills training for socially withdrawn/isolated children. In P. Karoly & J. Steffen (Eds.), *Enhancing children's competencies*. Lexington, MA: Lexington Books.

Howes, C. (1981, April). *Patterns of friendship*. Paper presented at the biennial meeting of the Society for Research in Child Development, Boston.

Hoyenga, K. B., & Hoyenga, K. T. (1979). *The question of sex differences*. Boston: Little, Brown.

Huesmann, L. R. & Levinger, G. (1976). Incremental exchange theory: A formal model for progression in dyadic social interaction. In L. Berkowitz & E.

Walster (Eds.), *Advances in experimental social psychology* (Vol. 9). New York: Academic Press.

Huston, T. L. & Levinger, G. (1978). Interpersonal attraction and relationships. *Annual Review of Psychology, 29,* 115–56.

Ilgenfritz, M. P. (1961). Mothers on their own: Widows and divorcees. *Marriage and Family Living, 23,* 38–41.

Ispa, J. (1981). Peer support among Soviet day care toddlers. *International Journal of Behavioral Development, 4,* 255–69.

Izard, C. E. (1960). Personality, similarity, and friendship. *Journal of Abnormal and Social Psychology, 61,* 47–51.

Jacklin, G. N., & Maccoby, E. C. (1978). Social behavior at thirty-three months in same-sex and mixed-sex dyads. *Child Development, 49,* 557–69.

Jacob, S., & Jackson, S. (1980, November). *Strategy and structure in conventional influence.* Paper presented to the 66th Annual Meeting of the Speech Communication Association, New York.

Jacobs, S. C., Prusoff, B. A., & Paykel, E. S. (1974). Recent life events in schizophrenia and depression. *Psychological Medicine, 4,* 444–53.

Jacob, T. (1975). Family interaction in disturbed and normal families: A methodological and substantive review. *Psychological Bulletin, 82,* 33–65.

Janes, C. L., & Hesselbrock, V. M. (1978). Problem children's adult adjustment predicted from teachers' ratings. *American Journal of Orthopsychiatry, 48,* 300–9.

Janes, C. L., Hesselbrock, V. M., Myers, D. G., & Penniman, J. H. (1979). Problem boys in young adulthood: Teachers' ratings and twelve-year follow-up. *Journal of Youth and Adolescence, 8,* 453–72.

Johnson, D. W. (1980). Group processes: Influences of student–student interaction on school outcomes. In J. McMillan (Ed.), *The social psychology of school learning.* New York: Academic Press.

Johnson, D. W., & Johnson, S. (1972). The effects of attitude similarity, expectation of goal facilitation, and actual goal facilitation on interpersonal attraction. *Journal of Experimental Social Psychology, 8,* 197–206.

Johnson, S. M. (1977). *First person singular.* New York: Lippincott.

Jones, R. R., Reid, J. B., & Patterson, G. R. (1975). Naturalistic observations in clinical assessment. In P. McReynolds (Ed.), *Advances in psychological assessment* (Vol. 3). San Francisco: Jossey-Bass.

Jones, W. H. (in press). Loneliness and social contact. *Journal of Social Psychology.*

Jormakka, L. (1976). The behavior of children during a first encounter. *Scandinavian Journal of Psychology, 17,* 15–22.

Jourard, S. M. (1961). Age trends in self-disclosure. *Merrill–Palmer Quarterly, 7,* 191–7.

Jourard, S. M. (1964). *The transparent self.* New York: Van Nostrand.

Jourard, S. M. (1971a). *Self-disclosure: An experimental analysis of the transparent self.* New York: Wiley.

Jourard, S. M. (1971b). *The transparent self* (2nd ed.). New York: Van Nostrand Reinhold.

Jourard, S. M., & Landsman, M. J. (1960). Cognition, cathexis, and the "dyadic effect" in men's self-disclosing behavior. *Merrill–Palmer Quarterly, 6,* 178–86.

Jourard, S. M., & Lasakow, P. (1955). Some factors in self-disclosure. *Journal of Abnormal and Social Psychology, 56,* 91–8.

Jourard, S. M., & Richman, P. (1963). Disclosure output and input in college students. *Merrill–Palmer Quarterly, 9,* 141–8.

Kandel, D. B. (1978). Similarity in real-life adolescent friendship pairs. *Journal of Personality and Social Psychology, 36,* 306–12.

Kaplan, H. B., Burch, N. R., & Bloom, S. W. (1964). Physiological covariation and sociometric relationships in small peer groups. In P. H. Leiderman & D. Shapiro (Eds.), *Psychobiological approaches to social behavior.* Stanford, CA: Stanford University Press.

Kaplan, H. B., Cassel, J. C. & Gore, S. (1977). Social support and health. *Medical Care. 15.*

Karweit, N., & Hansell, S. (1983). Sex differences in adolescent relationships: Friendship and status. In J. L. Epstein & N. Karweit (Eds.), *Friends in school* (pp. 115–30). New York: Academic Press.

Kasanin, J., & Veo, L. (1932). A study of the school adjustments of children who later in life became psychotic. *American Journal of Orthopsychiatry, 2,* 212–30.

Keating, D. P. (1980). Thinking processes in adolescence. In J. Adelson (Ed.) *Handbook of adolescent psychology.* New York: Wiley.

Kellam, S. G. (1974). Stressful events and illness: A research area in need of conceptual development. In B. S. Dohrenwend & B. P. Dohrenwend (Eds.), *Stressful life events: Their nature and effects* (pp. 207–14). New York: Wiley.

Kelley, H. H. (1979). *Personal relationships: Their structure and processes.* New York: Wiley.

Kelly, J. B., & Wallerstein, J. S. (1975). The effects of parental divorce: I. The experience of the child in early latency. *American Journal of Orthopsychiatry, 45,* 253–4.

Kelly, J. B., & Wallerstein, J. S. (1976). The effects of parental divorce: II. The experience of the child in late latency. *American Journal of Orthopsychiatry, 46,* 20–32.

Kerckhoff, A. C., & Davis, K. E. (1962). Value consensus and need complementarity in mate selection. *American Sociological Review, 27,* 295–303.

Kohlberg, L. (1964). Development of moral character and ideology. In M. L. Hoffman (Ed.), *Review of child development research* (Vol. 1). Beverly Hills: Sage.

Kohlberg, L., LaCross, I., & Ricks, D. (1972). The predictability of adult mental health from childhood behavior. In B. B. Wolman (Ed.), *Manual of child psychopathology.* New York: McGraw.

Kohn, M. & Clausen, J. (1955). Social isolation and schizophrenia. *American Sociological Review, 20,* 265–73.

Kolvin, L., Garside, R. F., Nicol, A. R., MacMillan, A. Wolstebholme, F., & Leitch, I. M. (1977). Familial and sociological correlates of behavioral and sociometric deviance in eight-year-old children. In P. J. Graham (Ed.), *Epidemiology of childhood disorders.* New York: Academic Press.

Komarovsky, M. (1962). *Blue collar marriage.* New York: Random House.

Komarovsky, M. (1976). *Dilemmas of masculinity: A study of college youth.* New York: Norton.

Kon, I. S. (1981). Adolescent friendship: Some unanswered questions for future research. In S. Duck & R. Gilmour (Eds.), *Personal relationships: Vol. 2. Developing personal relationships.* New York: Academic Press.

Kuhlen, R., & Collister, E. G. (1952). Sociometric status of sixth- and ninth-graders who fail to finish high school. *Educational and Psychological Measurement, 12,* 632–7.

Kupersmidt, J. (1983, April). Predicting delinquency and academic problems from childhood peer status. In J. D. Coie (Chair), *Strategies for identifying children at social risk: Longitudinal correlates and consequences.* Symposium presented at the biennial meeting of the Society for Research in Child Development, Detroit.

Labinger, M. R., & Holmberg, M. C. (1983). *Dimensions of sharing and helping in preschool children with friends and acquaintances.* Paper presented at the bienniel meeting of the Society for Research in Child Development, Detroit.

Labov, W. (1972). *Language in the inner city: Studies in the black English vernacular.* Philadelphia: University of Pennsylvania Press.

LaGaipa, J. J. (1977). Testing a multidimensional approach to friendship. In S. W. Duck (Ed.), *Theory and practice in interpersonal attraction.* New York: Academic Press.

LaGaipa, J. J. (1981). Children's friendships. In S. W. Duck & R. Gilmour (Eds.), *Personal relationships: Vol. 2. Developing personal relationships.* New York: Academic Press.

LaFreniere, D., & Charlesworth, W. R. (1983). Dominance, attention, and affiliation in a preschool group: A nine-month longitudinal study. *Ethology and Sociobiology 4,* 55–67.

LaFreniere, D., Strayer, F. F., & Gauthier, R. (1984). The emergence of same-sex affiliative preference among preschool peers: A developmental/ethological perspective. *Child Development, 55,* 1958–65.

Lambert, N. (1972). Intellectual and nonintellectual predictors of high school status. *Journal of Scholastic Psychology, 6,* 247–59.

Langolis, J. H., Gottfried, N. W., & Seay, B. (1973). The influence of sex of peer on the social behavior of preschool children. *Developmental Psychology, 8,* 93–8.

Leakey, R. E. (1982). *Origins.* New York: Dutton.

Leary, R. (1957). *Interpersonal diagnosis of personality.* New York: Wiley.

Leavy, R. L. (1983). Social support and psychological disorder. *Journal of Community Psychology, 11,* 3–21.

Leik, R. K., & Leik, S. K. (1976). Transition to interpersonal commitment. In R. Hamblin & R. J. Rundel (Eds.), *Behaviorism in sociology* (pp. 296–320). New Brunswick NJ: Transaction.

Lennard, H. L., & Bernstein, A. (1969). *Patterns of human interaction.* San Francisco: Jossey-Bass.

Lever, J. (1976). Sex differences in the games children play. *Social Problems, 23,* 478–87.

Levin, E. A., & Rubin, K. H. (1983). Getting others to do what you want them to do: The development of children's requestive strategies. In K. Nelson (Ed.), *Children's language* (Vol. 4). New York: Erlbaum.

Levinger, G. (1972). Little sandbox and big quarry: Comment on Byrne's paradigmatic spade for research on interpersonal attraction. *Representative Research in Social Psychology, 3,* 3–19.

Levinger, G., & Huesmann, L. R. (1979). An "incremental exchange" perspective on the pair relationship: Interpersonal reward and level of involvement. In K. J. Gergen, M. S. Greenberg, & R. H. Willis (Eds.), *Social exchange: Advances in theory and research.* New York: Wiley.

Levinger, G., & Raush, H. L. (Eds.). (1977). *Close relationships: Perspectives on the meaning of intimacy.* Amherst: University of Massachusetts Press.

Levinger, G., Senn, D. J., & Jorgenson, B. W. (1970). Progress toward permanence in courtship: A test of the Kerckhoff–Davis hypothesis. *Sociometry,* *33,* 427–43.

Levinger, G., & Snoek, J. D. (1972). *Attraction in relationships: A new look at interpersonal attraction.* Cambridge, MA: General Learning Press.

Lewine, R. J., Watt, N. E., Prentky, R. A., & Fryer, J. H. (1978). Childhood behavior in schizophrenia, personality disorder, depression, and neurosis. *British Journal of Psychiatry, 132,* 347–57.

Lewine, R. J., Watt, N. E., Prentky, R. A., & Fryer, J. H. (1980). Childhood social competence in functionally disordered psychiatric patients and normals. *Journal of Abnormal Psychology, 89,* 132–8.

Levy, L. (1974). Social class and mental disorder. *Psychiatric Clinic, 7,* 271.

Lewis, M., & Rosenblum. L. A. (Eds.). (1975). *Friendship and peer relations.* New York: Wiley.

Lewis, R. A. (1972). A developmental framework for the analysis of premarital dyadic formation. *Family Process, 11,* 19–48.

Liddell, H. (1950). Some specific factors that modify tolerance for environmental stress. In H. G. Wolff, S. G. Wolff, Jr., & C. C. Hare (Eds.), *Life stress and bodily disease.* Baltimore, MD: Williams & Wilkins.

Lopata, H. J. (1973). *Widowhood in an American city.* Cambridge, MA: General Learning Press.

Lott, A. J., & Lott, B. E. (1965). Group cohesiveness as interpersonal attraction: A review of relationships with antecedent and consequent variables. *Psychological Bulletin, 64,* 259–309.

Lowenthal, M. F., & Haven C. (1968). Interaction and adaptation: Intimacy as a critical variable. *American Sociological Review, 33.*

Maccoby, E. E. (1980). *Social development: Psychological development and the parent–child relationship.* New York: Harcourt Brace Jovanovich.

Maccoby, E. E., & Jacklin, C. N. (1974). *The psychology of sex differences.* Stanford, CA: Stanford University Press.

Maccoby, E. E., & Martin, J. A. (1983). Socialization in the context of the family: Parent–child interaction. In E. M. Hetherington (Ed.), *Handbook of child psychology: (Vol. 4) Socialization, personality, and social development.* New York: Wiley.

Maddison, D., & Walker, W. L. (1967). Factors affecting the outcome of conjugal bereavement. *British Journal of Psychiatry, 113,* 1057.

Mahl, G. F. (1956). Disturbances and silences in patients' speech in psychotherapy. *Journal of Abnormal Social Psychology, 53,* 1–15.

Mannarino, A. P. (1980). The development of children's friendships. In H. C. Foot, A. J. Chapman, & J. R. Smith (Eds.), *Friendship and social relations in children.* New York: Wiley.

Margolin, G., & Wampold, B. E. (1983). Sequential analyses of conflict and accord in distressed and nondistressed marital partners. *Journal of Consulting and Clinical Psychology, 49,* 554–67.

Markman, H. J. (1977). *A behavior exchange model applied to the longitudinal study of couples planning to marry.* Unpublished doctoral dissertation, Indiana University, Bloomington.

Markman, H. J. (1981). Prediction of marital distress: A 5-year follow-up. *Journal of Consulting and Clinical Psychology, 49,* 760–2.

Marshall, H. R., & McCandless, B. R. (1957). A study in prediction of social behavior of preschool children. *Child Development, 28,* 149–59.

Masters, J. C., & Furman, W. (1981). Popularity, individual friendship selection, and specific peer interaction among children. *Developmental Psychology, 17,* 344–50.

Matthew, W. S. (1978). Sex and familiarity effects upon the proportion of time young children spend in spontaneous fantasy play. *Journal of Genetic Psychology, 133,* 9–12.

McCarthy, B., & Duck, S. W. (1976). Friendship duration and responses to attitudinal agreement–disagreement. *British Journal of Social and Clinical Psychology, 15,* 377–86.

McCormack, B. L. (1982). Effects of peer familiarity on play behavior in preschool children. *Journal of Genetic Psychology, 141,* 225–32.

McCormack, S. H., & Kahn, A. (1980). *Behavioral characteristics of lonely and nonlonely college students.* Paper presented at the annual meeting of the Midwestern Psychological Association, St. Louis.

McDermott, J. F. (1968). Parental divorce in early childhood. *American Journal of Psychiatry, 124,* 1424–32.

McDermott, J. F. (1970). Divorce and its psychiatric sequelae in children. *Archives of General Psychiatry, 23,* 421–7.

McGee, P. E. (1979). *Humor: Its origin and development.* San Fransico: Freeman.

McGuire, J. M. (1973). Aggression and sociometric status with preschool children. *Sociometry, 36,* 542–9.

McMurray, L. (1970). Emotional stress and driving performance: The effect of divorce. *Behavioral Research in Highway Safety, 1,* 100–14.

McNair, D. M., Lorr, M., & Droppleman, L. F. (1971). *Manual for the profile of mood states.* San Diego, CA: Educational and Industrial Testing Service.

Medrich, E. A., Roizen, J., Rubin, V., & Buckley, S. (1980). *The serious business of growing up: A study of children's lives outside of school.* Berkeley: University of California Press.

Metettal, G. W. (1982). *The conversations of friends at three ages: The importance of fantasy, gossip, and self-disclosure.* Unpublished doctoral dissertation, University of Illinois, Champaign.

Miller, D. H. (1967). Retrospective analysis of posthospital mental patients' worlds. *Journal of Health & Social Behavior, 8,* 136–40.

Miller, N., & Gentry, K. W. (1980). Sociometric indices of children's peer interaction in the school setting. In H. C. Foot, A. J. Chapman, & J. R. Smith (Eds.), *Friendship and social relations in children.* New York: Wiley.

Miller, P. M., & Ingham, J. G. (1976). Friends, confidants, and symptoms. *Social Psychiatry, 11,* 51–8.

Miller, R. S. (1979). *An investigation of the behavioral correlates and function of interpersonal intimacy.* Unpublished doctoral dissertation, University of Waterloo, Ontario.

Mishler, E. G., & Waxler, N. E. (1968). *Interaction in families: An experimental study of family process in schizophrenia.* New York: Wiley.

Mitchell-Kernan, C., & Kernan, K. T. (1977). Pragmatics of directive choice among children. In S. Ervin-Tripp & C. Mitchell-Kernan (Eds.), *Child discourse.* New York: Academic Press.

Moely, B. E., Skarin, K., & Weil, S. (1979). Sex differences in competitive-cooperation behavior of children at two age levels. *Sex Roles, 5,* 329–42.

Moore, S., & Updegraff, R. (1964). Sociometric status of preschool children related to age, sex, nurturance-giving and dependency. *Child Development, 35,* 519–24.

Morgan, J. L. (1978). Two types of convention in indirect speech acts. In P. Cole

& J. L. Morgan (Eds.), *Syntax and semantics* (Vol. 6). New York: Academic Press.

Morton, T. L. (1978). Intimacy and reciprocity of exchange: A comparison of spouses and strangers. *Journal of Personality and Social Psychology, 36,* 72–83.

Mueller, D. P. (1980). Social networks: A promising direction for research on the relationship of the social environment to psychiatric disorder. *Social Science & Medicine, 14,* 147–61.

Murstein, B. I. (1970). Stimulus value-role: A theory of marital choice. *Journal of Marriage and the Family, 32,* 465–81.

Murstein, B. I., Cerreto, M., & MacDonald, M. G. (1977). A theory and investigation of the effect of exchange-orientation on marriage and friendship. *Journal of Marriage and the Family, 39,* 543–8.

Murstein, B. I., & Spitz, L. T. (1973–74). Aristotle and friendship: A factor analytic study. *Interpersonal Development, 4*(1), 21–34.

Myers, J. K., Lindenthal, J. J., & Pepper, M. P. (1975). Life events, social integration and psychiatric syptomatology. *Journal of Health and Social Behavior, 16,* 421–9.

Nahemow, L., & Lawton, M. P. (1975). Similarity and propinquity in friendship formation. *Journal of Social Psychology, 32,* 205–13.

Namache, G., Waring, M., & Ricks, D. (1964). Early indicators of outcome in schizophrenia. *Journal of Nervous and Mental Disease, 139,* 232–40.

Neale, J. M., & Oltmanns, T. F. (1980). *Schizophrenia.* New York: Wiley.

Newcomb, A. F., Brady, J. E., & Hartup, W. W. (1979). Friendship and incentive condition as determinants of children's task-oriented social behavior. *Child Development, 50,* 878–88.

Newcombe, N., & Zaslow, M. (1981). Do 2½-year-olds hint? A study of directive forms in the speech of 2½-year-old children to adults. *Discourse Processes, 4,* 239–52.

Newcomb, T. M. (1961). *The acquaintance process.* New York: Holt, Rinehart & Winston.

Nuckolls, C. G., Cassel, J., & Kaplan, B. H. (1972). Psychosocial assets, life crises and the prognosis of pregnancy. *American Journal of Epidemiology, 95,* 431–41.

Oden, S. (1980). The child's social isolation: Origins, prevention, and intervention. In C. Carteledge & J. Milburn (Eds.), *Teaching social skills to children: Innovative approaches.* Elmsford, NY: Pergamon.

Oden, S., & Asher, S. R. (1977). Coaching children in social skills for friendship making. *Child Development, 48,* 495–506.

Oden, S., Herzberger, S. D., Mangione, P. L., & Wheeler, V. A. (1984). Children's peer relationships: An examination of social process. In J. C. Masters & K. Yarkin-Levin (Eds.), *Boundary areas in social and developmental psychology.* New York: Academic Press.

Offer, D. R., & Cross, L. A. (1969). Behavioral antecedents of adult schizophrenia. *Archives of General Psychiatry, 21,* 267–83.

Olsen, P. H. (1977). Insiders' and outsiders' views of relationships: Research studies. In G. Levinger & H. L. Raush (Eds.), *Close relationships: Perspectives on the meaning of intimacy.* Amherst: University of Massachusetts Press.

Olson, D. H., & Ryder, R. G. (1970). Inventory of marital conflicts (IMC): An experimental interaction procedure. *Journal of Marriage and the Family, 32,* 443–8.

Omark, D. R., Omark, M., & Edelman, M. S. (1975). Formation of dominance hierarchies in young children: Action and perception. In T. Williams (Ed.), *Psychological anthropology*. The Hague: Mouton.

Opie, I., & Opie, P. (1959). *The lore and language of schoolchildren*. London: Oxford University Press.

Paloutzian, R. F., & Ellison, C. W. (1979). *Emotional, behavioral and physical correlates of loneliness*. Paper presented at Research Conference on Loneliness, University of California, Los Angeles.

Panaccione, V. F., & Wahler, R. G. (1984). *Child behavior, maternal depression and social coercion as factors in the quality of child care*. Unpublished manuscript.

Parker, J. G. (1984). *Making friends with an "extra-terrestrial": Conversational skills for friendship formation in young children*. Unpublished master's thesis, University of Illinois, Champaign.

Parker, J. G., & Asher, S. R. (1985). *Peer acceptance and later personal adjustment: Are low-accepted children "at risk"?* Unpublished manuscript, University of Illinois, Champaign.

Parlee, M. B., & the editors of *Psychology Today* (1979). The friendship bond. *Psychology Today, 13*, 43–54.

Parent, M. B. (1932). Social participation among preschool children. *Journal of Abnormal and Social Psychology, 27*, 243–69.

Patterson, G. R. (1982). *Coercive family process*. Eugene, OR: Castalia.

Pearlin, L. I., & Johnson, J. S. (1977). Marital status, lifestrains, and depression. *American Sociological Review, 42*, 704–15.

Pearlin, L. I., & Schooler, C. (1978). The structure of coping. *Journal of Health and Social Behavior, 19*, 2–21.

Pederson, D. M., & Breglio, V. J. (1968). Personality correlates of actual self-disclosure. *Psychological Reports, 22*, 495–501.

Pederson, D. M., & Higbee, K. L. (1969). Self-disclosure and relationship to the target person. *Merrill–Palmer Quarterly, 15*, 213–20.

Pemberton, D. A., and Benady, D. R. (1973). Consciously rejected children. *British Journal of Psychiatry, 123*, 574–8.

Peplau, L. A., & Caldwell, M. A. (1978). Loneliness: A cognitive analysis. *Essence, 2*, 207–25.

Peplau, L. A., & Perlman, D. (Eds.). (1982). *Loneliness: A sourcebook of current theory, research, and therapy*. New York: Wiley.

Phillips, E. L., Shenker, S., & Revitz, P. (1951). The assimilation of the new child into the group. *Psychiatry, 14*, 319–25.

Phillips, G. M., & Metzger, N. J. (1976). *Intimate communication*. Boston: Allyn & Bacon.

Phillips, S. L. (1981). Network characteristics related to the well-being of normals: A comparative base. *Schizophrenia Bulletin, 1*, 117–24.

Piaget, J. (1930). *The language and thought of the child*. Cleveland, OH: World.

Piaget, J. (1932). *The moral judgement of the child*. Glencoe, IL: Free Press.

Pitcher, E. G., & Schultz, L. H. (1983). *Boys and girls at play: The development of sex roles*. South Hadley, MA: Praegen.

Planalp, S., & Tracey, K. (1980). Not to change the topic, but . . . : A cognitive approach to the management of conversation. In D. Nimmo (Ed.), *Communication yearbook* (Vol. 3). New Brunswick, NJ: Transaction–I.C.A.

Pollack, M., Woerner, M. G., Goodman, W., & Greenberg, I. (1966). Childhood development patterns of hospitalized adult schizophrenic and non-schizophrenic patients and their siblings. *American Journal of Orthopsychiatry, 36*, 510–17.

Pollin, W., Stabenau, J. R., & Tupin, J. (1965). Family studies with identical twins discondant for schizophrenia. *Psychiatry*, 28, 60–78.

Price-Bonham, S., & Balswick, J. D. (1980). The noninstitutions: Divorce, desertion, and remarriage. *Journal of Marriage and the Family*, 42, 959–72.

Putallaz, M. (1981). *Predicting children's sociometric status from their behavior.* Unpublished dissertation, University of Illinois.

Putalluz, M. (1983). Predicting children's status from their behavior. *Child Development*, 54, 1417–26.

Putallaz, M. (1984). *Maternal behavior and children's sociometric status.* Manuscript submitted for publication.

Putallaz, M., & Gottman, J. M. (1981a). An interactional model of children's entry into peer groups. *Child Development*, 52, 402–8.

Putallaz, M., & Gottman, J. M. (1981b). Social skills and group acceptance. In S. R. Asher & J. M. Gottman (Eds.), *The development of children's friendships*. Cambridge University Press.

Putallaz, M., & Gottman, J. M. (1984). Social relationship problems in children: An approach to intervention. In B. B. Lahey & A. E. Kazdin (Eds.), *Advances in Clinical Child Psychology* (Vol. 6). New York: Plenum.

Rabkin, J. G., & Struening, E. L. (1976). Life events, stress, and illness. *Science*, 194, 1013–20.

Radke-Yarrow, M. (1985). *Affect in children and parental affective disorder.* Paper presented at the MacArthur Foundation Conference on Transitions from Infancy to the Second Year, Summer.

Radloff, L. (1977). The CES-D Scale: A self-report depression scale for research in the general population. *Applied Psychological Measurement*, 1, 385–401.

Raschke, H. J. (1977). The role of social participation in post separation and post divorce adjustment. *Journal of Divorce*, 1, 129–40.

Rasmussen, B., Gonso, J., & Gottman, J. M. (1980). *Observer's manual for coding children's interaction in classrooms.* Unpublished laboratory manual, University of Illinois, Champaign, IL.

Raush, H. L., Barry, W. A., Hertel, R. K., & Swain, M. A. (1974). *Communication, conflict and marriage.* San Francisco: Jossey–Bass.

Read, B. K., & Cherry, L. J. (1978). Preschool children's production of directive forms. *Discourse Processes*, 1, 233–45.

Reese, H. W. (1961). Relationships between self-acceptance and sociometric choice. *Journal of Abnormal and Social Psychology*, 62, 472–4.

Reid, J. B., (1970). Reliability assessment of observation data: A possible methodological problem. *Child Development*, 41, 1143–50.

Reisman, J. M., & Shorr, S. E. (1978). Friendship claims and expectations among children and adults. *Child Development*, 49, 913–16.

Reisman, J. M., & Yamokoski, T. (1974). Psychotherapy and friendship: An analysis of the communications of friends. *Journal of Counseling Psychology*, 21, 269–73.

Richey, M. H., & Richey, H.W. (1980). The significance of best-friend relationships in adolescence. *Psychology in the Schools*, 17, 536–40.

Rickelman, K. E. (1981). *Childhood cross-sex friendships: An investigation of trends and possible explanatory theories.* Unpublished honors thesis, University of Illinois, Champaign.

Ricks, D., & Berry, J. C. (1970). Family and symptom patterns that precede schizophrenia. In M. Roff & D. Ricks (Eds.). *Life history research in psychopathology.* (Vol. 1, pp. 31–9). Minneapolis: University of Minnesota Press.

Riskin, J., & Faunce, E. E. (1970). Family interaction scales: III. Discussion of methodology and substantive findings. *Archives of General Psychiatry, 22,* 527–37.

Robins, L. N. (1966). *Deviant children grown up.* Baltimore, MD: Williams & Wilkins.

Robins, L. N. (1972). Follow-up studies of behavior disorders in children. In H. C. Quay & J. S. Weery (Eds.), *Psychopathological disorders of childhood* (pp. 415–50). New York: Wiley.

Roff, M. (1957). Preservices personality problems and subsequent adjustments to military service: The prediction of psychoneurotic reactions. *US Air Force School of Aviation Medical Report,* No. 57–136.

Roff, M. (1960). Relations between certain preservice factors and psychoneurosis during military duty. *Armed Forces Medical Journal, 11,* 152–60.

Roff, M. (1961). Childhood social interactions and young adult bad conduct. *Journal of Abnormal Social Psychology, 63,* 333–7.

Roff, M. (1963). Childhood social interactions and young adult psychosis. *Journal of Clinical Psychology, 19,* 152–7.

Roff, M., Sells, S. B., & Golden, M. M. (1972). *Social adjustment and personality development in children.* Minneapolis: University of Minnesota Press.

Rolf, J., Knight, R., & Wertheim, E. (1976). Disturbed preschizophrenics. *Journal of Nervous and Mental Disease, 162,* 274–9.

Roopnarine, J. L., & Field, T. (1984). Play interactions of friends and acquaintances in nursery school. In T. Field, J. L. Roopnarine, & M. Segal (Eds.), *Friendships in normal and handicapped children* (pp. 89–98). Norwood, NJ: Ablex.

Rosenblum, L. A., Coe, C. L., & Bromley, L. J. (1975). Peer relations in monkeys: The influence of social structure, gender, and fantasy. In M. Lewis & L. A. Rosenblum, (Eds.), *Friendship and peer relations* (pp. 67–98). New York: Wiley.

Rothbart, M. K., & Derryberry, D. (in press). Theoretical issues in temperament. In M. Lewis & L. Taft (Eds.), *Developmental disabilities: Theory assessment and interaction.* New York: S. P. Medical and Scientific Books.

Rotheram, M. J., & Phinney, J. S. (1981, April). *Patterns of social overtures among preschool friends and non-friends.* Paper presented at the biennial meeting of the Society for Research in Child Development, Detroit.

Roy, A. (1978). Vulnerability factors and depression in women. *British Journal of Psychiatry, 133.*

Rubenstein, C., & Shaver, P. (in press). The experience of loneliness. In L. A. Peplau & D. Perlman (Eds.), *Loneliness: A sourcebook of current theory, research, and therapy.* New York: Wiley.

Rubenstein, J., & Rubin, C., (1984). Children's fantasies of interaction with same and opposite sex peers. In T. Field, J. L. Roopnarine, & M. Segal (Eds.), *Friendships in normal and handicapped children* (pp. 99–124). Norwood, NJ: Ablex.

Rubin, K. H., & Ross, H. S. (Eds.) (1982). *Peer relationships and social skills in childhood.* New York: Springer-Verlag.

Rubin, K. H. (1983). Recent perspectives on social competence and peer status: Some introductory remarks. *Child Development, 54,* 1383–5.

Rubin, K. H., Fein, G., & Vandenberg, B. (1983). Play. In E. M. Heatherington (Ed.), *Handbook of child psychology: Vol. 4. Socialization, personality, & social development* (4th Ed). New York: Wiley.

Rubin, Z. (1973). *Liking and loving*. New York: Holt, Rinehart & Winston.

Rubin, Z. (1976). Naturalistic studies of self disclosure. *Personality and Social Psychology Bulletin, 2,* 260–3.

Rubin, Z. (1980). *Children's friendships*. Cambridge, MA: Harvard University Press.

Rubin, Z., & Sloman, J. (1984). How parents influence their children's friendships. In M. Lewis (Ed.), *Beyond the dyad*. New York: Plenum.

Russell, D., Peplau, L. A., & Cutrona, C. E. (1979). *The revised UCLA loneliness scale: Concurrent and discriminant validity evidence*. Unpublished manuscript, University of Iowa, Iowa City.

Ryder, R. G., Kafka, J. S. & Olson, D. H. (1971). Separating and joining influences in courtship and early marriage. *American Journal of Orthopsychiatry, 41,* 450–64.

Rysman, A. (1977). How the gossip became a woman. *Journal of Communication, 27*(1), 176–80.

Sackett, G. P. (1977). The lag sequential analysis of contingency and cyclicity in behavioral interaction research. In J. Osofsky (Ed.), *Handbook of infant development*. New York: Wiley.

Savicki, V. (1972). Outcomes of nonreciprocal self-disclosure strategies. *Journal of Personality and Social Psychology, 23,* 271–6.

Savin-Williams, R. C. (1979). Dominance hierarchies in groups of early adolescents. *Child Development, 50,* 923–35.

Scanzoni, J., & Szinovacz, M. (1980). *Family decision-making*. Beverly Hills, CA: Sage.

Scanzoni, J. (1979). Social exchange in developing relationships. In R. L. Burgess & T. L. Huston (Eds.), *Social exchange in developing relationships*. New York: Academic Press.

Schachter, F. F., Kirschner, K., Klips, B., Fredricks, M., & Sanders, K. (1974). Everyday preschool interpersonal speech usage: Methodological, developmental, and socio-linguistic studies. *Monographs of the Society for Research in Child Development, 39* (Serial no. 156).

Schegloff, E. A. (1968). Sequencing in conversational openings. *American Anthropologist, 70,* 1075–95.

Schofield, J. W. (1982). *Black and white in school*. New York: Praeger.

Schofield, W., & Balian, L. (1959). A comparative study of the personal histories of schizophrenic and nonpsychiatric patients. *Journal of Abnormal and Social Psychology, 59,* 216–25.

Schutz, W. C. (1958). *The interpersonal underworld: FIRO*. Palo Alto, CA: Science & Behavior Books.

Schwartzman, H. B. (1978). *Transformations: The anthropology of children's play*. New York: Plenum.

Searle, J. R. (1975). Indirect speech acts. In P. Cole & J. L. Morgan (Eds.), *Syntax and semantics* (Vol. 3). New York: Academic Press.

Secord, P. F., & Backman, C. W. (1964). *Social psychology*. New York: McGraw-Hill.

Seidman, S. (1983, April). *Eventful play: Pre-schoolers' scripts for pretense*. Paper presented at the biennial meeting of the Society for Research in Child Development, Detroit.

Selman, R. L. (1980). *The growth of interpersonal understanding: Developmental and clinical analysis*. New York: Academic Press.

Selman, R. (1981). The child as a friendship philosopher. In S. R. Asher & J. M. Gottman (Eds.), *The development of children's friendships*. Cambridge University Press.

Serafica, F. C. (1982). Conceptions of friendship and interaction between friends: An organismic-developmental perspective. In F. Serafica (Ed.), *Social-cognitive development in context*. New York: Guilford.

Serbin, L. A., Tonick, I. J., & Sternglanz, S. H. (1977). Shaping cooperative cross-sex play. *Child Development, 48*, 924–9.

Shanteau, J., & Nagy, G. (1976). Decisions made about other people: A human judgement analysis of dating choice. In J. Carrol & J. Payne (Eds.), *Cognition and social judgement* (pp. 221–42). Hillsdale, NJ: Erlbaum.

Sharabany, R., & Hertz–Lazarowitz, R. (1981). Do friends share and communicate more than nonfriends? *International Journal of Behavioral Development, 4*, 45–59.

Shatz, M. (1978). On the development of communicative understandings: An early strategy for interpreting and responding to messages. *Cognitive Psychology, 10*, 271–301.

Shennum, W. A., & Bugental, D. B. (1982). The development of control over affective expression in nonverbal behavior. In R. S. Feldman (Ed.), *Development of nonverbal behavior in children*. New York: Springer-Verlag.

Sherman, L. W. (1975). An ecological study of glee in small groups of preschool children. *Child Development, 46*, 53–61.

Shulman, N. (1975). Life cycle variation in patterns of close relationships. *Journal of Marriage and the Family, 37*, 813–21.

Shuy, R. W., & Griffin, P. (1981). What do they do at school *any* day: Studying functional language. In W. P. Dickson (Ed.), *Children's oral communication skills*. New York: Academic Press.

Sole, L., Marton, J., & Hornstein, H. A. (1975). Opinion similarity in helping: Three field experiments investigating the bases of promotive tension. *Journal of Experimental Social Psychology, 11*, 1–13.

Solomon, L. (1960). The influence of some types of power relationships and game strategies upon the development of interpersonal trust. *Journal of Abnormal and Social Psychology, 61*, 223–30.

Soumi, S. J., Sackett, G. O., & Harlow, H. F. (1970). Development of sex preference in rhesus monkeys. *Developmental Psychology, 3*, 326–36.

Spanier, G. B., & Casto, R. F. (1979). Adjustment to separation and divorce: An analysis of 50 case studies. *Journal of Divorce, 2*, 241–53.

Sroufe, L. A. (1984). The organization of emotional development. In K. R. Scherer & P. Ekman (Eds.), *Approaches to emotion*. Hillsdale, NJ: Erlbaum.

Sroufe, L. A., Schork, E., Motti, F., Lawroski, N., & LaFreniere, P. (1985). The role of affect in social competence. In C. E. Izard, J. Kagan, & R. B. Zajonic (Eds.), *Emotions, cognition, and behavior* (pp.125–135) New York: Cambridge University Press.

Stack, S. (1980). The effects of marital dissolution on suicide. *Journal of Marriage and the Family, 42*, 83–91.

Stambul, H., & Kelley, H. (1979). Conflict in the development of close relationships. In R. L. Burgess & T. L. Huston (Eds.), *Social exchange in developing relationships*. New York: Academic Press.

Staub, E., & Noerenberg, H. (1981). Property rights, deservingness, reciprocity, friendship: The transactional character of children's sharing behavior. *Journal of Personality and Social Psychology, 40*, 271–89.

Stocking, S. H., Arezzo, D., & Leavitt, S. (1980). *Helping friendless children: A guide for teachers and parents*. Boys Town, NB: Boys Town Center.

Stone, L. J., & Church, J. (1957). *Childhood and adolescence*. New York: Random House.

Strain, D., Cooke, T., & Appolloni, T. (1976). *Teaching exceptional children: Assessing and modifying social behavior.* New York: Academic Press.

Strodtbeck, F. L. (1951), Husband–wife interaction over revealed differences. *American Sociological Review, 16,* 468–73.

Sullivan, H. S. (1953), *The interpersonal theory of psychiatry.* New York: Norton.

Suls, J. M. (1977). Gossip as social comparison. *Journal of Communication, 27,* 164–8.

Sussman, M., & Davis, J. (1975). Balance theory and the negative interpersonal relationship: Attraction and agreement in dyads and triads. *Journal of Personality, 43,* 560–81.

Sutton-Smith, B., Rosenberg, G. G., & Morgan, E. (1963). The development of sex differences in play choices during preadolescence. *Child Development, 34,* 119–26.

Szwed, J. (1966). Gossip, drinking, and social control: Consensus and communication in a Newfoundland parish. *Ethnology, 5,* 434–46.

Taylor, D. A. (1968). The development of interpersonal relationships: Social penetration processes. *Journal of Social Psychology, 75,* 79–90.

Terman, L. M., Buttenweiser, P., Ferguson, L. W., Johnson, W. B., & Wilson, D. P. (1938). *Psychological factors in marital happiness.* New York: McGraw-Hill.

Thibaut, J. W., & Kelley, H. H. (1959). *The social psychology of groups.* New York: Wiley.

Thoits, P. A. (1982). Conceptual, methodological, and theoretical problems in studying social support as a buffer against life stress. *Journal of Health and Social Behavior, 23,* 145–59.

Thorne, B. (in press). Girls and boys together . . . but mostly apart: Gender arrangements in elementary schools. In W. W. Hartup & Z. Rubin (Eds.), *Relationships and development.* Hillsdale, NJ: Erlbaum.

Tiger, L. (1969). *Men in groups.* New York: Vintage.

Tiger, L. (1974). Sex-specific friendship. In E. Leytan (Ed.), *The compact: Selected dimensions of friendship.* St. Johns: Memorial University of Newfoundland Press.

Tiger, L., & Fox, R. (1971). *The imperial animal.* New York: Holt, Rinehart & Winston.

Ting-Toomey, S. (1979). *Gossip as a communication construct.* Paper presented at the annual convention of the Western Speech Communication Association, Los Angeles, February.

Tinson, J., Goncu, A., & Kessel, F. (1982). *Metacommunication in preschoolers' pretend play.* Paper presented at the annual meeting of the American Psychological Association, Washington, D.C., August.

Tolsdorf, C. C. (1976). Social networks, support, and coping: An exploratory study. *Family Process, 15,* 407–17.

Tuma, N., & Hallinan, M. T. (1979). The effects of sex, race and achievement in school children's friendships. *Social Forces, 57,* 1265–85.

Turiel, G. (1975). The development of social concepts: Mores, customs, and conventions. In D. J. DePalma & J. M. Foley (Eds.), *Moral development: Current theory and research.* New York: Wiley.

Ullmann, C. (1957). Teachers, peers, and tests as predictions of adjustment. *Journal of Educational Psychology, 48,* 257–67.

Upton, G. J. (1978). *The analysis of cross-tabulated data.* New York: Wiley.

Valliant, G. E. (1977). *Adaptation to life.* Boston: Little, Brown.

Vandell, D. L., & Mueller, E. C. (1977). *The effects of group size on toddler social interactions with peers.* Paper presented at the biennial meeting of the Society for Research in Child Development, New Orleans, April.

Vandell, D., & Mueller, E. (1980). Peer play and peer friendships during the first two years. In H. Foot, T. Chapman, & J. Smith (Eds.), *Friendship and social relations in children.* New York: Wiley.

Vaughn, C. E., & Leff, J. P. (1976). The influence of family and social factors on the course of psychiatric illness: A comparison of schizophrenic and depressed neurotic patients. *British Journal of Psychiatry, 129,* 125–30.

Veitch, R., & Griffitt, W. (1973). Attitude commitment: Its impact on the similarity–attraction relationship. *Bulletin of the Psychonomic Society, 1,* 295–7.

Verbrugge, L. M. (1979). Marital status and health. *Journal of Marriage and the Family, 41,* 267–85.

Vondracek, F. W. (1969). The study of self-disclosure in experimental interviews. *Journal of Psychology, 72,* 55–9.

Vondracek, F. W., & Marshall, M. J. (1971). Self-disclosure and interpersonal trust: An exploratory study. *Psychological Reports, 28,* 235–40.

Vosk, B., Forehand, R., Parker, J. B., & Rickard, K. (1982). A multimethod comparison of popular and unpopular children. *Developmental Psychology, 18,* 571–5.

Waldrop, M. F., & Halverson, C. F. (1975). Intensive and extensive peer behavior: Longitudinal and cross-sectional analysis. *Child Development, 46,* 19–26.

Wallerstein, J., & Kelley, J. (1974). The effects of parental divorce: The adolescent experience. In E. J. Anthony & C. Koupernik (Eds.), *The child in his family: Children at psychiatric risk* (Vol. 3). New York: Wiley.

Wallerstein, J., & Kelley, J. (1975). The effects of parental divorce: Experiences of the preschool child. *Journal of the American Academy of Child Psychiatry, 14,* 600–16.

Walster, E., & Walster, G. W. (1963). Effects of expecting to be liked on choice of associates. *Journal of Abnormal Social Psychology, 67,* 402–4.

Wampold, B. E., & Margolin, G. (1982). Nonparametric strategies to test the independence of behavioral states in sequential data. *Psychological Bulletin, 92,* 755–65.

Wanless, R. L., & Prinz, R. J. (1982). Methodological issues in conceptualization and treating childhood social isolation. *Psychological Bulletin, 92,* 39–55.

Warnken, R. G., & Siess, T. F. (1965). The use of the cumulative record in the prediction of behavior. *Personal Guidance Journal, 31,* 231–7.

Watt, N. (1972). Longitudinal changes in the social behavior of children hospitalized for schizophrenia as adults. *Journal of Nervous and Mental Disease, 155,* 42–54.

Watt, N. E. (1978). Patterns of childhood social development in adult schizophrenics. *Archives of General Psychiatry, 35,* 160–5.

Watt, N. E., & Lubensky, A. (1976). Childhood roots of schizophrenia. *Journal of Consulting Clinical Psychology, 44,* 363–75.

Watt, N. F., Stolorow, R. D., Lubensky, A. W. & McClelland, D. C. (1970). School adjustment and behavior of children hospitalized for schizophrenia as adults. *American Journal of Orthopsychiatry, 40,* 637–57.

Wechsler, H., Thum, D., Demone, H. W., Jr., & Dwinnell, J. (1972). Social characteristics and blood alcohol level. *Quarterly Journal for the Study of Alcoholism, 33,* 132–47.

Weiss, R. S. (1973). *Loneliness: The experience of emotional and social isolation.* Cambridge, MA: MIT Press.

Weiss, R. S. (1974). The provisions of social relationships. In Z. Rubin (Ed.), *Doing unto others.* Englewood, NJ: Prentice-Hall.

Weiss, R. S. (1975). *Marital separation.* New York: Basic Books.

Weiss, R. S. (1976). The emotional impact of marital separation. *Journal of Social Issues, 32*(1), 135–45.

Weiss, R. S. (1982). Issues in the study of loneliness. In L. A. Peplau & D. Perlman (Eds.), *Loneliness: A sourcebook of current theory, research and therapy.* New York: Wiley.

Weiss, L., & Lowenthal, M. F. (1975). Life-course perspectives on friendship. In M. F. Lowenthal, M. Thurnher, & D. Chiriboga (Eds.), *Four stages of life.* San Francisco: Jossey-Bass.

Weitzman, L. J. (1975). To love, honor, and obey? Traditional legal marriage and alternative family forms. *Family Coordinator, 24,* 531–48.

Wellman, H. M., & Lempers, J. D. (1977). The naturalistic communication abilities of two-year-olds. *Child Development, 48,* 1052–7.

White, S. W., & Asher, S. J. (1976). *Separation and divorce: A study of the male perspective.* Unpublished manuscript, University of Colorado, Boulder.

Wiggins, J. S. (1973). *Personality and prediction.* Reading, MA: Addison-Wesley.

Wilkinson, L. C., Clevenger, M., & Dollaghan, C. (1981). Communication in small instruction groups: A sociolinguistic approach. In W. P. Dickson (Ed.), *Children's oral communication skills.* New York: Academic Press.

Wills, T. A., Weiss, R. L., & Patterson, G. R. (1974). A behavioral analysis of the determinants of marital satisfaction. *Journal of Consulting and Clinical Psychology, 42,* 802–11.

Wilson, W. (1967). Correlates of avowed happiness. *Psychological Bulletin, 67*(4), 294–306.

Winder, C. L., & Rau, L. (1962). Parental attitudes associated with social deviance in preadolescent boys. *Journal of Abnormal and Social Psychology, 64,* 418–24.

Wright, P. H. (1978). Toward a theory of friendship based on a conception of self. *Human Communication Research, 4,* 196–207.

Wright, P. H. (1984). Self-referent motivation and the intrinsic quality of friendship. *Journal of social and personal relationships, 1,* 115–30.

Wright, P. H., & Keple, T. W. (1981). Friends and parents of a sample of high school juniors: An exploratory study of relationship intensity and interpersonal rewards. *Journal of Marriage and the Family,* August, 559–70.

Yarrow, M. R., Campbell, J. D., & Burton, R. V. (1970). Recollections of childhood: A study of the retrospective method. *Monographs of the Study for Research in Child Development, 35* (Serial No. 138).

Yerkowich, S. (1977). Gossiping as a way of speaking. *Journal of Communications, 27*(1), 192–6.

Youniss, J. (1980). *Parents and peers in social development: A Sullivan–Piaget perspective.* University of Chicago Press.

Youniss, J., & Volpe, J. (1978). A relational analysis of friendship. In W. Damon (Ed.), *Social cognition* (pp. 1–22), San Francisco: Jossey-Bass.

Notes

Chapter 3

1. A parallel analysis was conducted using a median split rather than a mean split. The same children were designated to have hit it off in both cases.
2. A Sex by Condition ANOVA on these ratings indicated a main effect for sex [$F(1,40) = 12.57, p < .001$], but no main effect for condition and no interaction. Coders rated the parent conversations of girls (mean = 79.34, SD = 8.32) more highly than those of boys (mean = 67.96, SD = 12.34). For this reason, children were designated high and low using their within-sex mean. Results were unchanged when the within-sex median was substituted for the within-sex mean in this measure.
3. This model contained the following terms: hitting it off, sex of child, Panduit's skill, sex of child by Panduit's skill, and hitting it off by Panduit's skill.
4. This model contained the following terms: hitting it off, sex of child, Panduit's skill, and hitting it off by sex of child.
5. This model contained the following terms: hitting it off, sex of child, Panduit's skill, sex of child by Panduit's skill, hitting it off by Panduit's skill, and hitting it off by sex of child.

Chapter 4

1. This study was conducted in 1975; the sophistication of modern sociometric assessment is considerably greater than this median split permits. Nonetheless, there is considerable evidence for the validity of a high/low split on popularity. At a mean of 6.77 choices, the "low" popularity group in this study is certainly not comparable to "isolated" or "unpopular" children in other studies. Hence, the effects of this procedure should be considerably weaker than the extreme groups classifications currently used to study isolated, neglected, rejected, controversial, and sociometric star children. My experience with sociometric measures is that the unlimited-choice procedure used in this study gave results comparable to a fixed number of nominations when *mutual* choices correlated highly with the number of choices received ($r = .74$).
2. Chi-square statistics are based on non-independent data, as is common in observational research and sequential analysis. Statistics are therefore only

asymptotically chi square. This is not a problem (see Bishop et al., 1975). Also, chi-square comparisons across grade levels were computed in a statistically conservative fashion by adjusting observed frequencies downward to be consistent with the classroom with the least peer interaction. This is equivalent to truncation of all streams of interaction so that they have the same total amount of interaction, that is, the least (see Bishop et al., 1975). Hence, cross-sex interactions also decreased with grade level, but not as rapidly or as drastically as mutual cross-sex friendships, assessed by sociometric measures.

3. An earlier version of this study that had been circulated in preprint form had a smaller mean age for the younger cross-sex cell (3:7). The mean age for this cell contained a typographical error; it should have been 4:7 instead of 3:7.

4. The mother's presence or absence also had a set of marginally significant main effects on the exploration of similarity (GQAC→HAG; HFE→GAG). It had interaction effects with age on disagreement chains (GDG→HDG) and the reciprocity of humor (GJ→HJ). It had interaction with the sex composition of the dyad for establishing common ground (GWE→HAG) and for the reciprocity of gossip (HG→GG; GG→HG). And it had interaction effects with both age and the sex composition of the dyad on conflict resolution (HWEA→GAG).

5. The marginal main effects for the exploration of similarity (GQAG→HAG) had a similar pattern of disruption related to the mother's presence z(GQAG→HAG) = 4.21; (HFE→GAG) = .94 in her presence, compared with 2.36 and .21, respectively, in her absence.

6. The z-scores for younger children were 5.53 in the mother's absence and 1.86 in her presence; for older children these z-scores for younger children were 5.36 and 4.17, respectively.

7. The z-scores for younger children were .31 in the mother's presence, and .38 in her absence; for older children these scores were 1.56 and .03, respectively. The critical difference was 2.50.

8. The F ratios for the reciprocity analyses were as follows: (1) for fantasy, HF→GF [$F(1,24) = .41$], GF→HF [$F(1,24 = .32$]; (2) for gossip, HG→GG [$F(1,24) = .29$], GG→HG [$F(1,24) = .40$]; (3) for humor, HJ→GJ [$F(1,24) = 2.77$, n.s.], GJ→HJ [$F(1,24) = 1.62$, n.s.].

Chapter 8

1. The terms "directive" and "request" are often used equivalently, though in this case the term "request" includes a broader class of speech acts than it does when compared with "suggestions" or "demands." Directives or requests may be used to obtain goods or actions from others, attention, or information. We shall deal less with both attention bids and requests for information than with requests for goods or actions even though it has been demonstrated that requests for information are governed by many of the same factors that other directives are (Goody, 1978), particularly in the effect that status relations have on their use.

2. In another area, researchers who have studied children's use of tag questions have been preoccupied for the most part with whether children use universal tags such as "right?" or "OK?" or whether they use

forms that are grammatically dependent on the previous utterance, such as "isn't it?" or "won't you?" If one is interested in children's grammatical development, this classification is appropriate. Otherwise, worrying about whether children use "less advanced" or "more advanced" forms is pointless. Universal tags function interchangeably with grammatically dependent forms for the most part and knowing which children use is of little help in ascertaining whether children use tag questions strategically or to serve a variety of functions.

3. Unlike literal requests, requests in the context of fantasy were not affected by the speaker's status (host or guest) or the degree of acquaintanceship (friend or stranger), even when examined only in the context of fantasy discourse. In the context of fantasy, guests issued proportionately more requests than hosts among younger children. Among older children, hosts issued proportionately more requests than guests.

Requests for attention were excluded because they did not represent a separate strategy or form. Rather, they were directives seeking a different kind of response and so could not be entered in the comparison as if they represented a form. They were not subcategorized on the basis of the strategy employed in their presentation. The issuance of requests for attention was affected by host or guest status and by acquaintanceship in the same manner as requests for goods, action, or permission. Otherwise, they functioned differently. Requests for attention received relatively few overt responses, with very few refusals among them, and generally served to introduce other kinds of requests or information statements by the same child.

Although requests for help and offers were included in calculations of the proportion of utterances that were requests, they were eliminated from the total number of requests when the proportion of requests that used a given strategy was calculated. This was because they had different content than other requests and were not categorized by their form.

4. Chi-square analysis tested differences in the proportion of overt responses that were compliant between pairs of conditions (e.g., older hosts of strangers and older stranger guests).

5. Chi-square analysis of main effects was used to test between pairs of groups in the frequency of requests. Frequencies were adjusted in each group of subject pairs by dividing actual frequencies by the total number of utterances issued and multiplying by the total number of utterances in the group of subject pairs that issued the fewest utterances. This is a conservative method, and it was followed in the studies presented in this book.

6. To test variations in the proportion of overt responses that were compliant across the range of politeness for each condition, the range of politeness was divided into three types (bald-on-record requests, requests incorporating positive politeness, and requests including either deference alone or an off-record approach). In one case this range was curtailed.

7. Chi-square analysis tested differences between pairs of conditions in frequencies of requests of particular kinds. Frequencies were adjusted by dividing by the total number of requests issued in that condition and multiplying by the number of requests issued in the condition where fewest requests were issued in that age range.

8. Chi-square analysis tested differences between conditions in the proportion of all requests that were deferential or off-record.

Chapter 9

1. Divorced women in the final sample had completed more years in school than those who dropped out of the study [t (31) = 2.33, $p < .05$], with respective means of 16.16 and 14.00 years in school.

2. Divorced women with more education were less likely to be in emotional turmoil (Profile of Mood States, $r = -.418$, $p < .05$) and less likely to be depressed (Center for Epidemiologic Studies Depression Scale, $r = -.347$, $p < .05$). Divorced women who were Protestant rather than Catholic, Jewish, or other were less likely to be depressed (Center for Epidemiologic Studies Depression Scale, $r = 4.33$, $p < .05$).

3. The correlation between emotional turmoil (Profile of Mood States) and depression (Center for Epidemiologic Studies Depression Scale) was $r = .74$, $p < .001$.

Author Index

Subject index

coordinated play (*cont.*)
  as goal of friendship in early childhood,
    193–95
  Gottman and Benson study of, 145–53
  importance of emotional control to,
    200–1
  observational study of, 170–91
  in study of emotional, social
    development, 229–37
coping strategies, during stressful life
    events, 28–30
criticism:
  and negative-affect mindreading, 283
  and social support for divorcee, 369
Cronbach's alpha, 54–56
  for codes of extended MACRO system,
    95
  and observational study of cross-sex
    relationships, 174
cross-sex relationships:
  in adolescence, 210–11
  compared with same-sex relationships,
    143–45
  and conversations of young friends,
    153–70
  developmental pattern in, 179–81
  in early childhood, 143–145
  effect of mother's presence, absence on,
    177–79
  Gottman and Benson study of, 145–53
  initiation within, 151–53
  in middle childhood, 195–96, 195–97
  nature of, 139–141
  observational study of, 170–91
    discussion, 181–87
    method, 173–74
    older cross-sex friendships, 187–91
    results, 174–81
  and teasing, 210–11
  see also same-sex relationships; sex-
    related differences
cultural relativism, children's awareness
    of, 212–12

dating satisfaction, as predictor of
    loneliness, 368
declarative statements, and directives,
    requests, 323
deference, and complying with, issuing
    requests, 319–21, 322–26
delinquency, lack of friendships as
    predictor of, 21
demands:
  in child–child interactions, 306–8
  content codes for, 60t
  in mother–child interactions, 307
  see also directives; politeness

depression
  influence of friendship on, 22–23
  and lack of marital confidant, 36
  and loneliness, 24
  and loss of social support, 32–33
  in postdivorce adjustment, 356, 360
  and sex-related differences, 244–45
developmental psychology, observational
    research in, 3–4
diary record, 356–57
  in studies of sex-related differences,
    244
  of social activity and mood state, 349
differences, exploration of:
  and closeness between college
    roommates, 271, 272t
  effect of mother on determining, 177
  in establishing common ground, 68–69
  in friendship formation, 111, 182t,
    184–86
  see also similarities, exploration of
Dilemmas of Masculinity, 37
directives:
  adult use of, 316–22
  Brown-Levinson theory of politeness,
    319–21
  developmental literature regarding,
    322–27
  and development of children's
    strategies, 323–27
  and interactive constraints, 318–19
  study of children's strategies, 327–30
  used by children, 322–23
  see also politeness; requests
disagreement:
  in child–child interactions, 307
  content codes for, 61t
  proportion of, in friendship, 65–66
  and resolution of conflict, 69–70
disagreement with rationale:
  and conflict resolution, 69
  content codes for, 61t
distressed families:
  communication patterns in, 246–47
  interactions of, 65
distressed marriages:
  communication patterns in, 246–47
  and negative affect, 87
  and sex-related differences:
    in expressing grievances, 38
    in self-disclosure, 290–91
divorced parents, and loss of social
    support, 31
  see also postdivorce adjustment; social
    networks; social support
dominance:
  and lack of support for divorcee, 376